Ghosts of the Confederacy

GHOSTS
OF THE
CONFEDERACY

DEFEAT, THE LOST CAUSE, AND THE
EMERGENCE OF THE NEW SOUTH
1865 TO 1913

Gaines M. Foster

OXFORD UNIVERSITY PRESS
New York   Oxford

Oxford University Press
Oxford   New York   Toronto
Delhi   Bombay   Calcutta   Madras   Karachi
Petaling Jaya   Singapore   Hong Kong   Tokyo
Nairobi   Dar es Salaam   Cape Town
Melbourne   Auckland

and associated companies in
Berlin   Ibadan

Copyright © 1987 by Gaines M. Foster

First published in 1987 by Oxford University Press, Inc.,
200 Madison Avenue, New York, New York 10016

First issued as an Oxford University Press paperback, 1988

Oxford is a registered trademark of Oxford University Press

Library of Congress Cataloging-in-Publication Data
Foster, Gaines M.
Ghosts of the confederacy.
Bibliography: p.
Includes index.
1. Southern States—History—1865–1950.
I. Title.
F215.F694   1987   975′.041   86-11420
ISBN 0-19-504213-1
ISBN 0-19-505420-2 (PBK)

2 4 6 8 10 9 7 5 3 1
Printed in the United States of America

FOR
My Mother and Father

Acknowledgments

In writing this book, I have had assistance from many institutions and individuals, and I here gratefully acknowledge their contribution.

In working with manuscripts and gathering the illustrations, all of which date from the years covered by this study, the staffs of the following institutions provided much assistance: Alabama Department of Archives and History; Manuscript Department, University of Alabama Library; the Atlanta Historical Society; Manuscript Department, Perkins Library, Duke Univeristy; Historic New Orleans Collection; Special Collections, University of Georgia Library; Manuscript Division, Library of Congress; Manuscript Department, Joint Universities Library, Vanderbilt University; Manuscript Department, Hill Memorial Library, Louisiana State University; Mississippi Department of Archives and History; The Museum of the Confederacy, Richmond, Virginia; North Carolina Department of Archives and History; South Carolina Historical Society; South Caroliniana Library, University of South Carolina; Southern Historical Collection, University of North Carolina at Chapel Hill; Tennessee State Library; Archives Collection, University of Texas; Special Collections, Howard-Tilton Memorial Library, Tulane University; Union Theological Seminary Library; United States Army Military Research Institute; The Valentine Museum, Richmond, Virginia; Manuscripts Department, University of Virginia Library; Virginia Historical Society, and the Virginia State Library. A few individuals at these institutions deserve special mention. Allen Stokes of the South Caroliniana Library and Wilbur Meneray of Tulane were always knowledgeable and helpful; Michelle Hudson Ostby of the Mississippi Archives continued to answer research queries even after she had taken another job. During an early research visit to LSU, Stone Miller, Margaret Dalrymple, and Merna Whitley were unusually hospitable.

In addition to archivists, many other individuals offered assistance and advice. Lewis P. Jones of Wofford College first introduced me to some of the questions that shaped this study. The dissertation out of which it developed was directed by

Joel R. Williamson, who generously allowed me independence but still provided abundant support. Friends and teachers in and about Chapel Hill—Ruth Doan, Julia Hesson, John Kasson, Harry McKown, Michael Novak, Anastatia Sims, Scott Strickland, and Eric Walker—helped at crucial times. Charles Eagles exercised his considerable editorial skills on two early drafts. William Cooper, Anne Loveland, Burl Noggle, and Charles Royster, colleagues at LSU, read the manuscript and offered useful suggestions. Eleanor Canon and Martha Mikell assisted with the proofreading, as did Mary Mikell who also helped with the illustrations and in other ways. The book is much better for all their efforts.

J.P. Sacken and Willie Brooks typed various drafts, and a summer grant from the Louisiana State University Council on Research made possible a final research trip.

Baton Rouge   G.M.F
July 1986

Table of Contents

Ghosts of the Confederacy

Crowd for the unveiling of J. E. B. Stuart Monument in Richmond, Virginia, during the 1907 United Confederate Veterans' reunion. Monument pictured is the Robert E. Lee Monument (unveiled in 1890). The Davis monument in Richmond was also unveiled during this reunion. *The Valentine Museum*

Introduction

In the early twentieth century, during an intense celebration of the Confederacy, the small Mississippi town of Ripley, like many other southern communities, put up a Confederate monument, a marble soldier standing at ease and leaning on a rifle. In 1971 a delivery truck hit Ripley's Confederate monument, knocked it down, and in the process decapitated and disarmed the soldier. Only thirteen years later did the town get around to putting up another one. Modernity has not always dealt so harshly or so cavalierly with the symbols from the South's Confederate past, but unquestionably they have become less central to modern southern life than they once were. The lonely stone soldiers still stand on town squares, but southerners going about their days of buying and selling usually walk or ride past and pay them little attention.[1]

Such Confederate symbols still have their occasional uses, of course. Not many years before the accident in Ripley, in the early 1960s, a paunchy, whiskered old Confederate veteran was pictured on postcards and automobile tags that white southerners bought in great numbers. The little man, looking decidedly more defiant than dangerous, often clutched an unfurled Confederate flag, and the caption under him usually read, "Hell no, I ain't forgettin'!" Although more than a century removed from the calm dignity of Lee or the ferocious determination of Jackson, he symbolized quite well white southern attitudes at mid-century. Southerners still remembered the war, he announced. They suspect that the North has always been trying to push them around or put them down, and they do not like it. And yet the old veteran hardly appeared ready to fight, much less able to win. Exactly what he remembered about the war or what meaning it held for the present was not readily apparent. The old vet offered no marching orders, reminded no one of a powerful ideology. That remained true even when his card or tag carried a slightly more assertive caption, "The South shall rise again!" No one knew how or when or why it would. When later southerners interpreted the economic success of the sunbelt—with its commercial sprawl and business boosterism more in the tradition of Huntington,

Gould, and possibly Grady than that of Lee and Davis—they confirmed the lack of specifically Confederate content in the slogan.[2]

If asked how the South had adjusted to defeat, the good ol' boys and girls who bought the old vet's picture would most likely have been dumbfounded. The South was not defeated, they would have countered; it only wore itself out beating the Yankees. That they and most southerners in the twentieth century would remember the war but think of it almost as a victory was more than passing strange. Certainly, their bravado had its roots in continued defiance: You didn't and can't beat us, they said. On a deeper level, though, it suggested an important aspect of the South's view of its past. Southerners who had once fought and lost a nationalistic revolution but who did not seem to realize that they had lost must not have taken defeat too seriously. Especially if compared with the Scots or the Poles, modern southerners appeared almost nonchalant about their failed revolution. They remembered the battle but had forgotten its pain, its cost, and its issues.

The seeming ease with which twentieth-century southerners accepted defeat could have resulted from their forebears' lack of commitment to a Confederate nation in the first place. Some historians, Kenneth M. Stampp perhaps most systematically and skillfully, question whether all antebellum southerners supported slavery or favored the establishment of a Confederate nation. The deep and perhaps unconscious ambivalence of those who did not, he argues, helps explain the failure of Confederate arms. Stampp's hesitant Confederates would have had to make little concession in order to abandon the idea of an independent nation of slaveholders and would have found rejoining the Union far from difficult. Indeed, such southerners would have experienced defeat, at least on some level, with a sense of relief. Unquestionably, the Confederacy never displayed the unity of purpose its postwar celebrators recalled and may never have achieved the goal of creating a true nationalism. Yet the decision to secede, the will to fight for four long years, the willingness to sacrifice so many lives and so much treasure testified to the South's desire to preserve slavery in an independent nation. Some of the lack of support for the Confederate war effort, as James L. Roark's work on planters suggests, resulted from contradictions within these goals, not from a lack of commitment to them. Moreover, the anguish of individual southerners after Appomattox revealed the costs of defeat; few southerners seemed relieved by the demise of their nation or of slavery.[3]

Twentieth-century nonchalance about the war's outcome resulted not from the unimportance of its loss to the war generation but to the way in which that and the succeeding generation accepted defeat and interpreted the war in the years from 1865 to 1913. Their interpretation emerged in what has come to be called the Lost Cause, the postwar writings and activities that perpetuated the memory of the Confederacy. To modern eyes the Lost Cause appears at best excessive romanticism and at worst sheer craziness. A large number of white southerners participated in it and took it very seriously, though, and historians must as well. The central institutions of the Lost Cause were the postwar Confederate organizations: the memorial associations, the Southern Historical Society, the United Confederate Veterans, the United Daughters of the

Confederacy, and others. These groups sponsored much of the writing and oratory that helped shape southern perceptions of defeat. More southerners formed an understanding of their past through the ceremonial activities or rituals conducted by these groups than through anything else.

Out of the activities of these postwar Confederate organizations emerged the Confederate tradition, the dominant complex of attitudes and emotions that constituted the white South's interpretation of the Civil War. The tradition developed out of and in turn shaped individuals' memory of the war, but it was primarily a public memory, a component of the region's cultural system, supported by the various organizations and rituals of the Lost Cause. In order to understand the meaning and function of this tradition, the historian must examine who controlled these postwar Confederate organizations (and thereby served as keepers of the past), how southerners responded to these groups, what these groups had to say about the war, and what their rituals meant. Only then may the nature of the Confederate tradition become concrete and the southerners' sense of their past clear.[4]

No one interpretation of the war dominated all of the South all of the time, of course. A minority of white southerners never adjusted to defeat and continued to cherish wartime hatreds. Not all the talk of the "late unpleasantness" and of "damnyankees," however, should be accepted as proof of intransigence. One English visitor to the early twentieth-century South observed, "When a southern belle of to-day damns Yankees, she means by it, I judge, about as much, and about as little, as she does the kisses she gives young men who bear to her the felicitous southern relationship of 'kissing cousins.'" Hating Yankees and disparaging the North was fun, in other words, but for most southerners at least, fun of a more playful than passionate sort.[5]

Most white southerners, despite their alleged heedless romanticism and obsessive love of the past, were far too realistic to let bitter memories get in the way of rebuilding their society. Although they continued to champion states' rights and white supremacy, they abandoned forever their vision of an independent slaveholders' republic and did not long dwell on its passing. Southerners realized that they had to accept a new order without slavery and had to work within the Union. Even though they accepted these developments, they did not repudiate their decision to wage war on that Union. Rather, throughout the postwar years, they defended their actions in 1861–65 and insisted that the North acknowledge the honor and heroism of their cause.

Southerners' response to the first attempt to mobilize them in memory of the Confederacy demonstrated their resolve to accept defeat and their hesitancy to go off on romantic crusades. In the 1870s a coalition of organizations headquartered in Virginia began what amounted to a Confederate revitalization movement. Jubal A. Early and the other leaders of its constituent groups fit the stereotype of proponents of the Lost Cause. They brooded over defeat, railed against the North, and offered the image of the Confederacy as an antidote to postwar change. While not tied closely to the planter class, the leaders of this movement came from the prewar southern elite and from among the leaders of the Confederacy. They wrote much history that influenced the South's interpretation of the war, but they never created a successful movement. Their organizations attracted few members, and they failed to build an institutional base outside Virginia. Their vision of Confederate revitalization interested few southerners.

Extreme enthusiasm for and extensive participation in Confederate activities developed much later, toward the end of the 1880s. For the next twenty years or so, southerners celebrated the Confederacy as never before or since. Veterans all over the South joined not the Virginia organizations but a new group, the United Confederate Veterans. Nearly a hundred thousand southerners each year journeyed to one city for the UCV's reunion and a general festival of the South. The Sons and Daughters of the Confederacy also formed at this time. And most of the stone Confederate soldiers on town squares and courthouse lawns were put up during the same years. Although this Confederate celebration had its roots in persisting anxieties resulting from defeat, increasing fears generated by the social changes of the late nineteenth century provided the immediate impetus for the revived interest in the Lost Cause. In the public commendation of the Confederate cause and its soldiers, veterans and other southerners found relief from the lingering fear that defeat had somehow dishonored them. At the same time, the rituals and rhetoric of the celebration offered a memory of personal sacrifice and a model of social order that met the needs of a society experiencing rapid change and disorder.

The Lost Cause, therefore, should not be seen, as it so often has been, as a purely backward-looking or romantic movement. The Confederate celebration did not foster a revival of rabid sectionalism. With the exception of a few disgruntled and unreconstructed die-hards, its leaders and participants preached and practiced sectional reconciliation. Although in no way admitting error, their accounts of the war emphasized not the issues behind the conflict but the experience of battle that both North and South had shared. The Lost Cause did not signal the South's retreat from the future, but, whether intentionally or not, it eased the region's passage through a particularly difficult period of social change. Many of the values it championed helped people adjust to a new order; to that extent, it supported the emergence of the New South. To be sure, not all southerners accepted its message of sectional reconciliation and openness to change; the mind of the New South was "divided," as C. Vann Woodward maintained. Yet an understanding of the Lost Cause's role in reunion and the emergence of a new social order makes the New South advocates' enthusiastic support for it, which Woodward found curious, more understandable. It also renders the mind of the New South if not exactly unified at least less schizophrenic than the traditional interpretation of the Lost Cause, which stresses continued sectionalism and total allegiance to the past at the very time of reunification.[6]

The people most active in the formulation of this forward-looking Confederate tradition, especially the organizers and leaders of the UCV, came not from the ranks of the planter elite or even from the leaders of the Confederacy but from the urban and town middle class and the rank and file of the army. Most had accepted the new order and struggled to survive in it. Their leadership of the Lost Cause, an important part of the culture of the postwar era, therefore supports

Woodward's contention that new men from the cities and towns rather than the old planter elite dominated the New South.[7]

Once they started this movement, the new leaders of the Confederate celebration did not find it easy to perpetuate. After the Spanish-American War, the South received its long-desired vindication in the form of northern acknowledgment of its heroism and honor. About the same time, the fears of social change and disorder eased. The Confederate celebration continued for a time after 1900, but its unity and significance declined. By 1910 the veterans, their ranks thinned by death, began to pass control of the Confederate tradition to the next generation. They wanted the Sons of Confederate Veterans to accept this responsibility, but their sons were decidedly uninterested in maintaining the Confederate tradition—another sign of declining importance. The Daughters of the Confederacy, with some competition from the first generation of profession- al historians in the South, did try to take control. Neither group, though, commanded the attention of southern society the way the veterans had. The Lost Cause, it almost seemed, had served its purpose. Having reassured southerners of their honor and preserved the social order, it was no longer so important.

Interpreting the significance and meaning of the Lost Cause through the rhetoric and rituals of Confederate organizations differs somewhat from the more common attempt to understand southern culture through its fiction. The study of literature has yielded significant insights into southern history, but in this instance it seems worthwhile to investigate other sources. Fiction about the Civil War has already been extensively and expertly studied by Edmund Wilson, Daniel Aaron, Robert Lively, and others. Although these numerous studies sometimes differ among themselves and with the interpretation here, they reinforce the findings of a study of organizational behavior on three important points. First, they show that the theme of sectional reconciliation, so important in the Confederate celebration, was also prevalent in the fiction treating the Civil War. Second, they demonstrate that northerners wrote about the war as often as southerners, a fact suggesting that the fascination with and celebration of the war derived from something other than defeat or anything else unique to the South. And third, recent interpreters of the local colorists, particularly Thomas Nelson Page and others of the plantation school, argue that works of the local color writers appealed primarily because they offered an escape from the tensions of industrialization and a changing social order—a conclusion that fits well with the emphasis here on the roots of the Confederate celebration in the same developments.[8]

Along with not utilizing fiction for evidence, this study for two reasons avoids the terms "myth" and "civil religion" that have lately dominated examinations of the Lost Cause. First, neither term seems to have a clear definition within scholarly discourse. "Myth" is understood to mean everything from a creative falsehood to a disguised message that publicly presents "ordinarily unconscious paradoxes," while "civil religion," according to one recent study, has five distinct definitions in its literature. Having no generally accepted meaning, the terms "myth" and "civil religion" may confuse rather than clarify the phenomena they are used to describe. The term "tradition," defined as a cultural belief held over time, has less scholarly baggage but still conveys the cultural importance implied by "myth" or "civil religion."[9]

Second, both terms suggest that the Lost Cause had not just a temporary cultural importance but served as a permanent basis of social identity. Because of myth's most common definition in anthropological theory, its use implies that the Lost Cause was a tale about the origins of the southern people, a story that shaped their social identity. The concept of civil religion involves a similar but more explicit interpretation. Ever since Emile Durkheim's pioneering work, historians of religion have emphasized the religious nature of all attempts at the definition of society. In modern societies, which have a more complex social organization than the primitive one Durkheim studied, a difference emerges between what most people commonly think of as religion—the complex of concerns about the meaning of birth and death or the existence of a transcendental being—and beliefs that support a sense of social identity. The concept of civil religion was developed to acknowledge that divergence and in order to describe the beliefs that undergirded national identity in the modern United States.[10]

The scholars who consider the Lost Cause a form of southern civil religion make a case for its religious nature by pointing to its cultural importance and its use of religious symbols and metaphors. They probably take the metaphors too literally, but they are certainly correct about the cultural importance of the Lost Cause. It helped explain to late nineteenth-century southerners how and why they lost the war that marked the end of the Old South. It helped them cope with the cultural implications of defeat. It served to ease their adjustment to the New South and to provide social unity during the crucial period of transition. But once it had done these things, the Lost Cause declined in utility and therefore in importance. In the New South of the twentieth century, the Confederate tradition did not serve as a basis of social identity because it had lost much of its specificity and power to shape behavior. Like the old vet on the postcards, southerners were not forgetting: they remained defensive and defiant. But except for reinforcing those traits, the Confederate tradition played a limited role in modern southern culture.

Part One

COMING TO TERMS WITH DEFEAT, 1865 TO 1885

CHAPTER ONE

After Appomattox:
The Trauma of Defeat

The only chance General Robert E. Lee saw to save the Army of Northern Virginia, and ultimately the Confederacy, was to join with the forces of General Joseph Johnston in North Carolina. On 2 April 1865, Lee had disengaged his troops in Petersburg and moved west toward Amelia Courthouse. For six days federal forces had steadily pursued him and appeared to have closed off his means of escape. General Ulysses S. Grant had already sent communications asking for surrender. Near Appomattox Courthouse on the evening of 8 April, Lee and generals Fitzhugh Lee, John B. Gordon, and James Longstreet planned a final, desperate attempt to break through the Union lines and thereby save the army. The following morning General Gordon and his troops passed through the village of Appomattox and attacked the Federal lines beyond it. At first the Yankees gave way, but then they quickly began to turn the Confederates back. Gordon knew that his men could not go on. Informed of the situation, Lee concluded, "There is nothing left me to do but to go and see General Grant, and I would rather die a thousand deaths." Wearing a new gray uniform, red sash, and dress sword, Lee met a disheveled Grant at Wilmer McLean's house in Appomattox. There, with all the considerable dignity he could command, Lee surrendered the Army of Northern Virginia.[1]

The preceding week the Confederate capital at Richmond had fallen, and President Jefferson Davis had fled south in hopes of continuing the fight. In North Carolina, Johnston's command, to which a few of Lee's men escaped, still faced General William T. Sherman's forces, and Confederate armies also remained in the field in the deep South and the trans-Mississippi region of Louisiana and Texas. The combined disasters of the fall of Richmond and the surrender of Lee, though, left the Confederacy with little chance of survival. On 26 April Johnston surrendered his army, despite opposition from Davis, who held to the hope of eventual victory and continued his flight.[2]

Davis and a "tiny minority" of Confederates favored the adoption of guerrilla tactics as a means to continue the war. Lee and most military leaders opposed it as a futile and foolish attempt to prolong a war that had been hopelessly lost. Their soldiers concurred, although often for personal rather than military reasons. One Virginian counseled his son not to participate in any "irregular warfare in detached bands" that could only "reduce the country to anarchy, without a single element of settlement." "Nothing," he added, "can justify a gentleman becoming an outlaw." Another Virginian, Samuel H. Lockett, admitted that he "would be very much tempted to become a desperado and prey upon our enemy in every possible way that a strong feeling of hate and vengeance could devise. . . . But," he concluded, "with my little ones still living and looking so anxiously for my safe return, I must take care of myself and try to live to protect them, and care for them. . . ." Lockett's change of attitude—for he had allowed his little ones to wait during the war and had then been willing to risk losing his life— symbolized a general loss of corporate purpose that followed the military disasters and flight of the Confederate government.[3]

Soldiers had lost all will to continue the battle and turned from the cause to the protection of themselves and their families. Some still under arms wondered whether to "sacrifice their lives" simply to "gratify" what they now saw as someone's "ambition," and a few reportedly refused to obey orders. In early May an anonymous soldier in a Texas unit pleaded for an end to the fighting and accused his commanders of prolonging the war only to enhance their fortunes through cotton speculation. The soldier, who had heard of Lee's surrender, warned his commander that he and his friends were "not going into any more fights" where they might be killed. Were the country to be devastated, they wanted "to be left here in order to try to take care of our wives and little ones. . . ." Williamson S. Oldham, a Confederate senator from Texas who left Richmond when it fell and traveled through seven Confederate states on his way to Mexico, reported that not just the soldiers but the entire population considered any continuation of the conflict "madness." Everywhere he went, Oldham reported, he "found the same feeling and heard the same expression of public sentiment" and none were "in favor of the continuation of the war."[4]

Oldham also heard the rumors of foreign intervention that swept the South in late April and early May. Many reported France coming to the rescue of the South, while others cast Great Britain, Austria, Belgium, or a combined force from all four countries in the role of deliverer. A few reports even specified that the French had taken New Orleans or that the British had sailed up the Potomac. With no substance to them, the rumors of imminent rescue quickly died out. Their wide circulation indicated a deep desire to escape defeat, but their emphasis on foreign aid further testified to the Confederates' loss of faith in the possibility of victory. The only hope had become salvation from abroad.[5]

With the loss of corporate purpose and an absence of faith in the ability to triumph, the end came quickly. The few armies remaining in the field surrendered. On 4 May the last of the forces east of the Mississippi River abandoned the fight. Six days later a Union cavalry patrol captured Davis in Irwinsville, Georgia. On 26 May, General Edmund Kirby Smith surrendered the armies beyond the Mississippi. Within a month or so after Appomattox almost everyone throughout the South had accepted the end of the Confederate nation.[6]

. . . .

Though swift, the acceptance of irreversible defeat brought much pain. Deeply shocked by what they perceived as a calamity of unknown but awesome proportions, white southerners appeared demoralized and disoriented. Wives and sisters commented frequently on the disheartened attitude and discouraged appearance of the returning soldiers. Women lamented how "utterly hopeless" the former Confederates appeared, regretted how "exceedingly quiet" they seemed, and wondered if "all the dear 'men in gray'" felt "as crushed and disconsolate" as those they knew. The freed slaves, if recollections sixty years after the fact can be trusted, also noticed the changed countenances. "De sperrit dey lef' wid jus' been done whupped outten dem," one recalled. The veterans themselves occasionally substantiated the observations of the women and freedmen. In early May Confederate ordnance genius Josiah Gorgas confessed that "the total destruction of our government is of a character so overwhelming that I am as yet unable to comprehend it." He felt like "one walking in a dream, and expecting to awake." A month later, George A. Mercer of Savannah still had not "recovered from the stunning effect of mingled surprise and grief caused by the sudden prostration of our cause."[7]

The soldiers considered the civilians as "spiritless" as themselves. One veteran observed that during the first months after Appomattox all seemed "steeped in a fatal lethargy, unwilling or unable to resist or forward anything." Even the women, formerly the mainstay of Confederate morale, gave in to despair. "The demoralization is complete. We are whipped, there is no doubt about it," wrote a Georgia girl as she awaited the arrival of the Yankees in her town. A North Carolina woman admitted sleeping "endlessly" after hearing of Lee's surrender, and another in Virginia complained that she did not "feel much like doing any thing." Several diarists could not summon the energy or courage to record the traumatic events in their journals and abandoned them for weeks or months.[8]

Some southerners, males and females, experienced such agony and despair that they began to question their faith in God. He had, it seemed to them, first directed the Confederate cause and then deserted it in favor of the unjust. So devout a believer as Mary Jones, widow of a prominent Presbyterian minister of Liberty County, Georgia, admitted on one occasion that "[my] faith almost fails," and wondered if God had indeed "forgotten to be gracious." Mrs. Jones quickly felt reassured, but others with a less secure faith or a greater sense of loss did not readily find peace. Grace Brown Elmore of South Carolina, for instance, earnestly sought solace from God. Instead, she found, "Hard thoughts against my God arise; questions of his justice, of his mercy arise, and refuse to be silenced. . . ." She strove "night and day in every moment of quiet . . . to work out the meaning of this horrible fact, to find truth at the bottom of this impenetrable darkness." Her doubts persisted, and almost two months later she still bemoaned her wickedness in feeling "so rebellious against God."[9]

Few southern Christians wrestled so long, if they questioned God's will at all. For most, faith proved a source of comfort and consolation in the midst of the "impenetrable darkness." In the weeks and months after the surrender, ministers preached on such texts as "I will not leave you comfortless" or "Blessed are the poor in Spirit." Christians read in their Bibles the consoling passages of Job or the lamentations of Jeremiah. They found solace in a favorite hymn or religious poem. They rejoiced in the blessings God had provided, bringing them or a loved one safely through the battle or providing a comfortable home in such perilous times.[10]

Southerners' evangelical faith also offered the ultimate consolation: a promise of eventual vindication. In the first weeks after Appomattox, a few divines led their congregations to believe that God still intended the South to be independent. Like New Orleans Presbyterian Thomas Markham, however, most prophesied only that the "present afflictions which are but for a moment, shall work out for us a far more exceeding and eternal weight of glory." The loss of the war, in other words, was part of God's omniscient will for the greater triumph of the South. In believing this, most southern churchmen translated the scriptural promise that "all things work together for good for them that love the Lord" into an interpretation of the South's recent history.[11]

Even though their faith consoled many Christians, despair and demoralization persisted in the region. Through the summer and well into the fall of 1865, southerners complained that their fellow citizens remained disconsolate. Economic dislocations, especially the difficulty of hiring plantation laborers, and racial turmoil deepened southerners' fears and distress. In the antebellum South, slave revolt scares had frequently erupted during times of stress and uncertainty. As early as July 1865 reports of a black insurrection scheduled for Christmas were heard in white communities. The rumors spread through much of the region during the fall and peaked around the first of December. Christmas passed with no general uprising of the former slaves, but widespread fears testified to the despair and loss of confidence among white southerners.[12]

Even though fearful and disconsolate, southerners were not necessarily willing to submit to any changes dictated by the North, as Whitelaw Reid, a well-known northern newspaperman, concluded after a journey through the South in the first months after the war. Some southerners did talk of total submission, but Reid exaggerated the region's submissiveness. Other northern observers wrote of Confederates who waited only for an opportunity to strike again, and southern correspondence and diaries confirmed that a few talked of lying low only until a renewal of the conflict became feasible. Reid may have confused malleability with instability. It took time for southern society to return to normal; soldiers and refugees had to get home and resume a peacetime existence. The majority of Confederate leaders searched for months before securing new means of making a living, and less distinguished Confederates as well encountered difficulties adjusting. A number of southerners moved to new states during this period, although it is impossible to tell whether they moved right after the war or later in the decade. In summary, the disorientation brought on by defeat, compounded by the social flux of the immediate postwar period, made the former Confederates appear more open to change than they actually were. Reacting to events day by day, still adjusting to their loss, southerners had not really decided how to approach the future.[13]

In the months and years that followed, a semblance of normality returned to southern society, and the former Confederates began to adjust to defeat. A few of them, or maybe all of them some of the time, wanted simply to defy and damn the Yankees. They often did so in small ways. Women refused to walk under the American flag or crossed the street to avoid an encounter with a northern man. Ordered by federal authorities to display no rebel insignia, veterans covered their Confederate buttons with mourning cloth but left them on their coats. Both sexes enjoyed a popular ditty that expressed bitter defiance:

> Oh, I'm a good old Rebel,
>   Now that's just what I am;
> For the "fair land of Freedom"
>   I do not care a dam.
> I'm glad I fit against it—
>   I only wish we'd won.
> And I don't want no pardon,
>   For anything I done.

The song continued through stanzas expressing hatred for Yankees, the Freedmen's Bureau, the Declaration of Independence, and the Union. Its penultimate verse regretted that the southern armies and climate had not killed three million Yankees "Instead of what we got." Innes Randolph, the Virginia veteran who wrote the poem that was later set to music, may have intended to satirize the views of the common folk. The popularity of the song among all classes, though, suggested that on some level a great many southerners agreed with its defiance. Even in this humorous lyric of intransigence, however, a hint of acquiescence surfaced in the final verse: "I can't take up my musket, And fight 'em now no mo'. . . ."[14]

No matter how much southerners wanted to remain "good old rebels" who "did not care a dam," military power had failed, and neither defeat nor the Yankees would go away. Southerners had somehow to come to terms with that fact. Naturally, people reacted to the loss of the war and the demands of the North in different ways. A few chose to flee, either to a new country or into a private world safe from the pains of the postwar South. Most acknowledged defeat, realized the inevitability of a new order, and resolved to make their way in it. Of those who did, a small minority tried to work with the conquerors, but the vast majority strove to ensure all southern advantage in that new order.[15]

The first Confederates to flee to other countries did so shortly after Appomattox in order to escape federal prosecution—or persecution, as they saw it. They usually traveled first to Mexico or Cuba, then on to England, France, or Canada. Although a few never returned, these refugees rarely intended to become permanent exiles. Most settled along the Canadian border, monitored closely developments in the United States, and returned home when political conditions allowed.[16]

In the summer and fall of 1865 the Confederate exodus changed. No longer did it consist primarily of individuals fleeing federal justice. Instead, it consisted of organized groups of southerners seeking permanent settlement in Mexico,

Brazil, or, less often, some other Latin American country. Although the emigration movement continued into the 1870s, most émigrés left in 1866 and 1867. The colonies in Mexico, started by the Confederates who fled there in the last days of the war, continued to attract settlers into the first months of 1866. More than half the southerners who went to Brazil, the largest group of émigrés, did so during 1866 and 1867. Efforts to establish colonies in Venezuela and the British Honduras also began during this two-year period.[17]

The motivations of individual emigrants during this second phase varied. Some sought better economic opportunities, others could not face life in a society with free blacks, and a few simply longed for adventure in a strange new land. The movement as a whole might best be characterized as the "utopian dream" of Confederates who would not accept the results of the war. They chose to leave a South that they considered destroyed in order to recreate as close a replica as possible in a new country. The dream received its boldest and clearest expression in the plan of Matthew Fontaine Maury. This former Confederate naval leader sought to recruit two or three hundred thousand from the best families of Virginia—which in actuality would have entailed recruiting all the families of Virginia—for emigration to Mexico. They would bring with them a proportional number of "negro skilled laborers in agriculture" who would enter the country as "peons"—a concession that caused Maury to consider himself an abolitionist. Together, the best families and faithful peons would build a "New Virginia" in a part of Mexico that reminded Maury of the Valley of the Shenandoah.[18]

Southerners who went to Brazil, the site of the other major colonization scheme, operated from no such grandiose plan. Their selection of one of the few countries that still practiced slavery, however, indicated that they hoped to enjoy at least something of the antebellum order, and occasionally an immigrant there explicitly expressed a desire to reestablish another Old South. One, who wrote primarily to dispel rumors that slavery had been abolished, reminded the homefolks that his fellow Confederates in Brazil had "only to form communities large enough for the support of churches and schools, and to go to work to make money enough to support these well, to almost restore what we have lost in the U. S."[19]

None of the Confederate colonies came close to restoring the old order: Neither slavery nor Maury's peonage system took hold. The emigrants not only failed to recreate the Old South in the wilds of Mexico or Brazil, they rarely established any sort of viable community. Only in Brazil did a significant settlement survive, and it was small. A lack of capital, the hostility of local residents, and the rugged terrain of settlement sites contributed to the failure, but the settlers' own utopian dream did not help. Seeking a romantic Old South, most quickly tired of the reality of hard pioneer life and returned to the United States embittered and discouraged. With their negative reports and the rapid collapse of colonies, the Confederate exodus slowed and soon ended.

Accurate statistics on the number of southerners who emigrated did not survive, and reports of the number of people in any one settlement varied dramatically. Ten thousand southerners probably participated in the exodus, but the total may have been a quarter less than that. Even the higher estimate of ten thousand consituted less that two-tenths of 1 percent of the white population of the South. Compared to the number of loyalist refugees after the American Revolution (2.5 percent of the population), the Confederate émigrés seemed hardly significant at all. Southerners, one might conclude, must not have feared the aftermath of the war very much.[20]

A huge disparity between the few Confederates who actually emigrated and the many who contemplated doing so suggests a more complex conclusion. Countless southerners who never left the country filled letters and diaries with discussion of emigration. They swore that when they had the money they would go, or maintained that if only they were younger or did not have a family they would already have gone. The Virginia minister Robert L. Dabney, for example, for three years deliberated leaving the country. Unimpressed with the popular locations for resettlement, he and Confederate general Jubal A. Early investigated the feasibility of establishing a colony of prominent southerners in New Zealand. Early thought it a likely spot, since it had "no negroes" and was "a long way from Yankeedom." As in so many cases, however, nothing ever came of their plans.[21]

Anyone considering emigration did face many obstacles: federal hostility, opposition by such leading Confederates as Lee and Wade Hampton, the high cost of travel and relocation, negative reports by the first settlers—not to mention the dangers and hardships of pioneering. These impediments probably deterred few who were determined to emigrate, but most southerners who only discussed emigration probably never seriously intended to leave. Their talk of going to Mexico or Brazil differed little from that of a Georgia preacher who dreamed of finding "some soft green island, far out in the Pacific, a stray from the Tahitian group, or of like character, where no Yankee ever had come or could come, and [if I] could there remove together, enough to constitute society, that is the place to which I would pray be allowed to go, as an earthly heaven."[22]

Emigration apparently offered a means of psychological as well as physical escape from the consequences of the war. Only the determined, or maybe only the impetuous, actually left the South to create a world untouched by defeat. Southerners who contemplated joining them shared the dream and took solace in their talk of escape. They found the idea of emigration emotionally satisfying but knew it was unrealistic. The emigration movement suggested, therefore, that most southerners accepted the outcome of the war but still feared its implications. If they had considered the results of the war totally unacceptable, the scheme would have had more participants. Conversely, if southerners had been totally confident of their ability to control postwar developments, the dream would not have appealed to so many of them. Emigration served for a few as a total escape from defeat, and for many as a temporary, psychological one.

Rather than flee or dream of fleeing, other Confederates chose to withdraw into a private world safe from the traumas of life in a conquered South. Alcohol or drugs offered the most extreme means of avoiding the reality of defeat. Observers both from within and without the region commented on the prevalence of immoderate drinking among demoralized southerners. Between

1860 and 1920 southern whites also had an extremely high rate of opium addiction, and the psychological impact of defeat is said by one historian to be a minor contributing factor. In 1877 a New York opium dealer reported, "Since the close of the war, men once wealthy, but impoverished by the rebellion, have taken to eating and drinking opium to drown their sorrows." His observation, as well as those of people who decried widespread drunkenness after the war, cannot be substantiated, but that some southerners sought such a release seems probable.[23]

Despondent Confederates also chose more constructive ways of withdrawing from society. A few found the church a means of being in the defeated South but not of it. In late April 1865 Confederate soldier John Dooley despaired that all his desires had come to naught. He wished he "had followed the inspirations of my College days and entered the Society of Jesus," with its shelter from "the outside storms and cares of life," civil wars, and the fall of republics. The following September he became a Jesuit novice, only to die eight years later shortly before his ordination. Protestant ministers as well sometimes found the church a refuge. Episcopal priest Franklin Stringfellow, implicitly comparing his work for God with that for the Confederacy, took "great satisfaction in knowing that the gates *of hell* shall not prevail against *this* Kingdom." Other southerners retreated into their work and families rather than into the church. George Mercer, for example, claimed, "My profession and my books are my only pride and pleasure: my house my castle: my family my country."[24]

Ignoring politics, where southerners had to face both the Yankees and the harsh realities of defeat, constituted a less total but more common means of withdrawal. Many white southerners insisted that political matters no longer interested them. One Georgian argued that politics had become as useless to him "as diamond shoe-buckles would have been for Robinson Crusoe. . . ." An Alabaman maintained that he "lived in a very retired way" and had "turned away" from political discourse "with curses and disgust, as I would have done from the breath of a cur that had gorged himself on carrion." Such statements seemed calculated for effect, but numerous observers reported similar sentiments or commented upon the political apathy of the region.[25]

Like discussion of emigration, the talk of political withdrawal may have been more rhetorical than real. Yet many southerners apparently did refrain from voting, the most common and least demanding form of political activity. Voter turnout for the 1865 gubernatorial elections in the lower South declined dramatically from that of prewar levels. White voter registration also fell between 1860 and 1867, and disfranchisement may not have been the primary cause. Protests over nothern policies and fear of blacks contributed to the drop, a recent study has argued, but so too did weariness and defeat. Though far from definitive, this statistical evidence of decline in voting coupled with the disavowals of interest expressed in literary sources suggest that some southerners did withdraw from public involvement into a more private world in which politics played little or no part.[26]

Neither escape nor withdrawal—like the total defiance of "I'm a good old rebel"—proved practical as a permanent response to defeat. After all, most southerners had family and economic interests that could not be ignored. To protect them as well as to resume normal lives, the vast majority of southerners returned to full participation in politics and society. Those who did adopted various forms of two basic strategies. Some capitulated to the conquerors, while most accepted the defeat of their cause but continued to resist unacceptable northern demands.

Joining the Republican party constituted the most obvious form of capitulation, particularly after the passage of the Reconstruction Acts in March 1867. Of course, southerners became Republicans for various reasons, not all of which amounted to capitulation. Many from antebellum Unionist or upcountry backgrounds had always opposed the Confederate cause, so their Republican loyalty involved no radical change. For southerners who had ardently supported the Confederacy, however, becoming a Republican meant not just surrender but going over to the Yankees. Nevertheless, some did join the party because they believed membership in it to be the wisest strategy in defeat. Because of his prominence in the war and notoriety during Reconstruction battles in Louisiana, James Longstreet was the best-known of them. He argued that "reconstruction became a necessity when we turned from our arms" and that southerners had to accept the fact that they and their children would be part of the United States. Since they could not change that situation, Longstreet continued, southerners had best try to control the "revolution" to follow.[27]

Other Confederate leaders—James Lusk Alcorn, Amos T. Ackerman, Albert Gallatin Brown, Rufus Barringer, and M. Jess Thompson—took similar stands. Roger A. Pryor, an antebellum Virginia congressman and former Confederate general, urged his fellow citizens to accept defeat gracefully and to allow black suffrage. He then moved to New York City where he eventually entered law practice with Ben Butler, in that step going over to the devil himself in the eyes of most southerners. Surely many less-famous Confederates found a dramatic reversal of loyalties easier than did their leaders. The extent, social base, or geographical location of southern white Republicanism remains unclear, but many more southerners, even of the upper class, supported the party than southern folklore has implied. The Alabama Republican party contained at least 2,700 active white members, 85 percent of them natives of the state. Most lived outside the hill counties, nearly a fifth had served in the Confederate army, and more than half had lent some sort of aid to the southern cause. So sizable and identifiable a leadership group in one state suggests that a small but still significant number of southerners "went over" to the victors, at least far enough over to serve the Republican party.[28]

Some southerners who never went so far as to join the Republicans still demonstrated a flexibility in defeat rarely credited to southerners. In the first years after the war, a number of former Confederates went north to build a future—a move perhaps born of economic necessity but one that hardly represented utter defiance or demonstrated undying opposition to northern civilization. A few southern writers—George Frederick Holmes, Edward Pollard, and George Fitzhugh—rapidly adjusted their thought to the dominant intellectual currents of the North. In short, perhaps more southerners made significant adjustments to northern ways than has usually been thought. Yet only a minority capitulated to northern political or philosophical positions and when they did often found themselves ostracized by more persistent Confederates.[29]

The overwhelming majority of southerners never even considered joining the Republican party or making similar concessions to the victors. They realized nevertheless that southerners had lost the war and therefore had to act accordingly. Matthew F. Maury, once his colonization scheme failed, made precisely this point in a letter to his hotheaded son, who remained in exile. "Now my dear son, we have fought for our cause and we have lost it beyond the hope of recovery . . . ," he advised his grown child, who never passed up an opportunity to display Confederate sentiments or disparage anything northern. And "since we have been whipped and confessed defeat, it is proper that you should accept the consequences like a man." In 1867 Jabez L.M. Curry, a former Confederate senator, proffered similar advice to the Young Men's Christian Association of Richmond. "As a conquered people," he urged his audience, southerners should avoid hatred, acquiesce in the new political and labor system, and work to rebuild the South.[30]

Most southerners followed a course similar to that suggested by Curry. Northern observers agreed, for the most part, that the majority of Confederates accepted defeat, abandoned secession, and acquiesced in the abolition of slavery. In effect the 1865 state constitutions ratified this position, as did Robert E. Lee and a group of distinguished Confederate leaders in a public statement issued during the 1868 presidential campaign. Acceptance of defeat rarely included love for the North, enthusiasm for reunion, or tolerance of black social or political equality. Nor did it entail any abdication of local control or abandonment of local customs. In short, southerners returned to a loyal place in the Union without slavery, but struggled to retain as much political power as possible and fought to enforce white supremacy.[31]

To interpret their posture solely as continued defiance underrates the importance of the concession southerners did make: abandonment of their vision of an independent nation of slaveholders. It also oversimplifies the context of Reconstruction. Many northerners joined the South in opposing changes in the racial practices of the United States. Fights over federal enforcement of civil rights decrees in border states that had not seceded rivaled those in the former Confederacy. When loyal unionists acted in similar fashion, the southerners' opposition to black rights should not be considered a refusal to accept the results of the war. If equality never really became a northern war aim, southerners need not have been expected to interpret defeat as a mandate for racial progress. Southern intransigence over racial matters, therefore, probably should not be interpreted as a refusal to accept defeat.[32]

Too much emphasis on continued defiance over certain issues also obscures the very real trauma of defeat. The surrender at Appomattox left white southerners dazed and dispirited, aware of the futility of continuing the war but unsure of the implications of its unsuccessful end. After an initial period of confusion, individual southerners adjusted to defeat in differing ways. A few sought to escape to a new land or to withdraw into a private world. A small but perhaps significant minority capitulated to the conquerors by becoming Republicans or adopting northern ways. The vast majority remained loyal to old political values and to the principle of white supremacy, but even so accepted reunion and the abolition of slavery. Individuals in all three groups realized that the south had lost the war and had to abide at least some changes. They had all endured pain and confusion in coming to terms with defeat—a process that left its scars.

CHAPTER TWO

After Appomattox:
The Scars of Defeat

The dazed and distressed state of white southerners after Appomattox clearly revealed the trauma of defeat. Not so readily apparent but nonetheless real and important were the wounds that the loss inflicted on many individuals. Reestablishing a normal life left little time for dwelling excessively on the past and its pains, and the decision to accept the results of the war but to work within the Union for all political advantage discouraged public lamentations as well. The South could not afford to display weakness or confusion in the midst of sectional disputes. Defeat on the battlefield nevertheless begat anxieties that even the preservation of white supremacy and the redemption of state governments could not alleviate. Southerners began to wrestle with these anxieties in the months and years after Appomattox. They examined the justness of their cause and asked whether the South had been right to secede and to defend slavery. They worried that they had brought dishonor on themselves by losing the war and by meeting the demands of the conquerors. They struggled to reassure themselves about established conceptions of sex roles that the war had challenged.

As any people who had lost a war or revolution would do, southerners reexamined the justness of their cause after Appomattox. Good Protestants that most of them were, they sometimes condemned the sinfulness that had brought down the wrath of God upon them. They tended, though, to be rather vague about the nature of that sinfulness, usually dredging up the old failings of dance or drink. The would-be Jeremiahs seemed more committed to a theological form than troubled by any fundamental evil in their society. When the former Confederates considered the central issues of the war, secession and slavery, few talked of sinfulness. In the years immediately after the war, in fact, southerners reasserted the righteousness of the South's position on both these issues.[1]

Almost all southerners considered secession a dead issue, and a few even believed it to have been "unwise and inexpedient" in 1861. Rarely, though, did anyone proclaim it wrong. Instead, they rehashed the old arguments about northern violations of the original constitutional compact and the South's resulting legal right to withdraw from it. Like one Georgia woman, they concluded even "in the shadow of defeat and humiliation, that right and justice were ours." In seceding from the Union, southerners thought that they had acted morally and legally under the Constitution.[2]

The issue of slavery proved more troublesome. In theory, the Confederacy had abandoned slavery for independence when in the last months of the war it had recruited black troops with a promise of freedom. A few Confederates, including Davis and Lee, were willing to abolish slavery to win the war, but the recruitment effort hardly constituted a general repudiation of slavery. Only an administrative decree by President Davis offered the promise of emancipation. The act authorizing black enlistment, which passed by only one vote in the Confederate Senate, included the statement that "nothing in this act shall be construed to authorize a change in the relation which the said slaves shall bear toward their owners." Even with this caveat, the plan met with considerable opposition.[3]

After the war few southerners maintained that the Confederacy had voluntarily emancipated the slaves or even seemed aware that it had taken a step toward abolition. Rather, most continued to see slavery as central to the cause. A majority of the applications for pardon that southerners filed after the war termed slavery "the paramount cause of the Civil War." Similar affirmations appeared in postwar letters and writings, and a few northern travelers reported hearing statements to the same effect. Many southerners also commented on their fellow citizens' steadfast support throughout the war of the institution of slavery. Confederate captain Francis Dawson even blamed defeat on the unwillingness of southerners to sacrifice "their property." "Of course there were many exceptions," he wrote his father in June 1865, "but the majority would I am convinced rather have placed in the Army two sons than one negro."[4]

Nevertheless, once the war ended most southerners rapidly accepted emancipation. A few proclaimed it a benefit if not a blessing, but the majority only acquiesced without much enthusiasm. Southerners of both opinions, however, reviewed their long commitment to the institution. A few isolated individuals condemned it as a "moral cholera" and rejoiced that southern youth were now free of the "plague spot of African slavery." Columbus, Mississippi, Presbyterian minister James A. Lyon told members of his congregation to be thankful for their freedom from the sins of slavery, which he defined as a failure to reform the institution in accord with Biblical slavery and a refusal to adopt a plan of gradual emancipation. His sermon placed as much or more emphasis on the first failing, thereby echoing a not uncommon southern theme that God ended slavery in order to punish the South for abusing it. This interpretation had roots in the stewardship argument of the antebellum proslavery reform movement and had little to do with guilt over the owning of slaves.[5]

In fact, few southerners expressed any guilt over the owning or the mistreatment of slaves, even though they had been raised in a society that encouraged the public confession of sin. Certainly, public opportunities for repentance existed.

Northern Methodist and Presbyterian churches in the South required an admission of the sin of slavery for admittance to membership, yet few southerners took that opportunity to ease their consciences. Southern churches, which also emphasized open repentance, apparently did not feel a need to adopt a similar policy.[6]

Not only did few southerners repent of slavery, many reaffirmed their belief in its justness. Within a month of Lyon's sermon, the governing body of his denomination resolved that southerners "may have to lament before God, either for neglect of duty toward our servants, or for actual wrong while the relation lasted," but they have no need "to bow the head in humiliation before men, or to admit that the memory of many of our dear kindred is to be covered with shame, because, like Abraham, Isaac, and Jacob, they had bond-servants born in their own houses, or bought with their money. . . ." Most white southerners agreed. After offering a similar list of Biblical slaveholders, one declared that "Providence has no more condemned us on account of slavery . . . than it condemned Job, 'the perfect and upright man,' when he was permitted to be so sorely afflicted by Satan." Northern travelers reported similar sentiments. In July 1865 one asked a southerner if he expected retribution from God for waging an unholy war for slavery. The man looked "surprised and perplexed," and replied, "The people here look for some heavy visitation of Divine Providence upon you" of the North for mistreating the South. Calls for federal compensation for their freed slaves suggested that such confidence was not simply braggadocio in the face of the Yankees. Southerners still sincerely believed slavery a matter of property rights, not the immoral expropriation of the life and labor of another human being.[7]

Southerners, their defense of secession and slavery demonstrated, thought they had acted rightly in the war: Neither secession nor slavery had been wrong. Southerners therefore saw no reason to confess any guilt and seemed convinced of their good standing with their maker. And yet the need to consider and reconsider these questions, to defend so ardently the legality of a political right they admitted had no current relevance and the morality of an institution they accepted as abolished, indicated a persisting disquiet. Proud southerners still rankled at northern charges of treason and immorality and feared that someone might believe them. In the peace as so often in the war, southerners found themselves on the defensive.

As southerners reassured themselves that secession and slavery had measured up to God's moral standards, they worried that they had failed to live up to their own standards of public behavior—a concern that of course exacerbated their disquiet and defensiveness. Honor, as historians have increasingly come to argue, constituted an important component of the value system of the Old South. As described by historian Bertram Wyatt-Brown, honor involved an ethical system in which "judgments of behavior are ratified by community consensus" with family "integrity, clearly understood hierarchies of leaders and subordinates, and ascriptive features of individuals and groups" as "guides for those evaluations." Such important social standards, although rooted in the small rural communities of the Old South, did not simply disappear with the surrender at Appomattox. Indeed, many defeated Confederates consoled themselves that all had been lost save honor. Certainly, most wanted and needed to believe that was the case. Yet the code of honor in the Old South had made personal bravery and oath-taking central to a male's status. The war and its aftermath challenged southern males' self-image on both points.[8]

Defeat on the battlefield must have led soldiers raised in a culture that celebrated personal bravery and martial skills to question whether they had lived up to expectations, to question whether they had behaved honorably. One made these fears quite explicit in a poem addressed to his fellow southerners:

> Look not for hope or pity now,
> Nor joy, nor pleasure evermore
> Shall shine on your dishonored brow
> Dishonored aye, and in the dust laid low.

And he made clear where the fault for dishonor lay:

> Who forever struggling to be free
> Were crushed beneath the oppressors might
> And made such things of shame as we.

Few southerners expressed shame so explicitly, but an extreme testiness over war records suggested that others, even if not so convinced of their dishonor as the poet, still struggled with doubts about it. In the first years after the war, many former Confederates published defenses of their own, or their relatives', or their associates' honor and accomplishments. Jubal Early wrote about his final campaign partly "as an act of justice to myself," and Basil Duke intended in his *History of Morgan's Calvary* to record the heroism and "perpetuate" the fame of his leader and to "establish the true character" of the men who served under him. Often, a soldier felt that another's account dishonored him, and many literary duels between ex-Confederates resulted. The controversies sometimes had roots in wartime feuds or became embroiled in postwar politics, but they almost always had their basis in a question of personal honor. In a few instances they very nearly became physical rather than merely literary duels, but pistols were avoided.[9]

Much less frequently than they fought with fellow southerners, ex-Confederates challenged their former foes on points of honor. Wade Hampton questioned the account of the burning of Columbia given by William T. Sherman. Although the dispute had political ramifications, Hampton also considered Sherman's accusation that he was responsible for starting the fire an affront to his honor. Demanding a complete investigation, the South Carolinian explained, "My reputation is the only thing, that I have left, and I am jealous of its preservation." Another Confederate general, Nathan Bedford Forrest, nearly fought a duel with a northerner who stated publicly that Forrest could no longer consider himself a gentleman after a congressional committee found him guilty of the massacre of surrendered black troops at Fort Pillow. The northerner, however, ignored the challenge. Most Yankees' refusal to play by southern rules of honor further frustrated southerners.[10]

The North's demand that the former Confederates petition for pardon and take a test oath to participate in politics only increased fears of dishonor. Southern gentlemen resented swearing to their lack of devotion to the cause or begging forgiveness for their part in defending it. Many did so anyway because they admitted, with Josiah Gorgas, the right of the conqueror "to dictate terms." Even Gorgas blanched at his false request for pardon: "pardon for having done my duty in a cause I deemed the best on earth!" Others took the hated test oath in order to retain their property or to influence postwar developments. One Richmond politician told his fellow citizens that he could "conscientiously take that abominable test-oath" because "it is safer to trust my soul in the hands of a merciful God, than my country in the hands of the Black Republicans." In reaching their decisions to comply, southerners struggled to reconcile the necessities of the time with their sense of the justness of their past conduct. The exigencies of the situation forced them to swear falsely, but when they did, fears arose that they had further compromised their honor.[11]

When considering the question of personal honor, in sum, southerners acted very much as they had in evaluating the righteousness of their cause. Just as they had declared themselves sinless but felt a need to do so repeatedly, they proclaimed their honor secure and seemed inordinately determined to assert it. Indeed, their defensiveness rendered their claims to a secure honor a little less convincing than their affirmations of righteousness.

Similarly mixed signals emerged on the issue of whether or not the Confederates had preserved their manhood in defeat, an issue that was part of the larger question of the loss of honor. It can best be understood, however, in the context of the war's challenge to traditional definitions of masculinity and femininity and the dynamics of male-female relations after Appomattox. The value system of the Old South demanded that males demonstrate personal bravery and protect their women. It promised women not only that protection but the respect of all men in return for purity, piety, and submissiveness. The war and its aftermath led some men to question whether they had met these standards and some women to doubt their efficacy.[12]

The public controversy over reports that Jefferson Davis had been captured in women's clothes certainly suggested that on some level people perceived surrender as a form of emasculation. Northerners delighted in accounts of how the Confederate chieftain had tried to escape in female disguise. Cartoons pictured him dressed in hoop skirt and bonnet, and in his famous show P.T. Barnum displayed what he claimed to be the very clothes Davis had worn. Surely, the widely accepted accusation included a symbolic statement about Davis's and through him, the South's manhood. The insult did not escape the notice of Davis's sixteen-year-old son, who started a fight with a lad who repeated the accusation. Nor was it missed by Davis himself who, to disprove the charge, in 1869 went to the trouble of having his picture taken in the clothes that he had worn when captured. A young southern woman who began to cry when shown one of the cartoons by a northerner apparently considered it offensive, as did her male friend, who quickly eased her distress by burning it.[13]

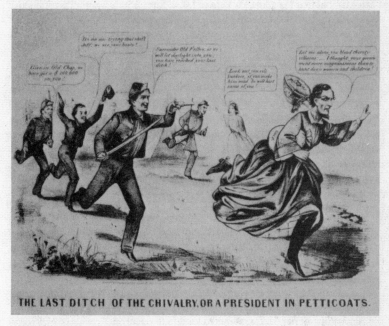

Northern cartoons depicting Jefferson Davis, dressed in women's clothes, attempting to escape. *The Library of Congress*

If Davis in bonnet and skirts offered a corporate and public symbol of emasculation, less-publicized tales of Yankees' ravishing southern women must have reminded southern soldiers of their failure to protect their women as their code of honor demanded. Males seemed reluctant to discuss northern barbarity—more so than females, in fact. On occasion, however, they did so in rather explicit sexual terms. One published story told of a Confederate scout who learned that during his absence a northern raiding party had visited his plantation. The Yankees "seized my tender flower, and with merciless hands stripped all the clothing from her delicate form, and then amid the brutal jests of twenty licentious men, she was forced to the harp, and ordered to play for them at the peril of her life." There were, of course, worse fates than harp playing, but the introduction to the story revealed that it had been made fit for publication. When the scout came home, his wife, who had escaped her tormentors, returned to die in his arms. He then proceeded to hunt down and kill the entire raiding party, one by one. The scout's tragedy may well have symbolized the southern male's fear that military failure had allowed the ravishment of his women, and the recounting of his successful revenge expressed the rage the idea evoked in him.[14]

The prospect that southern women might voluntarily choose victorious northerners over defeated Confederates was even more threatening to southern males. Jubal Early asked a friend to give his regards to the ladies of the family and "tell Miss Sallie if *she* marries a Yankee I shall lose entirely what little confidence I have left in human nature." His and similar comments usually contained an element of jest, but, as a story from a woman in Georgia suggested, they included an element of sexual doubt and jealousy as well. One day in 1865 while the husband of Mrs. E.G. Thomas of Richmond County was away, two northern males seeking to rent her house called on her. When her husband returned, Mrs. Thomas teased him that the callers had come with a letter of introduction. He became quite agitated, according to Mrs. Thomas's diary, and reprimanded her. "Suppose you had been walking on the street and had been joined by one of them how do you suppose I would have felt?" Mrs. Thomas quickly replied that "[I] did not know you thought me so fascinating," and added that southern men did not besiege her on the street. Her husband eventually calmed down, but his initial agitation revealed his apprehension that his wife might accept, if not welcome, northern advances or, more, his fear that others on the street might think that she had.[15]

Taken together, the controversy over Davis's disguise, stories of northern barbarity, and indications of southern sexual insecurities indicate that defeat had indeed undermined southern soldiers' confidence in their manhood. The postwar sense of powerlessness and despair certainly did not help restore it. Nor did the fact that their daughters or wives occasionally had to work outside the home, when before the war they had not. Males' failure as providers could only have added to their anxieties over not living up to the role expected of them.[16]

Almost no one, of course, admitted his doubts openly or even discussed sexual anxieties in general terms. But a Mississippi man lamented the sorry state of southern society, especially developments that could be summarized "by the

term 'his Comb was cut' or as you say his manhood was emasculated. . . ."
Robert Dabney, in an address to the literary societies of Davidson College, also
referred to the sexual implications of defeat. With the loss of the war and its
political aftermath, he explained, "the remnant of survivors, few, subjugated,
disheartened, almost despairing, and alas, dishonored," were "subjugated to every
influence from without, which can be malignantly devised to sap the foundation
of their manhood, and degrade them into fit material for slaves. If our women
do not sustain them, they will sink. Unless the spirits which rule and cheer their
homes can re-animate their self-respect, confirm their resolve, and sustain their
personal honor, they will at length become the base serfs their enemies desire."[17]

If women had turned against men, if they had revolted against the patriarchy
or male domination of southern society, perhaps southern males' doubts about
lost manhood would have been greater. But, as Dabney had hoped, southern
women did sustain their men in a process that began when wives comforted
despairing husbands. In response to what her husband admitted were not very
"manly" thoughts of despair, Julia Lockett wrote in May 1865, "We can not or
ought not repine—You have nobly discharged what was your duty as well as your
delight and as you say you can look any man in the face and call yourself his
equal." She added in closing, "I feel very much for you—but know your proud
heart and clear conscience will need nothing from me but loving sympathy and
all our noble men will find *that* at home from our still nobler women. . . ."[18]

Mrs. Lockett prophesied well, for women did enthusiastically and lovingly
welcome home the defeated troops. Whitelaw Reid reported that veterans were
mobbed on the streets of Savannah. "Many a stalwart fellow, in coarse gray," he
wrote, "was fairly surrounded on the sidewalk by a bevy of his fair friends; and
if without an arm or leg, so much the better—the compliments would rain upon
him till the blushes would show upon his embrowned cheeks, and he was fairly
convinced he had taken the most gallant and manly course in the world." In
another town, citizens honored the Confederates with a picnic replete with food,
dances, and women in finery. One unmarried woman, who did not really want
to go to a party, decided she would since "it was designed to welcome the
returned Rebels . . . I am glad to see the demonstration for the poor scarred
fellows," she added. "They deserve much praise for their perseverance and
fidelity." Such warm welcomes surely helped ease the veterans' doubts about
failure, sexual rejection, and lost manhood.[19]

As time went on, the reported ostracism of northern men by southern belles
should have further alleviated these anxieties. Reports of female hatred for and
avoidance of Yankees must not be taken at face value, however. Southern and
northern males both enjoyed the notion that southern women were intransigent.
Southern men wanted and needed to believe that nothing could shake the loyalty
of their women to them or to their cause. For northern men an intractable image
fit their sexual stereotypes and offered a chance to prove their own masculinity
through romantic conquest of the most hostile element in the South. "A man
may be reasoned and beaten out of a false opinion," explained northern
journalist John T. Trowbridge, "but a woman never. She will not yield to
logic, not even to the logic of events." An "appeal to their intelligence is idle,"

he concluded, but "they are vulnerable on the side of the sentiments; and many a one has been authentically converted from the heresy of state rights by some handsome Federal officer, who judiciously mingled love with loyalty in his speech, and pleaded for the union of hands as well as the union of States."[20]

Males of both regions, therefore, may well have exaggerated southern female hostility. One group of soldiers wandering through the mountains of North Carolina after the surrender encountered women with a very different attitude. When informed of the war's end, they went "into a paroxysm of delight" that the Yankees were on their way, thinking they would be able to find husbands among them. The mountain women were unusual, but the undying disgust for the Yankees professed by more typical women proved of questionable depth and sincerity. Hotheaded Augusta Evans Wilson, a Mobile, Alabama, novelist who constantly proclaimed her hatred of the Yankees and practiced ostracism as a religion, did not hesitate to take her brother to New York to secure the best medical care available, all the while decrying the decadence of Yankee civilization. Wilson also did not appear particularly insulted by the royalties her books earned from a northern publisher. Other women of seemingly intractable views were young, impressionable, and prone to hyperbole. They often admitted that association with Yankees proved less an unmitigated horror than their earlier proclamations had indicated. A few found they could socialize with the conquerors and even marry them.[21]

Although never as universally or as intensely as some accounts made it appear, southern women did dislike and shun northerners. They concurred with the author of the poem, "True to the Gray," who told of the death of a lover at Yankee hands. Such acts, the poem concluded, rendered northerners unsuitable mates for southern women:

> The girls who loved the boys in gray,
> The girls to country true,
> Can ne'er in wedlock give their hands,
> To those who wore the blue.

Many drew the line far short of marriage. They closed the shades and doors to evade the eyes of Yankees passing their houses, crossed the street to avoid meeting them on a stroll, shunned all social contact, and swore never to receive a northerner in their homes.[22]

Along with the hostility displayed toward Yankee soldiers and the warm welcome accorded the returning Confederates, other developments suggested that the war and defeat had done little to alter the patriarchy of the Old South. If Alabama was typical of the southern states, the region experienced a matrimonial boom in the first five to ten years after the war. The marriage rate in the state surpassed both the prewar level and that in the postwar North. Furthermore, if studies in two areas prove valid for the rest of the region, economic opportunities for women and their economic independence did not increase during the war. In Clarke County, Georgia, women had few new occupational choices after the war, and both there and in the Alabama black belt female land ownership increased only slightly or possibly even declined. Finally, no significant movement for women's rights developed in the South during Reconstruction to parallel agitation in the North. Failing to organize to fight for their rights, gaining little more economic independence, marrying more frequently than before the war, and embracing the returning soldiers, southern women surely launched no attack on the patriarchy and appeared to return happily to their status under the old code.[23]

Several factors made unlikely a substantial attack on male dominance during the social flux following Appomattox. Women felt concern and compassion for their loved ones and wanted to comfort, not confront, them in their anguish. A deep fear of the free black male encouraged white females to turn to their men for protection and thereby hindered any feminine revolt. The destruction and despair of defeat also discouraged the development of a women's movement, for females had to join with males to solve more basic problems of survival. Therefore no attack on the patriarchy developed, woman's role changed very little, and male anxieties began to ease. But particularly because so many factors made revolt unlikely, its absence did not mean women were totally at ease with their accustomed role in society.[24]

The women's extreme dislike of the Yankees, so reassuring to southern males, may have signaled a female disquiet rooted in a deeper, or at least different, resentment than that held by men. Naturally, women hated the invaders who had killed their relatives and despoiled their land. But the women seemed to display a more vehement hatred than men who had suffered similar losses. Many observers resorted to innate sexual characteristics to explain the more intense hostility: Women were simply more emotional, or "less forgiving than men." Others took into consideration the fact that women's experience of the war differed from men's. They had "more time to brood over the wrongs that had been done them," one woman of the era offered, and "had not had the excitement of battle to sustain them."[25]

Females not only had different experiences in the war, but those experiences and emancipation dramatically changed the daily lives of many southern white women and subtly challenged their traditional status within society. The abolition of slavery had an immediate influence on plantation mistresses and wealthy city dwellers, those who most often voiced hatred for Yankees. One Mississippian recalled the shock of women who awoke to find their slaves gone and no fire, no water, no breakfast. "Ah, then and there were hurryings to and fro' and gathering tears and tremblings of distress and cheeks all pale, their waterloos had come—face to face with a question never before presented in life. How to get a breakfast." Many households eventually secured black cooks and maids, but women still found their daily chores increased, and not all of them felt fulfilled by their new responsibilities. After the flight of her slaves, novelist Wilson complained of having *"to do our own work"* and dismissed as nonsense the idea that cooking a wonderful meal for a loved one was a great privilege. For her and other southern white women, emancipation altered their status by diminishing executive responsibilities in the home and increasing the difficulty and drudgery of the workday. Even in 1883 an Alabama woman complained before a congressional committee about the problems of running a household since emancipation, and, when pressed, she blamed the Yankees for her troubles.[26]

The war not only complicated the household work of women but also forced many to face personal danger as they rarely had before. Both at the time and later, women wrote of their anxieties when the men departed and they waited alone for the arrival of northern troops. Elizabeth Meriwether recalled how two Yankees stopped at her house, commented on how good she looked, and announced they would spend the night. Fearful, she resolved to leave occupied Memphis. When northern soldiers came to the front door of another woman, she admitted to being so frightened she could not move. She added that even the squeaking sound of the metal axle on the Yankee supply wagon "made every Southern woman tremble." Frances Doughty recalled that after the war when her family gathered by the fire and reminisced about the war, her father and grandfather recounted their "hairbreadth escapes, their hardships, the jokes of their camp life, or . . . a memorable interview with one of the great chieftains . . . ," but her mother and grandmother talked of their "clever household and toilet devices" and "of their anxieties." The war had exposed a personal, sexual vulnerability—a revelation women recalled long after the war.[27]

Southern condemnations of Sherman, Butler, and assorted Yankee "bummers," though frequent, caustic, and couched in rhetoric that suggested the ultimate violation, did not often include explicit accounts of rape or physical abuse of women. Instead, they stressed how Yankees had forcibly entered and ransacked homes and treated women with wanton disrespect. Perhaps entering the home served as discreet imagery for physical violation; certainly, rapes did occur, though exactly how often proves very difficult to determine. But southern women seemed sufficiently upset just by a literal interpretation of the stories of rude entry and rough handling. Their homes and their status as ladies, they had learned, did not always protect them. The protection and respect promised women in return for purity, piety, and submissiveness under traditional conceptions of femininity failed. Sherman, the other Yankee generals, and their men did not always follow those rules. In time of crisis, women learned, the domestic haven might be violated by any strange man, and pure, pious, even submissive women did not necessarily command respect. In the first years after the war, southerners heaped their greatest abuse on Butler—a tendency suggesting that respect was as much or more at issue than rape or the destruction of property. Called "the beast, the wretch, the reviler of women," Butler had in addition to his other transgressions threatened to treat loyal Confederate females in New Orleans as women of the street.[28]

Women gained a new appreciation not only of their vulnerability but also of the limits of their influence within the traditional feminine role. Their appeals to morality, their major source of power within the reigning conception of womanhood, often fell on deaf ears. One Alabama woman who detested Sherman for the outrages his troops committed in her area could not understand why her moral appeals to him failed. Experiencing a similar powerlessness, another despaired: "I think sometimes, that if I were *only a man*, and had the *eloquence* of Patrick Henry, I would certainly create a *stir*, if nothing else."[29]

The war and emancipation, in sum, had altered the household status of many women, had forced women to recognize their physical vulnerability, and had exposed the fragility of the protection offered by their moral femininity. Some simply accepted these developments and ignored their implications for the role of women in society. Others seemed vaguely aware of the challenge the war had brought but did not openly question the patriarchy, continuing to accept traditional definitions of the status of women. The Alabaman frustrated by her inability to reach Sherman continued to see woman as God's assistant in helping make men better and consoled herself that sometimes victory takes a long time. Although they did not rebel, these women did channel their frustrations into hatred for the men who had refused to proffer what they believed to be the proper respect and who exposed their vulnerability: the Yankees. Perhaps more than any other single factor, that explained the intense contempt for the Yankees women expressed after Appomattox and harbored for years to come.

Too much could easily be made of the anxieties and confusion southern white men and women experienced about their sex roles. The South did not become an open-air asylum for sexual dysfunctionals. Doubts and confusion did not incapacitate them. Rarely vocalized and only dimly perceived, these doubts distressed rather than debilitated. The women adjusted quickly to their old role, as their homage to the soldiers testified, and suppressed whatever doubts they may have had about it. As life returned to normal, they did not nurse their dissatisfactions. Their public signs of support for the men and their failure to attack the patriarchy reassured the former Confederates and began the process of easing their anxieties about their manhood.

The other anxieties of the southerners, about the righteousness of the cause and the preservation of honor, rarely had public airings after Appomattox either. Yet the disquiet remained, and even more than the southerners' need to repeat their assertions of righteousness, honor, and manhood, their defensiveness toward northerners revealed its existence. Southerners had good reason to treat with hostility visiting Yankees who sought to subvert the South's social order by helping blacks or supporting Republicans. But while some travelers on neither mission still found southerners aloof, others reported them quite gracious. One visitor attributed the differing receptions to the attitudes of the northerners rather than to those of their hosts. Mary A. Dodge, who traveled through the region in 1867, claimed that northern visitors who insulted southerners with "sympathy and pity" or who spoke too "loudly of the superiority of Northern to Southern society" awakened "antipathy" among them. Other northern travelers commented on how quickly southern manners improved when properly encouraged. John Trowbridge, a journalist hardly known for his pro-southern bias, received only curt responses from one disabled Confederate soldier until his plight moved Trowbridge to volunteer that he had a right to be bitter. The man's answers then lost "their explosive quality and sharp downward inflection." In most other instances, Trowbridge discovered that the hostility of southerners (South Carolinians excepted) "usually wore off on a short acquaintance." During her 1875 lecture tour, abolitionist and feminist mented on her hosts' "arrogance and readiness to take offense, and old slave driver ways [but] . . . at the same time faculty of 'subsiding' when they are properly met."[30]

The "readiness to take offense" coupled with the "faculty of 'subsiding' when . . . properly met" that Dodge, Trowbridge, and Dickinson all noted revealed much about white southern attitudes. Concerned about their honor, southerners met northerners prepared to assert it and to put the Yankee in his or her place. If the visitor appeared hostile or patronizing, in either case thereby displaying a lack of respect, southerners not only resented it but felt compelled to demonstrate their honor through contempt for the Yankee. But if the traveler met the southerner properly, in other words if he or she thereby acknowledged southern honor, the southerner reciprocated with a kind welcome and considerate behavior.

As the hostility directed toward the disrespectful traveler suggested, southerners valued northern respect. This sentiment found its clearest and most public expression in a column written by Charles H. Smith. A Georgia newspaper columnist who wrote as Bill Arp, Smith expressed southern feeling accurately throughout the war and became one of the region's most popular writers after it. In an 1865 open letter to Artemus Ward, intended to parallel a column addressed to him shortly after the attack on Fort Sumter, Arp admitted that the "rebs, so-called," realized that their country was dead. Southerners still found it "very painful, I assure you, to dry up all of a sudden, and make out like we wasn't there. . . ." Despite his own best efforts, Arp claimed, he would be unable "to subjugate myself to the level of surroundin' circumstances, so-called" until allowed to say something. Arp then affirmed that the South thought its course right and would take its chances with the deity. He also complained that since the war the North had not treated the South honorably. "We made a bully fite, and the whole American nation ought to feel proud of it."[31]

Bill Arp and the many southerners who agreed with him asked more of the North than could reasonably be expected. So soon after the conflict, northerners were unlikely to praise the nobility of enemies that they regarded as traitors and murderers. The demand for such deference obviously hindered the process of reconciliation and reconstruction, but it also revealed a sense of honor in need of assuaging. Under the old code a man might challenge anyone who questioned his honor, but he rarely chose to plead for respect through a public appeal in the newspaper—in dialect at that.[32]

Interpreting southern attitudes after Appomattox so nicely symbolized in Arp's letter is difficult. One might argue that southerners' repeated assertions of their righteousness and desire for northern praise revealed that they felt guilty over defending slavery and trying to destroy the Union. Yet to accept that conclusion requires that southerners' statements that they had acted rightly and did not fear God's judgment be ignored or interpreted to mean just the opposite. It also requires that the absence of any substantial confession of guilt over slavery or secession, even in the churches, must be seen as evidence that the guilt was so deep or unacknowledged that they could not confess it. Such a view is intellectually credible, but so is the opposite conclusion, that they felt no guilt. And in the absence of some compelling reason to disbelieve them, the southerners' assertion should be accepted. Faced with defeat, they judged their actions against their consciences and ruled themselves righteous.[33]

Another way of interpreting southern attitudes after Appomattox, an approach based on the idea that honor was central to southern values, would be to label the southern anxieties a sign of shame. Unlike guilt, in which southerners would have believed their behavior failed to meet an internalized standard, a sense of shame would have resulted from a perception of failure to live up to the expectations of their society. Knowledge of the latter failure would then come not from their consciences but from the opprobrium heaped on them by society. In some ways a more satisfying label for southern disquiet than guilt, shame still does not quite describe the pattern of southern belief and behavior. In a culture based on honor, the feeling of shame entails the acceptance of the condemnation offered by society. After Appomattox, southerners did not, for the most part, condemn the behavior of other loyal Confederates, as the women welcoming back the soldiers illustrated. Among other southerners they encountered little opprobrium and therefore had no reason to feel shame. Only the North offered condemnation, and southerners, as their reaction to northern travelers and the affirmation in Arp's column testified, refused to accept it. An interpretation that views southerners as overcome with shame seems only slightly more appropriate than one that portrays them as burdened by guilt. Southerners did not so much feel shame as they feared dishonor. They were determined that the honor they prized be acknowledged.

But if neither guilt nor shame accurately characterizes their attitude, southerners did clearly display disquiet and defensiveness. Perhaps their feelings can best be described simply as a damaged self-image. Defeat in battle and the exigencies of the war's aftermath wounded southerners' confidence in their righteousness, honor, and manliness. The wounds did not prove fatal; they did not destroy the sense of righteousness, honor, or manliness. Instead, as the antebellum code of honor demanded, southerners asserted to themselves and to the Yankees that they retained them. Soothed by these assertions, the wounds began to heal. But they left scars, scars that made southerners continue to be a bit defensive about their public image and more than a little anxious for reassurance.

CHAPTER THREE

Ceremonial Bereavement: Memorial Activities

Within an hour of hearing the news of Lee's surrender, Father Abram J. Ryan composed "The Conquered Banner," a poem that reflected the trauma and pain of defeat. Hardly a defiant statement of southern resolve, it expressed the despair of a defeated South and urged the furling of its flag because "there's not a man to wave it." Ryan later remarked that as he wrote his "mind was engrossed with thoughts of our dead soldiers and dead cause," and evocations of death filled the poem. The poem lamented that the hand that had "grasped" and the "hearts that fondly clasped" the Confederate flag were "Cold and dead and lying low." Ryan's poem closed with a plea to put away the fallen banner:

> Touch it not—unfold it never,
> Let it droop there furled forever,
> For it droops above the dead.[1]

Published under a pseudonym in a New York paper with southern sympathies, "The Conquered Banner" quickly became enormously popular in the South. One southern critic judged it "a poem in one respect, perhaps, unparalleled in literature:—it is a nation's dirge." When Ryan's identity became known, white southerners revered the poet as well as the poem, even though Ryan seemed a most incongruous hero. He had entered Confederate lines only in 1863 after his brother died in the Confederate army and he had himself been jailed overnight in Missouri for seditious statements. Ryan never actually joined the army or served officially as a chaplain, although he may occasionally have ministered to soldiers on the battlefields around his home in Knoxville. He was a Roman Catholic of decidedly mystical bent in an overwhelmingly evangelical society. In a culture that celebrated virility, he was a scraggly-haired, enfeebled, almost effeminate man whose appearance underscored the despair of his poetry. One woman who heard Ryan preach thought he looked as if he could not "live long" and commented on how "sad" it made her "to hear him speak, for he seems to have some deep grief weighing him down."[2]

Ryan's sad and deathly countenance perhaps only enhanced the appeal of his verse. In the first years after Appomattox southerners seemed fascinated with death, and "The Conquered Banner" became only one of many poems incorporating the theme. They filled southern magazines of the period, and many by less-polished or -ambitious authors went unpublished. Not just the poetry but, according to some observers, the very countenance of southerners suggested a fascination with death. Visitors to the region commented on how weighed down by grief southerners seemed. A northern minister, in fact, later recalled that during 1866 Virginia "looked not unlike a desolated country graveyard, and the people not unlike the sad spectres passing among the tombs."[3]

The pervasive melancholy, caught so well by the minister's somewhat exaggerated imagery, found various expressions. Naturally, relatives and friends mourned the loss of loved ones in battle, but defeat gave special poignancy to their grief. "We could bear the loss of my brave little brothers when we thought they had fallen at the post of duty defending their Country," wrote one woman in her diary, "but now to know that those glad, bright spirits suffered and toiled in vain, that the end is overwhelming defeat, the thought is unendurable." Some survivors not only mourned the dead but in diaries and poems expressed envy of them or confessed their own desire to die. Although sometimes reflecting frustration with the trials of Reconstruction, these wishes more often arose out of the general despair brought on by defeat.[4]

Edmund Ruffin wrapped himself in a Confederate flag, took a gun, and blew out his brains. His sad demise was atypical: Only a few suicides can be attributed to the war. The vast majority of southerners who wrote of their longing to die never acted out the wish and probably never considered doing so. The talk of death offered a temporary psychological escape not unlike that found in discussions of emigration, and especially discouraged Confederates even combined the two fantasies. In 1867 Jubal Early decided colonization in Venezuela was totally unrealistic, but admitted " . . . thinking that perhaps it might be better to go and be killed off by the climate so that there might be an end to my troubles in this world at last." Early never went to Venezuela and lived into the 1890s.[5]

In the first years after Appomattox, southerners' longing for escape through death and their mourning of dead soldiers and a dead cause was incorporated into a Confederate memorial movement and assumed thereby an importance transcending individual attitudes about death. As the first cultural expression of the Confederate tradition, the memorial movement began the process in which southerners interpreted the meaning and implications of defeat. Throughout the region, communities created cemeteries, erected monuments, and established a memorial day for the Confederate dead. These activities honored the dead and their cause, placed distance between the Confederacy and the daily lives of southerners, but also offered a vague hope of its future vindication. In the process, the memorial movement helped to ensure that the Confederate dead became powerful cultural symbols within the New South—gave power, in other words, to the ghosts of the Confederacy.

During the last half of 1865 women in Winchester, Virginia, first met to plan a cemetery for the Confederates killed in nearby battles. In January 1866, women in Columbus, Georgia, decided to hold a springtime memorial service for the Confederate dead. Two months later they published a newspaper appeal urging all southern towns to institute similar celebrations. In April and May 1866 memorial associations formed in communities throughout the former Confederacy. After this initial burst of organizational activity, memorial societies continued to form at a slower pace into the 1870s.[6]

A few associations credited the Columbus group with inspiring their formation, but the genesis of most appeared to be local. Often a leader of a women's wartime soldiers' aid society, a woman who in some cases had lost a husband or son in the war, called a public meeting to form an organization to memorialize the Confederate dead. Interested women met, organized a voluntary society, and often secured a charter from the state. Many local groups had only from twenty to thirty members, but in larger towns they sometimes boasted more than a hundred. The members initially chose a variety of names for their societies, but most quickly adopted the title Ladies' Memorial Association (LMA). Even so, no regional or statewide organizations emerged; the associations remained independent local organizations with common motives and goals.[7]

The name Ladies Memorial Association proved slightly misleading, since men played important roles in establishing many of the societies. In Richmond young newspaperman Francis W. Dawson claimed much of the credit for conceiving, organizing, and directing the early work of the prominent Hollywood Memorial Association. In Charleston and other cities males presided at the first meetings. Some LMAs allowed active or, more often, honorary male members. Others formed committees of men to provide advice and aid. Many recruited young veterans to perform much of the manual labor involved in their cemetery projects. And, most important, in all the groups men furnished financial assistance. In Raleigh, for example, a man gave the LMA land for its cemetery. Six men, but only one woman, became life members of the association by donating a hundred dollars each, and during its first two years male financial supporters outnumbered female members. Men clearly considered memorial work important. Yet few male memorial societies formed, and the ones that did usually did not long survive. One turned over its money to a woman's society after "recognizing memorial work as peculiarly fitting to women. . . ." In other words, southern males believed that memorial projects belonged to the realm of sentiment in which women had innate abilities and over which they had primary responsibility. Men therefore helped organize the societies and donated money to them but left the leadership of the groups and most of the work to women.[8]

The women directed their efforts almost entirely to the memorialization of the dead. Although a few LMAs met monthly, most convened only quarterly or yearly. Meetings involved little discussion of political or historical issues; members devoted their time to planning memorials and to figuring out how to finance them. Money came from male supporters, the members' own dues, and the proceeds of such projects as dances, other entertainments, and Confederate bazaars where wartime memorabilia were sold. In the decade after the war, LMAs in New Orleans and Richmond each raised more than $20,000, and those in Augusta and Montgomery more than $10,000. Smaller towns, naturally, had less success, but even in them a benefit held on two nights might yield as much as $1,000. With the money, the associations sponsored three major projects: creation of cemeteries, erection of monuments, and celebration of memorial day.[9]

Societies considered the proper burial of the Confederate dead their primary task. "These bodies bone of our bone, and flesh of our flesh," the Petersburg, Virginia, LMA maintained, "arise a spectre band before us, demanding a christian, an honorable sepulture." The LMAs usually accepted the responsibility of caring for the dead from battles in their area and the bodies of local soldiers sent home during the war. At least one society, though, appointed an agent to locate and bring home corpses from distant battlefields, and in the early seventies several cities reinterred Confederate dead from Gettysburg.[10]

In a few towns, societies sought to provide "an honorable sepulture" for the dead in the field where they had fallen. The effort in Winchester began when two women and a minister, upset because a farmer had accidently plowed up the remains of two Confederates, resolved to establish a cemetery for the Confederates killed in the many battles around their town. They formed a local association to carry out their plans, solicited financial assistance throughout the South, and by the spring of 1866 had enough money to purchase the land and begin reinterment of the corpses. The association buried the remains of 2,494 soldiers in state sections, with a mound in the center of the cemetery for the unknown dead. It then marked the individual graves with headstones and erected a wooden shaft to the dead of each state, with the expectation that the states would eventually replace them with more substantial monuments. When the group completed the work, it named the burial ground "Stonewall Cemetery" and dedicated it in October 1866. Women in towns around the battlefield at Resaca, Georgia, undertook a similar project at about the same time. They landscaped a part of the battleground, reinterred the dead in state plots, and marked their graves.[11]

Rather than placing them on a battlefield, LMAs more often sponsored cemeteries in their communities. They built Confederate sections in an existing graveyard, assumed responsibility for soldiers' burial plots started during the war, or created their own cemeteries. In Richmond, the management of Hollywood Cemetery, an antebellum graveyard overlooking the James River, opened a large tract for the Confederate dead. Under the auspices of the Hollywood Memorial Association, nearly eight hundred young men of the city spent a May day in 1866 "moulding and clearing the graves of the Confed[erate] dead." The women of the association then began collecting money to purchase memorial stones for each mound and to construct paved walks through the area. In Raleigh the LMA founded Oakwood Cemetery to have a place to bury the Confederates and donated the rest of the grounds to the city for a graveyard.[12]

Southerners manifested tremendous pride in the "cities of the dead" they constructed. Memorial associations boasted of their beautiful, dignified landscaping and built paths or streets through them to facilitate visits by the living.

Confederate monument, Oakdale Cemetery, Richmond, Virginia (unveiled 1871). *Manuscript Department, Perkins Library, Duke University*

"The first question you are asked on entering a southern city is: 'Have you been to the cemetery?'" one northerner reported. Even when not showing them off to strangers, southerners found solace and inspiration in the cemeteries. Resaca, according to one LMA historian, became "a sort of pleasure ground in the midst of a devastated land" that served as "a great resort for rustic lovers on Sunday afternoons." Dolly Blount Lamar of Macon, Georgia, remembered as a little girl spending Sunday afternoons in the local graveyard with her father who "would read [her] the tombstone inscriptions and discourse on the dead with considerable pomp and oratory."[13]

Once they had cemeteries in proper order, most LMAs sought to provide a monument to the Confederate dead, perhaps to provide less imaginative fathers than Dolly Lamar's with inspiration. A lack of money or loss of interest kept some groups from erecting monuments during the first two decades after the war. The monuments completed by 1885, though, differed significantly from the later ones that usually featured a Confederate soldier atop a tall shaft on the courthouse lawn. Instead, the early monuments incorporated themes of ceremonial bereavement: Over 90 percent of them had some funereal aspect, either in placement or design.[14]

Between 1865 and 1885, southerners placed approximately 70 percent of their Confederate monuments in cemeteries. Usually a town's memorial society or even a public meeting made the decision to put it there rather than in the center of town. Southerners apparently agreed with the historian of the Charleston LMA who maintained that "a memorial of a lost cause" should "not be a triumphal memorial. Placed in the City of the Dead, and near the entrance, the sight of it cannot fail to call back the memory of the sad history which it commemorates."[15]

The designs most frequently chosen for early Confederate monuments also evoked death and grief. Approximately 75 percent were of funereal design—that is, they resembled cemetery statuary and evoked mourning rather than featuring a Confederate soldier. Adopting a death memorial from another culture, the Hollywood Memorial Association of Richmond constructed in the Confederate section of the cemetery a massive, forty-five-foot rough-granite pyramid, an unusual but compelling monument. A few associations chose romantic Victorian cemetery sculpture, such as the statue in Savannah that depicted a robed woman with her finger pressed to her lips indicating silence. Most common, however, was some form of a classical obelisk, often with an urn or drape on top, that featured simplicity, even dignity, in an era when heavy-handed symbolism bordering on the maudlin still reigned in sepulcher sculpture.[16]

The addresses delivered at the unveilings of these monuments reinforced the theme of bereavement revealed in their placement and design. J.H. Hudson, speaking in Cheraw, South Carolina, at the dedication of perhaps the first Confederate monument, evoked the "mournful silence" with which "we approach this spot to erect and dedicate this simple monument. . . ." "Darkness has come upon us—poverty is our lot, and a sigh our song, . . ." he continued. "The land that once blossomed as a garden, and flowed with milk and honey, is

Confederate monument, Hollywood Cemetery, Richmond, Virginia (unveiled 1869). *Manuscript Department, Perkins Library, Duke University*

now draped in sorrow and desolation. . . ." Having acknowledged the South's gloom and grief, Hudson then offered hope. "In the economy of an all wise God, we may have become the chosen instruments of fulfilling his wonderful plans, though in a manner different from what we supposed."[17]

A similar grief tempered by obscure hope was symbolized in the final activity of the memorial associations: celebration of Confederate Memorial Day. The custom probably had its roots in the practice of individuals' placing flowers on the graves of loved ones who had died in the war. While returning from doing so in 1866, Lizzie Rutherford of Columbus suggested having a public ceremony. She had been reading the Baroness Tautphoeus's novel, *The Initials*, which described a Catholic custom in Germany of decorating the churchyard's graves on All Saints Day. Rutherford and her friends decided to institute a similar custom for Confederate graves, but to celebrate the day in the spring. The Columbus women published an appeal for all communities to adopt the practice, and the custom spread quickly. Later, other towns claimed to have first celebrated Memorial Day, and it may well have had several independent origins. In any case, its popularity indicated that it expressed deep and widespread southern sentiments.[18]

Communities that adopted the custom selected various spring days. The deep South almost universally recognized 26 April, the day of Johnston's surrender, while towns in South and North Carolina chose 10 May, the anniversary of Stonewall Jackson's death. Virginia societies selected days ranging from 10 May to the middle of June; in Richmond one memorial association celebrated on 10 May and another on 30 May. On whatever day chosen, sponsors of the event intended that most of the residents of their community take part. To encourage them, some merchants closed their stores for part or all of the day. The ceremonies themselves invariably featured the decoration of the Confederate graves with greenery and flowers. Other practices, however, varied. Most towns staged a formal procession to the cemetery and conducted a service of prayer, hymns, and an address by a minister or revered veteran. Some chose to hear the speech in a hall in town or not to have one at all. A few communities held no formal program, but simply had people gather at the cemetery to decorate the graves.[19]

If they were a part of the celebration, speeches usually enunciated themes common to the memorial movement. They evoked the South's despair at the end of the war, praised the accomplishments of the Confederate dead, and defended the nobility of their actions and the purity of their motives. The orators devoted limited attention to accounts of the war or sectional issues. "We are not here today to listen to political utterances," William Nelson Pendleton, a veteran and rector in Lexington, Virginia, said on one occasion. The addresses did, however, go beyond defense and celebration of the dead to hold out the hope of future vindication. "Here let us look away from the gloom of political bondage, and fix our vision upon a coming day of triumph, when principles, born of truth and baptized in the blood of our brothers, shall out live the persecution of a merciless enemy and the treachery of unhallowed ambition," urged Georgian Henry D. Capers in an 1869 memorial address. Echoing a theme heard in many

Confederate monument, Cross Creek Cemetery, Fayetteville, North Carolina (unveiled 1868), probably decorated for Memorial Day. *The Museum of the Confederacy*

southern churches after the war, Capers maintained that God would ensure this triumph, but other orators offered a more secular version.[20]

Addresses, however, constituted only a small and perhaps not very important part of the memorial movement. The emphasis remained on the process of bereavement: the creation of cemeteries, the erection of funereal monuments, and the springtime decoration of the graves. These activities incorporated attitudes about death common in nineteenth-century Victorian American culture. The North, in fact, quickly adapted the southern custom to celebrate its own dead. Northerners, however, had a triumphant Fourth of July as well as a memorial day and had an active, political veterans movement as well as ladies' memorial associations. In the South memorial ventures were virtually the only cultural expression concerned with the meaning of the war. To the extent that the movement accurately reflected southern sentiment and commanded broad popular support, it offers significant insight into the way the South began to come to terms with defeat.[21]

If southerners undertook memorial activities only because they feared federal opposition to more direct displays of Confederate sentiment, if they put monuments in cemeteries only because they thought the North would object to them in town, the movement did not accurately reflect southern attitudes. Occasionally, a southerner attributed the emphasis on bereavement to federal opposition to other activities, but little evidence exists to support the claim. During the first years after the war a few federal commanders did issue orders prohibiting celebration of any acts committed by the former insurgents and forbidding the erection of monuments of the Confederates. Their bans usually included memorial activities, so if southerners had been extremely sensitive to northern pressure they would have abandoned memorial work, too. In fact, federal objections were at most sporadic, and curtailing the celebration of the Confederate past never had high priority with northern forces. Southerners need not have worried much about federal opposition, and memorial associations certainly did not appear to plan their activities to accord with northern wishes. That they continued to place monuments in cemeteries well after Reconstruction ended indicated that fear of northern opposition was not a major factor in deciding to put them there. Memorial ventures genuinely expressed southern attitudes and were not a clever subterfuge for celebrating the southern cause without incurring federal wrath.[22]

Memorial work was not only a sincere expression of southern sentiment but a broadly popular one. Communities near battlefields, such as Winchester, Richmond, Petersburg, and Resaca, were for obvious reasons more likely to create cemeteries. Nevertheless, almost all areas of the South experienced some memorial activity. Furthermore, the success of memorial associations in raising large sums of money in a distressed economy offered evidence of significant support but testified primarily to the involvement of the well-to-do. Social elites probably were over-represented among the membership of the memorial associations. The roster of the Charleston LMA, for which membership records are extant, contained such well-known Carolina low-country names as Gaillard, Grimball, Manigault, Middleton, Porcher, Ravenel, and Rutledge. In the period 1866–79, male honorary members of the Charleston LMA came primarily from the city's business and professional elite. Factors and commission merchants were most numerous among them, but a number of physicians, lawyers, and ministers also belonged, as did at least a few area planters. In all, more than 85 percent of the males involved came from proprietary and high white-collar occupations. Fewer then 3 percent had working-class backgrounds. A similarly low percentage of the female members had working-class husbands. More of the women than men had middle-class backgrounds, but more than half of those, too, came from the upper class. The organizational strength of the Charleston LMA clearly rested in the city's elite.[23]

Although both the Charleston records and impressionistic evidence from other areas suggest that the wealthy sponsored the memorial movement, the reports of large crowds attending Memorial Day services and monument unveilings indicate wide popular support. Southerners claimed that large, dignified crowds participated in the ceremonies. Usually agreeing that much of the population took part, northern visitors sometimes offered a different assessment of those involved. Abolitionist Anna Dickinson described an Atlanta Memorial Day throng as "ignorant looking" and complained that most of the people in it "*stank*" and needed a bath. She may have thought all southerners unkempt and odoriferous, but her slurs on the appearance of the crowd suggested that it included poorer whites as well as the fashionable set. Some southerners stated specifically that the crowds included people from all classes.[24]

Because of the broad public support they received, memorial activities illuminate southern attitudes toward the war in the years after Appomattox. Memorial work provided opportunities to express grief at the loss of relatives and friends, but its rituals had specific corporate significance as well. Grief and mourning accompany social change as well as personal loss. Bereavement, social theorist Peter Marris writes, is an effort to "assimilate disruptive change. Grief, then, is the expression of a profound conflict between contradictory impulses— to consolidate all that is still valuable and important in the past, and preserve it from loss; and at the same time, to reestablish a meaningful pattern of relationships, in which the loss is accepted."[25]

Confederate memorial activity began the process Marris describes. By honoring the dead, whom some considered especially heroic because they never surrendered, southerners preserved what they considered part of the best of their recent past. And, of course, their praise for the pure motives and noble sacrifices of the fallen redounded to their own credit as well. At the same time, the services for the dead helped the South begin to reduce, or at least to alter, its commitment to the Confederacy. With memorial exercises the major expression of Confederate sentiment, the South ritualistically acknowledged the death of its cause. By placing memorials to the wartime heroes outside the normal living and working areas of the community, southerners symbolically placed distance between their daily lives and their lost cause. Memorial activities thereby helped the South assimilate the fact of defeat without repudiating the defeated.[26]

Memorial Day rituals took the process of adjustment still further by offering hope for the future. The Columbus women decided to decorate graves in the spring rather than in the fall. Even though they chose different days for it, all associations followed the same practice. In fact, the later dates selected in the upper South insured that flowers would be in bloom by the appointed time. The South clearly associated Memorial Day with the rebirth of spring. What southerners did on that day evoked similar associations. Every celebration centered on the practice of bringing flowers and greenery to the graves, symbolically bringing life to death. Memorial Day orators simply echoed themes inherent in the ritual when they spoke of future vindication emerging from the existing gloom of defeat.

According to a simile offered by one orator, Memorial Day resembled a rainbow, a sign of better times to come. If a fascination with, even longing for, death helped inspire the memorial ventures, the ritual in the cemetery enabled southerners to glimpse a future outside the city of the dead. The rituals aided the process of healing the wounds of defeat. Public reassurance of the justness of the cause eased defensiveness and fears of lost honor. The public respect displayed by southern women for fallen fellow soldiers helped reassure men of their loyalty. By offering hope for the future and easing the pain of the past, memorial activities moved southerners beyond the despair expressed in Ryan's "Conquered Banner."[27]

The memorial movement, however, did not lead the South to unfurl that conquered banner. It offered only a sign of, not a program for, eventual triumph. The promise of vindication remained vague and distant; neither rituals nor orators explained what form it would take. More important, by placing the celebration of Memorial Day under the charge of women and hence within the realm of sentiment, southerners further reduced any political or ideological implications. That some blacks, even ones active in politics, could contribute to the memorial work also indicated how little political content it had.[28]

Memorial activities did not offer a coherent historical interpretation of the war and therefore did little to define the Confederate tradition. Nevertheless, they still helped to insure that it had an influential role in southern culture. Organized bereavement strengthened a natural tendency for the dead to have influence on the living. Primitive and European societies during earlier centuries often believed that the ancestral dead returned to earth to influence the living. By the late nineteenth century, Americans did not believe their ancestors actually walked the earth shaping events, but, like people in most societies, they did recognize some influence exerted by the dead through legendary heroes who served as national symbols or role models. The Confederate dead might well have attained such status in any event, but the memorial movement insured and enhanced their cultural importance. Southerners did not adopt the belief of earlier centuries in ancestral spirits. But the Confederate dead did become important cultural heroes, who were perhaps more important to the South than departed heroes in many other societies, and who could be invoked to sanction values and behavior.[29]

White southerners often commented on the persisting influence of the Confederate dead. Virginian John W. Daniel, for example, employed a strange mixture of modern and ancient imagery in asserting to one Memorial Day crowd that "electric wires" stretched from the graves of the Confederate dead "into all the huts and habitations and hearts of men. . . ." On another Memorial Day, Georgian Charles C. Jones, Jr., exclaimed, "How voiceful the graves of those who died for freedom and country!" Memorial activities during the first two decades after the war increased the importance of the voice of the Confederate dead—gave authority to the ghosts of the Confederacy. But the South had not yet decided who would speak for the ghosts of the Confederacy and to what larger purpose.[30]

CHAPTER FOUR

Ghost Dance:
The Failed Revitalization Movement
of the Virginians

The process of giving voice to the ghosts of the Confederacy, of defining the Confederate tradition, progressed slowly in the first years after the war. Major social institutions in the South did little to establish a view of the past, so the task fell first to individual writers, a few southern magazines, and a scattering of veterans' associations. None of them developed a comprehensive definition of the meaning of the war or commanded the attention of the white South. In 1870 the death of the region's premier hero, Robert E. Lee, stimulated new interest in Confederate matters and spurred the formation of a loose coalition of Virginia organizations that did systematically attempt to define and exploit the Confederate tradition. Its leaders not only codified an explanation of the war and defeat but also launched a Confederate revitalization movement, a sort of Confederate ghost dance. Later groups would incorporate much of the Virginians' historical interpretation into the tradition, but in the 1870s southerners appeared largely uninterested in their vision of revitalization.

The established social institutions of the postwar South did little to define the Confederate tradition. State governments, even when not under Radical control, made no attempt to interpret the meaning of the war or celebrate its heroes. Nor did the churches undertake the task of interpreting the war, even though the major denominations, except for the Episcopalians, remained independent of their northern counterparts after the war. The southern churches' refusal to repudiate the Confederate war effort or condemn those who aided it implied their approval, but they took no direct role in defining the tradition. Perhaps chastened by their total commitment to the failed cause, they avoided the involvement in secular and political matters such an effort would have entailed.[1]

Educational institutions played a slightly larger role in preserving the southern view of the recent past than did the states or churches. Private schools, often headed by former Confederate officers, incorporated elements of the Confederate past into their programs. Military academies, which had existed before the war, now dressed cadets in gray and adopted other symbols from the war. A few schools did more to integrate the history of the conflict into education. Founded shortly after the war by prominent local women, the Confederate Home School in Charleston, South Carolina, enrolled fifty or sixty daughters of the struggling antebellum aristocracy of the state. There they were educated, according to one fund-raiser for the school, to be teachers who would be trusted with "the training of Southern youth" and to be mothers who would imbue their children with "just pride in their descent from the Confederate soldier" and with a reverence for such heroes as Jackson, Johnson, and Lee. Schools so thoroughly dedicated to preserving the past were rare, and even the more common military academies with Confederate pretensions were far from ubiquitous.[2]

A few colleges as well as secondary schools attempted to integrate elements of the Confederate past into their programs. The University of the South, which the Episcopal church reopened during 1867 in Sewanee, Tennessee, had several Confederate leaders on its faculty and tried to inculcate in its students the values of the Old South. Washington College in Lexington, Virginia, called Robert E. Lee to its presidency and gathered other ex-Confederates on its campus. Although few had as many as these two, other southern colleges also had former Confederate leaders on their staffs. These men exercised considerable influence on a generation of college students, and some of them became important historical spokesmen within the larger society. Yet they and the institutions they served had only a limited role in shaping southern attitudes about the war. Even at Sewanee and Lexington the memory of the Confederacy constituted a small part of the educational program. Only a miniscule number of southerners attended Washington (later Washington and Lee) or the University of the South, and in fact very few attended any college.[3]

The Ku Klux Klan, an informal, indeed extralegal, institution, more often than the schools or churches has been credited with first enshrining Confederate values. Although the Klan itself later occupied a central place in southern folklore, it did very little during the early postwar period to shape the Confederate tradition. The founders asserted their ties of brotherhood as former soldiers, but the Klan made limited use of Confederate imagery and history. Historians have stressed the KKK's incorporation of knightly and romantic themes, but its major symbolism had fascinating ties to the southern celebration of the dead. Klansmen dressed as ghosts and often claimed to be the Confederate dead of Gettysburg or some local battle. While attempting to play on what they perceived as the superstitions of the black populace, perhaps they unconsciously acknowledged their own fear that the Confederate dead were more powerful and awesome than the survivors of the war. In any case, the hooded ghosts devoted their efforts to ensuring white supremacy and left the job of interpreting the war to others.[4]

In the first decade after the war, in short, the established institutions of society did little to define the Confederate tradition. A host of individuals, however, did begin to try to explain the white South's position. Many former Confederates incorporated interpretations of the war into personal memoirs, while others offered sustained defenses of the southern cause or even comprehensive histories of the war. Not all these books, though, had a significant influence on the development of the Confederate tradition. Edward Pollard's *The Lost Cause*, a history of the war that gave its title to postwar Confederate activity and has been much cited by modern historians, did not. Many critics thought Pollard praised his own Virginia too quickly and too often, although natives of the state tended to criticize him as readily as did others. Former Confederate officers considered Pollard a mere journalist lacking in the military expertise needed to judge men and battles.[5]

Less well-known than Pollard's, but more significant in shaping the Confederate tradition, were three other books published in the first five years after the war. In *Is Davis a Traitor?*, published in 1866 as a defense of the then-imprisoned Confederate president, Albert Taylor Bledsoe argued that the Constitution rested on a compact theory of government that allowed secession. Long before Fort Sumter the North had abused the Constitution and abandoned the compact, Bledsoe continued, so in seceding southerners had not committed treason but only undertaken a legal defense of their rights. The following year Bledsoe's fellow Virginian Robert L. Dabney published *A Defense of Virginia*, an adamant Biblical defense of the morality of slavery and a justification of secession as well. In 1870 Alexander H. Stephens, former vice president of the Confederacy, published his two-volume *Constitutional View of the Late War*. Like Bledsoe, Stephens argued stridently for the validity of a compact theory of the Union that assumed every state had the right to withdraw from the agreement. In seceding in 1861, he concluded, the South was legally exercising its right, after being hounded and oppressed by northerners throughout the antebellum period. Perhaps because of Stephens's status in the Confederate government as well as the greater force of his argument, Stephens's work became the most influential of the three in the development of the southern interpretation of the causes of the war.[6]

Much of the other southern writing that shaped that interpretation appeared in magazines rather than in books. Several journals with a special emphasis on southern themes began publication in the decade after the war. Two, *The Southern Review* and *The Land We Love*, offered sustained defenses of the southern cause. *The Southern Review* was the personal pulpit of Bledsoe, who in its pages expanded many of the arguments first begun in *Is Davis a Traitor?* In 1866, Daniel H. Hill, a former Confederate general from North Carolina, founded *The Land We Love* in Charlotte as "the organ of the Army" and as a means "to vindicate the truth of history." At first it espoused reunion and economic development, but by 1868 Hill's magazine shifted to a more defiant stance and warned that the North sought to destroy "the manhood, the independence, and the integrity of the [southern] people." The following year *The Land We Love* was absorbed by *The New Eclectic* of Baltimore, which later changed its name to *The Southern Magazine* and remained influential in the 1870s.[7]

Although these books and magazines contributed to the development of a southern interpretation of the war and served as sources for those who codified it in the 1890s, they had a very limited public influence at the time. Neither

Bledsoe's nor Dabney's book sold well. The first volume of Stephens's *Constitutional View* did, but few people purchased the second. Postwar southern magazines had few subscribers, encountered difficulty securing contributors, and usually folded quickly. *The Land We Love*, which apparently had a wide readership outside the South, reportedly had 12,000 subscribers, but the others had only between 1,000 and 5,000. Perhaps southerners simply did not read magazines or had no money to purchase them, but the editors always attributed their troubles to a lack of public support. Bledsoe dismissed the argument that the "Southern people are too poor to subscribe for reviews, or to purchase books" as "more specious than solid," and a survey conducted by D.H. Hill revealed that southerners bought far more northern magazines than southern.[8]

Ultimately more important than books or magazines in shaping the Confederate tradition were various Confederate organizations, although they initially received little more public support than did the writers. In the first years after Appomattox, a few local benevolent associations with ties to militia units formed, and officers from at least one wartime regiment organized and met annually for dinner. In 1869, three avowedly historical societies formed. Two of them, the Confederate Survivors' Association of South Carolina and the Confederate Relief and Historical Association of Memphis, operated locally, accomplished little, and soon disappeared. The third, the Southern Historical Society, headquartered in New Orleans, survived and eventually became important in the development of the Confederate tradition.[9]

Virginian Dabney H. Maury, one of many leading Confederates who had settled in New Orleans after the war, first suggested the formation of a Confederate historical society in the city. After preliminary discussions perhaps as early as 1868, Maury, Richard Taylor, Braxton Bragg, and a few other former army leaders issued in April 1869 a call for a public meeting. On 1 May 1869 the Southern Historical Society (SHS) organized formally. Benjamin Morgan Palmer, a New Orleans minister who had preached the southern cause, became president, and Dr. Joseph Jones, a New Orleans physician and son of Georgia slaveholding minister Charles Colcock Jones, served as secretary-treasurer. Hoping to expand throughout the South, the group appointed prominent Confederates vice-presidents for each of the southern states. These included Robert E. Lee and several men already involved in historical work: Wade Hampton, president of the Confederate Survivors' Association of South Carolina; Isham G. Harris, president of the Confederate Relief and Historical Association of Memphis; and D.H. Hill, editor of *The Land We Love*.[10]

Like Hill's magazine, the SHS sought to ensure the acceptance of what its members considered to be a true history of the war. "No Southern man who reads the very personal and partisan chapters of the 'Lost Cause,' or the unjust and unreasonable history of the late war as compiled by Northern writers for the deception of the world and its posterity, can be satisfied," one announcement of the society's founding proclaimed. The society sent out 6,000 circulars and tried to enlist the aid of influential individuals and newspapers. *The New Eclectic*, the Baltimore literary magazine that had bought Hill's *Land We Love*, praised the

SHS's goals and became its official organ. Even with the publicity, the SHS gained little popular support outside New Orleans. After several months, Jones admitted that the "movement has as yet met with no general or material support from the Southern people." Fewer than a hundred had joined, he reported, "and of this number, little more than one-fourth attend the regular meetings." At the start of the second year, only forty-four members paid dues.[11]

A timely funeral helped spur interest in Confederate history, but a new group of leaders, rather than the ones who had formed societies in 1869, would seize the opportunity. On 12 October 1870 General Robert E. Lee died at his home in Lexington, the small Virginia town to which he had gone to be president of struggling Washington College. There he had avoided public controversy and preached political moderation, reunion, and rebuilding. Lee played an important role in leading southerners to accept defeat and to seek reunion. The general did so primarily out of his well-known sense of duty; he himself apparently found the adjustment painful. At least two visitors to Lexington commented on the "hidden sadness in his countenance," and Lee never brought himself to write the history of the conflict that he felt it his duty to provide. In 1867 he confessed that he had "little desire to recall the events of the war" and claimed to have read no "work that has been published on the subject."[12]

Lee's role in the emergence of the Lost Cause proved more ambivalent than that in sectional reconciliation. He did avoid and sometimes discourage memorial ceremonies, monument campaigns, and other Confederate activities. Yet, after his death, several of the more ardent and unreconciled Confederate historians had good reason to believe they were following the lead of their commander. Lee, after all, proclaimed it a duty to ensure that "the bravery and devotion of the Army of N[orthern] V[irgini]a be correctly transmitted to posterity." Although urging them to tone down their rhetoric, Lee gave his approval to books by Early and Dabney and strongly encouraged Bledsoe in his defense of the South. Lee also promoted the argument, which these men would help make a part of the Confederate canon, that the South succumbed only to overwhelming numbers.[13]

While Lee lived, however, his followers did not organize Confederate socieites, not only because of his potential opposition but because they would not and could not usurp his leadership. Although some of his fellow officers expressed doubts about his military genius, Lee had become the South's premier hero even before his death. When he traveled, wildly enthusiastic crowds treated him as a conquering hero. The people, in the words of a North Carolinian writing in *The Land We Love*, saw him "bathed in the white light which falls directly upon him from the smile of an approving and sustaining God."[14]

When Lee died and joined the honored Confederate dead, his stature among southerners increased. Upon hearing the "painful intelligence," one Alabaman observed that "the greatest man living in the United States is dead" and "the country has lost a treasure and a father." Throughout the South stores and businesses closed and towns held public memorial services. At one such meeting in New Orleans, Palmer described Lee as "the true type of American man," a "Southern gentleman," and a "second Washington." A resolution by the South

Carolina survivors' association also compared him to Washington and praised his "nature," which "like the circle . . . defies analysis or comparison. It presented a fullness, a completeness, a grandeur of development that offered nothing to censure, and left nothing to desire."[15]

A dead and perfect Lee, of course, made a more useful hero than a live and perfect one. From the grave he was no longer able—no matter what southerners may have thought about his divinity—to discourage Confederate activity or mar the images made of him. In the months after his death, various memorial associations formed, and from two of them organized in Virginia emerged the first sustained movement to define and exploit the Confederate tradition.[16]

On the day of Lee's death, a group of former Confederates met in the Lexington courthouse and organized a memorial association to care for Lee's grave and erect a monument over it. The leaders of the society were veterans of the Army of Northern Virginia and friends of Lee in Lexington: William Nelson Pendleton, rector of the Episcopal church Lee attended; J. William Jones, minister of the local Baptist church; and William Allen and William Preston Johnston, professors at the college. Mrs. Lee supported their efforts and decided to bury her husband's body in Lexington.[17]

Not long after the Lexington association organized, two competing groups formed in Richmond. Several women organized a Ladies' Lee Monument Association to raise funds for a memorial in their town. For many years they refused to cooperate with other efforts and quietly continued their fund-raising activities. The second group, which shared the goal of locating a monument to Lee in the Virginia capital, resulted from the efforts of Jubal A. Early. Unable to attend Lee's funeral because of a business meeting, Early later consulted Pendleton but decided to act independently of the Lexington association. He issued a call to all former soldiers of the Army of Northern Virginia for a November meeting in Richmond to adopt a plan to honor their commander. In a private letter, Early assured Pendleton that his call was "not intended to be in opposition to the place of a Memorial Association started at Lexington, but in furtherance of it," but added he could not at that time explain his plans.[18]

Learning of the call, Bradley T. Johnson, a Richmond politician and former Confederate general, sent Early a proposal. "We have been preparing for some months, an organization of the Society of the Army of Northern Virginia," he informed Early. The planners (Johnson never explained who else was involved) had thought first of having Lee at its head, "but supposing he w[oul]d decline had fixed on you for the real leadership and command." With Lee's death, Early would be the unquestioned choice for "Chief," Johnson added. The society, he explained, would be "a simple organization to preserve our old friendships[,] to collect materials for the history of the Army, and to cherish the name and fame of our dead comrades—and our abiding faith in the justice of the Cause for which they died." Johnson suggested making the monument the society's first project.[19]

Early liked the idea of a society to perpetuate the fame of the cause but still wanted an independent association to sponsor a monument. On 3 and 4 November 1870, during state fair week in the Virginia capital, Confederates gathered for both purposes. On the first day they heard speeches by Jefferson Davis, John B. Gordon, and other Confederate leaders, and then organized a monument association. Despite a plea by William P. Johnston and heavy lobbying by the Lexington association, the new group dedicated itself to the task of placing a statue to Lee in Richmond. The following day, many of the same people met and formed an Association of the Army of Northern Virginia (AANVA) and elected Early its first president.[20]

After the Richmond conclave, Early sought to broaden the movement. He wrote the survivors' association of South Carolina that the Lee statue was "not intended to be a mere state monument but a Confederate one" with the Confederate capital "the most appropriate place" for it. He also urged the South Carolina association to cooperate with the AANVA but warned that any who "have *deserted since the close of the war*, however high their previous position may have been," must be excluded from the ranks. The South Carolinians, however, never coordinated their efforts with Early's group. The only state division of the AANVA to form at this time, in fact, was in Virginia. It first met in November 1871 with Fitzhugh Lee, another former Confederate general active in Virginia politics and nephew of "Marse Robert," presiding, and B.T. Johnson making the first motion.[21]

Soon thereafter, the Lexington and Richmond memorial associations began to work together. After the Richmond meeting, Early's group and the Lexington forces had competed quietly for the memorial dollars, with neither side publicly condemning the other but each arguing that its cause deserved priority. Early and others in his group resented what they considered Pendleton's exploitation of Lee's name in raising funds for his church. Early also maintained that a Lexington statue would celebrate Lee the college president, not "Lee, the great, good, and glorious commander of the Confederate armies." In December 1871, however, W.P. Johnston invited Early to deliver an address at Washington and Lee, and apparently the overture helped change Early's attitudes toward the Lexington effort. In the October 1872 meeting of the AANVA he introduced a resolution that praised the Lexington monument and established a committee to raise money for it. Early in 1873 Early claimed that he regretted calling the Richmond meeting and proclaimed "the memorial tomb . . . the most practical scheme for the present," and thereafter he labored in its behalf. Why Early and others shifted their priorities remains unclear. The Richmond group had sought initially to have the Lee tomb in its city. When it accepted the finality of Mrs. Lee's decision to leave Lee's grave in Lexington, its members may have decided to honor the gravesite first. Early's comment that the monumental tomb was the more "practical scheme for the present" indicated that he may have realized southerners were more likely to donate money to a memorial tomb than an equestrian statue in a public place. For whatever reason, by early 1873 the Virginians had closed ranks.[22]

The same year the New Orleans leaders of the by-then-moribund SHS decided to hold a meeting outside their city in hopes of generating greater public interest. They even discussed moving the headquarters to Richmond, since they felt New Orleans was too isolated from the rest of the South, too involved with

Reconstruction politics, and too obsessed with commercial matters. In May 1873 the secretary of the SHS informed Early, who had become vice-president for Virginia after Lee died, that the society would meet that summer in White Sulphur Springs, West Virginia, and asked him to appoint from two to five delegates. Early promised to do so and agreed later to deliver the opening address. "Old Jube," though, interpreted his instructions differently, writing Pendleton that he could appoint as many delegates as he wished. In August a large number of "Gentlemen, distinguished in the civil and military history of the South" gathered to revive the SHS at the springs of Virginia, antebellum vacation spot of the southern aristocracy. They listened to various speakers, including Jefferson Davis, and reorganized the society with Early as its new president.[23]

Whether or not the New Orleans members had intended it, Early and his Virginians took control of the SHS. In the following months, Early called two more meetings, another at White Sulphur Springs and one in Richmond. Perhaps to emphasize the regional character of the society as well as its ties to the Confederate leadership, the occasions featured speeches by prominent wartime figures from other states, Raphael Semmes of Alabama and Wade Hampton of South Carolina. Most who attended and joined the society at these meetings, however, were Virginians. Consolidating his control, Early appointed an all-Virginia executive committee chaired by Dabney H. Maury, who had originated the idea of the SHS while in New Orleans but had since moved back to Richmond. Thomas Munford, another Virginian, became the SHS's salaried secretary, and, when he resigned late in 1874, J. William Jones, who had been active in the Lexington memorial association, replaced him. The SHS headquarters moved from New Orleans to rent-free quarters in the state capitol in Richmond. At first the new regime made the *Southern Magazine* of Baltimore its official organ, but in 1876 it began to publish its own *Southern Historical Society Papers (SHSP)*.[24]

By taking control of the SHS, the Virginians completed the formation of a coalition of Confederate organizations made up of two monument associations, a veterans' group, and a historical society. The *SHSP* endorsed both the Richmond and Lexington monuments, and the SHS and AANVA established especially close ties. Each held its meeting in Richmond during the state fair. One night the association gathered at the capitol to hear a prominent Confederate speak on some wartime matter, then adjourned to a hotel for an elegant banquet replete with numerous toasts to the Confederacy. The next day the SHS held its business meeting. In fact, as Fitz Lee commented during the 1874 meeting, the AANVA served as the social wing of the movement and left historical matters to "the Southern Historical Society, over which presides the indomitable and 'always-tell-the-truth' Genl. Jubal A. Early."[25]

Early was the central figure of the Virginia coalition and of early attempts to control the Confederate tradition. The Confederate general had fled the South after Appomattox and vowed to return only under a Confederate flag of triumph, but four years later a lack of funds forced him to come home to Yankee rule and resume the practice of law in his home town of Lynchburg. Later he made a quite comfortable living adding Confederate dignity and legitimacy to the drawings of the corrupt Louisiana Lottery, although he continued to reside in Lynchburg in a small room surrounded by his books and documents on the war. He stalked the town attired in Confederate gray, Confederate flag cufflinks, and the hat that he had worn during the war. Dressed for the part, Early became the prototypical unreconstructed Rebel. If he ever renounced "the cause for which Lee fought, and Jackson died," Early proclaimed, he wanted "the lightening of Heaven" to "blast" him and "all good women and true men" to scorn him. He loathed Yankees and blacks, but reserved the greatest measure of his not inconsiderable hatred for southerners who had "deserted since the war."[26]

As his rhetoric suggested, defeat had left deeper scars on Early than on most southerners. He drank a good deal and seemed inordinately defensive. One fellow southerner described him as a porcupine whose "quills stick out aggressively in all directions when any thing disparaging to Lee or Southern skill and valor is mentioned." Early was most prickly on issues of personal honor and spoke frequently of preserving the South's "manhood." He himself presented something less than a manly image and appeared a bit concerned about it. One not entirely unbiased observer reported that Early bore no physical resemblance to a soldier and spoke in "a piping treble" that often had "a long-drawn whine or drawl." Cruelly disappointed by a northern fiancee before the war, Early never married. Yet he pointed out to a visitor where the "accomodating" women of Lynchburg lived, and he smoked cigars rather than cigarettes because, he claimed, the latter impaired one's virility.[27]

Most of the other leaders of the Virginia coalition—B.T. Johnson, Fitz Lee, Maury, Jones, W.P. Johnston, and Pendleton—had backgrounds, though perhaps not insecurities, similar to Early's. All were Virginians. None had been leaders in secessionist agitation, and Early and perhaps others had opposed secession. Except for Lee, most had either controversial or undistinguished war records. Early and Johnson had been involved in notorious destruction of civilian property on northern raids. Early had been relieved of command toward the end of the war, and the military skills of Johnson and Pendleton had been questioned publicly. Johnston and Jones had done little either to generate questions or merit praise. After the war, most of them took a similar political stance in Virginia. Johnson, Early, and Lee were active in the traditionalist wing of the state's Conservative party and became ardent funders in the decade-long fight over the state debt.[28]

The common background of the leaders of the Virginia coalition suggests much about their personal motives. Those who had supported secession against their better judgment seemed to want reassurance after the war that they had acted rightly. For almost all of them, an undistinguished or at least disputed military record rendered them anxious to defend southern martial valor. And their battles in Virginia politics against men they believed had abandoned the old traditions for which the South fought exacerbated their fears about an uncertain future. Consequently, the Virginians sought to justify their own conduct by ardently defending the actions of the South, or, as they would have put it, by establishing the truth of history.[29]

The personal problems and motives of the Virginians should not, however, obscure their movement's basic character. Early, Johnson, and Lee, after all, had held high command in the Confederate war effort and remained important and respected leaders in their state. By holding their meetings in the former capital of the Confederacy and inviting such figures as Davis, Hampton, and Semmes to address them, the Virginians further strengthened their movement's association with the Confederate command. These trappings, the eloquent banquets, and the occasional gatherings at White Sulphur Springs testified to their ties to the region's elite. Early members did come primarily from the upper class. Of its Richmond members, more than half came from high white-collar or proprietary occupations—the upper class—while less than 10 percent had working-class backgrounds. Some of the non-Richmond members may have been planters (the addresses listed by a few members suggest that), but the leadership and most of the members were not. Nevertheless, the Virginia coalition remained rooted in the Confederacy's and the South's older elite.[30]

These members of the older elite sought not just to defend themselves and their region in what Early called the "ordeal of history" but to counteract what they perceived as the humiliation and transformation of the South that had followed northern victory. The Virginians feared that their fellow citizens were abandoning the traditional southern values exemplified by the Confederacy. Maury explained that he founded the SHS because southerners had "become so familiarized with the odious names and the odious light" in which northern accounts presented them that they "were fast losing . . . self-respect and seemed ready to acquiesce in all the degradations thus prepared" for them. Bradley Johnson similarly argued the need for the AANVA as a means to preserve self-respect as well as to protect southerners from "the moral consequences of conquest." In an 1874 speech in Atlanta, one agent claimed that the SHS would necessarily "possess a vitality and exert a moral influence through the whole South, which will steadily and irresistibly expand into an antagonism powerful to repel the insidious advances of those vicious principles which are now so fearfully undermining the civilization of the North."[31]

In seeking to "repel the insidious advance," the Virginians did not launch a political movement; they formed no party, offered no coherent political program or ideology. Rather, they started what might best be termed a revitalization movement. A revitalization movement, as defined by anthropologist Anthony F.C. Wallace, is a "conscious, deliberate, organized effort on the part of some members of society to create a more satisfying culture" by restoring "a golden age"—an attempt "to revive a previous condition of social virtue." Often the attempt takes millenial form, but some revitalization movements involve a less apocalyptic view of cultural revival. These "rational revivalistic nativistic movements," in Ralph Linton's words, are "almost without exception, associated with frustrating situations and are primarily attempts to compensate for the frustrations of the society's members. The elements revived become symbols of a period when the society was free, or, in retrospect, happy or great." The post–Civil War period, with the trauma and scars of defeat, was certainly a time of great frustration for the Virginians. They looked back to the war years as a glorious era and offered a heroic vision of the Confederacy as an antidote to the changes they perceived in the postwar South. In doing so, they refought the issues and battles of the war, seemingly searching for a way out of defeat and the world it had brought. In the process, their movement became less rational and more like other magical or millenial revitalization movements.[32]

The Virginians refought the war in their meetings, their speeches, and especially the pages of the *Southern Historical Society Papers*. They defended almost every aspect of Confederate behavior. If accusations arose concerning conditions in southern prisoner of war camps, Jones and the *SHSP* absolved the South of all blame and offered evidence of worse conditions in northern prisons. If northerners repeated allegations that the Union army had captured Davis in female disguise, the *SHSP* disputed the contention. Along with their mobile defense, however, the Virginians tried to establish a few heavily defended and, they hoped, impregnable points. They asserted fervently the justness and nobility of the Confederate cause and developed a general apologia of southern military capabilities. In the latter, they rationalized defeat in two ways: the overwhelmed-by-numbers explanation and the Longstreet-lost-it-at-Gettysburg excuse. They also rested much of their claim for the superiority of Confederate ability and culture, despite its defeat, on the sterling examples of Generals Jackson and Lee.[33]

In his address to the SHS at White Sulphur Springs, Early warned his fellow Confederates that they could not "escape the ordeal of history" and would be considered "either as criminals—rebels and traitors . . . —or as patriots defending our rights and vindicating the true principles of the government founded by our fathers." In establishing their claim to patriotism, the Virginians added little to Bledsoe's and Stephens's defenses or, for that matter, to what most southerners already thought. They merely helped codify the accepted interpretation that secession was a legitimate, constitutional exercise of state power to which the South resorted only after the North had shamelessly abandoned the constitution. The Virginians did, however, prove slightly more dogmatic than many southerners in maintaining that slavery had nothing to do with the South's decision to fight.[34]

The Virginians' defense of southern military capabilities influenced regional perceptions more heavily than did their ratification of commonly accepted attitudes on secession. In the first few years after the war, southerners had not agreed on the reason for their loss at arms. They offered countless explanations but usually stressed one of two general themes, either that the South had succumbed through internal collapse or that it had fallen to overwhelming numbers and resources. The Virginians adopted the overwhelming-numbers explanation and established it within the Confederate tradition. In speeches and articles Early, Jones, and others in the SHS continually referred to the disparity of numbers. The *SHSP* ran a series on the southern deficiencies in men and supplies and attacked any northern work that dared imply even a near-equality of forces. This rationalization had the advantage not only of explaining the loss but also, in the process, rendering the Confederate fighting men the best in the world. *Our Living and Our Dead*, the magazine of the North Carolina branch of the SHS, stated in its first issue that it would show "beyond controversy . . .

that the soldiers, of the Confederate Armies accomplished more in proportion to their numbers, and the resources at their command, than was ever before accomplished by the same number of men similarly opposed."[35]

Unsatisfied with the popularity and utility of the overwhelming-numbers explanation, the Virginians sometimes offered another reason for Confederate defeat. They claimed that General James Longstreet, by failing to carry out Lee's alleged order for an early attack on the second day at Gettysburg, lost that battle and ultimately the war. Jubal Early, in the 1872 address at Washington and Lee that helped close the breach between the Richmond and Lexington groups, opened a campaign against Longstreet that Pendleton then continued in fund-raising appearances throughout the South. In 1876 Longstreet counterattacked publicly, and the conflict became savage. Early, Pendleton, Fitz Lee, Jones, and others coordinated their efforts and utilized the *SHSP* in them. Not all Confederates, even among those who supported the Virginia organizations, believed the charge, but Early and company proved amazingly successful at convincing doubters.[36]

A variety of factors propelled the Virginians to attack Longstreet. He had encouraged it by publicly and privately questioning Lee's competence; yet his carping preceded Early's speech by more than five years. If Early and the other Virginians had simply revered Lee and felt compelled to defend his reputation, they probably could have done so almost as well by avoiding controversy. But Longstreet had "deserted since the war," had become a Republican and urged others to accommodate themselves to northern rule, and he thereby made himself a target too inviting to ignore. In one of the published condemnations of Longstreet, Fitz Lee mentioned, but did not deny, the charge that political motives were behind the criticism, and private correspondence of several of the Virginians revealed plainly that Longstreet's Republicanism influenced the severity of the attack.[37]

The Virginians also seized on the alleged late attack by Longstreet because it offered an appealing explanation of defeat. In 1872 Pendleton reportedly told friends that Longstreet's failure "lost us a victory that would have definitely established our independence." Six years later, at the height of the controversy, Fitz Lee wrote in the *SHSP* that if Longstreet had not been late, "the historic 'rebel yell' of triumph would have resounded along Cemetery Ridge upon that celebrated 2nd July, 1863, and re-echoing from the heights of Round Top, might have been heard and heeded around the walls of Washington, Baltimore, and Philadelphia." Still later, Jones stated flatly that if Lee's orders had been followed, "we would have won that field, crushed General Meade's army, rescued Maryland, captured Washington and Baltimore, and dictated terms of peace on Northern soil." The South, in short, would have "won Gettysburg, and Independence, but for the failure of *one man*." Jones and the other Virginians found the Longstreet-lost-it-at-Gettysburg excuse an appealing explanation for defeat because, more than the overwhelming-numbers explanation, it allowed them to believe success had been possible. To rewrite Faulkner's well-known phrase, for the Virginians it was always not yet dawn on 2 July, Longstreet was not yet late, and it all still hung in the balance.[38]

While attributing defeat to a disadvantage in numbers or the failure of a single individual, the Virginians also sought to defend their cause by celebrating its major heroes. In 1883 Jubal Early advised a group of veterans in Baltimore, "when called upon for a defense or justification of the cause in which you were enlisted . . . point proudly and confidently to the character of the great leaders whom you followed—Lee and Jackson—for your complete vindication."[39]

Thomas Jonathan Jackson, who had the advantage of dying during the war, became the first great southern hero and perhaps the only one ever to rival Lee. Southerners praised his character but gloried particularly in his battlefield success. Robert Dabney even argued that God had purposefully removed Jackson at the peak of his fame as "a singular mark of Heaven's favor" and because he could never have been defeated or subjugated. In 1875 Virginia dedicated a lifesize statue to Jackson on the State House lawn in Richmond. Although the statue was the gift of a British admirer rather than the product of a popular fund-raising effort like those started for Lee, on the occasion of its dedication southerners demonstrated their adulation. Moses Hoge, a local minister, delivered an address in fulsome praise of Jackson's character, command, and heroic accomplishments.[40]

Especially after his death, Robert Edward Lee was the supreme hero of the Virginians. They proclaimed his character flawless, particularly praised his unfaltering sense of honor and duty, but also celebrated such other character-istics as obedience, responsibility, accountability, and religious faith. His soldiers' unquestioned devotion testified to his nobility and became yet another theme stressed by the Virginians. Lee was "the grandest thing in all the world to us," said one former soldier in an 1875 speech, "when he loved us like a father and led us like a king, when we trusted him like a providence and obeyed him like a god. . . ."[41]

More central to the Virginians' portrait of Lee than his character or his soldiers' devotion were his unsurpassed abilities as a military commander. Lee had not been, Early maintained in 1872, "conquered in battle, but surrendered because he had no longer an army with which to give battle." His army "had been gradually worn down by the combined agencies of numbers, steam-power, railroads, mechanism, and all the resources of physical science." Not Lee, but his army, Early argued, had been worn down. "Our beloved chief stands, like some lofty column which rears its head among the highest, in grandeur, simple, pure and sublime, needing no borrowed lustre." Early and his associates did not even stop at making Lee an undefeated commander; they seemed determined to make him virtually incapable of error, as their attacks on Longstreet demonstrated.[42]

As Early's defense of Lee (to some extent at the expense of the reputation of his army) suggests, the Virginians never explicitly praised the Confederate private as loudly or as often as they did Jackson and Lee. Speeches or articles mentioned the private soldier's valor as part of a discussion of military campaigns, and annual dinners usually included a stirring toast to the Confederate private. But not until 1885 did the AANVA have a formal address on him, and only rarely did articles in the *SHSP* focus on the experiences of the men in the ranks. Praise for the common soldier can be found, of course, but the Virginians never really celebrated the private as later veterans' movements would. They did not even do much to counteract, and sometimes they actually contributed to, the rather popular image of the common soldier as lacking in discipline and careless of property. The Virginians' heroes, like their leadership, came primarily from the Confederate elite.[43]

In the Virginians' vision of Confederate history, heroic leaders inspired armies who fought valiantly in a war over constitutional principles. Their view all but prevented a revolutionary tradition forming about the Confederacy. The extremely conservative Virginians wished to draw no radical implications from the past. Their historical interpretation, in fact, supported an aristocratic social order resting on deference to leaders and duty to society. Indirectly, it supported white supremacy as well, but, somewhat surprisingly, the extreme anti-black views of the Virginians rarely surfaced in their historical work. Most important, the Virginians publicized a Confederate past of heroic proportions, one in which victory seemed as likely as defeat.[44]

When the Virginians' historical vision simply promoted older aristocratic values, their efforts constituted a rational revivalistic movement. They employed the Confederate tradition to revive an earlier culture, to urge a return to the ways of a better time. But as the Virginians continually refought the war and obsessively battled the Yankees, their activities took on a less rational tone. They seemed to be searching for some factor that would have changed the results of the war: If only they had not faced overwhelming numbers, if only Longstreet had been on time. They appeared captivated by a dream of victory, a dream of a return to an undefeated Confederacy. This aspect of their historical vision does not appear very different from another revitalization movement of the late nineteenth century, the Ghost Dance among the Plains Indians. The Ghost Dancers preached that white culture would disappear if only Indians believed and danced. Similarly, the Virginians seemed to believe that if they wrote their articles and kept southerners from deserting after the war, the Yankees and all that had occured after Appomattox would simply disappear. One can easily imagine a gathering of Early and company, wearing their gray ghost shirts and clutching volumes of the SHSP that Jones promised would be impervious to the slings and arrows of northern slander. Formed in a circle about a statue of a recumbent Lee, the true believers dance in and back, chanting, on one foot, "overwhelmed by numbers," and on the other, "betrayed by Longstreet"— waiting for an undefeated, marble Lee to rise and lead them to victory.

Especially in the Confederate ghost dance, in this surrealistic vision of a victorious Confederacy, but even in their symbolic use of the war to revive older values, the Virginians acted as the traditional interpretation of the Lost Cause would suggest. They clung to the past, defended old values, and dreamed of a world untouched by defeat. If the Virginians had mobilized large numbers of southerners in their revitalization movement, the New South might have been different. Certainly the Confederate tradition would have functioned as a romantic and essentially reactionary force. Only a few southerners, however, joined the ghost dance—only a few supported the Virginians' revitalization movement.

The organizations of the Virginia coalition never succeeded in mobilizing the South. The AANVA probably had no more than 200 members at any one time, with the majority of them from Richmond itself. Despite Early's attempts to broaden the coalition, few other veterans' groups associated themselves with its operations or goals. The Society of the Army and Navy of the Confederate States in the State of Maryland, founded by the AANVA's own Johnson, who was a native of that state, did maintain some ties. The Association of the Army of Northern Virginia, Louisiana Division, organized in New Orleans in 1874, never coordinated its activities with the Virginia Division and devoted itself to very different goals. Primarily a benefit society, it provided dues-paying members with money when unemployed and medicine when sick, and it raised money for a grand tomb for its members. The other handful of veterans' groups that formed in the seventies displayed a similar lack of interest in historical work and never affiliated with the AANVA. The Virginians had only slightly more success in extending the SHS, the other major organization in the coalition. South Carolinian Wade Hampton served as an agent for a time, and when Jones took over as secretary he dispatched several representatives throughout the South to form local groups and enlist *SHSP* subscribers. Only a few branches formed, however, and none remained active for long. Nor did many southerners subscribe to the *SHSP*; in November 1876 it had only 1,560 subscribers.[45]

Even the Lee monuments, the projects most likely to gain wide support, generated limited public enthusiasm. After two years one group had raised only a little more than $10,000 from the entire South. Only Georgia had donated more than $3,000, and Mississippi, Kentucky, South Carolina, and Virginia each donated about $1,000. The Lexington association took ten years to raise $22,000, and William W. Corcoran, a Washington banker of southern sentiment, gave nearly 10 percent of that. In contrast, many small cities in the South raised as much as $1,000 for their Confederate cemeteries in a single campaign, and both Richmond and Louisiana memorial groups nearly matched the Lexington total in the same period without a regional drive. Southerners apparently gave local memorial efforts higher priority than the Lee monuments.[46]

Many factors contributed to the Virginians' failure to mobilize the South in support of their causes. Confusion, if not corruption, plagued both the membership drives of the SHS and fund-raising for the monuments. The contentious personalities of Early and Pendleton made cooperation with other groups difficult. The aristocratic bias of the groups surely discouraged popular response. Even the *SHSP* appealed not to a mass audience but to an educated elite with time to read long, detailed discussions of military tactics—and with three dollars to spare for a subscription. These problems alone, however, fail to explain the failure of the Virginia coalition.[47]

The Virginians were prominent members of the Confederate leadership elite, worked hard to spread their organizations throughout the South, and received considerable public exposure. That they nevertheless failed to gain widespread support must have resulted from the majority of southerners' rejecting their use of the Confederate past. Most southerners were far more comfortable with the

Confederate memorial movement, which allowed them to honor the Confederacy and those who died in its behalf but at the same time distance themselves from the cause, than they were with the Virginians' revitalization movement, which encouraged them to dream of a return to the Confederate past. Unlike the Virginians, most southerners did not wish to keep alive the passions of the war by refighting its battles and issues.

Despite their limited following, the Virginians remain important because their speeches and articles did help establish points that would be accepted by later veterans' movements and become part of the Confederate tradition: that the South waged not a revolution but a legal war for constitutional principles, that it succumbed only to overwhelming numbers and resources, that it boasted uncommonly grand heroes in Jackson and Lee. But if southerners accepted these points of interpretation, they still rejected the stridency with which Early and company put them forth and the power with which they tried to invest those efforts. Most southerners had little interest in revitalization based on a Confederate vision. Some other group would give voice to the ghosts of the Confederacy.

CHAPTER FIVE

Toward a Reunited Nation: Signs of Reconciliation

The unenthusiastic response to the Virginians' revitalization movement revealed that white southerners had begun to come to terms with defeat. Developments in the late 1870s and early 1880s hastened the process. Rather than seize the electoral crisis of 1876–77 as an opportunity to renew the battle, the South responded calmly and cautiously. The election of a Democrat to the presidency eight years later confirmed white southerners' growing belief that the South had a political future within the Union. Signs of respect from former foes and northern publishers made acceptance of reunion easier. By the mid-eighties, most southerners had decided to build a future within a reunited nation. A few remained irreconcilable, but their influence in southern society declined rapidly.

If the South had wanted to renew the battle for independence, the disputed presidential election of 1876–77 offered a splendid opportunity. A succession crisis not quite twelve years after a major revolt might logically have led to a resumption of fighting, especially when the defeated side still proclaimed itself under the despotism of the victor. Just after Appomattox some southerners had hoped for such a chance to return to the battlefield. A few clung to the dream into the 1870s and predicted the demise of the American union if the abuses of Reconstruction continued. In an 1873 introduction to a collection of his columns entitled "Peace Papers," the usually calm Bill Arp hinted at the possibility of revolt. "Now, its useless and hipocritikal to cry pease, when there aint no pease. We may all mix and mingle, and trade, and joak, and carry on together, but away down in our bowels there is a burnin going on, and if our northern brethrin dont do sumthin to put the fire out, it will break loose sum of these days, and play the devil generully."[1]

The early return to white Democratic control of several southern state governments banked the fires of revolt, and the possibility of electing a Democrat president in 1876 offered hope of extinguishing them altogether. In New York

Democrat Samuel J. Tilden the South had a candidate it could support with both an expectation of victory and at least mild enthusiasm. Southern Democrats, some of whom had shown little interest in politics since the war, worked hard for Tilden. On the day after the election, their efforts seemed to have succeeded, and southerners rejoiced at Tilden's and the Democratic Party's apparent triumph. "We feel," Jabez L.M. Curry recorded in his diary, "as if the days of Federal tyranny were numbered. Praise God from whom all blessings flow."[2]

Twelve days later, the attitude of Curry and the white South had changed. "Still much uneasiness about the Presidential election," Curry noted. "Universal distrust of Pres. Grant and his party. Fraud or usurpation not considered beyond their purpose or capability." The Republicans had challenged the returns in three states with enough electoral votes to elect their candidate, Rutherford B. Hayes. Rival Democratic and Republican claimants to the state houses of Louisiana and South Carolina confronted one another, and a peaceful resolution of either the national or the state dispute was not imminent.[3]

During December and January, several men active in the Virginia revitalization movement discussed how best to respond to the crisis. Early, Fitzhugh Lee, and William H. Payne at first advocated an aggressive policy. Payne, a Warrenton, Virginia, lawyer active in the AANVA, especially relished the idea of resistance. He did think southerners

> should be cautious in the extreme. Now is the time to wear the fox's skin, but I believe we will soon doff it for the Lion—It will never do to submit, if it can be avoided, to the loss of our victory—The South, except in weapons and organization, is in many respects better off than she was in 1861—We are poor, unhappy and unemployed—A whole generation has grown to manhood since 1865, who know nothing of the honor of man—and are by no means reluctant to learn for themselves.

Payne worried, however, that "the belief, too studiously cultivated, that we can't help our Northern brethren and are crazy for peace" might discourage northern action.[4]

Bradley Johnson, more cautious than Payne, argued initially that the South should aid the northern Democrats if they tried to prevent any illegal inauguration of Hayes. By January he had become convinced they would not act, and he therefore urged the others to seek a constitutional and legal settlement. In the end, the Virginians followed Johnson's cautious policy rather than indulging Payne's fantasies of renewed war. Agreeing on the importance of inaugurating Tilden, they still believed that before forcing the issue they should await northern Democratic action. They debated but rejected a plan to hold a meeting of leading Confederates to show northern Democrats that the South would support them. Instead, they sent no signal and simply waited for events to transpire.[5]

The Virginians evaluated the available options the way other southern leaders did. Southern congressmen decided to deal with the Republicans, a recent study demonstrates, because northern Democrats refused to take a decisive stand or consider military action. Faced with northern timidity, the southerners agreed to the Election Commission Bill as the best chance to secure office for Tilden. When the supposedly neutral Judge David Davis resigned and all hope was lost, they were unable to repudiate the bargain.[6]

Southerners knew that without northern aid they could accomplish nothing through force but could easily bring the nation's wrath down upon their region. John Reagan, a Texas congressman and former Confederate postmaster, made this argument in a telling analogy. "We might admire the courage of the little bovine who, standing on the track of the railroad and viewing an approaching engine and train, would face them and stand his ground, bellow out his defiance, bow his neck and paw the crossties until the collision came; but the mangled and scattered steaks and sirloins would hardly attest that his judgment was equal to his courage." Although all southerners did not endorse Reagan's view, many considered an independent revolt futile. Such pragmatism indicated that the praise for the extraordinary ability of Confederate armies was a chant of the ghost dance, not an actual assessment of strength.[7]

The basic approach of southerners since 1865, of course, had been to acquiesce in the inevitable while noisily striving for the best advantage under existing conditions—bellowing a bit, but remaining on the hoof. In the electoral crisis, however, much southern moderation seemed more than just a tactic necessitated by northern timidity. Payne, who visited Washington at the height of the crisis in February, admitted that the Electoral Commission offered the South its only hope, since the "cold-blooded bond-holder" Tilden would not fight and the South fighting alone would be "left exposed to defeat, and to the odium of an abortive attempt to inaugurate a new rebellion." But Payne felt southerners "were *creating* disorganization and demoralization in the democratic party, and then using the *consequence* of our *own* conduct to excuse our advocacy of a tame and spiritless course." He suspected, in other words, that some southerners wanted to defuse the conflict, even if that defusing meant an unfavorable solution; they encouraged rather than yielded to the northern Democrats' hesitancy.[8]

Many southerners apparently did want the crisis resolved without violence even if it meant Tilden's defeat. The Richmond *Daily Dispatch*, which claimed to fear military intervention by Grant above all else, consistently praised the commission plan as being "on the side of law, and civility, and peace— eminently so—and puts to flight all ideas of violence." In urging caution, both the *Dispatch* and Johnson emphasized that the South must follow the laws and constitution—principles, Johnson declared, more important than the outcome of an election. This advice followed logically from the southerners' legalistic interpretation of the origins of the Civil War. If they believed their resort to arms in 1861 had been only for constitutional principles and in harmony with the laws of the nation, then in 1876 they should again follow a peaceful, legal course unless threatened by an unconstitutional usurpation of power. Their denial of a revolutionary interpretation of the war left the Virginians and the South as a whole with no radical tradition on which to draw in the electoral crisis.[9]

Despite the continuity in southern tactics and seeming inevitability of the outcome, the electoral crisis still represented an important milestone on the road to reunion. In 1876–77 the nation survived a major political crisis without violence or southern disloyalty. Home rule came to two states still under Republican control—a crucial real and symbolic victory, and the withdrawal of the remaining federal troops in the South constituted a significant stage in the North's gradual retreat from Reconstruction.[10]

One Mississippian considered President Hayes's order to remove the troops a consolation for the "bitter disappointment" that "Tilden was cheated out of his seat in the White House." What southerners "wanted was a friend," she affirmed, and "it mattered little from whence he came, his [Hayes's] was the first friendly hand stretched out to them, and gratefully they accepted it." Most southerners, though, were not ready to grasp the hand of any Republican president, even one who at first tried to modify his party's policy toward the South. When four years later Republicans once more waged a bitterly anti-southern presidential campaign, their readiness hardly increased. The South did express sympathy and regret after the assassination of the victor of that race, James A. Garfield. Richmond minister Moses D. Hoge even voiced the hope that the succeeding days of sorrow would be a time "for the inauguration of a new era of harmony and true unity." Garfield's successor and party, however, continued to exploit racial issues for political gain, and southerners rarely considered men who adopted such tactics to be worthy leaders of a truly united nation.[11]

For southerners only the election of Democrat Grover Cleveland in 1884 established reunion, or, as one of them phrased it, allowed the South's "escape from captivity and humiliation." Towns throughout the region held parades, fired cannons, lit bonfires, and generally rejoiced. Cleveland's victory, observed Curry, "produced a satisfaction, nay, an exhilaration of feeling in the South which has not been felt for many years." It allowed "an opportunity for the display of the patriotism which really exists," he added, and made "the Southern states feel that the Union is really restored." Democratic control in Washington also meant the elimination "of the negro problem from national politics" and a return of local patronage to white control, "a happy riddance of scalawags, ignoramuses, and dishonest men," as C.C. Jones, Jr., put it.[12]

If the election of Cleveland helped convince southerners that they had a political future within the union, it did not necessarily extinguish all of the "burnin way down in [their] bowels." Not just political acceptance but northern respect was needed to heal the wounds of defeat. The North had to acknowledge the heroism and nobility of the Confederate war effort, the honor of the South, before southerners would be totally at ease within the Union. In the late seventies and early eighties, a tentative rapprochement with northern soldiers and an acknowl-edgment in national publications of southern heroism indicated that a few northerners were willing to proffer such respect.

Soldiers, according to contemporary observers and some later historians, served as key agents in reconciliation because they had developed respect for one another in war. Confederates who had experienced total defeat on the battlefield were more quickly reconciled than other southerners, and veterans of both blue and gray displayed greater regard for the feelings of the other side than the non-combatants of either section. Such observations often rested on insidious comparisons southerners made between conservative federal officers and radical Republican politicians, but in other instances they seemed based on faith in the healing power of violence and war.[13]

Contemporary observers and historians gave the battlefield too central a role in reconciling the sections, however. The postwar expressions of mutual respect and rapid reconciliation among prominent Confederate and Union military leaders, the principle evidence offered to support the argument, owed more to antebellum friendships at West Point or on active duty than to the experience on the battlefield. More important, a large number of soldiers from each side came through the experience of battle with their hatred intact. Some of the more intransigent and bitter southerners, such leaders of resurgent Confederate sentiment as Early, Johnson, and Hill, had seen a great deal of action. Many northern combatants, too, remained bitter. An early Grand Army of the Republic ritual had each recruit kneel before a coffin bearing the name of a victim of Andersonville—an exercise hardly reflecting respect or admiration for former foes. Well into the eighties members of the organization responded with enthusiasm to Bloody Shirt campaigns. The battlefield did not, apparently, transform all soldiers into peacemakers or imbue them with love and respect for the other side.[14]

Issues of the war, especially slavery and secession, still divided the mass of soldiers on both sides. So too did bitterness toward enemies who had killed comrades and who had inflicted suffering on prisoners. Such personal hostilities, in fact, took longer to dissipate than the political ones. Time and a tendency when reminiscing to downplay the war's violence and gore, however, helped center the veteran's memory on the courage and camaraderie of battle rather than on its political implications or bloody consequences. As this happened, soldiers of blue and gray came to believe they had much to share, since both sides had experienced the heroics of battle and rigors of camp life. Mutual respect, then, emerged not so much out of the immediate experience of battle as out of a carefully refocused memory of it.[15]

The end of Reconstruction reduced the political importance of the issues of the war and thereby began the process of refocusing. A series of meetings between the veterans of the two sides continued it. In 1881 the First Division, Louisiana State National Guard invited a New York national guard unit to New Orleans for Mardi Gras. The Washington Artillery, a state militia unit with many former Confederate soldiers among its members, entertained the visitors, who also met with a delegation from the Association of the Army of Tennessee, Louisiana Division, a Confederate veterans' group. The New Yorkers, in the words of one journalist, "saluted the monument of the Confederate dead," placed a wreath on it, and "extended the right hand of fellowship and locked palms with their brethren of the South in one everlasting grasp of friendship." Later the same year, a New Jersey Grand Army of the Republic post and a group of Knights Templars from Boston and Providence came to Richmond, where the latter group paid its respects in Hollywood and put a wreath on the city's statue to Jackson.[16]

In 1882 a contingent of Richmond ex-Confederates paid a return visit to the New Jersey post, and Union and Confederate veterans first met together at Gettysburg. Over the next five years veterans held at least nineteen formal Blue-Gray reunions, as the meetings of Union and Confederate soldiers came to be called. They included another well-publicized exchange of visits between Richmond and New Jersey units and a second gathering at Gettysburg in 1887. The latter, sponsored by the Philadelphia Brigade and Pickett's Division, was marred by northern opposition to the placement of a Confederate monument within what had been Union lines. Nevertheless, some of the southern participants helped organize another reunion the next year for the major armies that had fought there and even supported the erection of a monument to American heroism at Gettysburg.[17]

In New Orleans, Richmond, and a few other communities, former foes also joined to celebrate Memorial Day. As early as 1882 in New Orleans, groups of Union and Confederate veterans paid homage to the dead of the other side. In 1887 the Hollywood Memorial Association of Richmond moved its celebration of Memorial Day to "the 30th of May which is the day observed throughout the United States by the Union Soldiers as their Decoration Day." The Richmond women urged other memorial associations to adopt the same practice in order to "foster the sentiments of brotherly love which have been so freely expressed of late by the former wearers of the blue and gray." A few societies agreed, but most continued to observe a purely Confederate day.[18]

As the dispute over the monument at Gettysburg and the refusal of most towns to change the date of Memorial Day demonstrated, Blue-Gray reunions and joint ceremonies for the dead did not mark the end of all sectional animosities. Sporadic outbursts of recrimination flared in the eighties. In 1887 the GAR objected strongly when President Cleveland ordered captured Confederate battle flags returned to the South, and it forced him to rescind his order. The incident, along with the politics of the next election, led to a brief renewal of sectional hostility. Sectional relations at this point remained extremely fragile; attention shifted all too easily from common experiences to divisive issues or the war's bloody cost.[19]

Events involving the blue and the gray nevertheless demonstrated that sectional reconciliation had begun and speeded it further by helping focus the veterans' attention on their common wartime experiences. Most important for southerners, however, the joint reunions offered tacit testimony and occasional explicit salutes to their honorable conduct in the war. When a reunion lacked such symbolic statements of northern esteem, in fact, southerners refused to participate. Most reunions did include them, though, and the joint reunions and common decoration of graves constituted the first signs of the respect Bill Arp had demanded in 1865 and helped ease the "burnin'" he and other southerners still felt.[20]

Northern writers and publishers offered additional assurances of increasing respect for southern sacrifices and accomplishments. Almost immediately after the war, northern novelists had offered the olive branch and, despite some condescension, portrayed most southerners as dignified, devoted adherents to their cause. More influential than novels in shaping late nineteenth-century public opinion, however, were popular magazines. In the first postwar decade, most major northern journals continued to display prejudice against the South. In the mid-seventies, particularly after *Scribner's* published Edward King's "The Great South" series, their tone changed. The middle-class mass market magazines began to publish the work of many southern authors and a number of favorable stories on southern topics.[21]

The single most important series in the new journalistic homage to the South appeared in *The Century* between 1884 and 1887. Its "Battles and Leaders of the Civil War" presented a wide-ranging history of the conflict in a series of articles by authors from both sides. "No time could be fitter," the editors maintained in introducing the series, "for a publicaton of this kind than the present, when the passions and prejudices of the Civil War have nearly faded out of politics, and its heroic events are passing into our common history where motives will be weighed without malice, and valor praised without distinction of uniform." The editors worked hard, however, to ensure that the series engendered no passions or prejudices of the war. They rejected as a title for it "Men and Events" because "events" might have suggested they "were going into, say, the condition and actions of the freedmen—the Emancipation Proclamation—and other events not connected with battles." These "political questions" were the very questions they wanted to avoid.[22]

To promote reconciliation, the editors instead stressed "contemplation of sacrifice, resourcefulness, and bravery in foes." They instructed authors to "give the non-military reader a vivid idea of the actual conflict of arms—of the picturesque features of the battle, special incidents of gallant conflict, in short the characteristics of the engagement—its color as well as its form." Everything, a cynic might add, but its cause and its gore. In giving "the characteristics of the engagement," the editors added, authors should avoid the "official report style" and "give, as it were in fatigue dress, such facts as you would be likely to state if you should set out to tell the story of the battle to your own family about your fireside."[23]

The articles in the two-year series, therefore, ignored or soft-pedaled divisive issues and instead emphasized the experience of battle itself. Southerners welcomed them for that reason and because they provided additional testimony of northern respect for southern martial efforts. Each issue included an article by a Confederate and one by a Union soldier, and the implied equality signaled to the South that the North recognized its achievements even if it did not applaud its motives. Moreover, the articles also achieved the editors' goal of praising valor "without distinction of uniform" and of stressing the "sacrifice, resourcefulness, and bravery" of former foes. A few controversies, mainly among former comrades rather than among former enemies, did grow out of the series, but in general it served to lessen sectional tension and spur the redefinition of the war's meaning. Although the South "won" in that respect, its "victory" in *The Century* and other northern magazines did not mean that the Lost Cause triumphed over a North it had failed to vanquish on the battlefield, as some historians have argued.[24]

By the mid-eighties most southerners did not want that kind of victory. The peaceful solution to the electoral crisis of 1876 testified to the South's growing loyalty to the Union. Cleveland's election assured the region a president sympathetic to its interests and promised full participation in the national government in the future. Blue-Gray reunions and favorable portrayals in northern magazines began to reassure southerners that northerners respected their wartime efforts. In both North and South memories of the war began to focus less on divisive political disputes and more on shared battle experiences that rendered the possibility of continued reconciliation more likely. All of these developments encouraged the spirit of reunion.

In the decade after the disputed election many prominent southerners began to preach reunion both in the North and at home. In 1877 Virginia politician and former Confederate soldier John W. Daniel spoke to the literary societies of his state university on the topic, "Conquered Nations." He reminded them of the beneficial effects of conquest and called on the South to accept fully "the decrees of fate" and to work "to conquer the souls of our Northern brethren. . . ." In 1885 in the center of postwar Confederate sentiment, the annual meeting of the AANVA, Daniel H. Hill proclaimed his "adoring reverence" for God's "decree which destroyed our hopes of Southern independence." He would "not reverse His decree" if he could, Hill admitted. "All honorable Confederates render the truest allegiance to the obligations imposed upon them by the surrender." The following year Charlestonian Edward McCrady, Jr., touched by northern contributions to his city after a devastating earthquake, told the same group that he regretted "neither the war nor its results."[25]

Apparently much of the southern population joined in the spirit of reconciliation. Several observers in the late seventies and early eighties commented on the South's rapid and thorough adjustment to defeat. Sir George Campbell, an Englishman who toured the region in 1876, maintained that he knew of "no people in the world who accept defeat in so thoroughly good-humored a way." Seven years later Virginia liberal Orra Langhorne reported that in the Shenandoah Valley the war "seems almost forgotten and the bitterness which was the natural result of such a revolution, has softened into a far nobler sentiment of regret for the sacrifice of so many lives of those who should have been friends instead of enemies." Observers usually acknowledged that such attitudes did not mean that southerners had repudiated their past or admitted error. Rather, they meant only that southerners no longer, as Alexander K. McClure put it, "talk of the past as a guide for the future."[26]

In abandoning the past as a guide and accepting defeat, southerners made a pragmatic assessment of their prospects and committed themselves to a brighter future—an approach quite at odds with the southern image of romanticism and devotion to the past. In 1880 one southerner called upon the rising generation to "bury in oblivion all useless regrets over these spectres of the past, and with a strong heart grapple with the stern realities of the present, and, we fear, the sterner realities of the near future." The two most prominent reconciliationists of the war generation, L.Q.C. Lamar and J.L.M. Curry, justified their position with a similarly realistic analysis.[27]

In 1874 Lamar, a United States senator from Mississippi, gained national attention when he delivered from the Senate floor a moving eulogy to abolitionist Charles Sumner. His speech both praised his former colleague and stressed the need for sectional reconciliation. When some southerners expressed dismay, Lamar argued that he spoke only out of a "concern for the Southern people, a love for them with their helpless families which is a stronger feeling in my heart than the indignation I feel for their undeserved wrongs. At least I try to rein in the last feeling in order to obey the dictates of the former." Lamar had made a pragmatic decision that in the long run the South would be best served by refusing to dwell on the injustices of the past and by looking instead to the future.[28]

Curry made a similar argument in a speech three years later. He urged his listeners at a fair in Lynchburg, Virginia, to "rise above the savage delight of cherishing animosities and hatreds and realize that we live in the present and not in the dead past." Several years later while criticizing the tendency of SHS secretary J. William Jones "to take delight in cultivating animosities," Curry explained his own approach to his son. "Crushed, subjugated, impoverished we were by the war, insulted, tyrannized over, outraged by Reconstruction Acts," Curry admitted, "but of what avail is it to keep alive passion and cherish hatreds." He still believed in the "abstract right" of secession, Curry concluded, but "To go about shaking our fists and grinding our teeth at the conquerors, dragging [with] us a heavy weight, the dead, dead corpse of the Confederacy is stupid and daily suicidal. Let us live *in* the present and *for* the future, leaving the dead Past to take care of itself, drawing only profitable lessons from that and all history."[29]

In a letter critical of the likes of Lamar and Curry, Jubal Early asked Jefferson Davis, "Are our leading Southern representatives, and bitterest revilers of the North, about to resolve themselves into a mutual admiration society, leaving such 'irreconcilables' as you and myself out in the cold?" The developing reconciliationist sentiment in the South had become so influential that Early and others like him were increasingly "out in the cold" in the eighties. To remain irreconcilable a southerner had to sustain hatred with considerable determination and to avoid the emerging reunion in politics and business. Early did so with single-minded determination, but others adopted positions along a spectrum from extreme and sincere intransigence to an almost humorous pseudo-defiance.[30]

Former Confederates somehow isolated from the changes of the era sustained defiance in its purest forms. A. Dudley Mann, a Confederate commissioner in Europe during the war, avoided the changes altogether as an expatriate in Paris. From his exile Mann condemned developments in the South, damned citizens of the United States as the "most debased, politically, of any upon the earth's surface," and awaited "the vengeance of Heaven" against the North for its "perfidy" to the South. Former commissary general of the Confederacy Lucius B. Northrop, from his isolated retreat in Minor Orcus, Virginia, also wrote of his hatred for the United States and the paganism of the present era. Mann's and Northrop's geographic isolation and, perhaps more important, their lack of public involvement or responsibility made it easier for them to maintain and to espouse such intransigence.[31]

A few southerners, of course, cherished such hatred even while remaining active in the South, although some of them, too, felt increasingly isolated. Robert L. Dabney, author of the postwar *Defense of Virginia*, wore the gray, literally and figuratively, long after the war. "Drawing upon his apparently inexhaustible reservoir of rancor," a recent biographer has written of Dabney, he "defended slavery and secession against a deluge of 'Yankee lies,' denounced public education in the South as a devilish Yankee trick, opposed ecclesiastical reunion with the 'Yankee' Presbyterian Church, and endlessly reminded southerners of the miseries suffered at the hands of barbarous Yankee hordes." In the early 1880s, fearing that his church had begun to drift toward reunification with its northern counterpart and realizing that his own influence in it and the Virginia seminary where he taught had declined, Dabney moved to Texas. There, despite ill health, he taught, served the church, and railed against the Yankees until his death in 1894.[32]

Fewer and fewer southerners active in the world concentrated so totally on their bitterness as Dabney did. William H. Payne, the lawyer who participated in the Virginians' discussions during the disputed election, provides a good example of an irreconcilable who made some concessions to defeat and the new order. In rhetoric sometimes equalling Mann's or Dabney's in virulence, Payne condemned the "lies and cant since the war" and lamented that the South kept "flinging herself into the arms of the North, weeping upon that icy bosom, and indifferent to the kicks and disgust with which her fawning is repelled." When invited to the 1888 reunion at Gettysburg, Payne replied that he "could not hold a carnival with the Yankees over the graves of the 100,000 dead who died to avert such a scene." He had, Payne added, "accepted reluctantly but fully the legitimate results of the war, but to rejoice over our defeat and love the Yankees was not included. If I joined this mockery, I should feel accursed and haunted by the dead." Payne's acceptance of the "legitimate results" of the war and his service as a railroad lawyer indicated that, despite his rhetoric, he occupied at least a middle or ambivalent position between defiance and acceptance.[33]

Jefferson Davis displayed similar ambivalence. Perhaps more than any other southerner, the former president of the Confederacy had a right to be bitter. Charged with treason after the war, he spent two years in a federal prison and another two awaiting trial before the government finally decided to drop the case. After sojourns in Canada and Great Britain, Davis tried the insurance business, but his company failed. Finally, the former president retreated to what became his home, Beauvoir, a plantation on the Mississippi Gulf Coast. There he remained in relative isolation while he wrote his *Rise and Fall of the Confederate Government*.[34]

Davis's two volumes, published in 1881, displayed no ambivalence whatsoever, but instead offered an unrelenting, and seemingly unending, defense of the South. Davis's interpretation of the war differed little from that of Bledsoe, Stephens, and the Virginians. He argued the righteousness and legality of secession under a constitution that preserved state sovereignty and maintained that the North had forced the southern states to exercise their sovereignty. He considered slavery a property right and denied that it had been a cause of the war. He subtly incorporated the overwhelming-numbers argument and, although really uninterested in using it (partly because he would not admit the South had lost at Gettysburg), bowed toward the Longstreet-lost-it excuse.

The tone of *Rise and Fall*, however, was as strident as the histories that preceded it and seemed more so in the context of the growing sectional reconciliation of the eighties. Davis blamed the North for "whatever of bloodshed, of devastation, or shock to republican government has resulted from the war" and claimed that the Yankees pursued the battle "with a ferocity that disregarded all the laws of civilized warfare." The "Attila of the American Continent" is what Davis called the United States government at one point. Only on a few occasions did he acknowledge any skill or heroism within the Union armies, while he almost invariably lauded the Confederate forces. Davis admitted no southern errors in the sectional conflict. He seemed to have rethought, much less regretted, nothing, and he believed that the battle over principles continued.[35]

Davis was not so utterly irreconciled as the *Rise and Fall* made him seem, however. One northerner who visited him at Beauvoir after its publication did not find the bitter recluse he expected. Davis's "discussion of the relations of the two sections was thoroughly philosophical and statesmanlike," reported Alexander McClure, "and while he will remain the one adjudged stranger to the Republic, he hopes yet to see the South prosperous in common with a prosperous North, and the scars of war and the bitterness of sectional dispute healed forever. Next to a Southern Slave Confederacy, he believes a free Union the best government for the Republic."[36]

Although possibly using Davis to make his own case for reunion and commercial growth, McClure caught the former Confederate president's ambivalence well. Davis thought the Confederacy had been a blessing to the South, believed it should have survived and thrived, and hoped for the eventual vindication of its principles. He therefore published his massive defense of the Confederacy and praised its cause in most of his public appearances. On the other hand, he sometimes acted or spoke for reconciliation. On several occasions he quietly endured assaults on his personal honor—no mean feat for the proud Davis—in order to minimize sectional hostility. His last public speech in Mississippi City in 1888 echoed themes enunciated by Lamar and Curry in charging his youthful audience to look to the future of the South. "The past is dead; let it bury its dead, its hopes and its aspirations," he urged them. "Let me beseech you to lay aside all rancor, all bitter sectional feeling, and to make your places in the ranks of those who will bring about a consummation devoutly to be wished—a reunited country." Davis's public wish hardly constituted intransigence, and perhaps by the end of his life he had moved toward the less belligerent end of the spectrum of irreconcilables. Intellectually, Davis realized the merit of his advice, but emotionally, he could never fully reconcile himself to defeat. He clung to and defended the dreams of the past but expected and prodded others to live in the realities of the present and to plan for the future. [37]

Charles C. Jones, Jr., the Georgian often grouped with Dabney and Davis as utterly irreconcilable, displayed an even greater ambivalence. In print and in frequent speeches he praised the Confederacy and, more heartily, the Old South. Yet, to recoup his fortunes after the war, Jones practiced law in New York City for twelve years—hardly a posture of total defiance. After returning to Georgia in 1877, he sought an appointment to West Point for his son, became a friend and political supporter of reconciliationist John B. Gordon, wrote a flattering eulogy to Henry Grady, and at one point considered work with ample remuneration perhaps "with Railways or other large corporations." [38]

Jones, Payne, and, to a lesser extent, Davis illustrated that responsibilities in the world usually entailed at least minimal concessions on reconciliation. Much of the continued intransigence in the South, of which too much has been made, was therefore private and essentially trivial. A relative of writer Grace King refused to celebrate Thanksgiving because she considered it a "Yankee institution." Her display of Confederate loyalty, King pointed out, only denied her kinfolk "all chance of a good dinner on that day." A Richmond Episcopalian expressed her continued hatred by refusing to pray for the president of the United States. When her congregation reached that section of the prayerbook, her grandson reported, "she would sit erect in her pew and glare around at the congregation, and it was only when this part of the prayer was finished would she kneel on the footstool and try to compose her mind to religious meditation." [39]

Miss M.A.H. Gay practiced an extreme form of intransigence in a house full of Confederate mementoes in Decatur, Georgia. As late as the 1890s she displayed pictures of Jefferson Davis and Queen Victoria there. "After Jefferson Davis," she explained, "I had no President; so in my heart I gave allegiance to Victoria as my sovereign. We southerners are of pure English blood." She did keep a picture of Cleveland, but though believing him an honest man she refused to acknowledge him as her president. Yet in her *Life in Dixie During the War*, an 1894 reminiscence not especially colored by bitterness, she affirmed that since the South had "come back to the United States, and means to stay in it, let the provocation to depart be what it may, I would not put into practice an iota of war-time feeling." The difference between Miss Gay's private practices and public unwillingness to "put into practice an iota of war-time feeling" suggests the unimportance of her intransigence as a social force. Most southerners found her, King's grandmother, the Richmond woman who refused to pray, and others like them quaint and amusing, but did not follow or even take their example very seriously. [40]

Southerners treated the better-known irreconcilables with similar disregard. By the 1880s the irreconcilables were disgruntled old men, celebrating the past and damning the present. Like Mann or Northrop, many lived in relative isolation and obscurity. Others, though admired and listened to, exercised little influence on political or social developments. Davis had become more a symbol than an actor in history. Early, Dabney, and Jones remained active, but fewer and fewer people looked to them for leadership.

In their works and letters some of the irreconcilables offered acute critiques of an impersonal, capitalistic America, but their analyses displayed little true understanding of the past and failed to offer an alternative vision of the future. Dabney especially rested his critique on a romantic notion of the merits of a slave society, a contempt for democarcy, and an almost feudal faith in a hierarchical society. He and the other irreconcilables seemed guided more by vitriol and hatred than by a commitment to a better world. A society built on their beliefs would have been as flawed as the one they condemned, though in different ways.[41]

In the final analysis, the irreconcilables remained isolated and unimportant to the development of the New South. Even when they offered a valid critique of the direction in which their society was headed, few listened. A minority of white southerners would continue to share their hatred and intransigence, but by the mid-eighties the majority had come to terms with defeat and embraced a future within the Union. Nothing revealed their feelings more strikingly than the behavior of the region during the electoral crisis. After it, nurtured by greater respect from former foes, most southerners pragmatically decided to put the war behind them without repudiating their past or forgetting its pains. The new order they accepted, however, brought its own tensions and strains.

Part Two

CELEBRATING THE CONFEDERACY, 1883 TO 1907

CHAPTER SIX

Toward a New South:
Social Tensions

The many southerners who came to terms with defeat in the eighties cast their lot with a society troubled by unusual tension. The beginnings of industrialization and integration into a national system threatened traditional patterns of life, and a disagreement between the advocates of a New South and defenders of an Old certainly reflected and probably exacerbated public disquiet growing out of these developments. At the same time a lonely but vocal racial liberal, disgruntled farmers, and rebellious workers attacked the social order. The social changes and open dissent strained social cohesion within the South.

Historians do not agree on the extent of change involved in the transition from the Old South to the New. Some emphasize continuity, either by portraying antebellum planters as capitalists in a modernizing South who had to make few adjustments after the war or, conversely, by portraying the planters as pre-capitalist landholders who controlled postbellum change. Other historians stress the differences between a prewar traditional slave economy and the postwar modern market economy and argue that new men with new values came to power after the war. The debate cannot be resolved in a study of the Lost Cause, but the argument here does stress discontinuity over continuity. Moreover, it assumes that in the eighties and early nineties many southerners both experienced a change in the pattern of their lives, particularly as they found themselves more often and more thoroughly enmeshed in a national market economy, and perceived an increase of disorder in their society.[1]

Growth in manufacturing and mining was the most dramatic change they witnessed. The South had begun to industrialize before 1880, but in the next two decades the pace quickened. In seven of the eleven former Confederate states, the number of manufacturing plants more than doubled between 1880 and 1900, and in nine the number of workers employed by such firms increased at least threefold. Richmond, Durham, Birmingham, and much of the Carolina piedmont became manufacturing centers. Despite the industrial growth, though, the South remained primarily an agricultural region, but not the same agricultural region it had been. The postbellum economics of cotton production forced changes in the selling of cotton that left farmers more directly involved in the market than ever before and also spurred the development of small crossroads market towns. Along with the less numerous mill villages, these market centers introduced a new town culture into the formerly rural, isolated South. In seven former Confederate states the population living in what the census defined as urban environments more than doubled between 1880 and 1890. In six, the rate of increase exceeded that of any other decade between 1860 and 1970. The figures probably underestimated the change because, in many towns too small for inclusion by the Census Bureau in the "urban" category, southerners still had to adjust to a different pattern of life.[2]

In the new town environment, shopkeepers, lawyers, physicians, small businessmen, and other professional people became increasingly influential. Constituting a new middle class, they shared the outlook of their big city cousins. A doubling of railroad mileage during the 1880s brought them into close touch with these cousins. The massive construction and eventual consolidation of rail lines integrated as never before the small towns of the South into the national transportation and communication network. The great symbolic moment in the process occurred one Sunday in 1886 when the Louisville and Nashville road moved two thousand miles of track to conform to the gauge used above the Mason-Dixon line.[3]

The rise of an important industrial sector, the expansion of the market economy and a town culture, the growth of the middle class, and the integration into national systems all intensified later; the eighties marked the inauguration, not the culmination, of most of these trends. Because some people celebrated these trends loudly and others condemned them, however, they had an immediate impact in the late eighties and early nineties. A group of New South publicists conspicuously championed many of the changes. Henry Watterson, Walter Hines Page, Henry Grady, Richard H. Edmonds, Daniel A. Tompkins, and others advocated national reconciliation and integration. They espoused diversified agriculture, but they preached more fervently the benefits of industrialization and the merits of commercial values. With changes in southern attitudes and the aid of northern capital, they promised, a business and industrial revolution would transform the South into a land of untold riches and power. Their movement even had its own rituals: industrial and commercial exhibitions, which promoted a vision of a wondrous future. Atlanta held the first in 1881, but others followed in Louisville, in New Orleans, and again in Atlanta before the end of the decade.[4]

The New South advocates and the exhibitions affirmed loyalty to the southern past even as they offered a vision of a very different future. Henry Grady, an Atlanta journalist and best-known of the publicists, claimed, "The new South is simply the old South under new conditions." He promised that the new order would always honor the Confederate dead and cherish "the memory of the old regime, its tradition and its history." Former carpetbagger Hannibal I. Kimball, the director of the first Atlanta exhibition, sought unsuccessfully to get Jefferson

Davis to attend, appointed the irreconcilable Charles C. Jones, Jr., a vice-president, and commissioned the poet laureate of the old order, Paul Hamilton Hayne, to write an ode for the exhibition. The Southern Exposition in Louisville, held two years after the first in Atlanta, had a War Memorial Exhibit with Civil War relics from both sides.[5]

Despite these and other gestures, many proponents of the New South found it difficult to suppress their scorn for the Old South or their impatience with its defenders. The Atlanta Exposition offers a good illustration. Kimball did not like Hayne's ode, only reluctantly agreed to its presentation, and apparently delayed payment for it. In an article on the exposition, Edward Atkinson, a northern industrialist who supported the New South movement, argued that the exposition offered the South an opportunity both to impress visitors with progress being made in overcoming "legitimate not malicious" past errors and a chance to prove how much like the rest of the nation the South was becoming. The exposition's closing ceremonies echoed Atkinson's view. Kimball's address stressed that the key word for the South was *improvement*, and the New Yorker who wrote the poem for the occasion included these lines:

> We stand to-day between the Old and New;
> The past is dead—the Future full in view.
> Behind, the Deluge—but before, the Sun
> Gilds with her light your glories one by one.

Atkinson, Kimball, and the poet baldly enunciated the antagonism between past and future inherent in the attitudes of many southern advocates of industrial progress.[6]

The phrase "New South" itself implied an invidious comparison with the old and suggested a need to abandon the latter. Some New South prophets made both comparison and need explicit. Early in the eighties two of the best-known, Henry Watterson of Kentucky and Walter Hines Page of North Carolina, attacked the old order. In an 1882 *Century* article entitled "Oddities of Southern Life," Watterson portrayed the Old South as an indolent, violent, and generally unpleasant place. With its passing, he seemed to suggest, the South will be better off. The following year, Watterson criticized the Old South more explicitly. It wasted its energies "upon trifles," he said, and took "pride in cultivating what it called 'the vices of a gentleman.'"[7]

More vehemently than Watterson, Page criticized the persistence of such Old South values since the war. His article, "A Study of an Old Southern Borough," appeared a year before Watterson's and ended with a plea for preserving the best of the old civilization. Prior to the conclusion, however, the article criticized savagely a small southern town's failure to embrace modern commercial values. A few years later Page moved to New York, and from there he more forthrightly expressed his disgust with the past in a series of letters to a North Carolina newspaper. In the most strident of them, Page vented his frustration with state officials who opposed the creation of an industrial school. Calling them "mummies," Page claimed that North Carolina's leaders "do not speak out what they think, but submit (as no other people ever submitted) to the guidance of the dead." The "time has come," he asserted, "for independent action, for a declaration of independence from the tyranny of hindering tradition."[8]

Not all southerners agreed on the need for freedom from tradition. In 1882, around the time Watterson and Page published their articles in the *Century*, Robert L. Dabney analyzed the New South in a speech during graduation weekend at Hampden-Sydney College. The reigning New South ideal, Dabney stressed, rested on a false notion of equality that led only to greater inequalities of wealth and ultimately to the financial despotism of New York. Of course, Dabney added, there has to be a New South, but he urged the students as they created it to avoid becoming like the conquerors, withdrawing from society, or, more important, forgetting the principles and "ennobling" examples of the past. Dabney closed his speech with a sentimental description of the dedication of the statue to Stonewall Jackson in Richmond, from which he concluded "There is Life in the old land yet."[9]

Even at a small denominational college in Virginia Dabney's defense of tradition did not go unchallenged. The next day Moses D. Hoge, a Presbyterian minister from Richmond, offered a more favorable assessment of the New South. Fighting sentiment with sentiment, Hoge offered his own anecdote from the festivities in honor of Jackson. He recounted how the general's young daughter had been held up before the crowd of veterans. They greeted her, Hoge recalled, with wild exuberance. "For why?" he asked. "General Jackson was dead, but his daughter still lived. The Old South was dead, but the New South was alive; and though now like the slender girl standing on the frail railing of a temporary platform, yet through the loyal devotion and loving service of these young men, she shall yet stand before the world like the bronze Athena. . . ." Dabney reportedly cried during Hoge's comments.[10]

In most instances, the occasional open renunciations of and implied condemnations of the Old South drove southerners still loyal to the old regime to rage or frustration, not tears. By the end of the eighties many considered the term "New South" insulting and the society it represented uninviting. In an 1887 speech at the unveiling of a Confederate monument in Smithfield, North Carolina, Alfred Moore Waddell claimed that the "phrase, the 'New South,' is tantamount to an insinuation that there is something about the ante bellum South to be ashamed of, and which has been remedied by contact with a higher civilization. And both the allegation and the insinuation are false, and degrading to us." Other southerners, particularly among those active in the Virginia coalition, liked the ways of the New South no better than the implied insult to the Old. William H. Payne urged his friend Early "to lay up something for old age" because "the 'New South' is a pitiless race and will have no forbearance with dependence." Bradley Johnson, relaying a comment by D.H. Hill that "our late enemies have discovered a new country or Island they call the 'New South,'" added, "I have some acquaintances but no friends there."[11]

In the last years of the decade, the dispute between advocates of the Old and the New Souths surfaced during Memorial Day celebrations in Augusta, Georgia. In 1887 local organizer Charles C. Jones, Jr., one of the ambivalent irreconcilables, asked Governor John B. Gordon to deliver the memorial oration. Jones wanted Gordon to place "the glories of the Old South and of our struggle for constitutional right . . . in noble contrast to all the modern bosh about a New South." Gordon, recently elected governor as the candidate of Henry Grady, initially refused the invitation. After Jones badgered him, he finally agreed to deliver an address, but not exactly the one Jones had in mind.[12]

Speaking in a hall in town, Gordon urged southerners to challenge northern misrepresentations of their motives and actions in the Civil War. If allowed to stand, he argued, they would reduce the self-image and self-respect of the South, lead to a "gradual but certain retrogression and impairment of our manhood," and eventually result in a loss of sectional distinctiveness. Yet on the question of slavery Gordon deflected rather than repudiated northern accusations of south-ern immorality. He admitted that there had been wrong in the institution, but claimed that slavery was far from an "unmitigated evil" and praised the civilization built upon the plantation home. That "peculiar and characteristic civilization," Gordon argued, ended with slavery, however. Industrial progress and the wealth it would bring in the next decade were inevitable. The South had only to ensure that in the new industrial civilization it retained the best of the old values, particularly honesty in politics and a sense of moral worth above "mere wealth."

After Gordon's address, the Memorial Day crowd adjourned to the Confed-erate cemetery, where Jones himself spoke. He began with the usual praise for the dead and their sacrifice, but went on to discuss developments in the South with much less equanimity than Gordon. Although welcoming prosperity, railroads, and commerce, Jones explained, "in the midst of such material growth, I would covet a remembrance and an observance of the patriotism, the purity, of the manhood, the moderation, and the honesty of the days that are gone." He wanted a New South "purged of all modern commercial methods" and believed the values of the Old South the best defense against the effects of commercial-ism.[13]

Gordon had called for a leavening of the new industrial society by traditional southern values; Jones sought to purge new "commercial methods" through loyalty to the Old South. Probably few in the audience paid much attention to the distinction, and even Jones praised Gordon for his fine and patriotic address. Yet Jones's dissent arose from a deep disgust with the New South and a fear of the loss of respect for the Old. Three weeks before Memorial Day, Jones had written Payne of the threat posed by "this New South, so called" to southern identity, which he felt depended upon reverence for the Confederate dead. The New South "is but another name for a free field in which speculators, *developers!* and sharpers may range, operate, and entrap the unwary," Jones continued. "There are two words in common use which I detest more than all others—they are *The New South*, and *Boom*."[14]

Two years later in another Memorial Day address Jones publicly attacked the new ways. In a speech on the unequalled contribution of Georgians to the Confederate war effort, Jones began with a requiem to the arcadia that had been antebellum Georgia. He praised its agricultural accomplishments, its patriarchi-cal civilization based on slavery, its lack of social tensions, its fair and honest business practices. Jones then developed his argument about Georgia's contribution to the Confederacy, but interrupted it later to criticize the society that had replaced the bucolic and bountiful antebellum order.

The accomplishments of the war generation, Jones observed, have been ignored in "this epoch of commercial methods—of general and increasing poverty in the agricultural regions of the South—of absorption by foreign capital of favored localities, and of the creation in our midst of gigantic corporations intent upon self-aggrandizement—in this era of manifest modification, if not actual obliteration of those sentiments and modes of thought and action which rendered us a peculiar people. . . ." Jones specifically condemned the commercial values, obsession with personal profit, worship of money, and unequal distribution of wealth that he considered characteristic of the New South. The South, he argued, would be better off with the "occupation of the planter lying at the foundation of all engagements and constituting the normal, the indispensable, the legitimate, and the honorable avocation of the masses," or in other words, would have been better off if the war had not destroyed the prosperous, stable, agrarian society of the prewar years.[15]

Jones thought his address well received, "although some of the plain truths announced were not entirely palatable to the blatant New South School championed by such Bohemians as Henry W. Grady." He sent copies to many people and had an unusually large number of responses. Gordon claimed he read the speech "with not only great pleasure but with an admiration that has rarely been produced to the same degree by anything spoken by any of our Southern people since the war." He said, however, nothing at all about its critical social commentary. Clement A. Evans, a political ally of Gordon's in Georgia, took a similar tack. Former general P.G.T. Beauregard of New Orleans closed his congratulatory letter, "We are however, already on the road to prosperity and ere long the South shall have regained the influence it formerly asserted in the Councils of the Nation. . . ." He seemed to miss the fact that Jones thought the South was on the wrong road. All three supporters of a New South concurred with Jones's celebration of the Confederacy and simply ignored his jeremiad.[16]

Other correspondents, however, commended the criticism and shared Jones's disenchantment with the New South. George A. Mercer "particularly" admired his "views of our simple, patriarchical system and life, as contrasted with the present vulgar struggle for wealth at all hazzards. . . ." Texan W.H. King, who claimed that he wept as he read the speech, agreed fully with its condemnation of the southern "tendency to ape the genuine Yankee race in active but unscrupulous, mean and greedy Schemes for personal, pecuniary and political advancement, without regard to honor and integrity, or the interest and rights of others."[17]

Stephen D. Lee, a Mississippian who held vaguely New South views, also had doubts about developments since the war. In his letter to Jones, Lee first praised the historical section of the speech and then concurred in Jones's apprehensions about the present. "You are certainly correct," wrote Lee, "and if no check is put on the tendency of the new order of things, our government will be wrecked in 20 years more." The rapid consolidation of wealth "into the hands of the few" and "the impoverishing of the many" alarmed Lee. "Results will come more rapidly than in Europe for our very freedom, is not only conducive to the success of speculators but also to rapid work of [the] masses, when they get thoroughly aroused and see how they have been overreached."[18]

The fact that Lee, a New South sympathizer, responded favorably to Jones's celebration of the Old South suggests that it constituted no real challenge to the new order. The essential friendliness of all the letters, the absence of major differences between the rhetoric of Gordon and Jones, and Jones's continued political support for Gordon further reinforce the idea that no major conflict of world views was involved. Nor did the larger debate between proponents of the Old and the New Souths seem to involve such fundamental issues. Watterson and Page clearly thought the South needed to adopt values more compatible with the new economic world; they resented the adamant opposition to change of Dabney and Payne, who just as thoroughly resented them. Most southerners, though, did not identify completely with either side. Rather, they worried that the social changes they only dimly perceived but apparently feared they could not avoid would somehow undermine southern character. They focused most intently on "commercialism," a vaguely defined anxiety that the new order entailed, in King's words, a scramble "for personal, pecuniary, and political advancement, without regard to honor and integrity, or the interest and rights of others." They directed their attacks against the publicists of the New South, but they saw the degeneration brought by commercialism throughout their society and, probably, in themselves. Even New South booster Gordon appeared apprehensive: He added to his celebration of the new order a plea for retaining some of the old values.

Lee even more deeply than Gordon shared Jones's fears. He in fact worried that not just individual character but social stability itself would be undermined by the changes. In the late eighties and early nineties, attacks on the southern social order by a racial liberal, irate farmers, and organized laborers made Lee's fears seem justified. In a series of speeches and articles, New Orleans novelist George W. Cable dramatically challenged both the South's racial practices and its view of the past. In an 1885 *Century* piece, "The Freedman's Case in Equity," Cable called for equal rights for blacks. In a later article, Cable condemned the institution of slavery, which he considered both the foundation of the Old South and the cause of the Civil War.[19]

Cable's articles had little influence on southern race relations or the Confederate tradition, but they did upset many southerners. One claimed to have been "overcome with nausea" by the first article; another criticized its "cringing, crawling, dirt-eating spirit." Henry Grady, a New South spokesman, and Charles Gayarré, an Old South loyalist, both published condemnations of Cable's racial views. Arch irreconcilable Robert L. Dabney ignored Cable's comments on race and condemned Cable for acting "like a good child" who thanked the "conquerors for whipping the folly and naughtiness out of him, although with whips dipped in hell-fire." Dabney marveled that Cable failed to realize that slavery was but "the circumstance of the attack," not the cause of the war, and attacked him for repudiating the Confederacy. If he knew himself to have been wrong in 1861, Dabney wrote, "he would be ashamed, and not proud," as Cable seemed to be. "Of one thing we are sure, if we had committed so enormous a blunder and crime as Mr. Cable now says he committed in 1861, and that, after being so positive we were right, if we had persisted in our error four years, and sealed it with human blood falsely shed, when at last we found out our delusion, we should have hidden our heads and laid our hands on our mouths for the rest of our natural lives. . . ."[20]

Rather than respond directly to his critics, Cable addressed another article to what he called the Silent South, and in it he sought to use the Lost Cause in support of his plea for racial toleration. He offered the "sainted Lee" in support of his call for letting the better instincts of the South reign. If a Silent South of better instincts existed, it chose not to respond to Cable's appeal. His attack on southern racial and historical orthodoxies aroused only his opponents. They and others in the South feared what such dissent would do to the South's social order.[21]

A second and more important challenge to the southern social order, a revolt by farmers, proved more threatening than Cable's. In the late eighties, the Farmers' Alliance first advocated a cooperative, agricultural social order based on producer values as an alternative to the emerging commercial, industrial South. After 1892, its successor, the Populist party, continued to espouse its alternative vision and challenged the dominance of the Democratic party as well. The social and political battles that followed left many southerners uneasy about the future of their society.[22]

Organized and militant labor constituted a third threat. The outbreak of strikes along major rail lines in 1877, which inaugurated a period of violent labor unrest in the nation, left the South relatively untouched. In Louisville, however, violence erupted, and to control it the mayor formed a special force of citizens. Former Confederates Basil Duke and Bennett Young, both of whom were active later in the veterans' movement of the nineties, were among the first recruits. Sporadic outbreaks of labor unrest recurred in Kentucky in 1879, in the spring of 1881 New Orleans cotton workers struck, and during the remainder of the decade labor agitation occurred in other parts of the South. In 1883–84 workers walked out of the Birmingham steel mills and staged additional strikes there over the next ten to fifteen years. By 1885 the Knights of Labor began to organize disgruntled southern laborers, and the union led a particularly long and well-publicized strike of Augusta textile workers in 1886. Between 1885 and 1888, slates of workingmen's candidates, some with ties to the Knights, ran in more than twenty-five municipal elections in the region. In Richmond, one of them briefly took control of the city council, and in a few other towns they had similarly short-lived successes.[23]

Southerners not only experienced the stirrings of labor unrest in their midst but in the late eighties and nineties anxiously followed outbreaks in other areas of the country. Labor rebellion, perhaps even more than the farmers' revolt, threatened the sense of order in the South. It probably exacerbated lingering fears of the dangers inherent in industrial society as well as persisting racial anxieties, since workers were black as well as white. It may even have presented a more alarming vision of disorder than the woolhat boys at the polls. A few southerners lumped both threats together and feared for the future of their society. In 1889 James Wood Davidson, a southern journalist of the old school, considered his native South Carolina under siege. Davidson saw a need to "arrest the spirit of radicalism" that "appears in various shapes but always the same—trade unions, labor reforms, alliances; hostility to whatever *is*, especially if respectable; a restless desire to change, to overturn, to level down; all leading towards strikes, communism, anarchism, and ruin." Although Davidson considered Tillmanism, the farmers' revolt in South Carolina, a particularly dangerous manifestation of "the spirit of radicalism," in general he identified the unrest with the principles of northern society.[24]

Although unusual in the thoroughness with which he discussed his anxiety and the inclusiveness with which he listed the threats, Davidson was not alone in his apprehensions. The South had experienced the beginnings of industrialization, the emergence of a town culture, and increased integration into a national society. A debate between proponents of an Old and a New South expressed and exacerbated the anxiety such dramatic changes engendered. At about the same time, Cable, the farmers, and organized labor challenged various aspects of the social order. Southerners feared for the stability of their society and the maintenance of community in the midst of such challenges and worried about their own values in the face of increased commercialism. These anxieties, as much if not more than the heritage of defeat, spurred a redefinition and redirection of the Confederate tradition between 1880 and 1895.

Two letters written in response to Jones's Memorial Day address illustrated the shift away from the issues or outcome of the war to the concern with the social order. Lee, who had avoided involvement in veterans' activities until the late eighties but became a leader of them in the nineties, both commended Jones's historical vision and shared his fears for the South. Jubal Early, the irascible leader of the Virginia coalition that had thus far dominated Confederate historical matters, also wrote Jones about his speech. Significantly, Early ignored the critique of the New South but criticized Jones for praising Joseph Brown too highly and for claiming James Longstreet as a credit to Georgia. Early still refought the war; Lee worried about the social tensions of the present. Men like Lee would be more influential than men like Early in the development of the Confederate tradition in the eighties and nineties.[25]

CHAPTER SEVEN

The Confederate Tradition in Transition: Developments in the Eighties

On 28 June 1883, from eight to ten thousand people gathered on the campus of Washington and Lee College in Lexington. They came to witness the unveiling of a statue to General Lee placed over his tomb by the Lee Memorial Association, one of the organizations within the Virginia coalition. Because the association's president, Joseph E. Johnston, was sick, Jubal Early presided. The association had asked both Jefferson Davis and John W. Daniel to speak. Davis declined the invitation because he thought his old nemesis, Johnston, would preside, so Daniel became the sole speaker. A Virginia politician crippled in the war, Daniel had maintained close personal ties with Early and others active in the Virginia coalition but had not really participated himself. Moreover, as his 1877 speech on "Conquered Nations" revealed, Daniel had more fervently embraced reconciliation and reunion than had most of the Virginians.[1]

Initially, Daniel had been asked to speak only on Lee's postwar life, perhaps to balance Davis's treatment of the war or to exploit the general's connection with the college. When Davis withdrew, Daniel devoted his address to Lee's entire career. In celebrating Lee's military genius and personal character, the speech followed the pattern set by the Virginians over the previous decade. But Daniel also incorporated themes less characteristic of earlier treatments when he commended Lee's postwar activities and briefly celebrated reconciliation. Following Daniel's speech, Father Ryan, author of "The Gently Furled Banner," read another of his well-known poems, "The Sword of Robert E. Lee." Early then led a procession into the chapel, where Stonewall Jackson's daughter unveiled the dignified, sleeping Lee chiseled in marble by Edward V. Valentine, a well-known Richmond artist. The crowd did not cheer but exclaimed "Majesty in repose," "Sweet Rest," "Marse Robert Asleep."[2]

The Lexington ceremonies were the last dominated by the Virginians and featured both old and new aspects of a changing Confederate tradition. The participation of Father Ryan, the placement of the monument over the tomb of Lee, and the statue itself of a sleeping Lee easily taken for dead echoed the

Edward Valentine's statue of a recumbent Robert E. Lee (unveiled June 28, 1873) in the Memorial Chapel, Washington and Lee University, Lexington, Virginia. *The Museum of the Confederacy*

feelings of bereavement so prevalent in the early postwar South. The monument had been all along the project of the Virginia coalition. Its leader Early presided; Daniel celebrated views it had championed; and the participation of the daughter of Jackson symbolically united the two heroes about whom the Virginians had built their movement. The inclusion of a discussion of Lee's postwar career, the choice of Daniel to deliver the address, and his allusions to reconciliation, however, all represented new themes in the Confederate tradition.

The increased spirit of reunion along with the anxieties that accompanied social change, and perhaps the simple passage of time as well, helped reshape the tradition. In the 1880s the bereavement of the early memorial movement gave way to greater celebration of the Confederacy. An openness toward the North and an emphasis on the experience and camaraderie of battle replaced the Virginians' militant sectionalism and obsession with the war's issues and outcome. Confederate activities in Augusta, Louisville, and New Orleans incorporated the new themes, and even a Richmond veterans' group that embraced them formed. Seemingly out of touch with the times, the Virginia coalition lost much of what influence it had. After the reemergence and eventual death of Jefferson Davis and the unveiling of the Lee Monument in Richmond at the end of the decade, the celebration of the Confederacy began in earnest under new leadership.

. . .

In 1878, a Confederate Survivors' Association organized in Augusta. Charles C. Jones, Jr., who had just returned to the city from his New York law practice, became its first president and remained its spiritual leader for the next fifteen years. The CSA, according to its organizers, sought to encourage friendship among surviving soldiers, to protect recollections of the past, to promote "the practice of manly virtues," and to provide for members in "seasons of sickness and distress." The CSA, however, never seriously undertook the broad program such goals suggested but rather in its first years functioned more as a memorial society than anything else. It held its annual meeting on Memorial Day, sent a special detail to the funeral of any member, and adopted as a badge a black silk ribbon about three inches wide with the letters CSA stamped in gold.[3]

Within a few years, though, the CSA changed. The association replaced its black ribbon with a badge of bright Confederate flags that symbolized "at once . . . national unity and . . . martial glory." In 1882 Jones began using his annual Memorial Day address to discuss historical issues rather than simply to memorialize the dead. Five years later, the CSA held the "first public reunion since the organization of the Association" and invited "representative Confederates" from Georgia and neighboring states. That year the CSA enrolled seventy-four new members, the largest increase in any single year of its history save the first. They joined a group that had shifted its attention ever so slightly from memorialization of the dead to the celebration of the war and that in the process had attempted and apparently succeeded in reaching out to a broader constituency. The CSA did so at the time Jones worried about the direction of the New South—the first public ceremony was the one to which Jones invited Gordon—and in the year following the protracted Knights of Labor strike in Augusta. Although no direct tie can be established, the social tensions of the eighties appear to have influenced Augusta's renewed interest in celebrating the Confederacy.[4]

Louisville, another city that had experienced labor unrest, also had an upsurge in Confederate activity. In 1882 a branch of the SHS that had formed in the Kentucky city began to publish a magazine, *The Southern Bivouac*. Jubal Early soon criticized it for being too sensational and for printing articles by obscure Confederates. The *Bivouac* did offer fewer analytical military histories than the *SHSP* and many more personal reminiscences and bits of "wit and humour of the bivouac." Within a year the sponsoring SHS disbanded, and the *Bivouac* changed owners twice before being placed under the management of Richard W. Knott, of the *Home and Farm*, and Basil W. Duke, a former Confederate officer who would remain active in Confederate veterans' affairs well into the twentieth century. Under their guidance, the *Bivouac* began to advocate the creation of a New South, though with the caveat that its roots must be in the Old, and ran several editorials on the danger of labor unrest. It evolved into a general rather than a historical or war journal, and in 1886 it ceased publication when bought out by the *Century*. In its brief life, the *Bivouac* had enunciated themes becoming important in the Confederate tradition: an emphasis on the experience of battle, approval of the New South, and apprehension about organized labor.[5]

Some of the themes emerging in Augusta and Louisville also surfaced in New Orleans, a city whose veterans would lead the Confederate celebration of the next decade. Interest in Confederate activities had increased significantly in the Crescent City since the SHS had left in 1873 for a more hospitable environment. By 1883, New Orleans had become, according to Fitzhugh Lee, the "headquarters of Confederate sentiment, feeling, and action." Two major veterans' groups, the Association of the Army of Northern Virginia and a similar Association of the Army of Tennessee, which formed in 1877, accounted for much of the enthusiasm. Both groups administered substantial programs of aid and relief for their members but dedicated much of their attention to securing a group tomb. In the 1880s both completed their projects and dedicated them—an accomplishment that left the groups free to focus on other activities.[6]

In 1884 New Orleans also dedicated a public memorial to General Lee. Fund-raising efforts, independent both of the Virginia enterprise and of the city's veterans' groups, had begun in 1870 but languished until the latter part of the decade. When the sponsors had sufficient money, they secured a statue and invited people from all over the South to a public unveiling on 22 February 1884. Fifteen thousand people attended, but only a few contingents came from other states. As the ceremonies began, a downpour scattered the audience, and officials canceled the program and simply presented the statue in a nearby building. Southerners did not judge the rain a sign of divine displeasure, although on other occasions they often interpreted good weather as testimony to God's favor, but instead considered the thunder "the salvos of Heaven's Artillery" in honor of the event. Consistent theology was the hobgoblin of loyal Confederates.[7]

As in Lexington, the unveiling in New Orleans suggested a Confederate tradition in transition. The main address prepared for delivery praised Lee's character, defended the cause for which he fought, and offered the overwhelmed-by-numbers argument. It clearly reflected the Virginians' interpretation if not their direct influence. On the other hand, the scheduling of the ceremony for Washington's birthday rather than a Confederate anniversary and the participation of a local Grand Army of the Republic camp betokened the growing emphasis on reconciliation. The statue itself involved a bit more public celebration than the one at Washington and Lee. It was placed in the business district rather than in a memorial chapel and portrayed Lee standing rather than lying down.[8]

Although—or, better, because they were—unrelated, the flurry of Confederate activities in Augusta, Louisville, and New Orleans testified to an increasing interest in the memory of the war. It suggested that new concerns generated such interest and substantiated the emergence of new themes within the Confederate tradition. Since the Virginians had always had only limited success outside their own state, developments in the other cities constituted little challenge to the power of the Virginia coalition. It had already begun to lose what little influence it had, however, and a new Confederate organization that formed in Richmond itself hastened its decline.

The *Southern Historical Society Papers*, the voice of the coalition, lost more

Robert E. Lee Monument, New Orleans, Louisiana, on the day of its unveiling, February 22, 1884. *The Historic New Orleans Collection, 533 Royal Street, Acc. No. 1974 25.24.128*

than 1,100 subscribers in the year before July 1877, and for that and other reasons had trouble paying its printer. Fund-raising lectures at the Springs of Virginia and the formation of a few new but short-lived local SHS branches failed to reduce the debt. Jones then approached Jefferson Davis about a speaking tour in behalf of the SHS, but the former president agreed to deliver only one address. In April 1882 he told a New Orleans audience that the South needed to preserve the record of its past and praised the SHS's efforts. The SHS had hoped Davis's endorsement and appearance would result in an endowment of $50,000, but the event raised only $1,500. Later that year, Fitzhugh Lee, one of the Virginia coalition's early leaders, did speak for the Society in several cities in South Carolina and Georgia. Except in the New South center of Atlanta, southerners received him warmly and contributed to his cause. In 1883 Lee raised $3,500 on a tour through Alabama, Louisiana, Texas, and Tennessee.

Together the various fund-raising appearances eased, but did not eliminate, the financial problems of the SHS.[9]

As the SHS coped with its financial difficulties, its sister society, the Association of the Army of Northern Virginia, faced a different kind of challenge: another major Confederate organization in Richmond, the home of the Virginia coalition. In April 1883 veterans there organized Robert E. Lee Camp #1, Southern Veterans (soon changed to Confederate Veterans). They invited "the cooperation of all veterans regardless of state, creed, or condition" and adopted as their first project the establishment of a home for Confederate veterans. Exactly why they chose to organize a new society rather than work through the AANVA remains unclear. Perhaps they did so because veterans of units other than the Army of Northern Virginia could not join the AANVA or because the older group showed no interest in a soldiers' home. Much more seemed involved, however, and the decision to act independently was an important development in the Confederate tradition. Lee Camp had a very different membership and expressed a view of the past rather different from that of the AANVA.[10]

Not one of the thirty-nine veterans who signed the Lee Camp roll the first night had belonged to the AANVA, and the new members were not only different men but different kinds of men. The AANVA had drawn its membership from the upper and middle classes. The first commander of Lee Camp was a lawyer, and one of the members of the committee on permanent organization was a physician. They would have been quite at home in the AANVA. The other four members of the committee probably would not have been: One was a grocer, two were carpenters, and the other was a coach painter. The leadership reflected the membership, since more than half the first members came from the working class, with the others split almost evenly between the upper and middle classes. Lee Camp drew its members from lower ranks of the social order than did the AANVA.[11]

As Lee Camp enrolled more members, the proportion of members from the working class dropped and that from the middle class rose. Still Lee Camp's social base differed from the AANVA's. In its first two years, the AANVA had drawn more than half its members from the upper class; in its first two years Lee Camp drew only a quarter from the elite. Both groups had about the same percentage of men from proprietary and low white-collar occupations, although Lee Camp had slightly more. But where the AANVA had almost no working-class members (fewer than 10 percent), Lee Camp attracted a substantial number (just under 30 percent) from the lower classes. More of the new recruits than organizers came to Lee Camp from the AANVA, but throughout their history the two organizations had relatively few members in common—only around 7 percent of the total membership of the two organizations.[12]

The groups appealed to different constituencies because they espoused different goals. The newspaper announcement of the first meeting of Lee Camp said, "Naturally enough time had to mellow the bitter feeling that the struggle engendered before southern soldiers took steps to effect any organization looking to a perpetuation of the hardships, struggles, and deeds of valor that marked their conduct in the strife for southern independence." In the next day's paper, the new commander of Lee Camp promised that it would provide nothing but "comradeship" and aid for the sick and needy. Over the next few years, the group displayed limited interest in establishing the truth of history or rationalizing defeat, and members seemed more concerned with remembering, or maybe even recreating, the experience of the war. Unlike the AANVA, they sought not revitalization, but "comradeship."[13]

Also in contrast with the AANVA's purposes was Lee Camp's embrace of sectional reconciliation. Its first commander stated that the Camp would avoid the "animosities" of the war and would extend courtesy to the former foes. In its first year, Lee Camp did participate in several activities with Grand Army of the Republic groups. It also appealed to the GAR and other northerners for aid in building the veterans' home. Responding to a gift by one GAR post, Lee Camp proclaimed these northern veterans "a band of brothers, bound to us by deeds greater than those won on the field of battle or the forum, Deeds of brotherly love and charity." Jubal Early, who must have turned gray at such effusions, criticized requests for northern money to build a Confederate home. Lee Camp persisted and gained support from a "Joint Committee of Conference (G.A.R. and Ex-Confederate)" headquartered in New York and chaired by former Confederate general John B. Gordon. He presided over a successful fund-raiser in New York City. Gordon also endorsed and Lee Camp sponsored a series of so-called romantic plays that toured major cities in the Southeast. The efforts paid off: The veterans' home opened only two years after the fund-raising began.[14]

The touring plays and other fund-raising efforts also generated publicity that no doubt encouraged similar associations to form. In June 1883, Lee Camp discussed the possibility of organizing such groups in other Virginia towns and of forming a statewide organization. The next spring it created a "committee on charters and subordinate camps" to begin the process. A second camp formed in Richmond within a year, and others followed elsewhere in the state and even as far away as Chattanooga.[15]

The success of Lee Camp apparently accelerated the decline of the AANVA and, less directly, the influence of the Virginia coalition. In 1885 the AANVA had 18 percent more members than it had had in 1873–74, but its growth had peaked. In the next fifteen years, membership dwindled as more than half the members stopped paying dues. In 1891 the executive committee bemoaned the "waning interest" in the society but made no changes to rekindle interest. Members continued to quit to join other groups, with several going to Lee Camp. The percentage of new AANVA members from Richmond dropped dramatically after 1885 as most new recruits came from other towns in Virginia or even from out of state.[16]

The influence of the SHS, too, declined, partly because of its worsening financial problems. By 1884 they had become so severe that Dabney Maury considered turning over custody of the Confederate records collected by the SHS to the state of Virginia. He blamed Jones for the difficulties, claiming he ran the society "practically for the benefit and convenience of Rev. W. Jones." Maury's report, however, suggested that a general loss of enthusiasm among the leadership and a decline in subscriptions were actually at fault. That matters worsened after Jones resigned in 1887 confirmed it. R.A. Brock, a man who already served as secretary of the Virginia Historical Society but had little standing among the veterans, succeeded Jones. During Brock's tenure the *SHSP*, once the primary voice of the Confederate tradition, became little more than a Confederate clipping service, mostly publishing stories that had first appeared elsewhere. By 1889 even Early despaired at the SHS's decreased importance. He thought Brock had "very little knowledge of war history" and accused him, incorrectly, of not even having served in the army. Since Jones's resignation and Maury's appointment to a diplomatic post, Early lamented, "the work of the Society has been very much neglected, as it is very difficult to get persons to fill their places suitably."[17]

By the late eighties, the transition within the Confederate tradition was well under way. Increased visibility for Confederate activity in New Orleans and the formation of Lee Camp in Richmond itself challenged the domination of the Virginia coalition, and its two main organizations began to decline. At the same time, a spirit of sectional reconciliation developed, in part fostered by a new emphasis on remembering the experience and camaraderie of wartime. Finally, southerners appeared more ready to celebrate the Confederacy than ever before. Two developments in the latter half of the decade nurtured the impulse toward celebration: the public reemergence and death of Jefferson Davis and the unveiling of the statue to Lee in Richmond.

A new role for and attitude toward Jefferson Davis emerged in the late eighties. At the end of the Civil War, many southerners had been extremely critical of Davis. Sympathy for his postwar imprisonment checked their hostility but, even so, few embraced him enthusiastically as a hero. The Virginians did admire Davis and frequently asked him to address their gatherings, but only occasionally did Davis make speeches or appearances. In 1886, however, he agreed to his first extended public tour since the war. A Montgomery, Alabama, citizens' committee invited Davis to speak at the laying of the cornerstone of a Confederate monument on the Alabama statehouse grounds. When New South advocate Henry Grady learned Davis had accepted, he asked the former Confederate president to come to Atlanta following the ceremony. Grady wanted Davis to participate in the dedication of a monument to Benjamin H. Hill, a former Confederate senator from Georgia. Davis agreed, and the Atlanta editor apparently seized the opportunity to promote his candidate for governor of Georgia, John B. Gordon.[18]

Gordon served as unofficial guide and spokesman for Davis during the latter's stay in Alabama and Georgia. While the Georgian waited at the station for the former president's train to arrive in Montgomery, he made a few brief remarks that appeared to explain the terms under which he escorted Davis. Gordon reminded the crowd of his own efforts at sectional reconciliation and assured them that "there is nothing in the honor paid our leader inconsistent with our duty as citizens of a re-united country." In fact, Gordon added, he welcomed any condemnations that might arise from "honoring this man who has been made to suffer for us. . . ." The next day both Davis and Gordon spoke during ceremonies at the Alabama statehouse. Gordon then accompanied the former Confederate president on what amounted to a whistle-stop tour from Montgomery to Atlanta. In many towns, large, enthusiastic crowds, sometimes encouraged if not organized by Grady, met the train amid considerable festivity. At one point Gordon urged Davis not to tire himself by delivering too many speeches, and Davis replied, "I am like Moses of old, and want an Aaron." At the next stop, he appeared before the crowd, placed his hand on Gordon and announced, "This is my Aaron; let him speak for me." When the train arrived in Atlanta, Gordon, again at Davis's request, addressed the large crowd awaiting them.[19]

The following day, however, Gordon remained in the background during one of the largest of the postwar Confederate celebrations. Nearly eighty thousand people gathered in downtown Atlanta to witness the unveiling of the Hill statue and to see the former Confederate president. The main address, by Major J.C.C. Black of Augusta, celebrated the life and accomplishments of Hill, defended the Confederate cause, lauded southern contributions to the nation, damned Reconstruction, and praised both Lee and Davis. With the former president on the platform, Black argued that Davis's conduct in prison and private life since the war illustrated how "human virtue can be equal to human calamity." He praised Davis for "bearing majestically the sufferings of his people, and calmly awaited the summons that shall call him to the rewards and glories of those who have suffered for the right." After Black spoke, Henry Grady introduced Davis. Grady too made reference to Davis's suffering and offered an analogy that suggested that it had ended in triumph for both Davis and the South. "This moment, in this blessed Easter week," Grady observed, "witnessing the resurrection of these memories that for twenty years have been buried in our hearts, has given us the best Easter that we have seen since Christ was risen from the Dead." Davis then made a few brief and perhaps inevitably anticlimactic remarks.[20]

After the ceremony, Davis journeyed on to Savannah for another appearance, where his statements proved less cautious than those made earlier in the trip. Several northern papers attacked what they considered a renewal of Confederate sentiment, and even a few southern ones criticized Davis for having learned nothing in twenty years. On the other hand, some intransigent old Confederates criticized the tour as undignified or complained that it awakened painful memories. Most southerners, however, celebrated the resurrection of memories of the past that, as Gordon announced from the first, could be cherished without disloyalty to a reunited nation. For most, Davis no longer inspired visions of lost independence but rather symbolized southern suffering since Appomattox. "He Was Manacled For US" read the inscription on the flowers placed on his train at one stop. When southerners cheered him, they cheered the Confederate past and ultimately themselves. "There never has been anything at the South equal to the ovation which Mr. Davis has received," D.H. Hill wrote his son. "You know that I have no reason to like Mr. Davis, but he has suffered for us and is our representative man. We ought to honor him in order to honor ourselves." This homage paid Davis in public, Bill Arp concurred, left him filled with "a peculiar pride and independence." Arp rejoiced that times had changed and that the South "can dare to indulge in self-respect. . . . We have asserted our manhood boldly and freely before the world, and it will command more respect than all the truckling and fawning and apologizing of time servers for the last twenty years."[21]

Southerners indulged their self-respect and asserted their manhood by honoring not only Davis but also his daughter Varina Anne. The twenty-one year old Winnie, as his younger daughter was usually called, was at Davis's side in Montgomery and accompanied him on the tour. In West Point, Georgia, Gordon introduced her as "the daughter of the Confederacy . . . the war baby of our old chieftain." The appellation followed her the rest of her life as she assumed an increasingly public role. Late in 1886 Winnie Davis appeared before a thousand admiring veterans in Richmond when Lee Camp made her an honorary member. Through J. William Jones, who spoke for her, she assured the throng that the former soldiers need feel no dishonor for having fought in a just cause. In 1887, she and her married sister, Margaret Davis Hayes, accompanied their father to a Confederate reunion in Macon, Georgia, where a ball was held in Winnie's honor. When ill health prevented the former president from going on to a scheduled appearance at a fair in Athens, the two daughters went in his place. During their visit, an assembly of Confederate veterans formed facing their carriage. Winnie Davis and her sister were introduced, and one veteran approached them carrying a Confederate flag. He dipped it toward them; they kissed its folds. The veteran then cut out two stars and presented them to the women.[22]

After these first public appearances, Winnie Davis frequently attended Confederate activities and almost always received a tumultuous but respectful reception. The veterans' affection for Winnie exceeded the regard one would expect to be granted the daughter of a former leader. Lee's daughter did not command similar devotion, and northern veterans did not bestow it upon the daughters of their generals. Even Winnie's older sister, who had been born before the war, never received equal adulation. Winnie's physical appearance probably did not inspire enthusiasm; one reporter described her as "a tall brunette, not decidedly pretty at first sight, but she improves rapidly on acquaintance." The title that Gordon bestowed on her, "daughter of the Confederacy," however, explains much about her popularity.[23]

Varina Anne Davis was born during the war to the leader whom northerners after the surrender had caricatured as a woman. She therefore offered visible evidence of a virility of the South's representative man and through him of the Confederacy, thereby reassuring southern soldiers of their manhood. Winnie's words and actions during the early appearances made such assurance explicit. In Richmond she told the veterans they should be ashamed of nothing. Kissing an upraised Confederate flag held by a veteran at the very least testified to her great faith in the cause and its troops, but on some level it may also have signaled her respect for the veterans' manhood.

Winnie Davis's affirmation of Confederate virility remained less important than, and of course dependent upon, her father. Jefferson Davis himself, however, proved a troublesome symbol as long as he was alive. As in Savannah, he sometimes spoke rashly, revived sectional animosities, and embarrassed men like Gordon. In December 1889 ex-president Davis died during a visit to New Orleans. The entire South went into mourning, and many cities and towns held memorial serivces. The "tearful demonstrations and many eloquent utterances, from pulpit and platform" surprised J.L.M. Curry, who "hardly anticipated such unanimity, but [Davis] was *the* representative of the 'Lost Cause.'" A few of the speeches expressed lingering sectional hostility, Curry added, but most were "generally free from partisan bitterness and impudent utterances." Southern leaders and prominent ex-Confederates from all over the South went to New Orleans for the funeral, at which Gordon served as honorary marshal.[24]

Death completed the transformation of Davis's image: He became less the partisan leader and more the "representative man." When southerners celebrated him in unprecedented fashion during his 1886 tour and upon his death, they celebrated themselves and the Confederate past. In his younger daughter veterans found evidence for the virility of the Confederacy and a young woman who would praise their accomplishments and manhood. Finally, Grady and Gordon, men committed to a New South and sectional reconciliation, not the leaders of the Virginia coalition, who had always considered Davis their own, presided at the new presentation of both father and daughter.

Less than six months after the Davis funeral, southerners gathered to unveil a statue to Robert E. Lee in Richmond. The festivities marked the emergence of the Confederate celebration, and the developments leading up to them testified to the declining influence of the Virginians. When the Virginia coalition in the early 1870s shifted its primary effort to the Lexington monument, it had not lost interest in the plans to place another in Richmond. Controversy and contention plagued the campaign, however, beginning in 1877 when a public dispute prevented a decision on a design for the monument. The Richmond women's association that had raised the most money rejected all the models and steadfastly refused to give up control of its funds. An 1884 attempt to consolidate it with the other organizations raising money for the monument failed, but two years later Virginia governor Fitzhugh Lee worked out a successful agreement. It created a new board of directors, called the Lee Monument Association (LMA), composed of representatives from the government and the women's association. Lee vigorously pushed the fund-raising toward completion, and the newly created board began the process of selecting a sculptor. Almost from the beginning, it leaned toward awarding the commission to Frenchman Jean Antoine Mercié.[25]

An increasingly disgruntled Jubal Early, who had agreed to the consolidation even though he still felt the statue his group's project, did not like the idea. He hated Mercié's early design, which he thought had "General Lee on a 'bob tail horse,' looking like an English jockey," and suggested that if it were erected he might gather "the survivors of the 2d Corps" and blow the statue up. Early thought Edward Valentine, the Virginia sculptor who had done the recumbent statue at Washington and Lee, should be chosen. To give the task to a foreigner over Valentine, for whom it would be a labor of love, Early felt would be

Funeral procession for Jefferson Davis through the streets of New Orleans, Louisiana, December 11, 1889. *The Historic New Orleans Collection, 533 Royal Street, Acc. No. 1985 125.1*

sacrilege. Sarah N. Randolph, the Richmonder who spearheaded the search for a sculptor, was unimpressed with appeals to state loyalty or Confederate sentiment. "Genius is cosmopolitan," Mrs. Randolph countered, "and while the Virginia sculptors must have every possible chance for winning the prize they should only expect to do so by superiority of merit and not the accident of place of birth." Obviously impressed by Mercié's international reputation, she wanted him to do the statue. In the face of her determination, Early and his allies had little influence on her or on Governor Lee. Although an early leader of the Virginia coalition, Lee had been one of its first members to join Lee Camp when it formed. His relations with Early had become strained after the disputed election, probably because of his increasingly active role in sectional reconciliation. The committee selected a revised model by Mercié, which featured a dignified Lee atop a majestic horse that bore slight resemblance to Lee's small, quiet mount, Traveller.[26]

Another debate arose over where in Richmond to place the statue. The committee finally decided upon a site at the far edge of one of the city's newer suburbs—testimony to its faith in local boosters' promise of growth. With both monument and site selected, the LMA laid the cornerstone in 1887. Governor Lee assigned to Lee Camp the responsibility for coordinating the stay of military and veterans' groups—another sign of the AANVA's declining status. These groups selected P.G.T. Beauregard chief marshal, and Lee agreed despite Early's protests. Early, however, presided, and his ally Charles Marshall delivered an address heavy with the old themes that southerners did not wage a war for slavery and that the soldiers fought out of love for Lee, a noble warrior.[27]

Between the laying of the cornerstone and the unveiling of the monument two years later, a final controversy developed. Early objected to the use of Maine marble in the base of the statue. Fitz Lee explained that there had been no other choice, since the marble companies of Richmond had colluded to keep the price high; Confederate patriotism apparently had limits in some quarters. Lee calmed "Old Jube," and together Early and Lee Camp contributed enough money to complete the statue. Early was chosen to serve as master of ceremonies for the unveiling, but major arrangements for the celebration remained under the direction of Lee Camp.[28]

When the unassembled statue arrived in Richmond, the camp requested that citizens drag it by hand to the site, as had been done with the Washington statue before the war. More than 9,000 Richmonders turned out to help pull long ropes attached to the four boxes containing sections of the statue. All classes of people, according to a local journalist, joined in the enthusiasm: "men who are in counting-rooms; men who are members of the Tobacco and Grain exchanges; men who toil in the foundry of the city; men who, with nail and hammer, build the residences of the citizens, all were present, and though lookers on until the ropes came in sight, they caught the infection, and, with enthusiastic 'yell,' took hold of the hemp." Women and children, too, participated, pulling two crates by themselves. Once at the site, the crowd cut the rope into small sections. Individuals then placed a piece in a buttonhole or put it into a pocket, thus in some fashion taking home part of the day's activities. They had celebrated their long-dead leader and wanted a symbol of the ceremony.[29]

Three weeks later people from all over the South gathered in Richmond to continue the celebration with the unveiling of the monument. Residents had decorated the city with miles of bunting, pictures of Washington and Lee, and countless Confederate and American flags. Throughout Richmond, bands played "Dixie" or other old tunes that evoked memories of the war. The major Confederate organizations in New Orleans, Augusta, Chattanooga, and other cities sent representatives. Most of the leaders of postwar Confederate activity came: Early, Maury, Payne, J. William Jones, C.C. Jones, Jr., Gordon, and Daniel. In all, between 100,000 and 150,000 people participated in the ceremonies—the largest crowd yet for a Confederate celebration and from ten to fifteen times as many as had come to earlier Lee monument unveilings in Lexington and New Orleans.[30]

On the day of the unveiling, 29 May 1890, events began with a parade of honored guests in carriages, militia units, veterans' associations, school groups, and even a delegation from the Farmers' Alliance. Led by chief marshal Fitzhugh Lee, the line of march 15,000 to 20,000 people long stretched four miles. The parade ended at the monument, where the crowd gathered to witness the ceremonies, which opened with prayer followed by the playing of "Dixie." Jubal Early, who again presided, introduced Archer Anderson, treasurer of Tredegar Iron Works and a member of the LMA and Lee Camp, who delivered the address. Anderson portrayed Lee as a man of action and sketched his military career with emphasis on the fact that he always faced superior numbers. Anderson also praised the general's character, "the perfect union of Christian virtues and old Roman manhood," and closed with a charge:

> Let this monument, then, teach to generations yet unborn these lessons of life! Let it stand, not a record of civil strife, but as a perpetual protest against whatever is low and sordid in our public and private objects! . . . Let it stand as a great public act of thanksgiving and praise, for that it pleased Almighty God to bestow upon these Southern States a man so formed to reflect His attributes of power, majesty, and goodness!

As Anderson concluded, General Joseph E. Johnston approached the statue, and, after a dramatic pause, unveiled it. Cannons and muskets fired. The crowd cheered. A sham battle broke out between the formed infantry and cavalry, and some spectators rushed from the stands for a better view.[31]

The sham battle, the roar of the crowd at the unveiling, the parade, and the general festiveness of the occasion were more important than the speech. Anderson himself considered the celebration "a thing to be seen once in a lifetime. Of all the popular demonstrations that I have witnessed or read of none approached it in the elements of deep, unanimous and spontaneous feeling," he observed. "There was nothing official about it, no cheer answered to orders from above; but in every face of the 100,000 I think I looked at there was written a personal participation in the public commemoration." "I felt," one of the

Small part of the crowd cheering the unveiling of the Robert E. Lee monument, Richmond, Virginia, May 29, 1890. *The Museum of the Confederacy*

100,000 explained, "as tho I were assisting at a combined funeral and resurrection." When "the mantle dropped from the statue of their old commander," he added, the members of the Army of Northern Virginia "passed forever from the gaze of time—into history." But another observed that "Cheers such as we have not heard for a quarter of a century salute our noble chieftain, mingle with the thunder of artillery and the roar and rattle of musketry. It seems as if legions of heroes have risen from the dead and are fighting their battles again in defense of Richmond." The ceremonies brought the participants out of their day-to-day world and, for a ritual moment, returned them to a past peopled by glorious heroes. Community homage to Lee, and through him to the Confederate cause and ultimately to the individual particpants, united the participants in a bond that transcended not only time but the usual social division of society. It eased the pain of defeat and restored southern pride.[32]

The unity and pride did not result in a revival of the spirit of independence, as a Utah Republican paper, which would likely have condemned any hint of sectionalism, pointed out. "The ghost of the lost cause was called up and saluted," it reported, but the "sober men of the South, while calling up their ghosts and while giving way to their affection for their cherished dead, still in their hearts are forced to confess that it was best that their arm was broken and that their defeat was, in fact, a mercy in disguise." Not all southerners would have agreed that defeat was merciful, but most neither sought nor found in the celebration a means of rejuvenating sectional battles or ideologies.[33]

Many participants considered the Lee unveiling unique. It was the grandest of all the Confederate festivals, partly because of the special place Lee and Richmond occupied in the hearts of the former soldiers. Yet the celebration during the two decades following the Lee unveiling involved a similar creation of ritual time, with its concomitant feeling of unity, release, and restoration. The transition within the Confederate tradition during the eighties helped shape that celebration. A new emphasis on reconciliation and the comradeship of battle made it easier to "call up the ghosts" of the past without igniting sectional tensions in the present. The Virginia coalition, a group interested in keeping alive old hostilities and reviving Confederate culture, no longer dominated the Confederate tradition. Men like Gordon and the members of Lee Camp had come to play a larger role in keeping the symbols and traditions of the war. With their help, a new group that formed late in the decade would lead the Confederate celebration.

CHAPTER EIGHT

The Confederate Celebration:
Its Organizational Structure

The United Confederate Veterans, which formed in the year before the Lee Monument unveiling, exploited and guided the celebration of the war. It assumed control of the Confederate tradition in the 1890s, completing the transition from the leadership of the Virginia coalition. Over the next twenty years, the UCV and the organizations it spawned attracted greater support among both veterans and the public than the Virginians ever had. The apprehensions that accompanied the social tensions of the late nineteenth century, along with doubts about lost honor and manhood that persisted among the veterans, explained its success.

In the 1880s more Confederate army units held reunions than had in the previous decade, and a few of the meetings resulted in the organization of permanent veterans' societies. Additional groups formed through the influence of Lee Camp, the Confederate Survivors' Association of Augusta, and other existing associations. In the fall of 1887 a camp in Florida sought to organize the growing number of camps into a general association of Confederate veterans. It published plans for such an organization, wrote to prominent camps, and proposed a slate of officers. The other Confederate organizations considered the idea impractical, however, and nothing came of it. Nevertheless, in 1887 and 1888 three statewide associations formed. Richmond's Lee Camp, which had sought a statewide confederation almost from its beginning, launched a new campaign that led to the formation of the Grand Camp of Confederate Veterans of Virginia, a loose confederation of most of the societies in the state except the Association of the Army of Northern Virginia. A similar association formed in Tennessee, and a move toward one began in Georgia.[1]

The formation in New Orleans of the Benevolent and Historical Association, Veteran Confederate States Cavalry, in 1888 continued the trend toward a general association. George Moorman, a Louisiana politician and civic booster, envisioned initially an association only of his former command, but at the suggestion of others invited all cavalry soldiers to an organizational meeting. Only a few veterans from outside New Orleans or even Louisiana attended, but the group selected Mississippian Stephen D. Lee president and appointed vice-presidents for every state. Lee admitted that the meeting was "the first reunion of Confederates I have ever attended." He had, for reasons he could not explain, previously refused invitations to such events. "When I received the request from Col. Moorman to come I hesitated and said, 'Why go now?' But something took hold of me and my coming here was impelled by an irresistible impulse."[2]

Others seemed compelled by a similarly irresistible impulse, and a second and successful campaign to establish a regional Confederate veterans' association began in New Orleans the same year. Leon Jastremski, a druggist and politician from Baton Rouge but a member of the New Orleans AANVA, later claimed to have first suggested the idea to E.D. Willett. Jastremski had seen an "inspiring and suggestive" reunion of the GAR and thought Confederate veterans should have a similar occasion. Actual planning began with conversations among Willett, Fred A. Ober, Fred S. Washington, and a few other members in the AANVA meeting hall. Soon J.A. Chalaron and D.E. Given of the Association of the Army of Tennessee (AAT) joined the discussions. In February 1889 the AANVA, AAT, and the newly organized Confederate States' Cavalry all formally endorsed a plan for a general meeting of southern veterans, and each appointed members of a committee to organize it.[3]

In response to the committee's call, representatives from ten Louisiana, Tennessee, and Mississippi veterans' groups met in New Orleans in June 1889. J.M. Shipp of Chattanooga and Peter J. Trezevant of Shreveport joined with the early planners to lead the proceedings. Under their guidance, the representatives adopted a constitution and chose a name, the United Confederate Veterans (UCV). The UCV, not surprisingly, had many military trappings: The chief officer was called commander, all officers held rank, and local associations were called camps. It had a hierarchical organizational structure with a national office and officers, three geographical departments, state divisions, and virtually autonomous local camps. The delegates at first debated whether to elect a commander or to wait until constituent organizations had approved their plan. Jastremski argued that John B. Gordon, the man he had in mind for the job, would bring in thirty or forty thousand members by the next meeting, so he should be elected at once. Fred Washington said he had already secured Gordon's agreement to take the post, and the delegates elected him without opposition.[4]

Although very popular with the veterans, Gordon did not bring in so many members at once. At the second UCV meeting, held in Chattanooga in 1890, representatives from the Lee Camp in Richmond first participated, but few other new groups sent delegates. Following the third general meeting in Jackson, Mississippi, in 1891, Gordon named George Moorman adjutant general of the UCV. By all accounts, Moorman ran the UCV, or "lugged the whole pack," as one member put it. Gordon, explained another, gave the group "about four days" a year and Moorman "313 days of the year." In fact, Stephen Lee may have exaggerated only slightly when he called Moorman "the life of the UCV."

He "organized" it and "kept it alive," Lee added. Moorman certainly succeeded in taking a languishing organization and expanding it throughout the South. He first published an appeal by Gordon in every newspaper in fifteen states and sent hundreds of telegrams and letters to individuals telling them how fast the UCV was growing and encouraging them to join the movement. He asked one distinguished Confederate to let him announce his name as commander for his state in order to promote growth and promised that when five camps had joined the man could resign. Moorman's tactics yielded quick results: By the 1892 reunion 188 camps had joined the UCV. Of course, the rapid growth did not result solely from Moorman's boosterism. Many local camps formed independently and wrote to him to apply for membership. Other societies that had organized in the 1880s decided, with little or no urging from Moorman, to give up their purely local identity to join the larger organization.[5]

Publicity provided by the magazine *Confederate Veteran*, established in 1893 by Sumner Archibald Cunningham, also contributed to the success of the UCV. Owner and editor Cunningham had attended the organizational meeting of the UCV. A contentious fellow, he never got along well with the UCV leadership, perhaps because he remained less reconciled to defeat and more skeptical of "fraternization" with the enemy than they. His early opposition to the New South (in referring to the term he printed the word "N-w" as if an obscenity) probably caused friction too. Cunningham nevertheless remained a loyal supporter of the UCV and, despite occasional sniping, of Gordon. His magazine quickly received endorsements from many local veterans' groups, and in 1894 it became the official organ of the UCV.[6]

The *Confederate Veteran* served as the voice of the second phase of the veterans' movement, as the *Southern Historical Society Papers* had for the first, but the two differed starkly. The *Veteran* sold for the markedly cheaper price of fifty cents (later a dollar) compared with three dollars for the *SHSP*. Rather than the *SHSP*'s long, scholarly discussions of constitutional issues and military tactics, the *Veteran* featured shorter, illustrated pieces of human interest material, often on the experience of the war by troops and leaders. The *Veteran* also devoted considerably more space to the various Confederate organizations, monument unveilings, and other celebratory activities. Some of the differences stemmed from late nineteenth-century changes in the magazine business, but clearly the *Veteran* aimed more at a mass audience than did its predecessor. It certainly met with a far greater popular response. Circulation passed 7,000 by the end of its first year and peaked at more than 20,000 by the end of the 1890s. The magazine went to 4,209 different post offices in 41 states, 2 territories, the District of Columbia, and a few foreign countries. In 1909 one southern scholar judged it the most popular of all the magazines published in the postwar South.[7]

Spurred by the publicity of the *Confederate Veteran* and the organizational skills of Moorman, the UCV spread quickly throughout the South. By 1896 it boasted 850 local camps; by 1904, 1,565. The distribution of UCV camps roughly followed that of the surviving veterans. Virginia and North Carolina had relatively fewer camps than the percentage of the veteran population living in them would have indicated, Texas and Missouri slightly more, South Carolina and Kentucky dramatically more. Within certain states, the geographical location of camps paralleled that of wartime support for the Confederacy. In Texas almost all camps were in the eastern half of the state, which had been the center of Confederate sentiment, and in Tennessee the unionist areas of the east had fewer camps than the west. In North Carolina the eastern and western counties, areas of anti-war unrest during the conflict, had fewer camps than the central portion of the state. Nevertheless, 75 percent of the counties in the 11 former Confederate states had camps. In South Carolina they organized in every county, in Alabama, Florida, Georgia, and Mississippi in more than 85 percent of the counties.[8]

The exact membership of the UCV camps remains elusive because the UCV never released comprehensive membership statistics. Different means of computing the number of members yield totals that range from 35,000 to 160,000. One reliable study of veterans estimated active and inactive UCV members in 1903 at from 80,000 to 85,000, and the same year the *Atlanta Constitution*, without distinguishing between active and inactive members, reported 65,000. Determining what percentage of living veterans joined is even more difficult because accurate survival statistics exist only for 1890. Using a membership total of 80,000 for 1903 and a survival rate extrapolated from the 1890 census figures to estimate the number of living veterans who joined the UCV, one arrives at a figure somewhere between one in three and one in four.[9]

Members apparently came from a broad spectrum of southern society. Reduced dues or, in some camps, no dues at all for the poor enabled all but the extremely disadvantaged to join. Many members were farmers, and letters from rural camps to Moorman indicated that farmers who were far from affluent participated. More reliable membership records of three urban camps—the Association of the Army of Tennessee in New Orleans, the Frank Cheatham Bivouac in Nashville, and the Lee Camp in Richmond—also provide evidence of broad participation. In all three, nearly half the members came from occupations classified as proprietary and low white-collar, while another quarter came from professional and high white-collar classifications. The rest were skilled and unskilled workers. Not only did the first group predominate in absolute terms, but the percentage of men from proprietary and low white-collar occupations was twice that in the general Confederate veteran population. Professional and upper white-collar membership was roughly the same as in the population at large. Skilled workers were slightly underrepresented, and unskilled workers even more so. In other terms, the middle class, made up not only of the proprietary group but of some in the professional and high white-collar category, clearly dominated the organization, as would be expected. But the UCV also attracted a significant number of workers and members of the lower class.[10]

UCV membership was open only to veterans, but individual camps promoted auxiliary organizations that led eventually to the formation of groups of daughters and sons. Lee Camp in Richmond established a semi-autonomous Ladies' Auxiliary in 1888. At the urging of Frank Cheatham Bivouac, women in Nashville in 1890 formed an auxiliary to care for the inmates of the local soldiers' home; two years later it adopted the name Daughters of the Confederacy. Especially in Virginia, other veterans' groups also encouraged the formation of ladies' auxiliaries. In 1894 Mrs. Lucian H. Raines of the Ladies' Auxiliary of the Confederate Veterans' Association of Savannah, Georgia, and Mrs. C.M. Goodlett of the Nashville Daughters began plans for a regional organization of Confederate women. Advised by a member of the UCV, they modeled a constitution after that of the UCV and held an organizational meeting in the Frank Cheatham Camp Hall in Nashville. In 1895 representatives from a large number of women's groups met and ratified the plan for an independent organization of daughters. From that beginning, and with continued assistance from the UCV, the United Daughters of the Confederacy grew rapidly.[11]

The United Sons of Confederate Veterans, which also received aid from the UCV, formed in similar fashion. The New Orleans AAT, perhaps the first camp to form a group of sons, in 1889 sponsored both a sons' and a daughters' auxiliary. The next year Lee Camp organized its sons for the Lee monument unveiling and then decided to make the group a permanent organization. Soon other camps in the South organized male descendants either by enrolling them as affiliates in the camps or by forming independent groups. Moves toward a regional body began almost at once: At the 1890 UCV reunion a group of sons asked permission to establish an organization under the auspices of the UCV. Nothing came of the idea, but six years later an independent United Sons of Confederate Veterans did form. Horrified that people might confuse the abbreviation on their badge, USCV, with United States Colored Volunteers, in 1908 the Sons dropped *United* from their name.[12]

By the mid-nineties, the organizational structure to support the Confederate celebration had formed. The process had begun with the formation of Lee Camp in 1883 and continued with the emergence of state societies in the late eighties. In the early 1890s the UCV succeeded in organizing camps throughout the South. Although led by the middle class, it mobilized significant support among veterans of all classes. It also spurred the organization of male and female descendants. Finally, the official journal of all three groups, the *Confederate Veteran*, went monthly to a large number of subscribers throughout the region. In sum, the UCV and its constituent and allied societies had taken control of the Confederate tradition and in doing so had met with a popular response far greater and far broader than the Virginia coalition had even known.

The Virginians had little influence on this second phase of the veterans' movement, and some of them had strong reservations about its direction. The two major organizers of the Virginians' revitalization movement, Jubal Early and Bradley T. Johnson, were never active in the UCV; in fact, both reportedly opposed bringing their associations into it. Early left no explanation, but Johnson considered the UCV tainted by reconciliationist sentiment. "We don't believe in the 'Blue and Gray' business," he maintained, and "refuse to join the United Confederate Veterans because Gordon and his crowd have too much fraternization for us!" William Payne, a lesser figure in the coalition, expressed similar views of the *Confederate Veteran* when he called it "a gushing,

Gordon-like concern" that did not take his "fancy." The estrangement between the Virginia coalition and the UCV, however, was never total, particularly at the height of the Confederate celebration. Payne served for a time on the board of visitors of Lee Camp's soldiers' home, and Dabney Maury joined Lee Camp in the nineties. Wade Hampton, who had been on the periphery of the Virginia coalition, held high office in the UCV but served more as symbol than leader.[13]

The only two leaders of the Virginia coalition prominent in the UCV were Fitzhugh Lee and J. William Jones, both of whom had joined Lee Camp almost as soon as it formed. Lee, the most thoroughgoing reunionist of the Virginians, actually exercised very limited influence within the councils of the UCV. Jones became its second chaplain in 1896 only after demonstrating he had ceased to be too ardent a Confederate. Many of the veterans had wanted him all along, Moorman informed Jones at the time of his selection, but until recently UCV leaders had feared that his "intense Southern sentiment" would lead him "into extremes" and that he "would not be conservative enough for the constantly changing conditions of affairs. . . ." Only the Virginians who, like Lee and Jones, learned to check their Confederate loyalties fit comfortably into the new movement, and even they did not exert a great influence in it.[14]

Not only did different individuals, for the most part, lead the second phase of the veterans' movement, but different types of men did as well. Whereas the Virginians had come primarily from the Confederate leadership, the organizers and promoters of the UCV did not. None of the organizers—Jastremski, Willet, Ober, Washington, Chalaron, Given, Shipp, and Trezevant—had served as general officers. Of those for whom information remains, three had been lower-ranking officers, three enlisted men. Nor had their social backgrounds and postwar careers brought them to the attention of the South. Shipp, perhaps the most prominent of the early organizers, was considered "one of the pioneer manufactur[er]es of Chattanooga," working first for the Southern Pump and Pipe Company and then the Chattanooga Furniture Company. He also served a term as president of the city's board of trade and held various political offices, including that of sheriff. Jastremski, son of a Polish physician who had emigrated to Louisiana, had first become a druggist after the war. Elected mayor of Baton Rouge in 1876 mainly because of his role in keeping blacks from voting, he served three terms. When he left office he became a newspaperman and then established a printing business, where he used his contacts in the Democratic party to get a state contract. Trezevant, a contractor from Shreveport, served as clerk of the Louisiana House of Representatives. The other organizers had less success and changed jobs even more frequently than Shipp, Jastremski, and Trezevant. Ober's father had run a wholesale grocery in New Orleans before the war, and after the war Ober tried the grain business, sold life insurance, became a public accountant, and ended his career as the director of a Confederate home. Chalaron, who had been in mercantile pursuits before the war, tried planting for ten years after it. He then abandoned that to become an insurance agent and rose to be president of an insurance company. In the late eighties and early nineties he suffered severe financial problems with creditors hounding him and even seizing his furniture, before his position as head of the Confederate museum in

New Orleans became salaried. Washington, listed in the New Orleans city directory as a stevedore, apparently headed a cooperative or firm that hired longshoremen.[15]

The two men most responsible for the growth of the UCV, Moorman and Cunningham, had backgrounds similar to those of the organizers. Moorman had studied law before the war and served in the Confederate army without distinction but with perseverance: He was taken prisoner four times. After the war he married the daughter of the chief justice of Mississippi, dabbled in planting and politics during the late sixties and early seventies, and after that became a small-time promoter. Moorman tried the restaurant, resort, and telephone businesses, sold real estate and marble, and served as an immigration agent for Louisiana. Always active in Democratic politics, he became a federal marshal in the last year of Cleveland's first term, only to have his career cut short by the next election.[16]

Cunningham, less prominent and well-connected, displayed a similar tendency to change jobs. He had been a Tennessee farm boy, and before the war he taught in a military academy. He, too, had an undistinguished career in the Confederate army. After the war, he worked in the mercantile business in Tennessee and later wrote for various newspapers there and in Georgia. In 1883 Cunningham founded a monthly magazine of southern sentiment in New York, but he soon returned to a job on a Nashville paper. He brought to the movement his journalistic skills but not the demeanor of a gentleman of the old school. A North Carolina woman warned a friend that he was "not to be judged by the social standards of a gentleman" and added that one of her acquaintances had found him the "very roughest specimen that had ever sat at his table."[17]

None of the organizers or promoters of the UCV came from the traditional southern elite. Only two or three had been planters, and they had ceased to be that long before the formation of the UCV. A few had achieved some political success, although mostly on the local level. They came from the middle class and had chosen various commercial and business pursuits in the New South—indeed, several were small-time boosters—but most did not do particularly well at them. They were men who apparently had accepted the new order after the war but still struggled to make their way in it. They clearly differed from the more established elite leaders and organizers of the Virginia coalition.

In selecting John B. Gordon commander, the UCV organizers did turn to someone with a distinguished war record and an established place in the southern elite, but their choice still underlined the discontinuity of leadership in the two phases of the veterans' movement. If they had wanted only a military figure they could have chosen an officer of higher rank (Johnston, Beauregard, or Smith), even one who had been prominent in earlier Confederate activity (Early or Hampton). In Gordon they chose someone with an acceptable war record, orthodox opinions on southern questions, and a reputation for supporting the New South movement and sectional reconciliation.

Opinions of Gordon varied. His political enemy Rebecca Latimer Felton considered him a corrupt publicity hound, while a less biased and more calm J.L.M. Curry judged him neither "a statesman, nor a great man" but one with "some elements of popularity which he has used well." In many ways, like the organizers and promoters of the UCV, Gordon was a man struggling for success in a New South. He alternated stints of elective office with projects for private gain, none of which produced sufficient income. Except for politics, he probably succeeded best at being a professional southerner. In his later years Gordon made his living lecturing on the Confederate past.[18]

Gordon had much to recommend him for the post of UCV commander. Although when people in Georgia addressed him as the "hero of Appomattox" a truly unrepentent rebel might question whether that battle had any heroes, Gordon had acceptable credentials as a dashing soldier. Since the war he had repeatedly proven his loyalty to southern norms. Gordon worked with the KKK, helped redeem his state of Georgia from Republican rule, and at a post in Washington defended South Carolina during the crisis of 1876-77. Ever after he upheld southern racial orthodoxy, states' rights, and the Democratic party. Of course, he may have taken bribes from the Huntington railroad interest and may have traded his Senate seat for a plush railroad job, but that did not seem to bother many people. After all, Davis had called him his Aaron.[19]

Gordon's personal presence as well as his background and beliefs made him a logical choice for commander of the UCV. Contemporaries considered him a powerful and moving speaker. His friend Clement Evans claimed Gordon's speeches had "the same spirit of dash and vivacity which were natural traits of his character. By the strong force of his descriptive power and personal magnetism and sympathy he would draw his audiences to the heights upon which he stood, causing them to weep or laugh as he chose." His physical appearance and military bearing as well as his voice contributed to the effect. One southern woman described him as "handsome, compelling, and magnificent on a horse" and commented on the "cross scar on his cheek, one of the Antietam wounds, which by no means detracted from his appearance, making him, in fact, even more attractive." Georgia political opponent Robert Toombs argued that if that scar had been "somewhere else than on his face" Gordon would have been "a failure as a politician." The man who seconded Gordon's nomination for UCV commander alluded to all thirteen scars Gordon carried from the war, and, as one obituary writer put it, "the scar upon his face was itself enough at all times to create the wildest enthusiasm with Confederate soldiers."[20]

The scars of the war had not kept Gordon from working for a New South. Since Appomattox he had devoted limited time to the history of the war and had shown great flexibility in adapting to defeat. He had a reputation as a New South booster and enthusiastic advocate of reconciliation. Although he later had a falling-out with Grady, in 1886 Gordon had run successfully for governor of Georgia as the candidate of the Atlanta journalist and what one historian calls the "Atlanta capitalists." Both before and after the election, he had publicly advocated sectional reconciliation. He had chaired the joint GAR-ex-Confederate committee to raise funds for Lee Camp's Confederate home, and about the time he accepted command of the UCV had discussed with a northern general the formation of a Blue-Gray organization of veterans.[21]

In summary, Gordon had a formidable personal presence, a reputation as a

defender of southern orthodoxy on race and politics, and the status of a
Confederate leader. The last attribute made him more the equal of the
Virginians than the organizers who selected him or the promoters who backed
him. In fact, Gordon had maintained friendly relations with the Virginians and
occasionally attended their meetings. As a New South booster and ardent
advocate of sectional reconciliation, however, he differed from them in
fundamental ways. In selecting Gordon, organizers chose a man whose attitudes
differed dramatically from those of the Virginians, and the veterans soon ratified
the choice. Although occasionally a few attacked his efforts at reunion, Gordon's
outlook seemed to bother few of them. He became phenomenally popular with
the rank and file, served as the primary ceremonial figure in the Confederate
celebration, and remained commander of the UCV until his death in 1904.[22]

With Gordon's aid, the middle-class leaders of the second phase of the veterans'
movement succeeded in mobilizing public support as the aristocratic Virginians
never had. The UCV's approach to the war, with its emphasis on reconciliation
and the experience of battle, helped account for the greater response. So too did
the absence of an elitist bias. But the UCV leaders only helped guide an already
growing popular interest in the Confederacy. Such sentiment would logically
have been stronger shortly after the war, when memories were fresh and more
people who had experienced the conflict survived, rather than twenty or thirty
years later. Yet only after the mid-eighties did southerners really begin to
celebrate the Confederacy.

The timing might be explained by the fact that the aging veterans, anticipating
death and fearing their deeds would be forgotten, organized to establish their
contribution before they passed from the scene. In the eighties and nineties
veterans did speak frequently of the need to preserve Confederate history for
succeeding generations, but they had in the sixties and early seventies, too. As
the celebration began, many of them remained active in society and had not
become so old as to fear imminent death and a loss of the last chance to establish
their reputation. Members of the Lee Camp, the group that pioneered the new
developments, were fairly young when they first organized. Of the men who
joined in 1883-84, almost 70 percent were under 50, and more than 50 percent
between the ages of 35 and 44. Even in 1890, more than 60 percent of all
Confederate veterans were still under 55.[23]

Moreover, if apprehension regarding death had been central to the emergence
of the UCV, memorial work would logically have assumed a greater importance
in its early activities than it did. The *Confederate Veteran* printed obituaries from
the first, but did not incorporate them into a monthly department entitled "The
Last Roll" until 1897. A few UCV camps formulated burial rituals in their early
years, but not until well into the nineties did the UCV itself devote much
attention to honoring comrades when they died. Only in 1899 did the adjutant
general distribute a burial ritual and a memorial service become part of the
annual reunion. Even then, the service did not become a prominent feature. In
1905 the UCV commander suggested that it be dropped from the program
because it took up "3 hours of precious time" and only a few people attended.

The lack of participation suggested that death was not much on the minds of the aging veterans. Surely, the desire to establish their place in history contributed to the veterans' participation, but an increasing awareness of death hardly seems central to the celebration or crucial to its timing.[24]

The timing and to a lesser extent the intensity of the celebration owed more to a social tensions of the 1880s and 1890s. Nothing provides stronger evidence of this than the fact that the Confederate celebration was far from unique in its fascination with the past. Civil war monuments were erected in the North as well as in the South. In addition, the Grand Army of the Republic, the northern equivalent of the UCV, revived in the 1880s after a decline in the 1870s, and its numerical strength peaked at about the time the UCV formed. Still concerned with securing pensions and electing Republicans, the new GAR expanded its historical and celebratory activities. In the early 1880s it encouraged the formation of a Woman's Relief Corps and later a sons-of-veterans' group. In short, the GAR embarked on activities very similar to those of the UCV in the South, only it did so a bit earlier and mobilized possibly even more support among the veterans than did the UCV. Compared to one of every three or four Confederates who joined the southern group, as many as one of every two Union soldiers still alive joined the northern one.[25]

Nor was the Civil War the only historical event to inspire similar organizations. A host of veterans' and descendants' associations formed during the period: the Mexican War Veterans, the Sons of the American Revolution, the Daughters of the American Revolution, the Colonial Dames, the Society of Colonial Wars, and the Mayflower Descendants. Many of these groups had southern as well as northern support, and southerners founded other historical societies unrelated to the war, such as North Carolina's Virginia Dare Association and the Society for the Preservation of Virginia Antiquities. A similar intensified interest in matters past—what a recent book has termed the "invention of tradition"—developed in several European countries. Between 1870 and 1914, a period of increasingly rapid social change and growing social unrest, state and private groups in Great Britain, France, and Germany celebrated various historical figures, events, or eras. Like southerners, Europeans established new public ceremonies and erected numerous historical monuments.[26]

The UCV and the celebration it sponsored must be seen as a part of this wider interest in the past that developed in the late nineteenth century. In celebrating the Confederacy, southerners found relief from the tensions of a changing society, just as others did in commemorating the American Revolution or the fall of the Bastile or King Wilhelm. Industrial growth, the spread of a town culture, the encroachment of the market economy, and national integration threatened southerners' sense of community and continuity. These changes had been occurring gradually over the years and would continue, but the public debate over a New South helped make southerners particularly conscious of them in the late eighties and early nineties. The acquisitive values associated with the New South and demanded by an increasingly commercial society troubled some in the middle class, the class that supplied the organizers and much of the membership of the UCV. At the same time, labor unrest and Populist agitation raised the specter of disorder if not revolution and frightened middle-class as well as other southerners. Economic troubles further heightened the apprehensions of all. The UCV organized at about the same time the southern economy slid into a severe recession, and its major expansion came during the depths of the depression of 1893. Economic suffering made the dangers of the emerging society very real, as the threat of unemployment or mortgage foreclosure rendered the specter of failure in the new order more vivid than ever before.[27]

Although the fears generated by the era's social changes and disorder explained the timing of and contributed to the enthusiasm for the Confederate celebration, the continuing legacy of defeat also pushed veterans to embrace it and perhaps explains the peculiar intensity of the southern celebration of the war. Southerners no longer wanted to refight sectional issues; nor did they seek to escape from defeat, as the Virginians had. Many, however, did still worry that the loss of the war had somehow dishonored them. The war, said one, had "defaced" their lives. Another, himself a prominent symbol of reconciliation living and active in New York City, commented, "These pangs, these stings have filled the cup of all Southern men who adventured in this City after the Civil War." Even among those who have succeeded, he continued, "the scars have never grown over ever-bleeding wounds." For most the wounds healed enough to become scars, although they remained tender and sensitive. The movement of the eighties and nineties eased the pain by celebrating the scars as signs of rightful devotion to principle and order, as signs of brotherhood and unity. Gordon, the ceremonial leader, bore thirteen scars, including the most visible one on his cheek, which the veterans cheered.[28]

By 1890 the UCV Gordon led had taken control of the Confederate tradition from the Virginians. Formed and promoted by middle-class boosters with no standing as wartime leaders, the new movement succeeded in mobilizing a broad spectrum of the veteran population, spurred the formation of two societies of descendants, and directed a celebration of the Confederacy. It offered a salve for the scars of defeat and—what was more important for the future of the South— relief from the social tensions of a changing society. Both the reformulation of Confederate history and the rituals of the celebration testify to that dual function.

CHAPTER NINE

The Confederate Celebration:
Its Interpretation of the War

Not all southern whites joined in the celebration of the Confederacy. J.T. James of Louisiana, who described himself as "An Ex-Officer of Lee's Army, Cleansed and purged of Southernism in 1868 by the blood of Christ—and a minister of the Methodist Episcopal Church," circulated a tract entitled "Counsel for Old Confederates: The Confederate Reunions: A Call to Repentance." In it, James argued that the veteran should not be encouraged to celebrate Confederate history but rather "should be carefully instructed concerning the evil of the war he helped to wage—a war to destroy the American Union, and bind the most abject slavery on the country in this Christian era, and make the South a living hell for millions of poor souls and bodies: a war in which he helped the devil in his great effort to destroy the Church of Christ in the South and make a Sodom and Gomorrah."[1]

Rebecca Latimer Felton, a better-known southerner, agreed with some of James's points. She argued that secession had been wrong, that the war had been fought only over slavery, and that the leaders had all along misled their people into thinking otherwise in order to secure political office. In the same book in which Felton dissented from the common view, however, she commended the courage of the soldiers and women who supported the cause and urged that their story be told repeatedly. In criticizing the cause but applauding its followers, in condemning the celebration but echoing its praise, Felton testified to the power and utility of the Confederate tradition. Even one who sought to escape its hold, who thought evil men manipulated it, could never completely ignore or repudiate what southerners considered to be the heroism of the war.[2]

Since the war held such power over the minds of white southerners, its interpretation assumed added importance. Establishing an understanding of history acceptable to most southerners, despite the criticism of southern heretics like James and Felton and the scorn of irreverent Yankees, became an important part of the Confederate celebration. The UCV and the veterans accepted primary responsibility for preserving this history—in other words, primary responsibility for speaking for the ghosts of the Confederacy. They concurred with the Virginians on the legality of secession, on the overwhelming-numbers explanation, and on the heroic stature of Jackson and Lee. They devoted more attention than their predecessor, however, to Lee's postwar role, to Davis, and to the Confederate private and woman. The new emphasis, particularly the celebration of the private soldier, reflected the origin of the celebration in the social tensions of the eighties and nineties. Rather than a vision of Confederate revitalization, it offered support for the newly emerging order. [3]

In 1892 the UCV established a historical committee to promote a "proper" appreciation of the war. Its own annual report occasionally included a discussion of historical issues, but generally it passed judgment on the work of others. The committee compiled a list of recommended histories, noted the publication of new books, and condemned a few it considered unfair to the South. After their formation, the UDC and, less actively, the SCV joined the battle for what the UCV called "true" history. And local Confederate organizations, especially Grand Camp of Confederate Veterans of Virginia, did so as well. These groups devoted much of their effort to seeing that school children were taught only a southern understanding of the war. On a few occasions they supported student defiance in the cause of sectional loyalty. For instance, they lionized Laura Gault, a Kentucky girl who refused her teacher's order to sing "Marching Through Georgia" and supported other students who declined to read texts that were offensive to them. In general, though, the Confederate organizations tried to avoid such situations by making certain that schools assigned only those books that incorporated a southern account of the war. Those who operated the statewide adoption systems in most southern states usually heeded the opinions of Confederate organizations, and the crusade for orthodox history texts generally succeeded. [4]

The Confederate organizations also sponsored exhibits and museums, partly to preserve history for those who did not read books. At the Atlanta Cotton States and International Exposition of 1895 and the Tennessee Centennial Exhibition of 1897, UDC women and others displayed Confederate memorabilia. By that time permanent collections of wartime relics had been established in New Orleans and Richmond. In 1889 New Orleans veterans' groups organized the Louisiana Historical Association to oversee a Confederate Memorial Hall there. By the turn of the century, the hall drew from five to twenty thousand visitors a year. Plans for a museum in Richmond began in 1890 when the Hollywood Memorial Association formed a Confederate Memorial Literary Society to preserve Davis's wartime home as a repository for Confederate memorabilia. Six years later the association opened in the former White House of the Confederacy a museum that attracted nearly ten thousand visitors a year. Some people feared that local efforts might fail in the future and suggested that the South needed a central museum to commemorate the heroism of the Confederacy. In 1894 Charles Broadway Rouss, a former Confederate private who after the war had made not one but two fortunes as a New York City businessman, offered a challenge grant of $100,000 to create such a "Battle Abbey." The UCV accepted his offer and began to raise money for the project.[5]

Museums and exhibits served more to keep alive a respect for Confederate history than to preserve a specific interpretation. The UCV historical committee reports, the resolutions of the annual meetings of the UCV, UDC, and SCV, the speeches of their leaders, and articles in the *Confederate Veteran* and other publications did present a general outline of Confederate history. It resembled that developed by the Virginians two decades before, as the placement of the volumes of the *SHSP* at the top of the list of books recommended by the UCV testified. Nevertheless, the new movement's interpretation of the war differed in emphasis from that of the Virginians and introduced new themes, subtle alterations that reflected the Confederate tradition's utility in easing the tensions of change and in supporting the emerging social order.[6]

The leaders of the Confederate celebration grounded their interpretation of the war in the same defensive conviction of southern rectitude that their predecessors had. "It is not to be expected that those who fought on the Southern side will admit that they were wrong simply because they were beaten, or that the highest and noblest purposes of their lives are worthy of the execration of mankind," wrote Stephen D. Lee in the UCV historical report of 1897. "The nation cannot afford to have the people of the South lose their self-respect, or the future citizens of that large and most promising section of the country brought up without that pride in their ancestors which leads to noble and patriotic action." To maintain their self-respect, the veterans had to believe, with Bennett Young, that the "sword in and of itself never made any cause right, and the outcome of battles does not affirm the truth of political or even religious questions." They rejected, as many southerners had after the war, the notion that defeat constituted the judgment of God. Instead, they proclaimed defeat part of the mysterious working of providence that would bring about an ultimate, though delayed, triumph—although they rarely agreed on or even specified what form it would take.[7]

The spokesmen of the celebration did agree, as they almost had to do in order to believe in the justness of their cause, on the legality of secession and on the centrality of constitutional issues in bringing on the war. Clement A. Evans, a Georgia veteran who eventually commanded the UCV, maintained that "If we cannot justify the South in the act of Secession, we will go down to History solely as a brave, impulsive but rash people, who attempted in an illegal manner to overthrow the Union of our Country." But "we had a legal and moral justification," Evans quickly added, and need not "fear" the verdict of history. He and the other veterans left little to chance, though, and sought to ensure that the legitimacy of secession would be upheld. The UCV placed the constitutional defenses by Davis, Stephens, Bledsoe, and Dabney among the first ten books on its recommended list. In countless addresses and articles, veterans maintained adamantly that southerners had acted legally and honorably in seceding from the Union.[8]

The crusade to establish the legitimacy of secession included a new emphasis on the proper name for southerners and for the war itself. During the war and for a time after it, southerners had usually accepted the label "rebels" for themselves and "rebellion" or "revolution" for what they had done. By the turn of the century, only a few southerners still thought the South had fought a revolution or consented to be called rebels, although more accepted the label if it was pointed out that Washington and other fighters against tyranny were rebels too. The majority, however, considered the epithet insulting. "If secession was right, we were not rebels," wrote one veteran, "if it was wrong, then we were."[9]

Southerners who resented the implications of the term "rebel" objected vehemently to its use, particularly by Yankees. One wrote a fiery letter protesting the use of the term by a national newspaper. "To have you understand as well as I can how we resent the term 'rebels,' I will say that I have long tried to nurture a feeling of brotherhood for those at whom I used to shoot, and who shot at me, and I succeed quite well enough until I pick up the Tribune, and then the 'rebels,' 'rebels,' 'rebels,' gets into my blood and I begin to hate like I used to." More calmly, both the UCV and the UDC expressed reservations about the term, and the Sons found it particularly appalling. "Was your father a Rebel and a Traitor?" read one recruiting leaflet, with the words "Rebel" and "Traitor" in red. "Did he fight in the service of the Confederacy for the purpose of destroying the Union, or was he a Patriot, fighting for the liberties granted him under the Constitution, in defense of his native land, and for a cause he knew to be right?" Anyone willing to have his father "branded a Rebel and Traitor," the circular implied, need not apply.[10]

Agitation also developed over the proper name for the war itself, a point on which there had been little consistency since Appomattox. A few disheartened southerners, as folklore suggests, actually referred to it as "the late unpleasantness." When veterans began to celebrate their role and accomplishments in the war, that appellation seemed less appropriate. In 1894 the *Confederate Veteran* argued that the "late unpleasantness," "the late War," "the civil war," and "the war between the states" should all be abandoned since they lacked dignity. It considered "The Confederate War" more majestic and certainly less disloyal than the offensive "War of the Rebellion" that the federal government had adopted as the conflict's official name. In 1899 and 1900 both the UCV and UDC passed resolutions urging the substitution of "The War Between the States" for "War of the Rebellion." The former term acknowledged the legitimacy of secession, but the latter conceded the North's view, argued the woman who made the motion at the UDC convention. The federal government continued to use "The War of the Rebellion," and southerners themselves continued to apply a variety of names to the conflict. "The War Between the States" gradually became the most common, and the acceptance of the rationale behind that name—that the South had fought for constitutional rights—became even more so.[11]

Like the Virginians, participants in the Confederate celebration not only defended secession, they denied that slavery had been the cause of the war. The Confederates, they explained, fought a legitimate war for constitutional rights, not a war to preserve slavery. A few southerners dissented: In addresses at UCV reunions John W. Daniel and John H. Reagan each labeled slavery the prime cause of the conflict. Others hedged a bit by granting that the issue of slavery might have been the occasion for the war but was not its cause. The vast majority of southerners, however, vehemently denied that Confederate soldiers had fought to defend slavery. To admit that "however brave" the soldiers were, they were "actuated by no higher motive than the desire to retain the money value of slave property," wrote Hunter McGuire in a historical report for Grand Camp of Confederate Veterans of Virginia, would "hold us degraded rather than worthy of honor," and would mean "that our children, instead of reverencing their fathers will be secretly, if not openly, ashamed."[12]

While most participants in the Confederate celebration agreed with the Virginians that slavery had not been the cause of the war, they viewed its abolition with a great deal more equanimity than had Early and company. Even though "in the immediate quarrel the South was legally and Constitutionally right," wrote Episcopal theologian William Porcher DuBose in 1898, "No one questions now that Slavery had to be abolished. . . ." Echoing most ceremonial orators, Charles E. Hooker, in an address to the UCV that same year, agreed that no one in the South expressed any regret that slavery "has been forever abolished." A few did lament that abolition came without compensation or resulted in the horrors of Reconstruction. An occasional speaker even suggested that in time the South itself would have peacefully abandoned the institution. In admitting that abolition had been for the best, something the Virginians would never have considered doing, the celebrators of the Confederacy displayed a greater acceptance of the social changes that followed the conflict.[13]

Similarly, the new movement downplayed the Virginians' contention that the South had succumbed only to overwhelming numbers. At the 1904 UCV reunion the governor of Tennessee welcomed delegates as the "greatest army of individual fighters that ever went into battle. . . . If you had had equal resources with our brothers across the line to-day the stars and bars would float as the National emblem." The governor's remarks elicited a "Tremendous outburst of cheering and applause and cries of 'Go on,' 'Tell it again.'" On another occasion a kindly and sympathetic northern woman informed one veteran that the war had been settled in the province of God. "You must pardon me, ma'am, but I don't think God had much to do with this matter," the old man retorted. "Your people whipped us because you had five times as many men as we had, and all the money and rations you wanted, and I don't think I ever heard that God gave one half-starved man the strength to whip five fully-fed men." The two incidents testify to the continued hold of the idea that Confederate defeat had resulted from the disparity in numbers and resources. Fewer sustained defenses of that explanation, however, appeared than in earlier years. Perhaps fewer people wrote them because the argument was so generally accepted, but the leaders of the new veterans' movement also did not anxiously repeat the contention, as the Virginians had, in the hope that things might turn out differently. Rather, the overwhelming-numbers argument simply supported the claim for the heroism and ability of the armies and helped justify the celebration of the Confederate effort.[14]

The Longstreet-lost-it-at-Gettysburg excuse also proved less compelling than it once had. Accounts of Gettysburg now celebrated the glorious failure of Pickett's charge as often as they damned the opportunity lost because of Longstreet's alleged tardiness. Some critics still blamed the Georgian for the loss of the field, particularly after a battle of memoirs involving Longstreet, Gordon, and Mrs. Longstreet reopened old wounds. Yet even among Longstreet's detractors much of the fire had gone out of the accusation, and much of the apocalyptic sense of its importance had dissipated.[15]

The UCV leadership did dislike Longstreet and tried, as he suspected, to minimize his role in the celebration, but the veterans themselves greeted him warmly at Confederate gatherings. Longstreet received a tremendous ovation when he arrived to embrace Jefferson Davis during the Hill unveiling in 1886. At the ceremonies at the Lee monument in Richmond four years later he commanded, according to one observer, "a greater ovation from the old Soldiers than any other veteran, . . . showing that the old-time prejudice against General Longstreet's being a Republican had almost wholly disappeared. . . ." The "boys" welcomed him as warmly when he attended UCV reunions in 1892, 1896, and 1898. That the veterans' groups in New Orleans most likely to have nurtured resentment over his role in Reconstruction became his most ardent defenders suggested that his past political sins no longer seemed so damning. When he died in 1904, on the other hand, some Confederate groups did not express sympathy, and no UCV camp or UDC chapter ever adopted his name as its own. No statue to him was erected, even though the governor of Georgia and others proposed one when he died. Longstreet may not have been forgiven, particularly by the leaders, for his alleged failure at Gettysburg or his postwar role. But in a celebration of the bond among Confederate soldiers, Longstreet could be welcomed.[16]

Except for its ambivalence regarding Longstreet, the Confederate celebration honored the same leaders the Virginians had, but for slightly different purposes. The heroes no longer served as symbols with which to revitalize Confederate culture; rather, they became important role models for society and especially the young. So that the children of his town "should have good exemplars of character and conduct before them," William A. Courtenay of Newry, South Carolina, placed in the mill village schoolhouse a large panel that displayed "fine likenesses of Washington in the center, Lee on the right, and Hampton on the left." In other areas placing portraits of Confederate leaders in schools became a major UDC project. Not everyone agreed on which leaders merited enshrinement, and a sort of local option system of heroes existed. For example, Wade Hampton, as the panels in Newry demonstrated, became the most celebrated hero in South Carolina, rivaling Lee and other mortals for the people's affection and respect. Outside the Palmetto state, though, he never attained quite so much acclaim. In the South as a whole, only Robert E. Lee, T. J. Jackson, and Jefferson Davis commanded extensive and ecstatic adoration.[17]

Lee remained the South's premier hero, the man most universally respected and consistently offered as a role model. His picture adorned countless homes, schools, and businesses, and many people named their children after him. Beginning in the 1870s, but in larger numbers after the Lee monument unveiling in 1890, southern towns celebrated his birthday every 19 January. Four states eventually declared that date a legal holiday. In honoring Lee, the leaders of the Confederate celebration returned to themes developed by the Virginians. They proclaimed Lee a great commander, indeed a military genius, and praised his flawless character, as revealed in his loyalty, duty, honor, courage, modesty, and religious faith. In fact, people summoned up his memory for all sorts of causes—to urge greater attention to "money matters" or to condemn too great a reliance on the "Silliness and Shame of Swearing." He thereby resembled Washington, with whom his name was increasingly linked. In the first decade of the twentieth century, Lee even became something of a national hero, a development that would probably have engendered conflicting emotions in Early.[18]

The increasing northern regard for Lee owed much to the acclaim given by the leaders of the celebration to his postwar role—a decided addition to the portrait offered by the Virginians. The new spokesmen praised Lee's contribution to rebuilding the South through education and to strengthening the nation through support for sectional reconciliation. His postwar career also allowed them to make Lee slightly more of a model for everyman than his aristocratic background would otherwise have allowed. "Poverty had come; the utter wreck and ruin of all he held dear was around him, and again he refused to leave his people and his native state, preferring poverty with them to wealth and honor amongst others," observed an orator in an 1891 speech commemorating Lee's birth. "With quiet dignity he chose a life of honest toil, refusing wealth and ease, and once again set an example to his people worthy to be followed. Here then let us emulate him again."[19]

Many of the celebration's leaders linked Lee with his fellow Virginian, Jackson. A few labeled Lee the cavalier, Jackson the roundhead. Even those who did not see Jackson as a warring Puritan still celebrated his religious convictions along with his martial skills. Although below Lee in the southern pantheon, he was more approachable. Raised in a prominent family, Lee had obviously been born to greatness and was well on his way to a successful military career before the war. Jackson, on the other hand, had been a relatively unknown professor at a Virginia military college before the war. Starting without any advantage, he rose in two years during the war to highest military command, an advance that, in the mind of at least one southerner, made Jackson more remarkable than, though not the equal of, Lee. Many accounts of Jackson's life stressed his rapid rise from obscurity through hard work and self-discipline. A sort of Horatio Alger in gray, Jackson served as a more attainable example than Lee. A leaf of a "Stonewall Jackson Calendar, 1912," issued by a West Virginia UDC chapter, succinctly expressed the moral of Jackson's life in a quote taken from his own copybook and placed under his picture: "You can be whatever you resolve to be."[20]

The third of the heroes, Jefferson Davis, occupied a central place in the Confederate celebration. A move to erect a memorial to him began right after his funeral in 1889 and gained UCV support. The UCV and other Confederate groups urged all states to observe his birthday as Confederate Memorial Day, and a few cities and the state of Louisiana did so. Five other states made it a legal holiday, so in all two more states memorialized his birthday than did Lee's. Unlike Lee, Jackson, and most other Confederate heroes, Davis did not serve so clearly as a role model. Speakers praised his character and accomplishments, but treated him more as a representative than as an exceptional man. They emphasized that in his postwar imprisonment Davis had suffered for all. "Each man felt that Davis had suffered vicariously for him," wrote one Virginian. "If Davis was a traitor, so was he. If Davis should suffer the penalties of the law, so should he." Southerners did not believe Davis or themselves traitors, so they made him a hero of Anglo-Saxon constitutionalism, as John Daniel put it. Davis became, in short, a symbol of the South's righteous cause. Perhaps not by accident, the first design for the Davis memorial featured a classical temple, not a likeness of the man himself.[21]

Davis joined Lee and Jackson as the major heroes of the Confederate celebration. Likenesses of the three would eventually stand in a row along Monument Avenue in Richmond and ride together on the face of Stone Mountain in Georgia. Each served a slightly different function. Lee epitomized the aristocratic style and faultless character to which southerners aspired; Jackson stood for the opportunity everyone had to make something of his life; Davis symbolized the essential nobility of the defeated cause as well as the suffering it had brought in its wake.

In an 1892 speech one southerner admitted that southerners usually proclaimed the three as heroes of the war, but he contended, "The purest spirit, the deepest love, the greatest hero, the noblest manhood, was in the infantry private of the South." Few people in the South would have replaced Lee with the private soldier, but many agreed with the orator's description. Where the Virginians, partly because of their elitist attitudes and emphasis on political issues, had usually praised the private only in passing, the Confederate celebration made him a central figure in their account of Confederate history.[22]

Only a few orators of the Confederate celebration portrayed the private soldier as a chivalrous knight. Most simply lauded the private soldiers' humble origins, faithful and glorious service, and unmatched valor, dash, and tenacity in fighting. The soldiers "served, they suffered, they endured, they fought, they died for their childhood homes, their firesides, the honor of their ancestors, their loved ones, their own native lands," declared North Carolina industrialist and UCV leader Julian Shakespeare Carr. The emphasis on self-sacrifice, endurance, and martial glory is unsurprising; one would not expect the soldiers to be called cowardly clods. More interesting, if more peripheral, were three other qualities for which Confederate soldiers were praised: their submission to discipline, their respect for private property, and their contribution to rebuilding the South.[23]

In the first years after the war some southerners had commented on the lack of discipline in rebel ranks, but the celebration offered a different view. Industrialist Carr, perhaps, went farthest in praising the discipline of the Confederates: "The glory of the private Soldier of the South was that, an intelligent unit, he permitted himself, for duty and for love, to be made into the cog of a wheel." Other leaders credited the private with a bit more individualism and espoused a less mechanistic view of the source of authority. Discipline and order, argued a Raleigh Memorial Day orator in 1897, rested more in "the personal influence and example of the officer and non-commissioned officer, to the reciprocal esteem of private soldiers and their immediate superior in rank for each other" than in the formal structure of military government.[24]

One particular aspect of Confederate discipline, respect for private property, came in for special praise. Old Confederates still recalled with amusement the theft of a chicken or the requisition of milk from an available cow, of course, but orators argued that the private soldier generally displayed admirable respect for civilian property. "To their everlasting honor stands the fact that in their march through the enemy's country they left behind them no ruined homes, no private houses burned, no families cruelly robbed," one orator boldly asserted. He did admit to one exception, which he justified by the need to retaliate; Early's burning of Chambersburg left him and other Confederates a bit embarrassed. Comparison of southern and northern behavior, however, offered a handy way to minimize such incidents. Southerners almost delighted in recounting the tales of violence, destruction, and thievery that they claimed the armies of Sherman, Sheridan, and other northern generals directed against civilians. They especially enjoyed contrasting these tales with stories of the well-behaved campaigns of the Army of Northern Virginia and other Confederate forces. At least one leaflet juxtaposed an order by Lee barring destruction of civilian property with quotes by Sherman sanctioning it.[25]

John S. Mosby, who scorned much of the Confederate celebration, ridiculed a similar pamphlet. Lee issued the order not out of tenderness toward the enemy, Mosby claimed, but to ensure the maintenance of discipline. "His commissaries and quartermasters [still] took everything his soldiers needed." The emphasis on the destruction of property puzzled Mosby. The former Confederate guerilla leader could not understand "why so much more complaint is made of the wheat stacks Sheridan burned than of the young men in the South that he killed." Mosby underscored two important points. First, the Confederates had not behaved much differently from the Yankees they condemned. Second, destroying houses and fields seemed to be more terrible to southerners than the killing of soldiers. Denouncing the Yankees' barbarous ways of waging war had long been a staple of southern sectional rhetoric, but in the eighties and nineties it served the added purpose of reinforcing an image of a southern soldier particularly respectful of private property. To that extent, the emphasis reflected the anxieties of the end of the century.[26]

As the leaders of the celebration disassociated the Confederate soldier from the destruction caused by the war, they associated him with the economic and social revival of the South after the war. In an address opening the 1895 UCV reunion, Gordon termed the soldiers' rebuilding effort "a fitting climax to their splendid record in war." Other orators, like one at a Georgia monument unveiling, developed the theme with greater flourish. "I look around and see with pride the smoke stacks of factories, dotting the towns and villages of the South, and I hear with delight the hum of machinery as it turns the snowwhite cotton into completed cloth, and changes the metals of the hills into the steel and iron of industrial enterprise, and I am stirred to enthusiasms at the progress of our people." Rejoicing that southerners had returned to an active national role in "the professions and the trades," he declared that the "keenest pleasure of it all comes from the reflection that these things testify [to the] courage of the race, whose unrivaled heroism makes it [possible] to leave the battlefield, the hopeless victim of power and oppression, and rebuild in a few short years the shattered fortunes of a nation." A report by the Historical Committee of Grand Camp of Virginia stated the matter more simply when it reported that the Confederate soldier "has built the New South." He "laments the Old South as a parent that has passed away. He turns to the New South as to his child, and with affectionate solicitude he devotes his life to rear and protect it."[27]

Praise for discipline and respect for private property within the Confederate ranks, commendation of the veterans' role in rebuilding the South, and acclaim for the soldiers' sacrifice of self for the good of society served indirectly to protect the New South. All contributed to an image of the Confederate soldier as a solid, law-abiding, loyal common man—a most desirable type in the tumultuous late nineteenth century. Of course, the image of the Confederate private did more than just serve as a role model. It also emphasized the soldiers' skill and courage in battle, thereby helping to reassure the veterans at the same time it promoted desirable behavior among the general population.

While undoubtedly part of the general homage accorded women during the Victorian age, the glorification of southern womanhood within the celebration served a function similar to that of the glorification of the common soldier. "The woman of the South and the soldier of the Confederacy seemed to have been made for each other," declared one southern orator. "She had the utmost confidence in his manhood and valor, and the soldier loved her with the devotion that one pays to the soul's ideal of purity and womanliness." And well he should, for in the view of the Confederate celebration she endured great hardship, ministered to the needs of the soldiers, and remained loyal to the cause. When the battles ended, her loyalty as well as her willingness to sacrifice persisted. Another orator described the southern woman after Appomattox as "clinging closer and more tenderly to father and husband when the storms beat upon him, comforting as only such Christian women can comfort; smiling only as such heroines can smile; with 'toil-beat nerves, and care-worn eyes,' helping only as such women can help. In the schoolroom and behind the counter, over the sewing machine and the cooking stove, in the garden and field, everywhere showing the gems of Southern character washed from its depths by the ocean of Southern woe." The Confederate woman pictured in these accounts reassured the soldiers of female loyalty and offered a model for woman as the helpmate and servant of southern man. It glorified the new labors that followed emancipation and reinforced traditional conceptions of female sex roles that the war challenged. The Confederate woman of the celebration, a role model for southern females as the private was for males, trusted men to protect her and practiced purity, piety, and submissiveness.[28]

The Virginians would generally have agreed on the praise accorded the Confederate woman and private, although they never gave either such prominence in their accounts of the war. The Confederate celebration followed the interpretation of the Virginians much more closely on the basic points of Confederate history. The new leaders agreed with Early and company that the southern cause has been just and legal. Confederate armies had fought not for slavery but for constitutional rights, the principle of secession, and the preservation of their homeland. They had lost at the hands of overwhelming numbers not because of their own shortcomings, and, if pressed, most spokesmen of the celebration would have added that Longstreet had not helped any. They almost all enthusiastically embraced Lee, Jackson, and Davis as Confederate heroes.

The heroes' function in the Confederate celebration, however, hinted at a basic difference between the two phases of the veterans' movement. The second treated them more as models for present behavior than as symbols of cultural independence or revival. Moreover, discussions of heroes, the overwhelming-numbers argument, and the Longstreet-lost-it-at-Gettysburg excuse no longer seemed attempts to make defeat go away. The leaders of the celebration did not despair at the destruction of civilization in their society but commended Lee and the private soldier for rebuilding it. In short, the Confederate celebration accepted the basic historical interpretation of the Virginians, but without the goals or passion of the ghost dance. History functioned more as a support for the status quo than for revitalization.

In a letter written in 1895, George Moorman, approvingly quoting an address by John B. Gordon, clearly enunciated this view of the Confederate past:

> To cherish such memories and recall such a past whether crowned with success or consecrated in defeat, is to idealize principle and strengthen character, intensify love of country and convert defeat and disaster into pillars of support for future manhood and noble womanhood. Whether the Southern people under their changed conditions may ever hope to witness another civilization which shall equal that which began with their Washington and ended with their Lee, it is certainly true that devotion to their glorious past is not only the surest guarantee of future progress and holiest bond of unity, but also is the strongest claim they can present to the conscience and respect of the other sections of the Union.

Gordon thus paid his respects to a lost civilization but considered unimportant whether it could be matched, much less recreated. Rather, the ghosts of the Confederacy should be employed, Gordon added, as "living inspirations for future service to the living republic."[29]

Moorman's and Gordon's view of the past, like that of the veterans' movement they led, had its roots in the acceptance of defeat and reunion in the eighties. Defeat no longer seemed like death, but rather had become something to be transformed "into pillars of support for future manhood and noble womanhood." The participants in the celebration, who so dreaded the appellation "rebel," were more concerned in the eighties and nineties about threats to law and order than convinced of the need to maintain Confederate values. Portraying the war as a defense of constitutional rights and the soldiers as disciplined and respectful of private property helped bolster social stability. At the same time, southerners still sought the "respect of the other sections of the Union," still needed to defend their actions and accomplishments. The revised version of the Confederate tradition with its celebration of just conduct, martial ability, and glorious heroes met that need as well.

CHAPTER TEN

The Confederate Celebration: Its Ritual Activities

Even more than the revised historical interpretation, the public ceremonies of the Confederate celebration revealed the new power and purpose of the Confederate tradition. As the Virginians had never succeeded in doing, the second phase of the postwar Confederate movement mobilized most white southerners. Although few read history books, many participated in a variety of ritualistic activities: Memorial Day ceremonies, monument unveilings, and, perhaps most important, veterans' reunions. Like the historical interpretation of the war, the activities offered southerners relief from the social tensions of the period and from the pains of defeat. Participating in them, they enjoyed a renewed sense of confidence and experienced a deeper sense of social unity.

Southern towns had continued to celebrate Confederate Memorial Day since the initiation of the custom in the 1860s. In a few, interest in the memorial movement apparently declined in the late seventies and early eighties only to be revived in the late eighties and early nineties. Memorial Day became an integral part of the Confederate celebration. Surviving LMAs, often with the cooperation of local UDC chapters, continued to sponsor the service, and in communities without an LMA or where the LMA had become a UDC chapter, the Daughters of the Confederacy alone accepted responsibility. In either case, local UCV camps cooperated in the celebration of Confederate Memorial Day. Although in 1887 Lee Camp of Richmond campaigned for a uniform day of observance, regional variations in the ceremony and time of celebration persisted.[1]

Attitudes toward Memorial Day did seem to change, however. An 1889 poem, "Lines on Memorial Day," by Charles E. Jones, son of C.C. Jones, Jr., of Augusta, included verses that would not have been written two decades earlier:

Comrades: 'tis coming;
Memorial Day;
And soon we'll be humming
The Patriot's Lay.

Soon we'll be voicing
Our feelings of Pride,
In endless rejoicing,
For those who have died.

Soon we'll be wreathing
Their dear Graves with flowers;
And soon, too, unsheathing
That Brave past of ours.
. . . . . .

Yes, soon with the tolling
Of Funeral Knells,
Will mingle the rolling
Of Famed 'Rebel Yells.'

Be ready to meet it—
This Great Day so near,—
And zealously greet it,
Ye Citizens dear.

Jones hardly summoned his fellow citizens to mourning. In his poem, Memorial Day offered instead a chance to rejoice, to demonstrate pride, and to celebrate the past. Changes in the observance of Memorial Day were not nearly so stark as Jones's lines implied. It remained a solemn occasion, with the bringing of flowers and greenery to the graves as its central ritual. Yet the tone of the celebration resembled the spirit of the poem more than it did the melancholy of the years immediately after the war.[2]

Memorial Day addresses evoked the gloom of defeat less often than they proclaimed the heroism of the soldiers and the justness of their cause. They focused less on death and more on vindication and history. In 1884 the Raleigh LMA adopted a policy of having an address on some historical theme and recommended that other towns in the state do so as well. Although the service in the cemetery retained its solemnity, the occasion as a whole became more festive. In Winchester, Virginia, a Memorial Day crowd broke into cheers and waved handkerchiefs at the playing of "Dixie." In several towns bands and non-Confederate groups, such as the Daughters of the American Revolution or the Knights Templars, joined the parade to the cemetery. Memorial Day had become a more joyful occasion, one for celebrating the cause as well as mourning its dead.[3]

The monument movement also continued to be an important part of the Confederate tradition, but in it, too, ceremonial bereavement gave way to public celebration. In the late 1880s and 1890s, many communities resumed or launched campaigns to raise money for a Confederate memorial. Sometimes a committee of prominent citizens spearheaded the effort, but more often a local LMA, UCV camp, or, after 1895, UDC chapter took the lead. The group in charge usually succeeded in raising enough money, and many more towns dedicated monuments between 1886 and 1899 than had in the first twenty years after the war.[4]

In this period, the proportion of Confederate monuments placed in cemeteries declined from the 70 percent of the 1865-to-1885 era to just over half (55 percent). More towns chose to place their monuments along the city's streets or on courthouse lawns instead of in cemeteries. Southerners also more often avoided funereal designs in monuments, as the percentage of memorials with funereal motifs dropped from over 70 to just about 40. From 1886 to 1899, more than 60 percent of the new monuments featured a Confederate soldier.[5]

The increasing number of monuments placed in town testified to the growing importance of the Confederate tradition. The memory of the war was no longer relegated to the city of the dead. Rather, the Confederate monument now occupied a more public place within the daily patterns of life of the citizens, where all would see it and profit by it. The stone warriors atop these monuments had an aura of dignity and endurance, but otherwise they hardly seemed suited for a war memorial. The lone Confederate soldier usually stood at ease, with his rifle resting on the ground and his arms resting on it. He seemed anything but a dashing, daring knight and, in fact, hardly seemed martial at all. He had little individual personality: At a distance, one looked pretty much like the next, and, except for being less well-dressed, not unlike the statues to Union soldiers in the North. As time went on, more and more of the soldiers were mass-produced models purchased from monument companies. In 1915 North Carolina editor Clarence Poe claimed that most of these monuments did little to make "anybody's heart beat faster" or give "any child a vision of the spirit, heroism and pathos of our Civil War period." Later, William Alexander Percy, who grew up among the monuments, damned them as "pathetic" and unworthy of the men they honored. At the very least, like the historical interpretation of the Confederate celebration they lacked the passion of the war.[6]

Perhaps they were not supposed to evoke sectional passions; Confederate monuments no longer simply honored the dead and celebrated the cause. In a fund-raising speech for the statue to the private soldier on Libby Hill in Richmond, Moses Hoge maintained that they served as a form of history for people who did not read, particularly young schoolboys and workingmen. "Books are occasionally opened," he added, "monuments are seen every day, and the lesson of that lofty figure which is to tower over Libby Hill . . . will be . . . . : 'Live nobly; there is a reward for patriotic duty; republics are not ungrateful.'" Stephen D. Lee agreed that monuments were erected not only to remember the dead but more "for the sake of the living, that in this busy industrial age these stones to the Confederate soldier may stand like great interrogation marks to the soul of each beholder. Are you also ready to die for your country? Is your life worthy to be remembered along with theirs?" The passionless soldier atop these shafts probably served a function similar to that of

Confederate monument, Orange, Virginia (unveiled 1900). *The Museum of the Confederacy*

the historical interpretation of the private soldier as a disciplined, loyal supporter of society. Workingmen learned that republics, even in this industrial age, rewarded men who gave their lives for their country and—as Lee's comment on a worthy life suggests—honored those who served faithfully in peace as well. If the Confederate monuments did help create loyal workers for the age, their being mass-produced was unintentionally appropriate.[7]

The ceremony unveiling the monuments to the common soldier ritually aligned the common man with the social order. In 1894 Richmond unveiled its Soldiers' and Sailors' Monument, a memorial to the men in the ranks, with all the pomp that had accompanied the unveiling of the Lee Monument four years earlier. Once again 100,000 spectators gathered to watch a parade of 10,000 marchers, who included little girls representing the thirteen Confederate states, 1,000 children carrying Confederate flags, and numerous militia units, Confederate veterans, and sons of Confederate veterans. When the procession reached the site of the monument, spectators gathered about a stand filled with prominent people to hear a prayer, a poem, and a speech—all in celebration of the cause and the Confederate soldier. A bugle sounded, and two children pulled the cords to unveil a bronze soldier towering ninety feet above the city. Although the cloth did not fall perfectly, the crowds still cheered and the howitzers fired. Once more, according to a journalist, "The veterans were carried back to the days of real war, and their eyes flashed as of old."[8]

Increasingly in the 1890s and into the first decade of the twentieth century, communities throughout the South held similar ceremonies. Public participation, though not so large as in Richmond, still testified to the importance of the ceremonies. In small towns several thousand people usually attended (sometimes more than the town's population), and in state capitals or larger cities from fifteen to twenty thousand came. The typical ceremony began with a parade, gathered the community around the monument to hear poems and speeches, and climaxed with the unveiling of the statue amid cheers.[9]

The parade clearly demarcated a break in the normal sequence of time, and the festive gathering created a sense of community that, being outside the normal order of things, transcended the usual social and economic divisions of society. Within this special sense of time and structure, southern communities formed at the base of a statue honoring not a leading general but a likeness of the private soldier, the common man who had faithfully defended his fellow citizens. The ceremony and the speech delivered by a prominent citizen paid homage to this representative follower. The event reversed the order of society, as the common man became the focus of attention and praise. When the ceremony ended and people resumed their daily lives, when the ritual time closed, the order of society returned. But the temporary establishment of a special sense of community and the town's and its leaders' testimony of respect to the common man served to enhance the bonds of unity within society.[10]

The enhancement of unity helped ease the social tensions of the era, but the monuments also offered salve for the scars of defeat. For the veteran, the homage paid to the stone soldier symbolized his community's respect for him. The unveiling ceremony reminded him that he had acted with honor and nobility, had given of himself for the good of all. The statue celebrated not just the veteran but also his cause. It signified the South's conviction that it had acted rightly.

Even more than Memorial Day and the unveilings of the monuments, UCV activities epitomized the Confederate celebration. As a veterans' association, the UCV claimed to want to make the last days of the soldiers comfortable so as to demonstrate that republics were not ungrateful. Camps in New Orleans,

Confederate Monument, Baton Rouge, Louisiana (dedicated 1886). *Manuscript Department, Hill Memorial Library, Louisiana State University*

Nashville, and Richmond had extensive assistance programs for needy or aged veterans, but small camps rarely furnished much aid. A survey of more than a hundred camps revealed that almost three-quarters provided none at all. Assuming much of the burden, state government usually operated a home for veterans and paid small pensions. Acting more like their GAR counterparts than they would have cared to admit, UCV camps occasionally lobbied to improve the care rendered in the home or to increase the pension. In general, though, the UCV devoted limited attention to aid, and the rhetoric of respect generally exceeded the reality of relief.[11]

Although they did not always provide financial assistance, some camps did honor the individual soldier's contribution to the war through historical and memorial efforts that usually focused on his personal experience. Some encouraged the old soldiers to recount their wartime adventures, and a few published the talks or preserved them in an archive. Many camps had committees prepare formal eulogies to any member who died and thereby ensured even the lowliest veteran a moment of glory, albeit posthumously. Only the more active groups, however, had such historical and memorial programs. The more typical one met only once or twice a year, provided no aid for the needy veterans, and undertook no historical projects.[12]

Such camps existed solely to hold their own reunions and to send delegates to regional ones. Reunions constituted the central activity for them, but actually for the entire UCV. UCV reunions, unlike individual unit reunions, which were also held occasionally, brought together not men who had gone through the war as a group but everyone who had worn the gray and wanted to come. Their sense of community rested less on personal familiarity and shared experiences and more on a common memory of the war. Individual camp reunions were usually informal. A few had programs of parades and speeches, but most camps held only simple picnics or barbeques. The veterans invited relatives and townspeople to join them at the outing, and visitors usually outnumbered the members and were central to the affair. The "kindly intercourse between the people, neighbors and strangers alike, . . . lends to these annual gatherings their greatest charms," explained one veteran. Although also encouraging "kindly intercourse," state reunions were more formal than local camp picnics. Crowds of veterans and visitors gathered in a host city for a two- or three-day festival of parades, speeches, and social events.[13]

The annual meeting of the UCV served as the model for the state reunions and became the central ritual of the Confederate celebration. The first two annual meetings did not attract many veterans or stimulate significant public excitement. On the eve of the 1892 meeting in New Orleans, however, one bemused resident reported that:

The old Confeds are arriving in force, and tomorrow and [the] next day will own the town. Their hats are 'chalked.' Everything is free for them, drinks, shaves, cabs, theaters. The barbers, bar keeps, boot blacks are ordered to serve them free, and call on the Comm. for reimbursement. Just fancy 1500 Texans, well-primed with corn-whiskey, turned loose on the bully—and behind a half-dozen brass bands playing the Bonnie Blue Flag!

More than 10,000 veterans and visitors joined the revelry in New Orleans that year. The following year the depression forced the leaders of the UCV to cancel the reunion, but in 1894, 20,000 old Confederates gathered in Birmingham. A newspaperman covering the event reported that everyone was "surprised that the reunion should have assumed such colossal proportions." Succeeding UCV reunions attracted even larger and more enthusiastic crowds and commanded extensive press coverage as well.[14]

Southern cities competed fiercely to be chosen by the UCV to host so important an occasion. The winner formed committees to arrange accommodations and entertainment for the veterans and to raise the required $20,000 to $100,000. A few even built or expanded an existing arena to house the convention. Huge crowds necessitated such preparations. In 1896 an estimated 100,000 people crowded into Richmond for the reunion. The main thoroughfares of the city became "almost impassable," and the expanded streetcar service proved "totally inadequate." "Every hotel, boarding house, empty store and other possible place for housing strangers is crowded greatly beyond its capacity," noted one reporter. Two years later 60,000 went to Atlanta, and local officials claimed never, not even during the industrial exposition in 1895, to have entertained more people in a four-day period. The 1903 reunion in New Orleans outdrew Mardi Gras—strong testimony to public enthusiasm.[15]

Picture taken at an early twentieth-century Confederate veterans' reunion, a local one, probably in San Marcos, Texas. *Manuscript Department, Perkins Library, Duke University*

Veterans of all classes participated in the reunions. Both the sponsoring cities and local camps tried to make it possible for poorer veterans to attend. The cities often provided free board and lodging, and the camps financed transportation. Veterans, however, made up only a small part of the crowd. Of the reported 140,000 visitors in Dallas for the 1902 reunion, only 12,000 were former soldiers. Wives and children sometimes accompanied the members, and both the Sons of Confederate Veterans (SCV) and Confederated Southern Memorial Association (an association of LMAs founded in 1900) held coincident conventions. The UDC held an independent annual meeting, but many Daughters still participated in the reunion. Relatives, natural and organizational, therefore accounted for much of the crowd, but no doubt many from the general population came as well.[16]

With such broad participation the UCV reunions assumed a cultural importance far beyond that of a gathering of old soldiers. The veterans came for fairly obvious reasons: to visit with comrades not seen for years, to carouse and drink, to feel young again. The civilians, especially those too young to remember the war, came to honor the veterans and to learn from them. "Confederate Reunions are the finest of schools for us who didn't arrive in time to be part of the original excitement," observed one young woman. "Every man has his story to tell, and reunion ears listen willingly and reunion hearts are responsive," reported the *Confederate Veteran*. "Southern sentiment, Southern ideas and Southern manners are strengthened anew by these gatherings," one of the organizers of the UCV maintained. "Above all, the reunions tend to preserve in the South that respectful devotion to its splendid womanhood that the Southern manhood inherited from their chivalric ancestors." The reunion, all three observers agreed, taught Confederate history, intensified southern loyalties, and reinforced proper behavior. They served, as one organizer summarized it, as "the annual festivals of the South."[17]

The UCV business meeting was the main though not the most important event of the festival. It featured speeches by the UCV leaders and a major address by a prominent Confederate. Although each introduced his own variations, the speakers enunciated the basic themes of the revised historical tradition. The delegates from the camps also listened, or were supposed to, to reports on monument projects and other historical matters. They debated assorted resolutions, with perhaps the most vigor reserved for the decision on where to hold the next reunion.[18]

More important to the function of the reunion than the resolutions, reports, or even speeches was the general festivity of the occasion. For three or four days veterans and other southerners broke their daily routines to celebrate the war. They did not, apparently, seek to revive sectional passions. Decorations included many American flags, bands played national songs, and occasionally northerners addressed the meetings (despite repeated protests by a few members) and received a warm welcome. But the reunion did clearly seek to recreate the spirit of wartime. Bands played and people sang "Dixie" and other tunes of the war. Confederate flags and bunting decorated the meeting place and city streets; pictures of Lee, Jackson, and Davis were everywhere. Gordon and other beloved leaders met with the troops, some of whom wore the gray and all of whom had decorative badges testifying to their service. Even a few loyal blacks ready and willing to play the faithful darkey wandered about.[19]

Amidst the general festivity, the presentation of sponsors and the parade of the veterans proved particularly significant. The custom of inviting sponsors to the reunions, one that had no counterpart at GAR reunions, evolved with little central direction. Gordon and Moorman wanted women to attend the first gatherings but planned no formal ceremonies in their honor. In 1894 each state division chose a young woman to represent it in a tableau at the reunion. The tableaux portrayed a series of historical scenes that ended with one representing peace and a reestabished nation, and the veterans loved the show. In the next few years, apparently with Moorman's approval, almost every department, division, and camp started to bring a representative, or sponsor, to the reunions. These young, unmarried women, usually chosen on the basis of their family ties to a Confederate veteran or their past service to the camp, often came from socially prominent, wealthy families. At the reunion, leaders of the camp or division usually attended the sponsors, who attracted a great deal of attention and played a prominent part in the festivities. With so many of them, they did not participate in a tableau like the one in Birmingham, but usually at some point at least the major sponsors were presented to the veterans.[20]

Always considered too special to be a sponsor, Winnie Davis in many ways served as their model. At the 1898 reunion in Atlanta, a guard of honor escorted the Daughter of the Confederacy to the stage, where Gordon grasped her by the hand and presented her to the veterans. The crowd "went wild with joy." The cheering lasted for some time, and Miss Davis "gracefully bowed her acknowl-edgments with her eyes filled with tears." The band then struck up "Dixie," the cheers began again, and many veterans "broke down completely and cried like babies." Someone in the crowd yelled "Kiss her!" and Gordon replied, "I don't have to be reminded of that. I have already done that."[21]

Nearly as popular as Winnie Davis was Elizabeth Lumpkin, daughter of a Georgia veteran then living in South Carolina. She served as a sponsor at the 1905 UCV reunion and also addressed state reunions in South Carolina, Georgia, and Virginia, where her remarks caused pandemonium among the veterans. Lumpkin always acknowledged woman's steadfast devotion to man and praised in romantic rhetoric the heroism of the veterans. On one occasion she asked the veterans, "how can I find words to give you greeting when every pulsing heart beat says: I love you—you grand old men who guarded with your lives the virgin whiteness of our Georgia?" The daughters reveled in the esteem of the veterans, she continued, but envied "one honor our lovely mothers gloried in. We can work with tireless fingers, we can run with tireless feet for these men; but *they* could love and marry Confederate soldiers!"[22]

The presentation of Davis and sponsors like Lumpkin had several levels of meaning. By their enthusiastic reception of the daughters, the veterans indirectly honored the women who had been faithful during the war. Placed on pedestals as representative women and treated almost as lovely little (barely-) talking dolls, the sponsors reinforced traditional images of womanhood. Sometimes spokesmen made the message more explicit. In a memorial service for Winnie Davis after her death in 1898, one claimed she represented the ideal that home was the center of woman's life. He added that people who try to "make woman a competitor of man in the struggle of life, in the affairs of business, are lowering the ideal as much as those who regard her only as the drudge for service or the minister of animal pleasure."[23]

The women of the war or the ideal of true womanhood could have been affirmed by women of any age, yet the veterans chose young, usually pretty, unmarried women who were instructed to dress in white. The choice of symbolic virgins, the reception of Winnie Davis with calls for kisses, and Lumpkin's comments about marrying old veterans indicated the sexual connotation of the presentation. A ritual presentation of virgins to veterans, it assured the soldiers that the women of the South loved them despite their defeat and thereby indirectly affirmed their manhood. A speaker at the presentation of the sponsors during the 1898 reunion put it succinctly: "Soldiers of the South, is it not sweet to know that you are lovingly enshrined in such golden hearts as these, and that you are dearer to them in defeat than are the proudest victor heroes that ever trod the paths of glory into triumph? Such is the assurance which I bring to you tonight, warm from the hearts of these fair sponsors. They honor you; they love you; they cherish you. . . ."[24]

The sponsors also participated in the veterans' parade, on which, one observer wrote, the "interest of the whole reunion is always centered." Participants frequently referred to it as the "Most moving event" or the "most gorgeous feature" of the reunion. Moorman claimed the veterans "would not miss it for anything in the world" and usually scheduled the parade for the last day of the reunion so that the vets would stay through the entire proceedings. When a conflict with the local Memorial Day forced Moorman to change his policy at the Charleston reunion, many old Confederates did not remain for the rest of the festivities but left after the parade. At the 1900 meeting in Louisville, a minor rebellion occurred among delegates when Gordon canceled the parade because of heavy rain. By a small margin, the delegates voted to uphold his decision, but a thousand vets staged an impromptu march anyway.[25]

The veterans probably enjoyed the parade so much because more than any other activity at the reunion it placed them at the center of the celebration. The leadership of the UCV led the parade, which included sponsors and honored guests in carriages and groups of sons of Confederate veterans on foot. Interspersed along the line, marching bands played the old tunes of the war and, occasionally, national patriotic airs or contemporary ditties. The bulk of the line of march, however, consisted of as many as 10,000 old veterans, formed in order of their UCV departments, divisions, and camps. A few vets carried relics of the war, and many old and honored Confederate battle flags appeared in the ranks.[26]

The veterans usually marched with less than military precision. In one parade an old veteran repeatedly stopped to inform the spectators that he represented "nothing on God's green earth but the lost cause." Close behind him came a younger fellow pretending to be a horse—an act that amused the "ladies along the line who knew nothing of the silly antics soldiers used to play." The parade

Crowd for a Confederate Veterans' parade, Richmond, Virginia, 1907. *The Valentine Museum*

allowed these two men and all the veterans, in the words of one observer, to be "self-assertive." Yet at the same time they reveled in the acclaim of the crowd. At the 1896 Richmond reunion, "men, women and children welcomed the old battle-scarred heroes with yells (not cheers) of triumph and enthusiasm that knew no bounds," reported a northern visitor, who found the excitement much greater than that at a GAR reunion parade he had attended earlier in the year. Sometimes at UCV parades, young women ran "into the lines to hand [the marchers] flowers, to clasp them round the neck, to kiss the wrinkled faces." One vet, who had "suffered much pain" after a fall at the reunion, claimed "those glorious loyal, and Beautiful Women of the South by their demonstrative reception . . . made me forget that I was wounded." The adulation helped the veterans forget the real and psychological scars of defeat as well. The kisses and cheers of the women provided reassurance of their manhood. Like the monuments to them, the homage offered by the crowd to the private soldiers expressed symbolically the appreciation of society for the common man.[27]

At the same time, the parade reinforced respect for the leaders of society. The commander of the UCV and his staff rode horseback at the front of the line; the mounted leaders of each division and camp headed their units. The members, whether or not they had served in the infantry or the cavalry, walked behind them. The order of march thereby enacted the relationship of followers to leaders. Moreover, the superiority that southerners had long attributed to the man on horseback reinforced the leaders' dominance. When Gordon, or, after his death, the succeeding commanders, left the line to review the marchers, the parade itself took the form of a salute to the leadership. UCV officials once admitted they planned a parade so that Gordon would have "the greatest occasion" of his life.[28]

Both the celebration of the soldiers and the deference to the leaders occurred in a ritual situation that fostered unity in southern society. Veterans, sons of veterans, sponsors, and citizens along the street became caught up in an atmosphere that temporarily recreated the sense of wartime unity. The parade was, one reporter commented, "nearer like war times than anything ever gets to be in these piping days of peace." The old battle flags, which received cheers rivaling those for the marchers, also helped bring back memories of the war and served, as flags have in other cultures, as symbols of social unity.[29]

Social solidarity, deference to leadership, and homage to the common soldier were not the themes just of the parade but also of the reunion as a whole. For three or four days each year significant numbers of southerners and the attention of even more converged on the gathering of the UCV. There the veterans heard Confederate history interpreted, watched the presentation of the sponsors, participated in the parade. In these rituals they experienced the respect of society and demonstrated their reciprocal respect for it and its leaders. The veterans were told that they had not only been right, but brave and manly. And all southerners found relief from their lingering defensiveness regarding defeat. "These Reunions," one SCV leader claimed, "are a physical expression of the fact that the South was right."[30]

. . .

R. E. Lee Camp, Richmond, Virginia, on parade. *The Valentine Museum*

In the celebration of the war, epitomized by the UCV reunion, the Confederate tradition came to serve a new and complex function in the society of the New South. Not surprisingly, it supported southern racial and political orthodoxies. The presence of a few faithful black servants of the war years at the reunion and the paeans to the faithful slaves in historical addresses and magazine articles reinforced the white South's view of the proper place of blacks. *Confederate Veteran* editor Cunningham labeled the historical accounts lessons for "young negroes" whose "aspirations for social equality will ever be their calamity." They should follow the example of the "old-time negro" who "lives in the South to-day faithful to white people" and consequently has white friends to sustain him. Conversely, celebration spokesmen occasionally evoked the image of black assertiveness during Reconstruction as a warning to whites that they had to stand together to prevent its recurrence. In rare instances, veterans' groups became involved in the disfranchisement campaigns. Yet explicit rhetorical references to white supremacy, much less direct action to insure it, occurred less frequently in the context of Confederate activities than might have been expected during this period of intense racial conflict in the South. The Atlanta *Confederate Veteran Magazine*, which combined strident support for white supremacy with accounts of the history of the war, died within a year of its founding in 1890.[31]

The Confederate tradition also supported southern political orthodoxy. The historical interpretation of constitutional issues was used to sustain states' rights dogma, and the influential role of a few Democratic politicians in organizing the UCV suggests an even more overt political function. In principal, at least, they banned politics from the UCV, but the ban was sometimes violated. "Joe Kendall Camp No. 1747 of the Straight Democratic Confederate Veterans" made little secret of its allegiance. Moorman once told a reunion he wanted

STEPHEN D. LEE AT
LOUISVILLE, KY REUNION.

Stephen D. Lee, second commander of the United Confederate Veterans, receiving the salute of the veterans during the parade in Louisville, Kentucky, 1905. *The Museum of the Confederacy*

Gordon in the White House, and numerous politicians exploited the UCV or Confederate ceremonies for campaign purposes.[32]

Political hostilities, between Republicans and Democrats or between advocates of gold and silver, occasionally exploded within a camp or division. The disputes pointed up the failure of the UCV to exclude politics, but they also demonstrated that in calmer times people of varied views participated harmoniously in the Confederate celebration. Mrs. William H. Behan, leader of the Confederated Southern Memorial Association (CSMA), was the wife of a Republican mayor of New Orleans who himself played an active role in the UCV. John S. Wise, active in Republican politics in Virginia, belonged to Lee Camp for a time. One monument committee claimed "Democrats, Republicans, Populists, Prohibitionists, vied with each other in their contributions." Of course, the leadership and membership of the UCV always remained overwhelmingly Democratic, but the involvement of non-Democrats and the success in keeping politics out of the celebration appears more significant than the occasional failure to achieve the goal. Nonetheless, in so heavily Democratic a region, anything that increased unity redounded to the benefit of the Democratic party.[33]

The Confederate celebration did more than serve simply as a bulwark of the Solid South, though. On a deeper cultural level, it helped ease the personal and social tensions of the late eighties and early nineties. The middle class, which constituted the majority of its membership—struggling members of the middle class, if the organizers were at all typical—found in the UCV relief from the competition and acquisitiveness of an increasingly commercial society. Even more than other fraternal orders, the UCV offered a temporary escape from an individualistic and competitive world into one of community. One veteran joined a succession of fraternal orders only to discover in each that "'the tie that binds'" was "of artificial construction," and the societies were incapable of fulfilling his "expectations of genuine and lasting fraternity." He soon realized, however, that his years of Confederate service provided "a greater real fraternity than had ever existed before or probably ever will again. . . ." To reestablish it, he joined the UCV, "the most fraternal order now on the globe," and found what he had sought.[34]

In UCV activities, veterans found not only a sense of community but a reassurance that, no matter how competitive or acquisitive they felt now, no matter how great the strains or disheartening their failures in the new order, they had once sacrificed all for a cause greater than themselves and rooted in principle, not profit. Speeches on Memorial Day, at the unveiling of monuments, and at the reunions told them so. "When we feel that we have made poor crops, and mortgages and debts have pressed upon us, when we feel utterly discouraged and cast down—go and read our record," Stephen D. Lee told the veterans at the 1894 reunion. "You will rejoice that there is a country where honor is first, not wealth; where patriotic endeavor and duty are everything, riches only a secondary consideration." The veterans' recounting of their military careers at local meetings or their participation in the reunion parades let them make the point themselves. Each of his comrades in the parade, one veteran commented, seemed to say "'There was a time when I was more than myself. My life then lost its commonplaces. My individual being was swallowed up in the life of the whole. You might not think it, but once I glorified in self-surrender.'"[35]

The celebration not only eased middle-class southerners' fears about themselves but those about disorder in their society as well. Although the UCV charter did not, many individual camps dedicated themselves explicitly to the task of preserving order. "We propose to avoid everything which partakes of partisanship in religion and politics," read the constitution of Lee Camp and other groups, "but at the same time we will lend our aid to the maintenance of law and the preservation of order." Actually, the celebration did so in ways that the participants themselves probably did not perceive.[36]

In its rituals, southerners created a model of what was perceived as the proper social order. At the UCV reunion, "the annual festival of the South," thousands of non-veterans and veterans alike joined in a ritualistic affirmation of social unity and of deference to authority. The celebrations of the private soldier in speech, stone, and parades, with their emphasis on discipline and respect for private property, offered a model of the way the world should work and how the lower classes should behave. As southerners watched these rituals or, more important, participated in them, they learned and even acted out the values of social solidarity and deference that helped hold southern society together as it experienced the social tensions of the last two decades of the nineteenth century.[37]

Of all the functions of the celebration, the offering of a model for the common man is the most difficult to demonstrate, though in fact it may have been the most important. While it was undoubtedly sincere, the rhetoric celebrating the private soldier represented more than a simple evaluation of the private's worth and role. Southerners erected numerous monuments to a typical Confederate soldier, but precious few were dedicated to a specific enlisted man. Memorials to specific individuals almost always honored officers. Veterans claimed no higher glory than that of being a Confederate private, but members of the UCV were inordinately fascinated with the attainment of rank. One observer commented on how much more important rank was than the GAR, and southerners joked about men securing postwar promotions through the UCV. In sum, southerners praised an ideal private but honored real ones far less than they did officers. They described the ideal private in rhetoric that made it sound like a privilege to be one, but they preferred higher rank. The disparity between rhetoric and behavior supports the conclusion that the praise for the private arose in part to reinforce a model of proper behavior for the common man, not simply to express sincere esteem.[38]

During the economic unrest of 1894, the use of the Confederate tradition as a bulwark against rebellion became explicit. Shortly after Coxey's Army of unemployed marched on Washington, a Texas veteran told a reunion that "we would not join any band that would march upon Washington now," and urged his "fellow-soldiers" to stand fast against the "aggressions of government, against the aggressions of anarchy, against the aggressions of communism in every shape, come from whatever quarter it may. . . ." Later in the year, the violence and subsequent federal intervention in the Pullman strike evoked a similar but more widespread response. On the floor of the United States Senate, John Daniel of Virginia, a leading orator of the celebration, introduced a resolution approving President Cleveland's use of the army. Daniel's colleague, Gordon of Georgia, the commander of the UCV and virtual embodiment of the Confederate celebration, also rose to condemn the strikers and praise the use of force to maintain order. He assured his colleagues there would be "no division among us when the constituted authority called upon the people" to put down rebellion. "The men who wore the gray from 1861 to 1865, under strong convictions, will be found side by side with the men who wore the blue, following the same flag, in upholding the dignity of the Republic over which it floats, and in enforcing every law upon its statute books." A few months later, during a visit to Pittsburgh, which had also experienced rioting, Gordon discussed with reporters the danger of lawless mobs. Reminding them that he commanded the UCV, Gordon added, "If occasion requires it, I will march an army of old soldiers across the Long Bridge on the Potomac greater than Gen. Lee ever commanded, every man of whom will fight to the death to preserve the Union and command respect for the old flag."[39]

Many southerners supported the positions taken by Daniel and Gordon. At the next UCV reunion J. William Jones declared that both senators "but echoed the sentiments" of their "Confederate comrades." The Confederate Survivors' Association of Augusta, Georgia, had already assembled "at the base of the beautiful Confederate monument," "heartily" endorsed Gordon's "patriotic and noble utterances," applauded the action of President Cleveland in taking every step to put down the violence, and pledged themselves and their "'sacred honor' to sustain the Executive in every effort he may make to maintain the dignity of our great republic and suppress lawlessness in every section of the country." They all but volunteered to go to Chicago to straighten things out themselves. The Confederate tradition by the 1890s served the cause of order, not of rebellion.[40]

If the Confederate celebration had functioned only as a covert means of social control, it would probably never have mobilized so many veterans or generated such public enthusiasm. Its historical interpretation reminded southerners they had acted rightly in 1861; its orators and rituals reassured the old soldiers that their manhood and honor had survived defeat undiminished. The Confederate celebration served two interrelated social functions. It helped fade the scars of defeat while providing a ritual model of an ordered, deferential, conservative society. The Confederate tradition thereby helped the southern social order weather a period of social stress with a minimum of disruption and, more important, only a modicum of change.

CHAPTER ELEVEN

The South Vindicated:
The Spanish-American War
and Its Aftermath

The rituals of the Confederate celebration helped heal the wounds of defeat, but the need for northern respect and for a sense of full participation in the Union persisted. Southern participation in the Spanish-American War and the euphoric patriotism generated by the conflict did much to meet both needs, and a deeper sectional reconciliation followed. Moreover, the war spurred the North to offer symbolic testimony to Confederate heroism and nobility. As a result the white South felt vindicated in the early twentieth century as never before. It signaled its restored confidence in various ways, including the unveiling of an elaborate statue to President Davis, the vicarious sufferer of the South.

Southerners who sought both to vindicate the Confederate soldier and to reunify the nation might have staged the Spanish-American War if it had not come along when it did. As early as the 1870s one argued that a foreign war would foster reunion, and in 1887 John B. Gordon told a Cleveland audience, "I have sometimes thought that I would be willing to see one more war, that we might march under the stars and stripes, shoulder to shoulder, against a common foe." A few southerners hoped the opportunity for reunion by fire had arrived in 1891 when tensions arose between the United States and Italy over the lynching of Italians in New Orleans. Several groups of ex-Confederates offered their services to the War Department. One Georgian wired for permission "In event of war with Italy . . . to raise a company of unterrified georgia rebels to invade rome disperse the mafia and plant the stars and stripes on the dome of St. Peters." But the crisis passed quickly, and the South had to wait for another chance to prove its military mettle and dedication to the Union.[1]

The outbreak of the Cuban revolution in 1895 presented another opportunity. In a speech to the Association of the Army of Northern Virginia that fall, Clement A. Evans warned that "the South is now listening with boundless sympathy to the cry of Cuba, and on hearing the wail of this oppressed neighbor it inquires, Why shall all America be free and the beautiful Queen of the Antilles

be alone a slave?" During the remaining two years of the Cleveland adminis-
tration, two Confederate veterans were in position not only to hear the cry but
to urge their government to answer it. Hannis Taylor, ambassador to Spain, and
Fitzhugh Lee, consul in Havana, both advocated intervention. When William
McKinley took office, Lee remained at his Cuban post, less ardently advocating
intervention but still jealously defending American interests on the island.[2]

Not all southerners shared the enthusiasm of Evans and the diplomats for the
Cuban cause. In Florida, where war would expose ports to Spanish attack,
newspapers denounced the growing war fever, and in the rest of the South some
people thought the problems could be resolved without resort to arms. Many
southerners, however, became early supporters of American intervention. A few
believed the Cubans' battle for independence deserved assistance because of its
similarity to the South's in 1861. One Alabaman belittled the hypocrisy of
northern interventionists who "fought us four years to prevent our doing just
what they want the Cubans to accomplish to day" and prayed for their success as
he had for the South's. Other southerners made no historical analogies, but
supported aid to Cuba as a matter of humanitarianism or national honor. After
the explosion of the *Maine*, American honor seemed even more at issue, and
support for a crusade in Cuba grew.[3]

Shortly after President McKinley sent a war message to Congress on 11 April
1898, UCV leaders considered having Gordon publicly offer the services of the
"old Confederates." An organization to recruit manpower, founded by several
former Union officers, asked Moorman for help. He suggested that the UCV
commander issue a statement of support, but Gordon and Stephen Lee, who was
increasingly consulted on UCV matters, decided to wait for a formal declaration
of war. "We know," wrote Lee, "and the country knows, that we are patriots, and
whenever the Congress of the U.S. acts, and the President calls, we are for our
whole country, right or wrong, and that all of us who are physically able will be
ready to go to the front as any other citizen of the republic."[4]

Actually, some Confederate veterans were far from anxious to go to the front.
"We have not yet offered our services for the 'Spanish War,'" one wrote
Moorman, "thinking that as the President has such a *large* army of '*Pensioners*'
we will just let them adjust the little matter with Spain, and so *earn their pay*
and, *support.*" Other veterans claimed, no doubt partly in jest, they would not
enlist for fear that if they were killed wearing a blue uniform, their former
Confederate comrades in heaven would shun them as deserters. To appease
southern sensitivity, *Confederate Veteran* editor S.A. Cunningham advocated,
apparently in all seriousness, adopting brown as the color of the United States
uniform.[5]

Once the war started many Confederates decided they could don the blue
uniform without too much indignity. On 18 May the *Atlanta Constitution*
pointed out that most of them had supported the war all along and then
proclaimed that all former Confederate soldiers "are profoundly loyal to the stars
and stripes and are eager to exhibit their fidelity upon the field of battle." Five
UCV camps in New Orleans offered their services to the War Department, and
many individual veterans also sought to join the army. Those too old to fight,

as many were by 1898, encouraged the young to enlist. Despite his doubts about the war, a Virginia veteran argued "that those who have been looked up to by their fellow citizens as men who proved their courage and patriotism in the sixties as Confederate veterans may without claiming too much be assumed to have some special influence in stimulating their fellow citizens to measure up to the standard of patriotic duty erected in and by this emergency." Wealthy industrialist Julian Shakespeare Carr interpreted his duty in more concrete terms. He offered to pay the expenses of the families of men in two units raised in his home town of Durham, North Carolina. Other less well-to-do veterans saw the troops off or visited them in their camps, offering, as one young soldier put it, their "benediction" upon the cause.[6]

Sometimes literally but always figuratively following Confederate veterans, frequently singing "Dixie" or giving the old "rebel yell," young southerners marched off to war with typical American innocence and confidence. A Baptist preacher in Atlanta described their coming campaign as a "holy crusade" and called the "American sword . . . the sword of God." "Go forth, army of deliverance," he charged, "and bring us speedy peace; go forth from the north and the south, from the east and from the west, without regard to creed or color or party. Go forth singing the old battle song of freedom:

> "In the beauty of the lillies
> Christ was born across the sea,
> As He died to make men holy
> Let us die to make men free,
> While God is marching on!"

In Columbia an ex-Confederate echoed the minister's charge in a speech to a militia unit preparing for war. The American war effort, a newspaperman reported him as saying, was "guided not by the hand of man but by the hand of Providence, and is the onward march of Christianity and civilization and would . . . spread until it had circumvented the world and covered every island of the seas. . . ." Most southerners believed that the American armies would easily win the victories necessary for the worldwide spread of Christian civilization. "I believe an American soldier, whether in blue or gray, is better than any soldier in the world," one Confederate veteran maintained. "If they would turn the war over to the South," said another at the 1898 reunion, "it would be finished in six months."[7]

At the 1898 reunion this veteran and the other members of the UCV fervently endorsed the war, and Gordon championed the sense of mission expressed by the preacher and the veteran. In his opening address, the UCV commander lauded the "great ends . . . to be achieved in this war with Spain." Our "boys are to bear, wrapped in the folds of the American flag, the light of American civilizaton and the boon of Republican liberty to the oppressed islands of both oceans; they are to place on a higher plane than ever before the influence of America in the councils of the nations, and are to command for their country a broader and more enduring respect for its prowess on land and sea throughout the world." The war would also lead, Gordon continued, "to the complete and permanent obliteration of all sectional distrusts, and to the establishment of the too long delayed brotherhood and unity of the American people, which shall never be broken nor called into question no more forever." Later in the reunion Stephen Lee introduced a resolution of total support for President McKinley "as Commander-in-Chief of our Army and Navy, until an honorable peace is conquered from the enemy." The delegates passed it on a rising vote and ordered it sent to the president.[8]

The members of the UCV and other southerners saw the war against Spain not only as a chance to free Cuba and establish American influence in the world, but as an opportunity to free themselves of northern suspicions of their loyalty and to establish southern honor. "This crisis," observed one Alabaman, "will be looked upon by our northern brethren as the test of the South's professions of loyalty and patriotism. . . ." With a "glorious record" in the war, wrote another Alabama veteran, "we can show not only to this country but to the world that the South has not degenerated."[9]

The South reveled in its heroes of the war, few in number though they were, who demonstrated both the loyalty of the South and the fact that it had not degenerated. Fitzhugh Lee and Joseph Wheeler, former Confederate generals commssioned at that rank for the battle with Spain, received wide acclaim. So too did Richmond P. Hobson, a naval officer from Alabama who, with some of his men, sank the American ship *Merrimac* in Santiago harbor and thereby prevented the escape of the Spanish fleet. A newspaper account of his exploits suggests an important reason for southern praise of Hobson: "It begins to look very much as if even these fellows [in Washington] who have for years been coming to Congress and holding other offices on the strength of ability to fight the south with their mouths, will soon be forced to acknowledge that we have a place in the Union after all." Hobson, Wheeler, Lee, and the other southern heroes had demonstrated to the North the South's rightful claim to a place of honor and respect in the nation, or so southerners thought.[10]

The exploits of these men also offered testimony to the honor and heroism of Confederate soldiers. Southern accounts linked young men like Hobson to their Confederate forebears and thereby implied that they simply acted as their fathers had. The *Atlanta Constitution* began its account of Hobson's reception in Washington by describing him as "Lieutenant Richmond Pearson Hobson, the hero of the *Merrimac*, a southern boy, the son of a gallant Confederate soldier, himself a hero," and later letters to the editor compared Hobson's naval exploits to those of Confederates during the Civil War. Southerners did not have to make such connections with a former Confederate like Wheeler. His exploits in battle provided direct testimony to the heroism of the Sixties. "We are *all* so proud of you, Old Fellow. Every survivor—officer or private!" wrote fellow Confederate general E.P. Alexander. "You have had the chance to honor again the Old Cause, and you have availed yourself of it most nobly and gallantly." You came out of the recent war with the greatest reputation of any of the generals, Alexander continued, and "the South feels to you as if you had captured that prize for the memory of the Confederate Army—and you can't conceive the delight which all classes take in it." "In fact it seems that by and through you," wrote another southerner to Wheeler, "the whole South is to be recognized and rehabilitated." The honor paid to Wheeler and to all "our Southern men who have recently fought under the 'Stars and Stripes,'" added yet another, "have healed many scars, and all our people have rejoiced at the homage that has been paid by our nation to the people we regard as peculiarly our own."[11]

The Spanish-American War, in sum, allowed southerners to affirm their loyalty to the union and, of equal importance, to demonstrate their courage and that of the Confederate soldier. It thereby helped confirm the Confederate celebration. Southern behavior in the crisis with Spain also reflected the influence of the Confederate tradition. In the hands of Gordon and other leaders of the Confederate celebration, memories of the Confederacy blended readily and smoothly with American nationalism and mission. Having accepted the Confederate tradition's proclamation of southern righteousness, southerners, like other Americans, displayed little awareness of the possibility that the nation's cause might not be God's. Moreover, having learned from the celebration what heroic fighters Confederate soldiers were, they had no more notion of the possibility of defeat than did northerners.

Thus southerners' enthusiasm for the Spanish-American War indicates that the Confederate tradition served only to reinforce America's sense of innocence and omnipotence. On the other hand, southerners' reservations about the imperialism that followed the war suggest that they may have learned from their past. However, it is difficult to judge to what extent the South's sense of its past influenced its role in the debate over American imperialism. No southern position emerged on territorial expansion in general or the annexation of the Philippines in particular. Some southerners favored both; some opposed both. Others wanted to expand in the western hemisphere but not in Asia.

At least one southerner argued that the South's past rendered it especially qualified to lead American expansion. In 1895 Senator John T. Morgan of Alabama, the region's premier expansionist, wrote to a friend, "If, in the history of men, a nation has been 'set apart' and qualified by long suffering for the vicarious work of bettering the conditions of the world, that nation is the people of our Southern States. We have not suffered in vain, and we will not have to wait long for the revelation of the fact that we have supposed to redeem." During Congressional debates several years later, Morgan argued against independence for the Philippines on the grounds that a territory should not be given rights denied Alabama in 1861. Most southern proponents of expansion did not refer to the South's past, but rather offered justifications similar to those of other Americans. Some even defended keeping the territories solely on the basis of the right of conquest—a doctrine southerners had condemned during Reconstruction.[12]

Although many southerners supported the acquisition of territory and even the retention of the Philippines, their Congressmen voted overwhelmingly against the annexation of the islands. Fourteen of twenty-two senators from the former Confederate states voted against ratification of the treaty ending the Spanish-American War and providing for United States retention of the Philippines. Most also voted for the later Bacon Resolution, which would have promised independence to the Filipinos, and for similar measures introduced over the next three years. Consistent southern congressional support of Philippine independence could be interpreted as a display of empathy for fellow rebels by men who remembered their own region's attempt to gain independence. It might even be seen as southern dissent, forged in the travail of the defeat of their own rebellion, from America's sense of innocence and omnipotence.[13]

During the debate, however, southern congressmen rarely drew a parallel between their region's history and the Filipinos' position. On one occasion, Benjamin Tillman of South Carolina alluded to such a parallel, but only James H. Berry actually used the parallel to defend his position. In the debate over ratification of the treaty, the senator from Arkansas reminded his colleagues that he had fought for southern independence in 1861 and, though beaten, had not changed his mind about the right of the southern states to govern themselves. If "the doctrine that 'all just powers of government are derived from the consent of the governed' was true in 1861, it is true in 1898," he continued, and "I for one will never vote to force upon an unwilling people principles and policies against which Lee fought and to protect which Jackson died." Other southern congressmen, including Tillman, in most instances cited the American Revolution, not the Confederate's, in justifying the Filipinos' revolt. Only one aspect of the South's past clearly influenced southern congressmen: the memory of Reconstruction. Over and over again they argued against inflicting "carpetbag rule" on the Filipinos. Even if the government about to be established in the Philippines were "not ten thousand times better" than the carpetbag government in the South, contended Senator Edward W. Carmack of Tennessee in 1902, "may the Lord God have mercy upon the Philippine Islands." Such arguments demonstrated that their historical experience had rendered southerners more sensitive on a few policies than it had other Americans. But the debates and southern behavior in the Philippine war also suggested that wisdom gleaned from its tragic past had limited influence on the South's opposition to the annexation of the Philippines.[14]

In the final analysis, southern opposition had little to do with sympathy for fellow rebels or even memories of carpetbag government. Some southerners criticized annexation partly out of political partisanship: loyal Democrats, they relished attacking Republican policies. More important, southern Congressmen feared that annexation would bring millions of dark-skinned people under the government of and possibly into the United States. Tillman, who talked a great deal about the Declaration of Independence, at one point in the debate termed the race issue—or, as he so judiciously put it, the "injection into the body politic of the United States" of "ten millions of the colored race, one-half or more of whom are barbarians of the lowest types"—the "one issue in this whole proposition." His fellow southern Congressmen's comments during the debates bore out his observation.[15]

Southern response to the Philippine insurrections that followed ratification of the treaty also suggested that the Confederate past, at least as interpreted by the celebration, did little to cause southerners to question imperialism. Even before the treaty passed and fighting on the islands began, opponent John W. Daniel of

Virginia reminded his fellow senators that he believed in the doctrine "my country right or wrong" and admitted that the Filipinos, who were already armed, would become rebels as soon as the treaty was ratified. If then "they do not lay down their arms, it is the duty of the American president to order it, and it is the duty of the American soldier to shoot them to death and to make them lay down their arms under the penalty of execution in battle," he declared. Other southerners agreed. Upon hearing the news of the Filipino insurgent Emilio Aguinaldo's attack on Americans in Manila, the *Atlanta Constitution*, which opposed annexation, editorialized, "In the light of the thrilling news from Manila there now remains but one course for the American government to pursue and that is—To conquer the forces of Aguinaldo! . . . In our way and in our own time we can deal with the question of local government in the Philippines, but as long as an armed foe stands in the way the only work ahead of us will be to vindicate the authority of our flag." Even two of the senators who consistently voted for Philippine independence, Alexander Clay of Georgia and Augustus O. Bacon of Alabama, stressed that the United States had to restore order and create a stable, responsible government before it could leave.[16]

Indeed, notwithstanding the opposition of its congressmen to annexation, the South supported the American war effort with enthusiasm. The anti-war movement had few spokesmen in the region; anti-imperialist agitation was centered in New England. Among southern congressmen, only Tillman and Carmack remained adamantly and aggressively anti-imperialist. And although some evidence suggested southern opposition to recruitment for the Philippine war, southern whites apparently volunteered for the cause as readily as did men from other sections.[17]

Many of the southern soldiers who did go off to suppress a rebellion in a faraway land seemed oblivious to their own region's rebellion, especially a Tennessean who argued that the troops "should . . . carry on a war as Sherman did in his march to the sea." Others found inspiration in the memory of the Confederacy. An Alabaman in the Philippines claimed that he served his country "with the devotedness which I think in my case can only spring from a holy love and reverence for the treasured memories wrapped in that symbol of the majesty in truth and purity—the Stars and Bars interwoven with the immortal banner of Humanitarianism—the Star Spangled unity of Bars and Stripes our glorious national Flag." Another southerner, an officer fighting in the Philippines, at one point called to his men, "Boys, I'm going to lead you across that bridge, and when I give the command I wish you to give an old-time Rebel-Yell. . . ." Apparently, many adopted the same tactic. "It would have pleased you to know and have heard the wild 'rebel yell' echoing from the ancient walls of Manila," the son of Virginia Confederate informed former Confederate general E.P. Alexander after the war. "We of the younger generation owe you of '61 a debt of untold gratitude and admiration for the noble examples & high ideals set for us to follow," he continued. "I know that the spirit of the fathers is in the sons too, through my own limited experience in the military service." In its battles, the First Tennessee Regiment "maintained the name given it in bloody baptism in the Army of Northern V[irgini]a." The irony of putting down rebels with a rebel yell seemed lost on these soldiers. For them, the Confederate soldier exemplified only martial courage and discipline.[18]

The celebration had kept alive few of the political passions that might have encouraged southerners to empathize with the Filipinos. The opponents of annexation acted less from sympathy for the Philippine cause than out of racist fears that the Filipinos would become part of the United States and thereby destroy it. The memory of their own rebellion did little to spur southerners to attack imperialism but did much to encourage their participation in the suppression of the Filipino rebellion. Instead of admiration for rebellion, the Confederate celebration had fostered national loyalty and respect for authority. Even many of the southerners opposed to annexation asserted that the Americans must suppress the rebellion, ensure stability, and then establish a proper government before they withdrew. The interpretation of the South's past offered by the Confederate celebration had limited influence on the region's opposition to the annexation of the Philippines. Rather than fostering southern dissent from the American sense of mission, the Confederate celebration facilitated southern participation in the crusade.

Southerners who shunned the Confederate celebration and remained irreconciled to defeat often exhibited the most sympathy for the Philippine rebels—a circumstance that reinforces the conclusion that the Confederate tradition undermined what might have been a natural southern empathy for fellow rebels. Tillman, the most vitriolic southern anti-imperialist, may be a good example. The South Carolinian had always scorned the celebration of the war, no doubt partly because it worked to the advantage of his political rivals. His comments in the Senate debate certainly revealed a continued and ferocious bitterness against the North. At one point, he corrected a northern senator who said most people in the South were glad that the Civil War had not permanently divided the nation. Tillman contended that not more than 5 percent felt that way and stuck by his view even when two fellow southerners disagreed. Some irreconciled southerners even pointed to the irony of southern participation in imperialism. One former Confederate, an expatriate living in Oregon who remained a vehement critic of reunion, condemned American actions in the Philippines, Cuba, and China as well as the very notion of an American empire. He reserved special scorn for southerners like Wheeler and Fitz Lee whom he ridiculed as former rebels who "afterward turn out to help a lot of d-d Yankee jamizaries hunt down other 'rebels' in far-off lands—'rebels' not against *us* or *our government*, but against Spain and Russia and The Emperor of China!"[19]

The sometimes acrimonious debate over the Philippines did little if anything to hinder the growing sectional reconciliation engendered by the Spanish-American War. In 1899 the UCV, keeper of the Confederate tradition, placed its blessing on the reunion effected by the war. "Once more the blood of North and South has been poured out together—no longer beneath contending standards in the bitterness of the war between the States, but beneath one flag, to the glory of one country," concluded its historical committee. "These dead, at least, belong to us all. The last hateful memory that could divide our country is buried with them. About their graves kneels a new nation, loving all her children everywhere the same."[20]

In the decade or so after the war, the North nurtured this southern sense that the nation loved "all her children everywhere the same." Like southerners, northerners apparently interpreted southern heroism in the war against Spain as a retroactive demonstration of the honor of Confederate soldiers. Through the federal government, the North paid its respect to the former foes in two highly symbolic ways: by caring for the graves of the Confederate dead and by returning captured Confederate battle flags to the South.

President McKinley, who reportedly made sectional reconciliation one of his war aims, toured the South at the end of the war and assured his audiences that the fighting had reunited the sections. During an Atlanta celebration of the Spanish-American War peace treaty, the president also praised Confederate heroism. "Every soldier's grave made during our unfortunate Civil War is a tribute to American valor," he declared. After the applause died down, he went on to say that the differences of the war "were long ago settled by the arbitrament of arms" and that the time had arrived "in the evolution of sentiment and feeling under the providence of God, when in the spirit of fraternity we should share with you in the care of the graves of the Confederate soldiers." The audience approved his offer with "Tremendous applause and long-continued cheering."[21]

A few former Confederates belittled McKinley's gesture as insincere or politically motivated. In the *Confederate Veteran*, however, Cunningham commended and even seemed moved by it, although he did add that it was long overdue. At the next UCV reunion Stephen Lee introduced a resolution to accept the offer of federal care for the graves and to urge southern congressmen to support implementing legislation. The committee on resolutions amended Lee's motion to call for federal oversight only for Confederate graves in the North, since those in the South were already under the care of devoted southern women. A few delegates still opposed the resolution. One claimed that by acting on an incidental remark by the president, the UCV appeared to be "asking for something from those who slew our men." When other delegates proposed changes, one of the resolution's supporters demanded to know if the veterans would "insult the Chief Magistrate of this nation." No, no, they shouted. It is our government, he then continued; why should it not take care of our graves? After additional discussion, the delegates voted in favor of federal care for Confederate graves in the North by a "decisive vote" according to the minutes, in near unanimity according to a reporter for the *Atlanta Constitution*.[22]

In what became a first step toward federal care for the graves, in 1900 a Washington, D.C., UCV camp convinced Congress to have the remains of 128 Confederate soldiers already buried in scattered sites in the capitol area reinterred in Arlington National Cemetery. A few UCV camps and Mrs. William H. Behan of the Confederated Southern Memorial Association thought the bodies should be returned to their states instead. Mrs. Behan asked Gordon and the governor of her home state of Louisiana to intervene to stop the plan. Both refused, and the latter told her he applauded the official approval implied by burial in the national cemetery. Reinterment in a Confederate section of

Arlington proceeded, and in 1903 the first Confederate Memorial Day service was held there.[23]

Congressional approval for federal care of Confederate graves in other parts of the North came more slowly. Congress had not acted by 1901, so the UCV unanimously reaffirmed its support for federal care. Mrs. Behan, who had become the leading opponent of the plan, then abandoned her protests. In 1903 and 1904 Senator Joseph B. Foraker of Ohio sponsored legislation to care for the Confederate graves, legislation that passed in the Senate only to die in the House. The 1904 and 1905 UCV annual meetings endorsed the Senate bill despite protests by a few members the second year. A UCV member who lived in Washington lobbied in its behalf, and its congressional sponsors apparently discussed it with UCV leaders. At one point in the floor debate, a senator urged that no amendments be made to the bill because "it has been gone over carefully by the committee and it has been carefully considered by General Lee. . . ." With UCV endorsement and aid, in 1906 Congress finally passed, and the president signed, a bill providing for federal care of Confederate graves in the North.[24]

While Congress was considering the graves bill, it voted to return captured Confederate battle flags to the South. In 1905 Congress approved their transfer to the states, and the following year it voted to send to the Confederate Museum in Richmond the flags that could not be identified as belonging to any state. In 1888 President Cleveland had had to rescind an order to return the flags after an angry public protest, which included a threat by then Ohio Governor Joseph B. Foraker to disobey if the president ordered his state to return the trophies of war. In 1905, however, the flags went back "without arousing a ripple of protest."[25]

The North's willingness to acknowledge southern honor had its limits, of course. Congress did not restore the citizenship of Lee or Davis for another half-century. Even hatred for the so-called arch-traitor Davis, however, had cooled. In 1907 Mrs. Behan of the CSMA organized a committee composed of the heads of the UCV, UDC, and other major Confederate societies to campaign for the restoration of Davis's name to the Cabin John Bridge in Washington. Davis had served as Secretary of War when the bridge was built, but during the Civil War the government had obliterated his name from its plaque. In 1909 the committee convinced President Theodore Roosevelt to order the restoration of Davis's name, thus symbolically returning him to at least part of his place in American history. Wielding new tools, a Confederate veteran stonemason chiseled in the name. A picture of the craftsman and the bridge adorned a widely-distributed postcard, and a bitter fight developed over which museum would receive his tools and which Confederate organization the credit for restoring Davis's name. Many in the South apparently thought it important that Davis's name be on the bridge.[26]

They also thought important the paeans to the Confederacy offered by various northerners, praise that reinforced the symbolic actions of the federal government. In 1901 Charles Francis Adams, of unimpeachable New England pedigree, began a ten-year celebration of Lee. In 1911 Charles E. Stowe assured a Nashville audience that the North shared responsibility for slavery and even

Ceremony accepting the return of captured Confederate battle flags, Tallahassee, Florida, 1905. From left to right: W.D. Ballantine of the Florida Division, UCV, Governor N.B. Broward, former Governor F.P. Fleming, and F.L. Robinson of the Florida Division, UCV. *The Museum of the Confederacy*

admitted that he did not blame southerners for their hatred of abolitionists. "In the minds . . . of pious, churchgoing, orthodox slaveholders, and many such there were, the abolitionists of the North were looked upon as we to-day regard the bomb-throwing anarchists of Chicago or the most radical wing of the socialist party—as the enemies of society and the enemies of God and his holy Word, the Bible, in which the pious slaveholder of the South found abundant authority for his beloved institution." Abolitionists' attacks, continued the son of the author of *Uncle Tom's Cabin*, forced southerners to identify slavery with states' rights, and the war resulted from the sections' inability to compromise the issue. An always magnanimous Cunningham printed Stowe's speech under the headline, "Honest Confession Good for the Country." The same year the commander of a Massachusetts GAR camp read a poem, "Let the 'Conquered Banner' Wave," to a Petersburg, Virginia, UCV camp. It began:

> Why furl it and fold it and put it away,
> The banner that proudly waved over the gray?
> It has not a blemish, it shows not a stain,
> Though it waved over fields where thousands were slain.
> O, why should we furl it and put it away?
> It's loved and respected by the blue and the gray.[27]

Southerners gloried in northern homage to their conquered banner and in all other signs of northern respect. Federal care of the Confederate dead, the inclusion of Confederate graves in the national cemetery, the celebration of Confederate Memorial Day there, and restoration of Davis's name to the Cabin John Bridge symbolically acknowledged the Confederates as legitimate contributors to the nation's history rather than rebels and traitors. The return to the South of captured battle flags, trophies of northern conquest, testified to the North's respect for the heroism of its former foes. The North had publicly conceded, as the South had wanted it to do since 1865, the honor and nobility of the Confederates' fight. The acknowledgment both sealed reunion and reaffirmed southern honor.

Voices claiming vindication abounded in the South after the turn of the century. A southern victory in the War Between the States "was not to be," Julian Carr calmly informed a Virginia audience in 1916. "The God of Battles ordered otherwise and His decree was that the North should have the victory and the South should reap the glory of that mighty conflict," said Carr. "So be it. We are content. I have yet to see or to hear of any Southern man who wore the Gray and did his brave devoir on stricken field who is not proud of the deeds of the sons of the South from the firing on Sumter to Appomattox." The contentment and pride displayed in such remarks derived from the interpretation of the past supported by the Confederate celebration and now endorsed by many in the North.[28]

Southerners believed they had fought a legal and moral war over constitutional issues, not over slavery. Nevertheless, after 1900 they openly proclaimed slavery a social institution beneficial to white and black alike. The UCV and many individuals discussed a monument to the faithful slave, and a few talked again of federal compensation for their lost slave property. The veterans also appeared firmly secure in their honor and manhood. Extrapolating an image of success from the overwhelming-numbers explanation, they hardly realized they had lost on the field of battle. "You know we never was whipped," wrote one, "but was over powered by an overwhelming numbers." A Blount County, Tennessee, veteran took the thought even further in a poem that closed:

> The Yankees did not whip us boys,
> No, never let it be said,
> We wore ourselves out by whipping them,
> And stopped for want of bread

The veterans probably did not believe this literally true, but the notion accurately reflected self-confidence in their martial accomplishments. They had not won, but they had given as good an account of themselves as they would have if they had won.[29]

Public signs of vindication bolstered and at the same time symbolized renewed southern confidence. The veteran who felt he had never been whipped had recently received a Cross of Honor from the UDC. A Georgia Daughter, just back from a UCV reunion, had first proposed an award for veterans, and in 1899 the UDC created the Cross of Honor. All its divisions established procedures to verify the war records of the veterans in order to determine who had served faithfully. On Memorial Day, Lee's or Davis's birthday, or some other Confederate occasion, the UDC then bestowed on each worthy a bronze badge in the shape of a cross. The Daughters awarded the first in Athens, Georgia, on Memorial Day 1900, and after that veterans all over the South received a Cross of Honor. A very few manifested so little sentiment as to pawn theirs, although, worse yet, one gave his to a Yankee. The majority cherished the badges as vindication of themselves and their role in the war.[30]

Nothing "could have been more appropriate" than the cross, one veteran observed. "Since the awful tragedy on [Calvary] Hill, [it] has been emblematic of virtue, truth and love. . . . It alike consecrates the palace and the hovel. It has in all ages emblazoned the breast of heroes and the scepter of Kings." Equally important, the badge symbolized honor, the intangible quality southerners had seemed so determined to assert since their defeat. In the ceremony, representative southern women ritualistically bestowed a sign of honor on each veteran and thereby reassured him he had not forfeited his honor in defeat. The same veteran explained the significance of the act to a group about to receive their crosses. "Comrades," he began, "you are to receive a full recognition of your patriotism, valor and your marvelous endurance." This insignia "will proclaim every-where the honorable part that you bore in our great civil war . . ." and

will heighten your pride at having been a Confederate soldier that wore the gray. It will strengthen your conviction that the cause you upheld was just, right and honorable. The rising generation will stand with uncovered heads in your presence, and thank God that our South land can produce such chivalric manhood.[31]

While the Cross of Honor served as a symbol of vindication for individual veterans, in the early twentieth century the Confederate monument came to serve more than ever before as a physical symbol of vindication for southern communities. In 1899 an association in Waynesboro, Georgia, moved its twenty-two-year-old monument from the cemetery to the town's main intersection. In another community, a cemetery monument destroyed by lightning was replaced by one at the courthouse. After the Spanish-American War, the trend away from funereal monuments, which had begun in the 1890s, increased. Only a quarter of the monuments erected between 1900 and 1912 had any funereal aspect. Almost 80 percent featured the lone Confederate soldier, and more than 85 percent were placed on courthouse lawns, downtown intersections, or other public places. Southerners apparently agreed with the spokesman of one monument association that decided to place its monument in town. A Confederate monument, he argued, "should be where all will see it: in daily view, familiar to the eyes of our people and commanding the attention of every stranger within our gates. We can mourn our dead in the silent cemeteries and commend their deeds from house tops." More towns than ever before decided to commemorate those deeds. About three-fifths of the Confederate monuments erected before 1913 were unveiled between 1900 and 1912.[32]

Perhaps the clearest sign of the southerners' sense of vindication came in the form of honor paid to the region's "representative man." After 1898, much of the effort of the UDC, CSMA, and other Confederate groups went into the campaign for a monument to Jefferson Davis in Richmond. During the long years of fund-raising, the sponsors discussed several designs and various locations in the city. In the end, the monument to Davis was placed on Monument Avenue not far from that to Lee. Smaller than some of the earlier designs, the Davis monument was still the grandest, most ostentatious of the major Confederate memorials. At its center stood an Edward Valentine statue of Davis with an arm outstretched as he lectured from a history book. A 50-foot, 13-column, semicircular colonade formed a backdrop. At both ends stood square piers, on each of which perched an eagle, and in the center directly behind the Davis figure rose a 67-foot Doric column topped by an allegorical figure of a woman. The entire monument, wrote the local newspaper, "typifies the vindication of Mr. Davis and the cause of the Confederacy for which he stood before the world. . . ." It did not appear a simple or reserved vindication.[33]

The unveiling was held on Davis's birthday in 1907 in conjunction with the UCV reunion. A crowd of between eighty and two hundred thousand—estimates varied considerably—gathered in Richmond, and at the request of the UCV commander some people in other parts of the South stopped their activities at the time of the unveiling. Resembling those for the Lee memorial, the ceremonies began with a parade of veterans to the monument. The crowd then gathered about it to listen to prayers, speeches by numerous people active in the fund-raising effort, and a lengthy celebration of Davis and his role in the war by Clement A. Evans. When Evans finished, Margaret Davis Hayes and the former president's two grandchildren pulled the cord to unveil the statue, and as usual the crowd responded with cheers and rebel yells.[34]

Jefferson Davis Memorial, Richmond, Virginia (unveiled June 3, 1907). *The Valentine Museum*

The Davis unveiling was far from usual; rather, like the Lee unveiling seventeen years before, it proved a milestone in the evolution of the Confederate tradition. It climaxed the Confederate celebration by honoring the southern hero most directly identified with the righteousness of the Confederate cause. In so grand a celebration around so elaborate a monument to the vicarious sufferer for all southerners, the South vindicated not only Davis and the cause, but itself. The vindication had begun with the Confederate celebration of the nineties, but the Spanish-American War had marked its full arrival. In that war's battles, the South proved to itself and to the North its loyalty to the Union and its heroism. In the aftermath of war, the North finally offered the symbolic testimony to the South's honorable course between 1861 and 1865 that Arp and all southerners had demanded, and needed, since Appomattox.

Part Three

THE WANING POWER OF THE CONFEDERATE TRADITION, 1898 TO 1913

Changes in the Celebration: The Declining Importance of the Confederate Tradition

The apparent vindication of the South that followed the Spanish-American War did much to make southerners less sensitive about the painful scars of defeat, and afterwards the veterans and other southerners seemed less in need of reassurance. The social tensions that had helped shape the Confederate tradition also diminished. With the election of William McKinley in 1896 and victory in the war with Spain, the United States began to come to terms with the new interrelated industrial order. Renewed confidence and greater social stability may well have contributed to a reduction in the need for fraternity and social unity so important to the early UCV and to the Confederate celebration as a whole.

In any case, divisions developed within the UCV and, perhaps more important, the nature of the Confederate celebration itself changed. Commercialism increasingly cheapened its rituals. The upper and middle classes, which had always dominated the celebration, seemed decidedly less interested in mobilizing the lower classes. And as the veterans who had led the celebration died, responsibility for the Confederate tradition shifted to a new generation of southerners. In a significant development, the Daughters, not the Sons, became the guardians of the tradition, and they sometimes disagreed with the Veterans on their role. None of these changes destroyed the celebration, but bickering, commercialization, and declining interest in a broad-based social movement did indicate that in the future the Confederate tradition would play a less crucial role in southern society than it had at the end of the nineteenth century.

Maintaining harmony within the Confederate celebration had never been easy. From the beginning, the UCV had experienced occasional fights, but none had seriously damaged the organization. In 1899, Moorman expressed amazement that no division had yet attempted "Secession." "If we can succeed in keeping the remains of the Confederacy intact it will certainly be a great feat," he observed. In the decade after Moorman made his comment, unity became even more precarious as disputes within the UCV and the Confederate celebration emerged over sectional reconciliation and over what might best be termed the spoils of vindicated defeat.[1]

A few southerners had never abandoned their bitter memories of the war and had always opposed sectional reconciliation. Some of these irreconcilables, the leaders of the Virginia coalition, for instance, had refused to join the UCV. Others, who supported the UCV's glorification of the cause though not its moves toward reunion, participated but still quietly grumbled and occasionally publicly questioned fraternization with former foes. Their complaints had little effect, however, and the spirit of reconciliation reigned essentially unchallenged in the UCV during the 1890s. At the beginning of the twentieth century, perhaps affronted by the celebration of reunion following the Spanish-American War, a few veterans did begin to attack fraternization.

At the UCV annual meeting in 1900 a resolution of fraternal greetings to the Grand Army of the Republic sparked an uproar. The "auditorium resounded with cheers and cries which swept back and forth through the long hall without abatement." Fondly recalling his wartime "ambition to run to earth the marauding bluecoats," one Virginia delegate declared that he did not "intend to coquette with, or in any way offer compliments to the Yankees now." In response, Stephen Lee defended the greetings, and Gordon endorsed Lee's remarks. When the angry Virginian rose to speak again, the delegates shouted him down and then voted in favor of the resolution.[2]

At least some of the defeated minority, however, did not abandon the hope of stopping "marauding" Yankees or subverting the UCV leaders intent on sectional reconciliation. Two months after the reunion a controversy arose following a Blue-Gray reunion in Atlanta where both Gordon and Albert D. Shaw, a leader of the GAR, spoke. Shaw urged southerners for the sake of patriotism to blot out all memories of the war. Teaching children that the cause of the South was right and just, he said, "is all out of order, unwise, unjust, and utterly opposed to the bond" that Lee had made when he surrendered. With his "lips . . . tightly compressed and his eyes . . . shining," Gordon, who had already addressed the group, rose to challenge Shaw. He would never teach his children that he had been wrong, Gordon declared. The South must cherish its memories. Chastened, Shaw lamely replied that he had "hoped that I had made clear to all of you precisely the point that General Gordon has made. I can heartily indorse what he has said."[3]

The *Confederate Veteran* published an account of the interchange between Shaw and Gordon but dismissed its importance and praised Gordon's response. In New Orleans the Association of the Army of Tennessee (AAT), however, took a different view. At the urging of J.A. Chalaron, head of a local Confederate museum and a founder of the UCV, it passed a resolution condemning Gordon for participating in Blue-Gray reunions where insults like Shaw's could be delivered. As an individual Gordon or anyone else had the right to go to such gatherings, it maintained, but Gordon should never attend as a representative of the UCV and risk embarrassment to its members.[4]

In an open letter published in major newspapers that August, Gordon informed the association that he fully intended to continue "the efforts which I have made for thirty years in the interest of sectional harmony and unity." Gordon added that "Whatever I can do will assuredly be done for the truth of history, for justice to the South, and to all sections for fostering our cherished memories and for the obliteration of all sectional bitterness and for the settlement of all sectional controversies on a basis consistent with the honor the manhood and the self-respect of all." Refusing to retract its criticism, the AAT publicly repeated its condemnation of Blue-Gray reunions and fraternization with the GAR but did add a statement in fulsome praise of Gordon.[5]

Only a few individuals and other camps endorsed the New Orleans protest, and even some members of the AAT thought the resolution made too much of the incident. Cunningham continued to praise Gordon's performance in Atlanta, although he added in one article that it "may as well be recorded in the Veteran, that Gen. Gordon and a number of other prominent Confederates, years ago adopted a policy represented conspicuously and with great ability by the lamented Grady, of conceding too much." Moorman and Lee, probably among those Cunningham felt conceded too much, commended Gordon. The adjutant-general also reported that "nearly all whom I have heard speak" of the incident thought Gordon had done "the proper thing exactly." Perhaps Moorman was right, because the controversy died down quickly.[6]

Another incident occurred the following year when Memphis officials planning the 1901 UCV reunion invited President McKinley. With Chalaron again in the lead, the AAT condemned the invitation for bringing politics into the association. Other camps passed similar resolutions, and Moorman distributed some of them. Gordon concurred with Moorman's decision to do so, since it would protect the leaders "from any suspicions of taking sides with the Memphis people against our own rules and precedents." The protestors appeared less worried about rules and precedents than upset by what they considered another attempt to pander to the Yankees. That the invitation went to a Republican politician, considered by many southerners to be the worst sort of Yankee, made them even angrier. Before lines were drawn, however, McKinley declined the invitation and the protest became moot.[7]

The counterattack against reconciliationist sentiment within the UCV then slowed. After the Memphis reunion, a Georgia veteran campaigned to have Gordon relinquish command of the UCV, but only the timing suggested any relation to the recent squabbles. In any case, his effort failed, and the next reunion reelected Gordon. Chalaron still agitated for an end to fraternization and a return to what he considered the true principles of the UCV. He never mobilized much support, and in 1905 his own AAT declined to follow his suggestion of seceding from the UCV. Neither Chalaron nor the other stubborn rebels in the UCV boasted any real victories.[8]

Despite its failure, the opposition to fraternization testified to a persistent hostility toward the North. Even as most southerners relished reunion, others inside, and more often outside, the UCV did not. They agreed with a Texan who claimed, "The only thing I regret about the war is that we *got wore out and had to quit the fight*. If I had my way—there would not have been left in all Yankeedom as much as a hen house standing." Not just disgruntled old veterans, but members of the postwar generation shared his hostility. In 1904, outraged by a Republican electoral victory and by the possibility of northern intervention in southern racial matters, Charlestonian Gustavus M. Pinckney preached defiance. "I believe," he wrote, "if the Southern People were alert and vigilant and wise they would hold a convention tomorrow" and declare that they "have the right to govern" themselves "without let or hindrance." The convention, he maintained, could argue that it acted out of self-preservation and explain its "stand is right and just and constitutional." If the North then accepted its demand, fine; if not, the South would have to resist an attack. Born in 1873, Pinckney seemed unaware the region had tried that approach once before.[9]

Some people, including Moorman and Lee, thought such rabid southern sentiment fairly widespread, within the UCV at least. The intransigents never won a vote in the UCV annual meeting, though, and the thoroughgoing reconciliationist Gordon remained at its head. Indeed, much of the irreconcilables' protests seemed frivolous—an SCV resolution protesting the insult of uniforming United States Mail carriers in gray, for instance. An English visitor to the early twentieth-century South discovered "little real bitterness" and discounted much of what he found as silly and insincere. He was unquestionably correct. But a very small minority of southerners did remain seriously irreconciled, and after 1900 these were more vocal than in the 1890s. Their challenge created, or better reactivated, a division within the Confederate tradition.[10]

The "secession" Moorman feared, however, resulted not from a difference of opinion over sectional reconciliation but from petty bickering among the veterans, primarily over the rewards that came with southern vindication. The most prominent dispute was over the location of a Confederate Battle Abbey to be built with money raised throughout the South. Veterans from Richmond, Nashville, Memphis, and New Orleans fought for the prize, but when the committee in charge announced its decision to place the Abbey in Richmond, those in New Orleans and Nashville demanded the return of the money they had contributed to the project. Out of the resulting squabbles emerged not one but two lawsuits. The museum still opened in Richmond in 1921, but the spectacle of veteran fighting and even suing veteran hardly did anything to promote fraternity or community.[11]

The Battle Abbey fight received more publicity, but infighting also plagued various UCV divisions. Between 1900 and 1907 the California division endured several serious squabbles. During the same period two factions in Tennessee battled one another, primarily for control of the state's Confederate pension system. In 1907 bickering broke out within the Louisiana division over the order of camps in parades and the allocation of state funds for monuments. The traditional antipathy between New Orleans and the rest of the state probably exacerbated the tensions. A slight to the honor of the division commander by the New Orleans LMA and accusations by his opponents that he had maneuvered himself into a job as state commissioner of Confederate records did not help, either. Eventually the Association of the Army of Tennessee and another camp in New Orleans "seceded" from the state organization.[12]

Strong leaders in UCV headquarters might have reduced tensions by intervening in the disputes. The dissension, however, coincided with a change in UCV leadership. Moorman died in late 1902, and a Mobile, Alabama, bookseller, William E. Mickle, succeeded him. By almost all accounts, Mickle was a less able administrator than Moorman and did not have his knack for calming troubled waters. In fact, Mickle himself became a controversial figure, although not altogether because of his own shortcomings. His chief detractor, Chalaron of New Orleans, who was involved in so many of these disputes, may have criticized him out of pique over not getting the job himself. Making matters worse, John B. Gordon, who might also have helped ease tensions, died in early 1904. The UCV lost both its organizational genius and its symbolic head within little more than a year.[13]

Stephen D. Lee, the Mississippian whom Gordon had all but anointed as his successor, replaced Gordon and served with considerable popularity until he died in 1908. With voting split along east-west lines, Georgian Clement A. Evans won a close election to replace Lee but held command for only two years. After he declined to run again, political intrigue and infighting accompanied the selection of the commander, further reducing harmony among the veterans. Angered that no one from the West had ever held the top post, in 1912 Dick Dowling Camp of Houston advocated the secession of the Trans-Mississippi Department. The department rejected the idea, but several individual camps did pull out of the UCV.[14]

Even taken together, the dispute over the Battle Abbey, the squabbles within certain divisions, and the politicizing of the commander's post never threatened the survival of the UCV. The organization maintained its strength; the total number of camps and delegates eligible to vote at the reunions remained stable between 1900 and 1910. Subscriptions to the *Confederate Veteran* did, too. And yet the bickering suggested subtle but important changes in the function of the Confederate tradition. Veterans involved in petty disputes hardly offered a model of social unity, and the fights for rewards and privileges hardly provided an example of self-sacrifice. When considered along with other changes, such as growing commercialism and decreasing participation by the lower classes, the bickering indicated not only a shift in function but a decline in the importance of the Confederate tradition.[15]

Ever since the war some businesses had tried to associate their products with the Confederacy in order to increase sales. The Daughters and other loyal Confederates occasionally attempted to stop such exploitation but rarely succeeded. In the early twentieth century, however, commercialism crept into the Confederate celebration itself. The trend was clearest, perhaps, within the monument movement. It had always involved a degree of commercialism, of course, but by the early 1900s the monument companies had become far more aggressive and influential than ever before. Some local groups still formed from a sense of duty and then bought a monument, but marble companies also aggressively encouraged the construction of memorials. The McNeel Marble Company of Marietta, Georgia, most actively exploited patriotism. It furnished UDC chapters advice on fund-raising techniques and offered liberal terms that allowed them to order a statue with very little cash on hand—lest dilatory contributors deprive soldiers of the honor due them before they died, of course. Not content to aid chapters that had decided to put up a monument, McNeel dispatched agents to encourage them to start a campaign. In 1910 it offered a free marble breadboard to any local UDC president or secretary who provided the company with the name of a chapter planning to erect a monument in the next year. Adopting other creative marketing strategies, McNeel introduced a Confederate memorial drinking fountain that it advertised as combining "Art, Sentiment, and Utility."[16]

The desire for financial gain crept into the annual meetings as well, and by 1911 a delegate on the floor "declared that the spirit of commercialism had entirely invaded the Reunion." Veterans increasingly complained of extortionate rates in hotels and boarding houses and in 1912 organized a boycott when "a clique of Macon men, through a 'trust'" conspired to raise carriage rental fees the night of a ball. The same year news leaked out that at least one city had quietly hired an agent thought to have special contacts to influence the delegates' choice of the next reunion site. Such developments led one veteran to conclude in 1915 that cities applying to host the reunion were "not always influenced by the highest and most patriotic of motives, but in many instances by the thought of the money that can be made out of the Reunion." No doubt, cities had always sought to make money as well as to honor the veterans. Yet the spirit prevalent in Macon differed significantly from that in New Orleans twenty years before when "all the veterans hats were chalked." By the end of the first decade of the twentieth century, serious profit-taking had become a far more important motive than in earlier years.[17]

Marble companies and businessmen in the reunion cities were not the only ones who tried to profit by association with the Confederate celebration. During the 1901 annual meeting in Memphis, a group of "old ex-Confederate soldiers and successful businessmen" organized the Confederate Mining Company. Perhaps because Cunningham had invested in it, the *Confederate Veteran* carried its announcement, but the magazine also printed numerous other advertisements with Confederate sales pitches. Some, logically enough, hawked Confederate mementos or pictures of war leaders. Others had only a tenuous connection with the Confederacy. An ad for Ayer's Hair Vigor proclaimed in large type, "The Blue and the Gray," then explained, "Both men and women are apt to feel a little blue, when the gray hairs begin to show. . . ." "The Old Gray Jacket," according to the headline of the advertisement for the Phillips and Burthoof Manufacturing Company of Nashville, "was famous for wear—so is the National Steel Range," read the smaller type. Getting worse rather than better, the copy continued: "When you 'Pass over the River and rest under the shade,' Ye battle scarred heroes: As your children 'rise up and call you blessed,' may it always be from a bounteous table and a meal prepared on the National, a Southern-made range—the best effort of a sturdy member of the 'First Tennessee.'"[18]

A float in a parade at a Nashville reunion proved the most shameless instance of commercialism in the celebration. Drawn by four black horses, it carried a "realistic imitation of a marble sarcophagus" draped with a Confederate flag. At one end of the sarcophagus stood a daughter of the Confederacy in a long dress, at the other the son in a gray uniform. "Your Sons and Daughters will forever guard the memory of your brave deeds," the sign below read. Beneath it appeared another: "National Casket Co."—the name of the sponsor of the float, which won first prize in the commercial division. In the *Confederate Veteran* the company published a picture of the casket company's entry and promised to provide a free twelve-by-eighteen-inch print on request. Honoring the Confederate dead, once the most sacred of duties, was now used to advertise, of all things, a "National" casket. This and other signs of commercialism appeared not in the ads of some irreverent northern company or in the pages of the popular press but in the Confederate celebration's own publications and rituals.[19]

Even more than the perhaps inevitable commercialization, a shift in the social base of the celebration suggested a change in its function and a decline in its importance. A reduced interest in including all of southern society in the celebration is indicated by a subtle shift in the focus of the UCV reunion and by the dramatic difference in the membership of the SCV and UDC compared with that of the UCV. Early reunions had included various social activities, especially for the sponsors, but at the turn of the century their number and prominence in the festival increased. In 1900 Louisville officials decided to add a Grand Ball for the sponsors. The following year Memphis continued to practice and staged, in addition to the march of the veterans, a parade of floral floats. In 1902 Dallas placed the Kaliphs, a local social group that sponsored an annual celebration much like Mardi Gras, in charge of a similar parade and allowed them to participate in the dance. The "kaliphates in their costumes," according to one observer, "gave the scene at times a bizarre cast and afforded considerable amusement." Costumed Kaliphs seemed inappropriate for a celebration honoring the martyrs and servants of the southern cause, but the reunion was becoming less and less a purely Confederate festival. In 1903 a reporter observed that "there is a distinct and growing social side to the Confederate reunion." Two major balls and a host of smaller parties became standard.[20]

The social emphasis resulted in greater distinctions being drawn between the leaders and men of the ranks. At the 1906 reunion in New Orleans a newspaperman discovered "two centers of Reunion life marked clear-cut and distinct" that represented "the two great phases of the Reunion." In the fashionable St. Charles Hotel, "beautiful women, stately, well-clad wearers of the gray and the 'fair women and brave men' of the old Confederacy gathered— with music and laughter and gayety. Down in the Hotel Royal, where ghosts of the past seemed lurking even in the glare of gas and electricity—bivouacked 3000 old soldiers." There the reporter found mostly "men who came from the ranks," wearing "plainest" garb, eating "simplest" fare, and sleeping on cots.[21]

Beginning at the turn of the century veterans complained increasingly that the public's attention centered on the St. Charles. Criticizing the treatment he and his comrades received in New Orleans, one participant concluded "that the

Picture of a float, sponsored by a casket company, that won a prize in a Confederate veterans' parade. *The Confederate Veteran*

Reunions of the Confederate veterans as latterly conducted are not for them, and that society events are the leading features of these gatherings." Four years later a Florida veteran objected that at the Memphis reunion the leaders were "banqueted, wined, dined, and quartered in the very best hotels," but the private had to "shift for himself, stand around on the street, or sit on the curbstone." The Florida vet was not alone in his resentment. Many other veterans, according to commander Stephen Lee, objected to the "prominence of social features to their exclusion and comfort." One woman, somewhat disappointed by her trip to the 1913 reunion, substantiated the veterans' observations. The numerous "social functions entirely independent of the old Veterans," she lamented, left her little chance to talk to the veterans about her father and "to enjoy an uplift of the spirit."[22]

Respect for the veterans and reverence for the past did not disappear from the reunion, but by the end of the decade social activities for the leaders, sponsors, and their guests had become a major, if not the prime, feature. The annual meeting of the UCV became less a public festival of social unity and more a social occasion—primarily for the middle and upper classes. Most of the veterans who attended the balls and parties probably came from the elite, and more certainly the Sons, Daughters, and others who participated with them came overwhelmingly from the middle and upper classes.[23]

Unlike the UCV, which attracted members from a broad spectrum of southern society, the SCV and UDC apparently drew, indeed only wanted to draw, their membership primarily from the middle and upper classes. All available evidence, including two instances in which the occupations of members of a UCV camp can be compared with those of an associated SCV camp, suggests that the Sons had significantly fewer members from the lower and working classes than did the UCV. At the 1905 annual meeting the SCV commander warned of the danger of the Sons becoming "a purely social organization, which judges a man more by his wealth or social position than by the record of his father as a Confederate soldier and his own personal worth and ability." "The son of a common laborer, who was a good soldier," he reminded the members, "is just as much in the intention of our constitution as the son of the mightiest in our land, and if we would accomplish anything we must utilize the common clay, the uncut stone, perhaps the diamond in the rough." The "common clay" probably found inhospitable an organization in which even those who championed the less affluent were patronizing at best.[24]

Although membership records are unavailable, literary evidence indicates that the UDC also had a primarily upper- and middle-class membership. Certainly, the UDC displayed an exclusiveness foreign to the UCV. Where Moorman had begged camps to join the UCV, prospective UDC chapters had to demonstrate their worthiness to unite with the national association. Each new group had to secure the endorsement of an existing chapter within the state so that, as one of the organizers explained, "an objectionable character" who might have the proper credentials but a "daily record" open to question could be kept out. Individual chapters also exercised greater discretion than did UCV camps. One UDC founder talked of accepting only those "to the manor born," and a later president argued that "chapters are not compelled to accept members who are personally objectionable to them, no matter how eligible they are." Most local groups required that applications have the signatures of two members and contain a one-dollar registration fee; the policy certainly discouraged poor strangers from applying.[25]

With a more exclusive membership and attitude within the SCV and UDC than within the UCV and with more obvious social divisions marking its central ritual, the Confederate celebration became more an upper- and middle-class phenomenon. Even though the celebration remained an important aspect of southern culture throughout the first decade of the twentieth century, the changes suggested that it might not continue to do so during the rest of the century. The restrictive membership requirements of the UDC proved particularly important because the Daughters eventually succeeded the Veterans as keepers of the Confederate tradition.

The UCV clearly hoped that the Sons, not the Daughters, would be the ones to keep alive the tradition. Despite occasional expressions of petty jealousy, the UCV supported the SCV in ways it did not support the UDC. In 1903 the Veterans and Sons even worked out an agreement to involve the Sons more fully in the UCV. The plan established a committee on cooperation, gave Sons floor rights at UCV business meetings, authorized them to serve as escorts for the Veterans in parades, and even permitted Sons to wear the gray (but no military rank). Although allowing associate membership for Sons in UCV camps, the agreement urged UCV camps to help organize separate groups of Sons.[26]

Even with the help of the Veterans, the SCV failed to mobilize second-generation Confederates. In 1903 the SCV had 16,000 members in 427 camps. Five years later the number of camps (membership statistics are unavailable) had risen to 580—still roughly a third the number in the UCV. Few of the camps were very active. Only 42 sent delegates to the 1905 reunion, and the celebration of the unveiling of the Davis monument in 1907 drew representatives from only 94. At that reunion Commander Thomas M. Owen of Alabama announced that just 10 camps had responded to a questionnaire he had sent out, and few of them reported any historical or monument work. "The future of the United Sons of Confederate Veterans," Owen wrote in a letter declining to seek reelection, "is not bright with any special promise. Those of us, who have labored in the organization from the beginning, had a right to expect a better result than has been realized." Other observers agreed with Owen that the SCV failed to develop support among male Confederate descendants who showed little interest in organized Confederate activities.[27]

While the Sons failed to organize successfully, many of these observers noted, the Daughters succeeded splendidly. A few independent groups existed, but most women joined the United Daughters of the Confederacy. By 1912 it boasted more than 800 chapters with 45,000 members—probably from two to three times the number of members in the SCV. The same factors that generated the Confederate celebration obviously contributed to the growth of the UDC, but its greater success than the SCV in the twentieth century suggests that more was involved. Not just descendants but women who had lived through the sixties joined the UDC. Women who right after the war had displayed greater hatred than men for the Yankees who had exposed their vulnerability and denied them respect apparently not only continued to harbor their resentments but passed them on to their daughters. Especially for them, but for all Daughters, the preservation and promulgation of the southern view of the war became and remained their goal and passion. The UDC directed most of its effort to the support of the Confederate celebration: It battled for "true" history, raised funds for Confederate monuments, sponsored the observation of Memorial Day and other Confederate holidays, and maintained Confederate museums or relic rooms. Almost every chapter also worked hard to inform its members about Confederate history, and after 1896 a few formed chapters of the Children of the Confederacy to make sure their offspring learned about it too.[28]

The Daughters' interest in education extended to a program to provide higher education for needy sons and daughters of Confederate veterans through a scholarship program at various colleges and universities. Aid went primarily to those who at least aspired to the middle class. On two occasions people asked the UDC to dedicate itself to the education of poor, illiterate whites, and both times it declined. Only the Georgia Division, which supported the Raben Gap Industrial School in the mountains of its state, undertook to help the masses.[29]

The educational work and even the historical activities appealed not only to women still bitter over the war but to those active in other women's clubs and organizations. For such women, many of them reformers, UDC activities constituted yet another form of public service and the emphasis on learning Confederate history yet another means to self-improvement. For Daughters who became leaders, particularly on the state and regional level, the organization even offered a chance to acquire skills not traditionally associated with the female role. They developed organizational and fundraising abilities, and UDC work forced many into the unfamiliar task of public speaking. Frequently, a member rose to address a gathering and confessed that she was "new to the business of speaking in public." At one convention the UDC president asked the members to remember their own "first experience and look lovingly on any mistakes" made by a novice speaker. In conventions leading Daughters also learned much about constitution-making and parliamentary procedure and often seemed to be debating and maneuvering pretty much for the sheer pleasure of it.[30]

Too much could easily be made of the way the UDC expanded the female role, however. Traditional social activities remained very important in the UDC. Many chapters met regularly in homes for tea and refreshments and held an occasional special reception. An Arkansas chapter once gave a party for which members dressed in costumes to suggest the name of a famous Civil War battle. When they arrived, the women played a game of Confederate charades by guessing which battle everyone else represented before they all sat down at an elegant table for a formal dinner. The decorum of the dinner, if not of the game, characterized many of the Daughters' meetings. Traditional social affairs and gentility persisted alongside the new activities.[31]

Many Daughters, in fact, clung to social gentility or traditional roles even when organizational activity called for another approach. A Texas member sent out a printed circular but added a personal note "to rob it of its stiff formality— too formal and too business like (according to my view) to be altogether appropriate for the *Daughters of the Confederacy*." Women who felt comfortable speaking to an assembly of Daughters did not always feel confident in a wider sphere. The UDC president had a man speak for her at the Davis unveiling because she felt that "a great speech should be made for the U.D.C. on this our great occasion. . . . And so well did he fill our wishes and expectations," she added, "that those who had thought I was wrong came to me afterwards and thanked me for asking him to do it."[32]

Moreover, no clear consensus developed within the group of women's issues. Some members apparently supported careers for women outside the home; others did not. Some advocated women's suffrage; others opposed it. In general, though, the Daughters seemed able—and content—to harmonize their expanded activities with the traditional ideal of femininity. "I love the United Daughters of the Confederacy," its president told the 1913 convention, "because they have demonstrated that Southern women may organize themselves into a nation-wide body without losing womanly dignity, sweetness or graciousness; that with a bedrock of sentiment and pride they do their altruistic work for the pure love of it, giving their time and talents without money and without price; their highest and only reward, success of the undertaking and the verdict of their fellow workers, 'Well done, thou good and faithful servant.'"[33]

Within the context of traditional femininity, the UDC offered outlets of expression for very different types of women. Women who still hated the Yankees for killing fathers, husbands, and sons and for violating the protections of the traditional female role found a forum in which to vent their persisting hostilities and to voice their continuing admiration for the men of the Confederacy. If content in traditional female roles, they enjoyed the social activities, approved of the celebration's placing women on pedestals, and found little that seemed unfeminine in the UDC. Others, who joined female reform societies as well as the UDC (and many women did), considered the Daughters' efforts in education and emphasis on patriotism simply another way in which active womanhood could better society. They probably looked upon the Confederate celebration's tales of women's heroic service in wartime as a perfect model. Thus the UDC's programs and view of history united women with somewhat different goals and attitudes. They allowed a significant expansion of women's activities outside the home in the name of conserving the past and without unduly threatening traditional values. They did so at a time when women, as SCV Commander Owen pointed out, had fewer organizations of any kind than men did. The relative scarcity of women's organizations alone may have explained the UDC's success compared with that of the SCV, but the UDC's special and varied functions in the lives of southern women in a period of social change probably was a more important factor.[34]

Because of their organizational strength, the Daughters would take charge of the Confederate tradition when it passed from the Veterans. Before 1913, however, the Veterans did not fully relinquish control, and the women often deferred to their wishes and usually acknowledged a womanly duty to care for them. At times, though, the UDC sought to assert its independence. Even after a public request by Gordon to meet during the UCV reunion, the UDC held its annual convention at a different time and place. When in 1899 the UCV asked the Daughters to cooperate with them in raising funds for the Davis monument, the UDC agreed to undertake the work only if given full responsibility. On occasion, the Daughters' spirit of independence led to disagreements with the Veterans. Two of these disputes, one over the song "Dixie" and the other over a monument to southern women, revealed much about the Daughters' attitudes as well as constituting another sign of declining unity within the celebration.[35]

In 1903 the Alabama Division of the UDC convinced both the Daughters and the Sons that the lyrics of "Dixie" should be changed. No definitive rationale for the revision developed as various proponents of the measure pointed to different problems with the original. Some labeled its Negro dialect more fitting for slaves than for white southerners. Others considered "Dixie" not quite genteel enough for the increasingly middle-class Confederate celebration. "The battle song of a proud and gallant people," claimed one, ought to be written "in the chaste, refined, and educated language of a refined and gallant people." Assuredly, "chaste" and "refined" had more to do with a decorous social world than with the blood and gore of battle. But battlefields were no longer at issue, and the critics sought words "suitable to be sung in parlors."[36]

A few Veterans agreed with the critics, but when the issue was raised at the 1904 UCV reunion one objected to changing the words to please the Daughters. "Dixie" had been the soldiers' song, he asserted, and it suited southern soldiers. The delegates then appointed a committe that studied the matter and the following year reported against revision. The UCV delegates agreed "with the wildest enthusiasm." A Daughter who had been present later told the UDC convention that "if you had heard those old men—and seen them—begging to leave the dear song 'Dixie' unchanged, you would never bring it up for discussion again." The UDC did abandon the idea, although occasionally thereafter individual members tried to revive it. The desire to rewrite "Dixie" revealed again the increasing upper- and middle-class bias of the Sons and Daughters. Historical accuracy, admittedly never of paramount importance in the celebration, now seemed less important than gentility.[37]

The other major controversy, over a monument to southern women, not only exposed differences between the Veterans and Daughters but testified to the division within the UDC itself. Efforts to raise funds for a memorial to the women of the Confederacy had begun in the late nineties, but only in 1906, after the money for the Davis memorial had been raised and the UDC endorsed the women's monument, did they begin in earnest. Unfortunately, the feuding did too. C. Irvine Walker, a Charleston veteran who headed the campaign committee, convinced the Sons, who accepted primary responsibility for the project, to adopt a plan to place one monument of the same design in each state. Not everyone liked his proposal, and major disagreements arose first over whether to have a monument at all and then over what its design should be.[38]

A minority within the UDC favored the establishment of a university or school for women rather than a statue. In 1906 Martha S. Gielow, president of the General Southern Educational Association, and Mrs. Virginia Clay-Clopton, perhaps the most prominent Daughter in the South, asked the SCV to use the money raised for the memorial for an industrial college dedicated to southern women. The Sons rejected the suggestion; some argued that there was not enough money for a school. A few Daughters continued to advocate using the available funds to establish scholarships for females or to support an existing school, but the Sons never reconsidered.[39]

The debate over the design for the monument proved more lively than the one over a school. Walker's committee proposed a statue of a robed woman holding

a sword in one hand and a flag in the other, but many veterans objected to the design. "The defiant expression on the woman's face and her stern hold on the flag are bad enough," wrote Cunningham, "but the sight of her clinched hand around the blade of the sword instantly pains. . . ." Cunningham also took exception to the phrase, "Uphold Our State Rights" at the woman's feet, since the "war is certainly over and our women are not in politics." Another critic agreed and added that the statue had not "a line of womanly grace or modesty or tenderness, not a hint of the dear old home keeper and home builder of the Southland, not a reminder of the sweet and gentle minister of mercy and comfort who bent over the hospital cot and soothed the pain of the wounded soldier and

Designs proposed for the monument to honor the Confederate woman. At left, the design rejected by the Veterans; at right, the Kinney design approved by the Veterans. *The Confederate Veteran*

left in his heart of gratitude forever a true picture of that noblest of all memories of the Confederacy, the patient, self-sacrificing, unwearied helper and comforter of the boys in gray." He hoped that the woman of the monument existed only in the mind of the artist, and apparently the delegates to the 1909 UCV reunion concurred. They rejected, in Cunningham's words, the "Amazonian proportions and warlike attitude of the figure [as] not conforming to the ideals of a true Southern woman." Instead, they selected a design by Belle Kinney of Nashville, which featured a woman representing fame cradling in one arm a "wounded and exhausted Confederate soldier" and with her other hand, as Cunningham described it, "placing a wreath upon the head of the Southern woman, whose every nerve is vibrating with love and sympathy for the soldier and his cause, as expressed by the palm she is trying to place upon his breast, thoroughly unconscious that as her reward a crown is being placed upon her own head."[40]

The UDC, however, objected to the Kinney design. Mrs. George H. Tichenor, a New Orleans Daughter who led the opposition, claimed not to recognize the Confederate soldier who left the field "with head aloft, heart undaunted, and mind resolved upon mastering the stern problems which confronted him . . . in the clumsy utterly prostrated, ignoble weakling of this gruesome design." She also saw nothing of the "lofty-souled woman of the war" in the "willowy, sentimental, frivolous girl with a palm branch in hand." Most of all, the "defeat and weakness" in the scene appalled her.[41]

Neither Tichenor nor other opponents among the Daughters persuaded the committee or the Veterans to abandon the design. Walker's committee succeeded in placing the Kinney design in only two states, however: Mississippi and Tennessee. The unity of the celebration certainly seemed precarious. The veterans clearly wanted a monument to celebrate the Confederate woman as the helpmate if not servant of man and objected to any design that even hinted at an active female role in politics. One group within the UDC opposed the whole idea of a monument because its members thought an industrial school more useful than a stone monument. Another worried not about female advancement but only the dignity of the southern woman and the defeated Confederate soldier.[42]

Neither the disagreement over the woman's monument nor the other disputes within and among Confederate organizations in the first decade of the twentieth century destroyed the Confederate celebration. Nor did the complaints of mistreatment of the old vets at the reunions, nor the growth of commercialism, nor the significant reduction in working-class participation in the Sons and Daughters destroy it. And yet taken together, these developments indicated that by 1913 fundamental changes had occurred in the nature and function of the Confederate tradition.

First, the celebration had become increasingly trivialized. When the Confederate dead were exploited to sell not just caskets, which had at least a logical connection, but stoves, the profound cultural importance of the Confederate tradition was diminished. Memorial drinking fountains with their blend of "Art, Sentiment, and Utility" hardly inspired or reflected reverence. Parties featuring Confederate charades and efforts to revise "Dixie" for Victorian parlors also indicated a frivolous attitude toward the past. So did the emphasis on balls and the participation of the Kaliphs in that most august of rituals, the Confederate veterans' reunion.

Second, the Confederate celebration no longer offered so splendid a model of social unity as once it had. After 1900 many rank and file members of the UCV felt ignored at reunions, which they saw as, and which increasingly were, soirees for the leaders and well-to-do. Neither the SCV nor the UDC attracted—or even seemed to want—members from the working class. As a result, the Confederate rituals and activities no longer mobilized the full participation of all levels of society, as they once had. At the same time, public feuds between the reconciled and irreconciled, fights over the spoils of vindicated defeat, and bickering within and among Confederate organizations disrupted unity.

Third, and perhaps most important, the Sons hardly seemed interested in accepting from their fathers responsibility for the Confederate tradition. The UCV had expected the SCV to succeed it, but males who came to maturity after the war apparently felt little need for a Confederate organization. The UDC did fill a special function within women's lives, so it attracted more members than did the SCV. As the stronger organization, the UDC came to share with the

UCV responsibility for the Confederate tradition. Since women traditionally have served as preservers of cultural values, the Daughters' role was possibly a normal development. But at the height of the Confederate celebration in the nineties, males had directed its activities, and in early twentieth-century America men still dominated public life. The transfer of responsibility for the Confederate tradition to women suggests that the tradition had become less central to society.

The trivialization of Confederate matters, the loss of the model of social unity, the failure of the Sons to accept responsibility—all pointed to the diminishing importance of the Confederate tradition within southern society.

CHAPTER THIRTEEN

Academic Missionaries:
The Challenge of the Professionals

In the twentieth century, the Daughters would not have unchallenged control of the Confederate tradition. At the turn of the century a new group of professional historians also laid claim to the responsibility of preserving the southern past. Most were southerners and shared many of the feelings that led to the celebration, but as professionals they adopted a somewhat different approach to the study of history than that of the Veterans or Daughters. During the first decade of the twentieth century, however, they maintained a tenuous peace with the leaders of the Confederate celebration and indeed participated in it. On the other hand, their emergence, like so many other developments during the period, threatened to disrupt the unity of the Confederate celebration and foretold its declining influence.

The professionalization of history in the South occurred gradually during the late nineteenth and early twentieth centuries. When the first professional historians trained in Europe or the new graduate schools of the North began teaching in the South toward the end of the 1880s, few southern colleges taught history and none offered courses in southern history. Over the next twenty-five years, more young historians, many of them products of Herbert Baxter Adams's seminar at The Johns Hopkins University and, later, of William A. Dunning's at Columbia, accepted positions at southern colleges and universities. These scholars expanded the teaching of history and, more particularly, southern history. In 1913, a survey of eleven universities in the South showed that six had courses in the Civil War and Reconstruction, state history, or some other aspect of southern history. At the University of the South, Vanderbilt, Trinity, Randolph-Macon, and other schools, professors supplemented courses on the United States or the South with active campus historical societies. By that time, too, Alabama, Mississippi, South Carolina, North Carolina, and Arkansas had established state archives for the professional management of historical records.[1]

The growing number of professional historians, archivists, and other scholars in the South included men of various attitudes and beliefs. Historian Yates Snowden of the University of South Carolina, for example, was probably as conservative and traditional a southerner as many of the leaders of the celebration. However, a small but active group of young historians and other scholars—Edwin A. Alderman, John Spencer Bassett, William E. Dodd, Edwin Mims, Samuel Chiles Mitchell, William P. Trent, and a few more—sought to use their professional training to transform the South. While still in college, Mims, who would teach English at both Trinity College and the University of North Carolina before going to Vanderbilt University, worried that being a scholar afforded too little opportunity to bring about changes in the South. When he finally decided to teach literature, Mims resolved to "be as much of a public man as time will allow—trying to reach the people. . . ." Mitchell, a prominent reformer as well as educator, argued that for his generation scholarship became "a form of statesmanship" and a "pragmatic" quest that, along with government and economics, "were the lights to the path of change." Bassett, in 1907 out of the region and living in Massachusetts, recalled that during the "high days of hope" when he taught at Trinity "we thought the redemption of the South was working in us till it was about to burst with its explosive power." Dodd, after he had left Randolph-Macon College for the University of Chicago, compared the study of history in the South to a call to the ministry—to missionary labor, in fact.[2]

Many of these missionary academics considered J.L.M. Curry, the leader of the educational crusade in the South, and Walter Hines Page, the southern critic and reformer who worked in New York publishing, as their mentors. Page in particular maintained close contact with several of them and frequently proffered advice and assistance. Although they never agreed among themselves on a specific program, the missionary academics, like their mentors, thought the "redemption" of the South would come through a combination of strong nationalism, industrial development, education, and progressive social engineering. Not just these men but almost all the new professionals agreed on another point: the need for freedom of thought and speech in the South, even, or especially, when discussing the region's past. They sometimes made their argument in the vocabulary of "scientific history," but as missionaries they themselves displayed little objectivity. Rather, they believed academics should function as social critics, attacking what they considered the excessive conservatism and sentimentality in the South's view of its past. They blamed much of the excess on the veterans and organizations of the Confederate celebration and thought that they themselves should replace the veteran organizations as keepers of the southern past.[3]

In a 1902 article in the *Nation*, William E. Dodd contended that the veterans and their sons who controlled the public conception of history demanded that all history teachers "subscribe unreservedly to trite oaths: (1) that the South was altogether right in seceding from the Union in 1861; and (2) that the war was not waged about the negro." The veterans' organizations, "without critical knowledge or even careful examination of the books used in schools and colleges," helped enforce compliance by making "out a list of authors whose works may be used." In another piece two years later, Dodd reiterated his criticism but escalated his rhetoric by claiming the Confederate veteran "works almost as great havoc in the field of history, although he unquestionably does some good, as does the union veteran in the neighborhood of the United States treasury." In an American Historical Association committee report on the teaching of history in the South, Vanderbilt historian Frederick W. Moore, one of the few northerners among the new professionals, also complained that the veterans controlled the South's perception of history. Like Dodd, he admitted that they did some good, and he expressed more appreciation than Dodd did for the defeated soldiers' need to shape their society's vision of its past. Nonetheless, Moore maintained firmly that the time had arrived for professional historians to assume responsibility for the study of history.[4]

When the new professionals tried to exercise that responsibility in their teaching or writing, they sometimes came under attack by their fellow southerners. During his first semester at the University of Georgia in 1891, John H.T. McPherson, an Adams student from Johns Hopkins, endured a newspaper attack on his choice of an "unsound" text for his history course. In 1892 William P. Trent's critical biography of William Gilmore Simms, a leading novelist of the Old South, provoked a wider controversy. Trent, who had also studied with Adams for a year before going to the University of the South at Sewanee, probably sought to challenge conventional historical attitudes. In the course of chronicling Simm's career, Trent condemned the antebellum South for failing to establish a good common school system and to support a "thrifty middle class." Slavery contributed to both problems, in his view, and was "wasteful and ruinous" as well as a "constant provocation to the indulgence of lowering passions." In the Civil War, southerners "did not and they could not realize that they were fighting, not for the true religion and the higher civilization, but for the perpetuation" of this "barbarous institution and of anarchy disguised." The war was therefore not a conflict between good and evil, Trent argued, but a battle between southern "primitives" and the forces of progress. Fighting for slavery, the South lost because it opposed "progress." The "forces of destiny," Trent believed, "made the North the instrument by which the whole country, North and South, was finally saved for . . . a glorious future."[5]

Few southerners thought Appomattox the place the North saved the South, admitted that the Confederates fought for slavery, or considered themselves "primitives." Many criticized the book and its young author. Trent reportedly doubted whether he could safely visit Simms's home city of Charleston. Even twenty-two years later a Charlestonian who entertained the idea of inviting Trent to speak there congratulated himself for being so open-minded. In Trent's own home town of Richmond, people shunned his mother on the street, and a local paper published a letter from one of his former professors at the University of Virginia questioning whether Trent should be allowed to teach southern youth. Trustees from South Carolina may have tried to remove him from the Sewanee faculty, but the board took no action.[6]

The "virulence of the criticism" surprised Trent but may also have chastened him. He became slightly more circumspect in his criticism of the southern past and in 1898 eagerly accepted an offer to write a biography of Lee. In it he could avoid political questions altogether, Trent observed, and would be able to "pay a tribute to a man of spotless character and great military genius and also incidently to prove to my friends, Southern as well as Northern, that I am not altogether a bloodless critic, but that I can praise generously when I feel praise is deserved." The resulting biography, published in 1899, certainly did praise Lee and in the process hewed a bit closer to the traditional southern interpretation of the war. Trent even criticized Longstreet's tardiness at Gettysburg and pronounced Lee a greater general than Grant. He concluded that there had "seemingly" been "no character in all history that combines power and virtue and charm" as Lee did. He is "with the supreme leaders of all time. He is with the good, pure men and chivalrous gentlemen of all time—the knights *sans peur et sans reproche*."[7]

The new professionals often pointed to the furor over the publication of Trent's biography of Simms as evidence of the need for free speech and inquiry in the South. But like Trent they may also have learned the advantages of avoiding open confrontation with the tradition. In any case, over the next ten to fifteen years the professionals rarely became involved in such public controversies. In 1901 a professor at Grant University in Chattanooga did cause a small stir when he claimed that the United Daughters of the Confederacy, like Emma Goldman, threatened union and order. Two years later Bassett, in a well-known incident, found himself under severe censure after linking Booker T. Washington and Robert E. Lee in an article in the *South Atlantic Quarterly*. Bassett's perfidy, though, had more to do with the violation of racial than historical orthodoxies.[8]

Most professionals not only avoided controversy but paid homage to Confederate pieties. In the decade after the Bassett affair the *South Atlantic Quarterly*, for example, published numerous articles in praise of Lee. Many of the professionals actually joined in the Confederate celebration. Thomas Owen, the Alabama archivist friendly with many of the professionals, and Walter Lynwood Fleming, one of the best-known of the professional historians, served as officers in the SCV. Others, including Dodd, delivered Memorial Day addresses or spoke to various Confederate organizations. Moore sent an article to the *Confederate Veteran*, and the professionals often read, reviewed, and praised the histories written by members of the war generation.[9]

Professionals also sought to involve the Confederate generation in some of their own projects. When Owen, North Carolina historian Stephen B. Weeks, and Hopkins graduate Colyer Meriwether in 1896 organized the Southern History Association to promote the study of the region's past, they brought together professionals, veterans, and amateur historians. The organization's shortlived journal, the *Publications of the Southern History Association*, provided information on the activities of monument and other Confederate organizations, along with book reviews by Dodd, Fleming, and U.B. Phillips— among the best of the young professionals. Its articles, written by older figures of the Confederate celebration as well as professional historians, rarely challenged historical orthodoxies. In fact, only to the extent that it made the Civil War a less central concern by publishing articles on many other aspects of the southern past did it dissent at all from prevailing views.[10]

In two other early twentieth-century publishing projects, the *Library of Southern Literature* and the *South in the Building of the Nation*, the professionals also worked with the veterans and other amateurs. More important, the *LSL* and *SIBN* testified to the professionals' own commitment to the celebration of the South. Charles W. Kent and C. Alphonso Smith, professors of English at the Universities of Virgina and North Carolina respectively, edited the *LSL*, although Joel Chandler Harris and Edwin Alderman loaned their names and prestige as co-editors. George Rines of the *SIBN*'s publishing company did much of the editorial work on it, but all save one of the nine editors for individual topics were professionally trained scholars. Many professionals contributed sketches to one or both of the projects, and several college faculties endorsed the *LSL*.[11]

The *LSL* offered sketches of southern literary figures—with "literary" being very broadly defined—along with selections from their writings. The sketches usually heaped praise upon their subjects, and the collection as a whole made a case for the significance of the region's contribution to the intellectual and cultural life of the nation. The compilers chose material from all periods of southern history, but the Civil War received special attention. The editors and writers deemphasized such divisive issues as slavery and secession, however, and celebrated national reconciliation.[12]

In the *SIBN*, discussion of literature and culture remained secondary to the goal of "trying to give a true and faithful picture of Southern life and progress and to show not only what the South has contributed in the past but to indicate what she is doing to-day." The editors wanted the volumes to "convey not only to the Southerner but to the Northerner as well, a true conception of the history and life of the Southern people" and a sense of the South's contribution to the nation. The title, said the introduction in volume one, explained the purpose. To establish that contribution, the *SIBN* included historical sketches of the individual southern states, of political and economic developments in the region as a whole, and of social and intellectual life in the South. It also presented brief biographical sketches of leading southerners and selections from the region's literature and oratory. Unlike the LSL, as a general history the *SIBN* could not avoid sectional issues. The volume on political history, which was edited by Franklin L. Riley of the University of Mississippi, included essays by U.B. Phillips on "The Slavery Issue in Federal Politics," by J.A.C. Chandler on "The South in the Interpretation of the Constitution," and by George Petrie on "The Principle of Secession Historically Traced." All three, written in a tone of detached scholarship, offered views easily harmonized with the Confederate tradition.[13]

The uncritical, indeed glowing, portrait of southern culture in the *LSL* and *SIBN*, the willingness of the professionals to participate in the Confederate celebration, and the overtures to and respect for the veterans as historians seem anomalous, considering the young professionals' call to free history from the stifling sentimentality of the veterans. Moreover, even though they demanded a more critical approach to the past, the professionals rarely attacked the

Confederate tradition. In fact, they did little to distance themselves from the commonly accepted interpretations of Confederate history.

A few historians rejoiced, along with some other southerners, that slavery had been abolished, and went further in labeling its demise an advance in morality and a step toward progress. Yet few of them actively condemned slavery, and Phillips, one of the best of the new professionals, would soon publish a highly sympathetic account of the institution. The academics rarely challenged southern views on the legality of secession, either, and generally joined in the celebration of the war itself. Always more irreverent than most, Trent said privately that serving on a faculty with two Confederate generals had removed any mystery as to why the South lost, but the others routinely praised the valor of the soldiers and skill of the leaders. Robert E. Lee, who was not considered a champion of slavery or secession and supported reunion after the war, received special praise.[14]

One explanation of the dissonance between the missionary academics' praise for the southern past and their pleas for rigorous criticism is that they failed to live up to their ideal in the face of hostile public opinion. Trent, Bassett, and Dodd eventually left the South, in part because of public hostility and a perceived lack of support for their work. Other southern intellectuals at times did seem slightly intimidated by public opinion. Trent's biography of Lee as well as the *South Atlantic Quarterly*'s publication of an inordinate number of articles on the general after the Bassett affair show that the missionary academics sometimes did seize opportunities to curry favor. But failure of will played only a minor role; the academics frequently displayed intellectual courage, particularly during the Bassett affair. Besides, if they had simply lacked courage, they could have praised the past and said nothing about the need for critical history.[15]

In an era of extremely low salaries for college professors, the money to be made from praising the past apparently influenced some academics. Certainly the scholars who helped with the *LSL* and *SIBN* did so partly for monetary gain. Fleming advertised his books in the *Confederate Veteran* and through the UCV—something that may explain why he castigated the Veterans and Daughters in correspondence but asked that his views be kept private. Although Franklin L. Riley championed scientific history along with the other professionals, when a school text he wrote became involved in an adoption struggle in Arkansas he told his son, who served as his agent there, to "hammer" the competing volume because it devoted more attention to Lincoln than Davis, slighted Jackson, and ignored Admiral Semmes. The competition "devotes nearly 27 pages to 'the heroes who saved the Union' . . . and only about 7 pages . . . to only one Southern hero of the War—General Robert E. Lee," Riley urged his son to remind the selectors. "No one can say that this is doing justice to the South. What will the little children think about the South after studying this book?"[16]

The divergence between the principle of criticism and the practice of praise, however, had more complex sources than either intimidation or financial need. The explanation lay not in a failure of character among the academics but in the social background and sense of mission that generated their desire to transform the South through scholarship. The missionary academics, indeed most of the first generation of professional historians in the South, had been born in the region. Growing up between 1865 and 1890, they had themselves endured the defensiveness of defeat and enjoyed the celebration of the Confederacy. Metaphorically at least, all shared the childhood experience of Wofford College's Henry Nelson Snyder, whose first suit of clothes, after the dresses of infancy, was cut from his father's Confederate uniform. When they left their native region for their professional education and adopted nationalistic attitudes, they did not turn their backs on their past. Like other provincials in a national society, many of them instead became more defensive about their region. Trent praised a speech by Mims for "letting our Northern brethren know that we are not so benighted as they sometime seem to think us," and Kent once criticized a northern publisher because of the absence of southern poets in an anthology of American literature.[17]

Their background, defensiveness, and goals led the academic missionaries to join the celebration of war. They realized that if they attacked the southern view of the Confederacy they denigrated their own heritage and reinforced northern stereotypes. Moreover, in seeking to make the South more like the rest of the nation, they could not afford to alienate its people. Consequently, the academics championed the principles of free and critical inquiry and questioned in general terms the veterans' control of the past, but they dealt carefully—except in Trent's biography of Simms and Bassett's comments on Lee—with the actual interpretation of the past. They paid special obeisance to the heroism and nobility of the Confederate armies and the leadership of Lee, themes of the Confederate tradition that had already been reconciled with nationalism.

With the academics participating in the celebration of the Confederacy, the leaders of the celebration supported the professionalization of history in the South. In 1901 the UCV's historical committee argued that the veterans should look to southern colleges and universities for aid in overcoming the prejudices and untruths surrounding southern history. Two years later, when the committee added eight representatives from the second generation, three of them—Owen, Riley, and R.H. Dabney of the University of Virginia—came from the ranks of the new professionals. The UCV and individual camps frequently advocated the establishment of chairs in American history in southern universities, and the UCV, SCV, and UDC endorsed the creation of state departments of archives.[18]

While harmony reigned between the Confederate organizations and most history professionals at the height of the Confederate celebration, the potential for conflict persisted. The academics' belief in free inquiry made them more tolerant of differing views of the southern past than were the more ardent members of the Confederate societies. In addition, the ideology of professionalism led the academics to consider themselves the only ones with the expertise to delineate the past properly, an attitude the nonprofessionals naturally resented. Between 1908 and 1913, three public confrontations occurred between the professionals and the Confederate organizations.

In 1908 Edwin A. Alderman, C. Alphonso Smith, and the president of

Columbia University served as judges for a UDC prize for the best essay on the War Between the States by a white student at Teachers College. The three awarded the prize to Christine Boyson of Minnesota for her paper on Robert E. Lee. In the *Confederate Veteran*, Cunningham objected to Boyson's contention that the southern people before the war were intellectually dead and ignorant, that Lee struggled with inferior assistants, and that western leaders of the army were incompetent. "It seems most unfortunate," he concluded, "that the prize paper given out by the United Daughters of the Confederacy, under the critical examination of the eminent scholars at the head of . . . highly reputable schools of learning" should praise "Lee at the expense of nearly all that is true of the South and her people." The historian-general for the UDC distributed a protest, and local UCV and UDC groups in almost every state condemned the award. Mrs. Norman V. Randolph, who led the attack in Richmond, raised most of the objections Cunningham had and added the charge that Boyson had labeled Lee a "traitor." Randolph considered Alderman and Smith, as southerners, especially culpable and demanded they provide an explanation. In the meantime, a relative of Smith's reported, the two became "the piece de resistance" of at least one tea in the city.[19]

The relative expected Smith to think the protests "funny," but neither he nor Alderman seemed terribly amused. A friend described Alderman as "slightly disturbed in his dreams" over the matter. Alderman and Smith published defenses in the local newspapers and later sent them to the *Confederate Veteran*. In his letter to the Richmond papers, Alderman began with a series of excuses as to why he might not have done a good job: He was ill, he was in a rush to leave for Europe, he had been given little guidance by the UDC about how to judge the essays. He explained that he did not hold college students to scientific standards and had made allowances because the essay had been written in the North. It included some misstatements and false generalizations, Alderman acknowledged. He assuredly did not agree with everything in it. But Miss Boyson was not mean-spirited and certainly did not label Lee a traitor. Alderman concluded with assurances as to his own orthodox opinion of the southern hero.[20]

Smith, who taught at the University of North Carolina but expected soon to join Alderman at the University of Virginia, sent his letter to the Raleigh *News and Observer*, which had placed Mrs. Randolph's charges on page one. Smith adopted a far less defensive tone, claimed to have done a conscientious job, and stood by the decision. He ignored all other charges against the essay and disputed Mrs. Randolph on the "traitor" issue. Boyson used the word, Smith pointed out, but in her protest Randolph misquoted Boyson by leaving out part of the sentence that made it clear that Lee was only a traitor to the extent Washington had been one. The theme of the Boyson paper, in fact, was the patriotism of both sides. If it had tried to show Lee or the "humblest soldier" as a traitor, Smith added, he would not have finished reading it. Like Alderman, he reaffirmed his own respect for Lee and then in effect wrapped himself in the Confederate flag. He had written this letter, he declared, under the gaze of the uncle for whom he was named, a soldier who had died following Jackson and whose portrait hung in his study. How could the Richmond chapter label one who bore his name a vilifier of Lee? Smith confidently concluded, "I submit the case, Mrs. Randolph, to every man and woman who knows the heritage of Confederate blood or who honors the simple justice of the Confederate cause."[21]

A few judged Alderman and Smith innocent of the charge of disloyalty. Several North Carolina UDC chapters, which apparently saw only two native Tarheels under attack by hostile Virginians, supported them. The Daughter who had first suggested the essay contest defended the award to Boyson on the ground that the offending passages could be explained. The statement about the South's having been ignorant before the war, for example, did not bother her once she realized it obviously referred to the great mass of people. The UDC convention, however, passed a resolution dissenting from the judges' decision. Cunningham, who had printed none of Smith's letter and only enough of Alderman's to dispute it, concluded in his "Last Words" on the subject that the "entire South agrees in its condemnation not of Miss Boyson or the opinions she held, but of the acceptance of these opinions by Southern judges." The opponents of the award had successfully challenged the idea of trusting the Confederate tradition to academics. Many professors, though, thought the defenses by Smith and Alderman heroic and the outcome a great triumph for the two. Some may have feared that the controversy would keep Smith from getting a chair at the University of Virginia and interpreted the fact that it did not as a victory. If victory it was, it came partly because the professionals defended themselves by reaffirming the basic tenets of the Confederate tradition, not by unabashedly championing the critical spirit.[22]

In 1911 Enoch M. Banks, a native southerner who taught history and economics at the University of Florida, learned that the critical spirit sometimes had its costs. In an article in a national magazine, the *Independent*, Banks asserted that slavery had led the South to put such emphasis on state sovereignty that the institution could be considered the "fundamental cause of secession and the Civil War." Slavery had been an anachronism and secession a bad policy, Banks continued. Since people who align themselves with the "best interests of an advancing civilization are in the right in the highest and best sense of the term right," Banks believed people of his day had to conclude "that the North was relatively in the right, while the South was relatively in the wrong." A state senator in Florida considered that conclusion and other statements in the article dangerous to the university and urged the Sons and Daughters to condemn Banks. The state president of the UDC called for Bank's resignation, and rumors circulated that the legislature might cut the university's funds. At that point Banks resigned. Ironically, he had published the article in part to demonstrate that "conditions are changing, and that the South is becoming more tolerant of a free discussion of its past and present policies."[23]

The same year a controversy that had quietly begun at Roanoke College in Salem, Virginia, spread to the rest of the South. In the fall of 1910, Judge William W. Moffett, a local Confederate veteran who served on the college's board of trustees, objected to the treatment of slavery and the Civil War in the text assigned to his daughter at the college, Henry W. Elson's *History of the*

United States. Moffett complained to Roanoke's president, John A. Morehead, who discussed the matter with the young woman's professor, Herman J. Thorstenberg, and assured himself that Elson's text was used "in such fashion that nothing unfavorable to the South would actually be taught in the classroom." Morehead relayed the assurances to Moffett and urged him to drop the matter. The judge refused, and after an unsatisfactory exchange of letters with Thorstenberg in 1911 convinced the local newspaper to demand the abandonment of Elson's *History.* The paper and other critics claimed that the book contained a variety of libels and errors. Elson's *History* maintained that slavery caused the war and used the term "slaveholder's rebellion." In a passage critics found particularly offensive, the text argued that masters slept with their slaves and, referring to a statement by a sister of James Madison, that "though the southern ladies were complimented with the name of wife, they were only the mistress of the seraglio."[24]

After the newspaper attack, the northern-born, Yale-trained Thorstenberg began to receive threats from local citizens, and many alumni complained about the use of the text. In a stormy session the board vindicated the professor but ordered that Elson's *History* no longer be used. Still unsatisfied, Moffett objected to the support for Thorstenberg and the fact that the offensive book remained in the hands of some students. He recruited local UCV and UDC groups for the fight, and criticism of the college and its president intensified. Over the next two months, the faculty, the president, and even the author of the text responded. The faculty strongly defended academic freedom but reassured the critics that "Roanoke College is a southern institution with southern traditions. . . ." It explained that the books had not been taken from the students because they were private property. The president, too, championed academic freedom, but added that he knew the South's case was strong enough to withstand scrutiny and quoted both Lee and Gordon on the need to avoid bitterness. He claimed he had suggested discontinuing use of the book not because it was dangerous but in deference to the feelings of the veterans and in the interest of harmony. In a letter to the newspapers, Elson admitted that his single·use of the term "slaveholder's rebellion" was illchosen, hedged his statements on miscegenation by saying only a "small" percentage of slaveholders was guilty of it, and argued that he never said southerners fought for slavery but only that the institution was the cause of the estrangement of the sections.[25]

Though conciliatory, none of the responses mollified the critics. The *Confederate Veteran,* which had entered the controversy, escalated its criticism of the college. Cunningham took little consolation from the removal of the book and dismissed the notion of academic freedom out of hand: "To a Southern man who is sane *death* would be preferred to *liberty* that licenses the use of that vile history in the schools of the South." He even printed an anonymous letter pointing out that much of the college's support came from the North and concluding that the president and "faculty think they must give a *quid pro quo.*" Many UDC chapters and UCV camps over the South joined the protest, and the 1911 annual meetings of the UCV, UDC, and CSMA passed resolutions condemning the use of Elson's *History.* Over the summer, the controversy at

Roanoke College burned itself out, fortunately before anyone learned that Morehead had originally offered Thorstenberg's position to Elson.[26]

Loyal Confederates in other areas soon learned of additional colleges that used Elson's *History*, and their professors had to defend themselves. J.G. de Roulhac Hamilton, professor of history at the University of North Carolina, and Yates Snowden, professor of history at the University of South Carolina, had to answer irate UDC women. Both men assured the Daughters that they already understood the problems in Elson's *History* and planned to discontinue its use. At the University of Texas, Eugene Barker of the History Department explained the adoption of the book to the university's president after he had received a complaint. Barker did lament the remarks about relations between masters and their female slaves but defended the book as "in the main a very useful one" and the author as "generally . . . fair." In closing, Barker reminded the president that Barker was himself a "southern man," a life-long Texan, whose grandfathers and uncles served in the Confederate army. "And you may assure [the complainant] that my desire to have students correctly informed in the history of our country is as strong as his own." Despite Barker's defense, the university board of regents informed the UDC that the book "will not be in use much longer," or at least so reported a Texas Daughter at the next convention.[27]

The controversy over Elson's *History* at the University of Texas had an interesting twist. George W. Littlefield, an extraordinarily wealthy Texas Confederate veteran, also asked Barker if the offending text was assigned to students there. Barker replied that it was, as one of eight or ten, and sent along a copy of his letter to the president. Several months later he wrote Littlefield again to discuss the dire need for an endowment to support a chair of southern history and to finance the purchase of books and documents in the field. Barker contended that the new generation of historians was almost totally free of sectional bias and would write truthful history if only they had the necessary materials. The South, however, lagged far behind the North in assembling them. "Until this collection is made," he warned Littlefield, "the resolutions and protests of patriotic societies against the misrepresentations of the South are 'as sounding brass and tinkling symbols.'" Barker closed saying he hoped such a project would "appeal to you, and that some means will occur to you for obtaining the necessary funds." Apparently, it did not. In April of the following year Barker took the occasion of Littlefield's forwarding a UCV camp resolution on another book to remind him money was needed to ensure fair histories of the South. In 1914 Littlefield gave $25,000 for the project, but two years later the shameless Barker once again asked for and received more money. The truth of history did not come cheap. The Littlefield Fund, however, proved a major spur to the professional study of southern history.[28]

The Barker-Littlefield interchange neatly symbolizes the relations between the new academics and the older keepers of the Confederate tradition as of 1913. Tensions had developed between the two, but enough of a shared sense of purpose existed for them to work together in preserving the heritage of the South. Young professionals, especially the missionary academics, had questioned the veterans' use and control of history but rarely challenged the reigning interpretations of the Confederate tradition. Consequently, relations between them and the older organizations remained generally harmonious. Yet UCV and UDC distrust of the views of the professionals developed and occasionally led to heated disagreements.

The growing tensions suggested that a time would come when southern scholars might not be considered trustworthy keepers of the tradition. In fact, many members of later generations of professionals did accept interpretations of the war considered heretical by an increasingly conservative United Daughters of the Confederacy. But perhaps more than dangerous, the professionals became irrelevant. Twentieth-century academics generally did not seek and assuredly did not play so prominent a role in society as the early professionals had. More and more, they talked to and wrote for one another, and less and less did the general public listen to or read them. The twentieth-century debate among professionals about the causes, nature, and meaning of the war, a contentious and continual one, had limited influence on the larger southern society.

Conclusion

A 1911 *Atlanta Constitution* headline, "Gray Veterans Limp in Parade," captured the effect on the reunion of the Confederate veterans' advancing age. Officials began to shorten the parade route, and the fear grew that some veterans might succumb along the way. That year, in fact, three did die during the reunion. However, by the time age became an important factor in the festivities, the Confederate celebration had helped convince southerners that the triumph prophesied since Appomattox had arrived. After half a century, the *Constitution* editorialized in 1911, the South "hails" the veterans in their reunion as "conquerors." "For the south today is a south with the smile of victory in her eyes, the beauty of peace and the lure of dawning destiny in her features. And these old men—tottering, maimed, but with spirits untouched by time—are the molders of that destiny, sponsors for a rehabilitation the world must yet live long to duplicate."[1]

During the next two years, the rehabilitation proceeded. In November 1912, southern-born Woodrow Wilson was elected President of the United States. Even before his victory, Edwin A. Alderman, one of the missionary academics, considered Wilson's national role "a sort of fulfillment of an unspoken prophecy lying close to the heart of nearly every faithful son of the South that out of this life of dignity and suffering, and out of this discipline of fortitude and endurance there would spring a brave, modern national minded man to whom the whole nation, in some hour of peril and difficulty would turn for succor and for helpfulness." Southerners flocked to Washington for the inauguration, and the rebel yell and "Dixie" greeted the approach of the southerners in the parade. As one historian has pointed out, Wilson's "election was a kind of vindication for the South," which had "'come back to rule the Union.'"[2]

In the summer after Wilson's inauguration, veterans of both armies gathered at Gettysburg to commemorate the fiftieth anniversary of the battle. There too ex-Confederates found vindication. In urging his fellow veterans to attend, C. Irvine Walker explained, "We, the people of the reunited nation, . . . held back from formally acknowledging the acceptance of the peace for several reasons. We thought that the overtures should come from the successful parties; we believed that it should be authoritatively offered; and above all, we only wanted it, if it was sincere." "The time seems to have come when we can honorably accept overtures of Peace and *I think we should*," Walker concluded. Many fellow southerners agreed. The UCV endorsed the reunion, and more than eight thousand Confederates joined more than forty-four thousand Federals on the battlefield. (Somewhere, no doubt, Early revelled in the North's overwhelming numbers.) The former foes reenacted Pickett's charge, heard a speech by President Wilson, and generally enjoyed one another's fellowship. "And as we came away there was this reflection and this sweet memory," wrote one ex-Confederate who participated, "There had been no apology, no explanation, no expression of regret, no humiliation, no retraction, no recanting. Each conceded to the other the well-earned right to boast his prowess, each honored the loyalty and zeal and skill of the other, each acknowledged that the other had been a 'foeman worthy of his steel.'"[3]

The sense of triumph southerners derived from such occasions involved little that had been at issue in the war. As the editorial in the *Constitution* made clear, "the smile of victory" reflected success in rebuilding southern society and southern influence within the nation. Southerners smiled too because such events as the Gettysburg reunion demonstrated that the North considered them worthy foes, not rebels and traitors. Southerners no longer thought the nation expected them "to dry up . . . and make out like [they] wasn't there," in Bill Arp's words of 1865. Finally, they believed, everyone realized the Confederates had "made a bully fite" of which "the whole American nation" felt proud.

The Confederate celebration had not only helped create this sense of triumph and confidence, in the process it had subtly influenced the development of the New South. The memory of the war helped bolster white supremacy, of course. Yet racism was not as overt in or as central to the Confederate celebration as one might suspect, and southerners employed its symbols in behalf of a wide spectrum of racial thought. After all, in the 1880s Cable had invoked Lee, albeit unsuccessfully, in the cause of racial liberalism. And although in 1900 a white mob in New Orleans gathered at the Lee monument before setting off on a murderous attack on blacks, six years later following a similar riot in Atlanta one racial conservative summoned the spirit of Lee in behalf of moderation and fair play. Nevertheless, the celebration did reinforce white supremacy. Accounts of good and dutiful slaves and the appearance of faithful blacks at reunions provided models intended to teach the "new Negro" born since slavery how to behave. And the celebration's symbols of unity could be and were employed in the fight for disfranchisement and segregation.[4]

In politics, as in race relations, the memory of the war could be employed in the service of widely varying goals. Farmers' Alliance lecturers and even a socialist newspaper editor attempted to ally their cause with the Confederacy's. Conservative Democrats, however, proved themselves the masters at evoking the Confederate tradition and did so in order to defeat the Populists and other groups that proposed alternatives to Democratic rule and the emerging order in the South. Grady's manipulation of Davis's 1886 visit to Atlanta in behalf of Gordon's campaign for the governorship proved only the most egregious example. Stories abound of the exploitation of the Confederate tradition, both before and after the celebration began, by Bourbon Democrats. Many a Democratic candidate in the late nineteenth century called on his fellow southerners to stand with him now as he had stood with those at Gettysburg or some other battlefield. If he could substantiate his claim by displaying an empty sleeve, his chances of victory improved, unless of course he campaigned against a one-legged veteran. In Louisiana, Francis T. Nichols, who had lost an arm and a leg in the Civil War, seemed unbeatable. Such evocations of and appeals to the memory of the war often succeeded. As Rebecca Felton pointed out, "the politicians on both sides have worked these war issues, *ad infinitum*, to keep the offices of the country in their own grasp." But, as Felton also commented, in the South Democrats shrewdly mixed pleas to remember the Confederacy with even louder calls to vote for them in order to maintain white supremacy or to prevent a return to Reconstruction.[5]

The Confederate celebration was primarily a cultural movement, despite the racial or political uses to which it was put. It helped create what Lawrence Goodwyn has aptly described as "patterns of deference," and in doing so contributed most significantly not just to Democratic electoral success but to the emergence of the New South. The model of social unity and the example of the loyal common man at the heart of the Confederate celebration's historical interpretation and its ceremonies helped hold southern society together during the social and economic tensions of the late nineteenth century. The acting out in its rituals of social solidarity, respect for loyal followers, and deference to leaders helped foster the cultural patterns that made political revolt or racial reform so difficult. The celebration thereby not only contributed to the failure of the Populists' challenge to the established order, it helped imbue the New South with values and attitudes that rendered it a particularly conservative society. The celebration prized order, deference to authority, and tradition—and so too did the New South. The Confederate tradition emphasized personal loyalty to leaders—an attitude that at least one historian has identified as important in shaping southern labor relations and that also characterized life in many small southern towns. It also taught unquestioning allegiance to the nation and encouraged a martial spirit—both characteristics of the twentieth-century South.[6]

Because it was used against political dissenters and supported patterns of deference did not mean that the Lost Cause was a delusion or a trick played by clever conservatives on the southern common folk. The Confederate celebration appealed to a broad range of southerners, and its popularity owed little to shrewd exploitation by an elite. Workers took the lead in organizing Richmond's Lee Camp and continued to join other Confederate societies. Members of the middle class founded the UCV and constituted its main strength. Indeed, a substantial cross-section of the southern population helped propagate the Confederate celebration. Southerners did so because it met certain needs. Members of the middle class who participated in such large numbers found in it a sense of community and a support for order in a world they perceived as fragmented and disorderly. Struggling in an increasingly competitive and individualistic economy and society and suffering the ravages of recession and depression in the late 1880s and early 1890s, they relished the memory of their self-sacrifice during the war, when money meant little and the common good almost everything. They as well as the veterans from the working class enjoyed the homage paid them in the celebration. The orators and monuments testified to their importance, to their heroism, to their honor. If they went to a reunion, huge crowds cheered them as they marched. In their local camps, they knew that when they died their death would be marked. To twentieth-century readers such things may seem paltry reward when weighed against the abuses of the Lost Cause by politicians. But Confederate soldiers scarred by battle and defeat found great personal satisfaction in them.[7]

Southerners supported the Confederate celebration, in sum, not because they lacked the sophistication to see through the trick played by conservatives but because they found its activities satisfying. It helped them cope with defeat and provided special comfort for the veterans. It allowed southerners to distance themselves from the issues of the war without repudiating the veterans. After the Spanish-American War, the North joined the celebration, resulting in a rapid reconciliation of former foes. The rapid healing of national divisions and damaged southern self-image, however, came at the cost of deriving little insight or wisdom from the past. Rather than looking at the war as a tragic failure and trying to understand it, or even condemn it, Americans, North and South, chose to view it as a glorious time to be celebrated. Most ignored the fact that the nation had failed to resolve a debate over the nature of the Union and to eliminate the contradictions between its equalitarian ideals and the institution of slavery without resort to a bloody civil war. Instead, they celebrated the war's triumphant nationalism and martial glory. Southerners participated in the celebration, even though they had lost the war. Surprisingly, they never questioned whether defeat implied something was wrong with their cause or their society. Their cause had been just and their failure the result only of overwhelming numbers, they concluded. Conceivably, defeat might have impelled them to question the morality of slavery and, in the process, of southern race relations. It might have led southerners to be more skeptical of their nation's sense of innocence and omnipotence. But it did not. Late nineteenth-century southerners gained little wisdom and developed no special perspective from contemplating defeat. Although it served to justify the cause and therefore its veterans, the Confederate celebration did not so much sacralize the memory of the war as it sanitized and trivialized it.

In the 1920s and 1930s many southerners still remembered and talked about the war, although probably intellectuals and artists did so more often than businessmen and workers. The decline in the social and cultural importance of the Confederate tradition, already visible in 1913, continued nonetheless. The Confederate celebration's interpretation of the war helped ensure that it would.

By helping secure the long-sought northern affirmation of southern heroism and by celebrating southern vindication it dramatically reduced persisting southern fears of dishonor. The social tensions of the late nineteenth century, another factor that had contributed to the need for the celebration, also declined. Even as it had helped ease the fears of dishonor and disorder, the Confederate tradition became commercialized, further trivialized, and divided. By 1913 the memory of the war was being used to sell cook stoves and caskets, to promote good roads and good language, to defend rabid white supremacy and racial moderation. The Veterans, Daughters, and the new professionals did not always agree on how it should be interpreted, much less on how it should be employed. Defused and diminished by so many diverse meanings and uses, the Confederate tradition lost much if not all of its cultural power.[8]

The tradition's decline in influence and importance owed even more to the fact that after 1913 little institutional structure survived to sustain the memory of the war. Fewer and fewer towns put up monuments. Confederate reunions continued to be held, but they were increasingly regarded as curiosities rather than important festivals. The SCV never became an important group, and the more successful UDC exercised only limited influence. Its annual conventions never had the hold on the South's population that the Veterans' reunions did. Both Sons and Daughters contributed to their own decline by limiting their activities to the middle and upper classes, and the professionals, too, spoke to a smaller audience as later generations of academics exhibited less interest than the first in missionary work among the people.

In the late 1920s schoolboys in three Alabama cities cited Lincoln more often than Lee as a historical or public character after whom they wished to model themselves—and both Lincoln and Lee ranked well below Washington and Lindbergh. A survey begun in the thirties found that southerners more often used "Civil War" rather than "the War Between the States" to designate the conflict of 1861–65. The concerns and shibboleths of the Confederate tradition had faded from public consciousness. By the time of the Civil War centennial, according to two historians who traced the persistence of the Lost Cause into the present, the memory of the war no longer touched southern lives as once it had. Recent survey data from one state confirmed their conclusion.[9]

To be sure, some southerners remained fascinated by the war. A few irreconcilables still railed against the Yankees and talked of winning next time. Civil War buffs studied the history of the war, roamed its battlefields, and collected its relics. Such writers as Faulkner transformed stories of the war into meditations on the South, history, and the human condition. Each group saw the war differently, though; each used the memory for its own purposes. And most southerners paid little attention to their efforts. The development of the Confederate tradition had not erased the memory of the war but had trivialized it and failed to establish one commonly accepted interpretation, thereby limiting its importance within southern culture.

Almost alone among postwar attitudes, southern defensiveness persisted. The Confederate celebration never completely eased southern disquiet. The comments of the Confederates who went to Gettysburg in 1913 implied a persisting need for reassurance. Even the missionary academics, the young southern professionals who thought themselves so far removed from the sectionalism of the 1860s, fell prey to it. After 1913, the North, which in the first decade or so of the twentieth century had joined in the South's celebration, did not always speak so highly of the region. American popular culture sometimes portrayed the South as a land of "moonlight and magnolias" or a place of grace and gentility, but usually set such images in the past. Often, northerners were decidedly less charitable about the southern present. In the 1920s H.L. Mencken parodied the region as "The Sahara of the Bozart," a desert devoid of culture, and a host of other journalists and academics attacked the South as a benighted, violent land. In the 1930s the region was seen as a place of poverty and suffering, in the 1950s as the home of Klansmen and rednecks. In the North a southern accent was no longer taken as a sound of rebellion but was often considered a sign of backwardness and stupidity. Twentieth-century southerners resented such stereotypes just as their forebears had resented being called rebels. Long after the memory of Appomattox had faded, the northern attacks on the South and southerners kept alive postwar defensiveness.[10]

In response, southerners still occasionally seized the symbols of the war in the form of cartoons of old veterans, Confederate monuments, and rebel flags. Such paraphernalia as well as the history of the Confederacy could be used to support almost any cause. Occasionally, liberals like James McBride Dabbs or C. Vann Woodward, like Cable before them, invoked the southern past to promote racial progress or some other change. More often, conservatives or reactionaries, such as the Confederate flag wavers in segregationist mobs, claimed it for their own cause. But when they did, the symbols of the Confederacy stood for no coherent ideology or tradition. They only symbolized defiance: "Hell, no, I ain't forgettin,'" they said. "You can't push me around. We southerners made our stand long ago and will again."[11]

The stand no longer had much to do with the memory of the Civil War because the manner in which the Confederate tradition had developed in the late nineteenth century eliminated its specificity and power. The New South of the twentieth century remained a land haunted by the ghosts of the Confederacy. The ghosts had helped make it a conservative, deferential society; they had contributed to an unquestioning patriotism and respect for the military. Sometimes they had supported the cause of reaction. They were not ancestral spirits who exercised constant or crucial influence, however. Rather, they were phantoms called forth from time to time by various people for differing purposes. The ghosts of the Confederacy had shaped the New South, but in the twentieth century they had become too elusive and ephemeral to define its identity.

Frequently Used Abbreviations

AANVA: Association of the Army of Northern Virginia
AAT: Association of the Army of Tennessee
CSA: Confederate Survivors' Association
LMA: Ladies' Memorial Association
SCV: Sons of Confederate Veterans/United Sons of Confederate Veterans
SHA: Southern History Association
SHS: Southern Historical Society
UCV: United Confederate Veterans
UDC: United Daughters of the Confederacy
CV: *Confederate Veteran*
CWH: *Civil War History*
DR: *DeBow's Review*
GHQ: *Georgia Historical Quarterly*
HMPEC: *Historical Magazine of the Protestant Episcopal Church*
JMH: *Journal of Mississippi History*
JSH: *Journal of Southern History*
LWL: *The Land We Love*
MQ: *Mississippi Quarterly*
NCHR: *North Carolina Historical Review*
NE: *The New Eclectic*
OLOD: *Our Living and Our Dead*
PSHA: *Publications of the Southern History Association*
SAQ: *South Atlantic Quarterly*
SB: *The Southern Bivouac*
SHSP: *Southern Historical Society Papers*
SM: *The Southern Magazine*
SR: (1867–81) *The Southern Review*
(1902–82) *Sewanee Review*
THQ: *Tennessee Historical Quarterly*
VMHB: *Virginia Magazine of History and Biography*

CSMA Minutes:	*Minutes of the Annual Convention, Confederated Southern Memorial Association*
HCMAS:	Confederated Southern Memorial Association, *History of the Confederated Memorial Associations of the South* (New Orleans: Graham Press, 1904)
Proceedings of Grand Camp:	*Proceedings of the Grand Camp Veterans, Department of Virginia*
UCV Minutes:	*Minutes of the Annual Meetings and Reunions of the United Confederate Veterans*
UCV General Orders:	*Orders, U.C.V., General and Special*, ed. William E. Mickle, 2 vols. (New Orleans: United Confederate Veterans, 1911–12)
UDC Minutes:	*Minutes of the Annual Meetings of the United Daughters of the Confederacy*
USCV Minutes:	*Minutes of the Annual Meetings of the United Sons of Confederate Veterans*
LHAC:	Louisiana Historical Association Collection
UCVA:	United Confederate Veterans Association
AG Lpb:	Adjutant General's Letterpress book
AG Lb:	Adjutant General's Letter box
ADAH:	Alabama Department of Archives and History, Montgomery.
UAL:	Special Collections, Amelia Gayle Gorgas Library, University of Alabama, University.
AHS:	Atlanta Historical Society, Atlanta, Ga.
Duke:	Manuscript Department, Perkins Library, Duke University, Durham, N.C.
JUL:	Manuscript Department, Joint Universities Library, Vanderbilt University, Nashville, Tenn.
LC:	Library of Congress, Washington, D.C.
LSU:	Manuscript Department, Hill Memorial Library, Louisiana State University, Baton Rouge.
MDAH:	Mississippi Department of Archives and History, Jackson.
NCDAH:	North Carolina Department of Archives and History, Raleigh.
SCHS:	South Carolina Historical Society, Charleston.
SCL:	South Caroliniana Library, University of South Carolina, Columbia.
SHC:	Southern Historical Collection, University of North Carolina, Chapel Hill.
TSL:	Tennessee State Library, Nashville.
Tulane:	Manuscript Department, Howard-Tilton Memorial Library, Tulane University, New Orleans, La.
UTSL:	Library, Union Theological Seminary, Richmond, Va.
UTX:	Archives Collection, University of Texas, Austin.
UVA:	Manuscript Department, University of Virginia Library, Charlottesville.
VHS:	Virginia Historical Society, Richmond.
VSL:	Virginia State Library, Richmond.

Notes

INTRODUCTION

1. Tupelo, Mississippi, *Daily Journal*, 3 February and 27 March 1984. I thank Charles R. Wilson for bringing the events in Ripley to my attention.

2. "Southerners" and "South" will be used here as shorthand for the more correct "white southerners" and "the white South." Obviously, black southerners had a different view of the meaning of the war. In many ways, the defeat of the white South was a victory for them. The qualifying word *white* will be added occasionally to remind the reader of the issue.

3. Kenneth M. Stampp, "The Southern Road to Appomattox," *The Imperiled Union: Essays on the Background of the Civil War* (New York: Oxford University Press, 1980), pp. 246–69; James L. Roark, *Masters Without Slaves: Southern Planters in the Civil War and Reconstruction* (New York: W. W. Norton, 1977), pp. 35–108.

4. The term "tradition" is used here essentially as it is defined in the dictionary. Michael Kammen, *A Season of Youth: The American Revolution and the Historical Imagination* (New York: Alfred A. Knopf, 1978) also uses tradition as a conceptual approach to the function of history. History plays a role in the culture of almost every society; the postwar South is far from unique in that respect (a fact that historians sometimes seem to forget). See Eric Hobsbawm, "The Social Function of the Past: Some Questions," *Past and Present* 55 (May 1972): 3. In a more recent work, Hobsbawm and others discuss what they term "invented tradition." Their findings on the role of these traditions in England and Europe parallel mine on the South on a number of points. However, they use "tradition" primarily to refer to the rituals rather than the body of cultural attitudes as I do, and I find the term "invented" not entirely satisfactory for describing the Lost Cause because of its deep roots in the needs and attitudes of a large part of the population. See Eric Hobsbawm and Terence Ranger, eds., *The Invention of Tradition* (Cambridge: Cambridge University Press, 1983).

For a helpful definition of *ritual* see Roland A. Delattre, "The Rituals of Humanity and the Rhythms of Reality," *Prospects* 5 (1980): 35–49. The approach to the study of rituals and ceremonial activities here owes much to the essays in Clifford Geertz, *The Interpretation of Cultures: Selected Essays* (New York: Basic Books, 1973) and other works cited later in the text.

5. Julian L. Street, *American Adventures: A Second Trip "Abroad at Home"* (New York: Century Company, 1917), p. 194.

6. C. Vann Woodward, *Origins of the New South, 1877–1913* (Baton Rouge: Louisiana State University Press, 1951), pp. 142–74.

7. *Ibid.*, *passim*. For a summary of the debate over this issue see James Tice Moore, "Redeemers Reconsidered: Change and Continuity in the Democratic South, 1870–1900," *Journal of Southern History* 44 (August 1978): 357–78; and Harold D. Woodman, "Sequel to Slavery: The New History Views the Postbellum South," *JSH* 43 (November 1977): 523–54. Jonathan M. Wiener, *Social Origins of the New South, Alabama 1860–1885* (Baton Rouge: Louisiana State University Press, 1978) portrays both the veterans' movement and the Lost Cause as part of the persisting influence of a planter ideology.

8. Edmund Wilson, *Patriotic Gore: Studies in the Literature of the American Civil War* (New York: Oxford University Press, 1962); Daniel Aaron, *The Unwritten War: American Writings and the Civil War* (New York: Alfred A. Knopf, 1973). On sectional reunion see Joyce Appleby, "Reconciliation and the Northern Novelists, 1865–1880," *Civil War History* 10 (June 1964): 117–29; Rebecca W.S. Lee, "The Civil War and Its Aftermath in American Fiction, 1861–1899, with a Dictionary Catalogue and Indexes" (Ph.D. diss., University of Chicago, 1932); Robert A. Lively, *Fiction Fights the Civil War: An Unfinished Chapter in the Literary History of the American People* (Chapel Hill: University of North Carolina Press, 1957), pp. 42–43, but cf. 48. On northern writing, see Lively, pp. 22–32; Sheldon Van Auken, "The Southern Historical Novel in the Early Twentieth Century," *JSH* 14 (May 1948): 157–91. On local color genre see Alfred Y. Wolff, Jr., "The South and the American Imagination: Mythical Views of the Old South, 1865–1900" (Ph.D. diss., University of Virginia, 1971); and Michael A. Flusche, "The Private Plantation: Versions of the Old South Myth, 1880–1914" (Ph.D. diss., Johns Hopkins University, 1973).

9. Use of the concept "myth" was pioneered by George B. Tindall, "Mythology: A New Frontier in Southern History," in *The Idea of the South: Pursuit of a Central Theme*, ed. Frank E. Vandiver (Chicago: University of Chicago Press, 1964), pp. 1–15. For its use in studies of the Lost Cause see Howard Dorgan, "Southern Apologetic Themes, as Expressed in Selected Ceremonial Speaking of Confederate Veterans, 1889–1900" (Ph.D. diss., Louisiana State University, 1971); Susan S. Durant, "The Gently Furled Banner: The Development of the Myth of the Lost Cause" (Ph.D. diss., University of North Carolina–Chapel Hill, 1972); Rollin G. Osterweis, *The Myth of the Lost Cause, 1865–1900* (Hamden, Conn.: Archon Books, 1973); and Waldo W. Braden, "Repining Over an Irrevocable Past: The Ceremonial Orator in a Defeated Society, 1865–1900," in *Oratory in the New South*, ed. Waldo Braden (Baton Rouge: Louisiana State University Press, 1979). Charles Reagan Wilson, *Baptized in Blood: The Religion of the Lost Cause, 1865–1920* (Athens: University of Georgia Press, 1980) uses the concept "civil religion." Lloyd A. Hunter, "The Sacred South: Postwar Confederates and the Sacralization of Southern Culture" (Ph.D. diss., St. Louis University, 1978) eschews the term but sees the Lost Cause as functioning in the same fashion. Braden uses the term "creative fiction;" quotation from Edmund Leach, *Claude Lévi-Strauss* (New York: Viking Press, 1970), pp. 52–86, on Lévi-Strauss's meaning of myth. Gail Gahrig, "The American Civil Religion: A Source for Theory Construction," *Journal for the Scientific Study of Religion* 20 (March 1981): 51–63.

10. Discussion based on John F. Wilson, *Public Religion in American Culture* (Philadelphia: Temple University Press, 1979); and Talcott Parsons, "Durkheim on Religion Revisited: Another Look at the Elementary Forms of Religious Life," in *Beyond*

the Classics? Essays in the Scientific Study of Religion, eds. Charles Y. Glock and Phillip E. Hammond (New York: Harper & Row, 1973), pp. 164–65.

CHAPTER ONE.

AFTER APPOMATTOX:

THE TRAUMA OF DEFEAT

1. Douglas Southall Freeman, *R.E. Lee: A Biography*, 4 vols. (New York: Charles Scribner's Sons, 1935–36), 4: 105–44.

2. The last days of the war are chronicled in many military histories; see the account and bibliography in Emory M. Thomas, *The Confederate Nation, 1861–1865* (New York: Harper & Row, Publishers, 1979). Rembert W. Patrick, *The Fall of Richmond* (Baton Rouge: Louisiana State University Press, 1960); Robert L. Kerby, *Kirby Smith's Confederacy: The Trans-Mississippi South, 1863–1865* (New York: Columbia University Press, 1972). On soldiers joining Johnston see Joseph T. Durkin, ed., *John Dooley, Confederate Soldier: His War Journal* (Washington: Georgetown University Press, 1945), pp. 176–77; and Memoirs, written in 1877, pp. 666–82, Berry G. Benson Papers, Southern Historical Collection, University of North Carolina at Chapel Hill.

3. On official support for continuation see Thomas, *Confederate Nation*, pp. 300–6, quotation on p. 302; "gentleman" from Robert Young Conrad to Charles F. Conrad, 27 April 1865, Holmes Conrad Papers, Virginia Historical Society, Richmond; S.H. Lockett to Wife, 19 April 1865, Samuel H. Lockett Papers, SHC.

4. David to William H. Pierson, 9 May 1865, Pierson Family Papers, Manuscript Department, Howard-Tilton Memorial Library, Tulane University, New Orleans; James M. Morgan, *Recollections of a Rebel Reefer* (Boston and New York: Houghton Mifflin Company, 1917), p. 237; "From Your Friend" to Ashbel Smith, 16 May 1865, Ashbel Smith Papers, University of Texas Archives, Austin; Williamson S. Oldham, "A History of a Journey from Richmond to the Rio Grande," pp. 78, 415, Williamson S. Oldham Papers, UTX. On loss of morale see Thomas, *Confederate Nation*, p. 284; Kerby, *Kirby Smith's Confederacy*, pp. 432–34.

5. Oldham, "A History," pp. 67, 116, 129, Oldham Papers, UTX; Virginia J. Mosby Diary, 19 April 1865, John S. Mosby Papers, Manuscripts Department, University of Virginia Library, Charlottesville; Beth G. Crabtree and James W. Patton, eds., *"Journal of a Secesh Lady:" The Diary of Catherine Ann Devereux Edmondston, 1860–1866* (Raleigh: Division of Archives and History, Department of Cultural Resources, 1979), pp. 699–700; Earl S. Miers, ed., *When the World Ended: The Diary of Emma LeConte* (New York: Oxford University Press, 1957), pp. 95, 97; Anna Maria Green, *The Journal of a Milledgeville Girl, 1861–1867*, James C. Bonner, ed. (Athens: University of Georgia Press, 1964), pp. 73–74. Robert L. Harris, "The South in Defeat: 1865" (Ph.D. diss., Duke University, 1956), pp. 186–190, also notes the existence of these rumors.

6. Thomas, *Confederate Nation*; Kerby, *Kirby Smith's Confederacy*.

7. C.H. Cary to William Walthall, 25 December 1865, William T. Walthall Papers, Mississippi Department of Archives and History, Jackson; John Q. Anderson, ed., *Brokenburn: The Journal of Kate Stone, 1861–1868* (Baton Rouge: Louisiana State University Press, 1972), pp. 363–64; Susan Bradford Eppes, *Through Some Eventful Years* (Macon: J.W. Burke Company, 1926), p. 278. See also Mrs. Eva B. Jones to Mary Jones, 14 July 1865, in Robert M. Myers, ed., *The Children of Pride: A True Story of Georgia and the Civil War* (New Haven: Yale University Press, 1972), pp. 1280–81;

Thomas Journal, 1 May 1865, Manuscript Department, Perkins Library, Duke University. Quotations are from Leon F. Litwack, *Been in the Storm So Long: The Aftermath of Slavery* (New York: Alfred A. Knopf, 1979), p. 108; Josiah Gorgas Journal, 4 May 1865, sec. III, p. 29, SHC; George A. Mercer Diary, typescript vol, "1860–1865," p. 230, SHC. See also Durkin, ed., *Dooley*, pp. 205–6; Diary No. 1, 16 June 1865, William H. Ellis Papers, Manuscript Department, Hill Memorial Library, Louisiana State University Library, Baton Rouge.

8. George W. Munford to Lizzie, 28 April 1865, G.W. Munford Letters, Munford-Ellis Family Papers, Duke; Durkin, ed., *Dooley*, pp. 200–201. On women, see Eliza F. Andrews, *The War-Time Journal of a Georgia Girl, 1864–1865*, Spencer B. King, Jr., ed. (Macon: The Ardivan Press, 1960; first published 1908), pp. 153–55; Crabtree and Patton, eds., *"Journal of a Secesh Lady,"* p. 695; Lucy Jane Thorp to Lucie Jane Gregory, 19 April 1865, Gregory Family Papers, VHS. See also Diary of Catherine B. Brown, 2 May 1865, typescript vol. 2, p. 44, SHC. On stopping diaries see Crabtree and Patton, eds., *"Journal of a Secesh Lady,"* p. 717; Journal of Meta Morris Grimball, 6 March 1865 and 20 February 1866, typescript, pp. 111–18, SHC; Anderson, ed., *Brokenburn*, pp. 368–76. Mary Elizabeth Massey, *Bonnet Brigades* (New York: Alfred A. Knopf, 1966), pp. 318–19, makes the same observation.

9. Mary Jones to Joseph Jones, 2 May 1865, Joseph Jones Papers, LSU; Grace Brown Elmore Diary, 10 May and 20 June 1865, South Caroliniana Library, University of South Carolina. See also Mary B. Goodwin Diary, 4 June and 2 July 1865, Virginia State Library, Richmond; C.C. Clay to Virginia Clay, 11 August 1865, Clement Claiborne Clay Papers, Duke; Cornelia McDonald, *A Diary with Reminiscences of the War and Refugee Life in the Shenandoah Valley, 1860–65* (Nashville: Cullom and Ghertner, 1935), pp. 267–71; Rufus B. Spain, *At Ease in Zion: Social History of Southern Baptists, 1865–1900* (Nashville: Vanderbilt University Press, 1961), p. 17.

10. Texts from A.E. Pendleton to Child, 18 July 1865, William Nelson Pendleton Papers, SHC; Abbie M. Brooks Diary, 14 May 1865, Atlanta Historical Society, Atlanta. See also Thomas R. Markham, Sermon, 4 March 1866, Thomas R. Markham Papers, LSU; M.D. Hoge, Sermon, "Revelation 2:17," 26 September 1869, Moses D. Hoge Papers, Union Theological Seminary Library, Richmond; David Macrae, *The Americans at Home* (New York: E.P. Dutton & Co., 1952; first published 1870), p. 135; John R. Dennett, *The South as It Is: 1865–1866*, Harry M. Christman, ed. (New York: Viking Press, 1965; first published, 1866), p. 12. On Bible reading, etc., see Myrta Lockett Avary, ed., *Recollections of Alexander H. Stephens: His Diary Kept When A Prisoner at Fort Warren, . . .* (New York: Doubleday, Page and Company, 1910), pp. 183, 262; J.A. Campbell, untitled journal of captivity, Campbell-Colston Papers, SHC; Miss M.G. Cobia to Edward McCrady, Sr., 29 July 1865, Edward McCrady Papers, South Carolina Historical Society, Charleston; Julia Peterkin to W.N. Pendleton, 28 September 1865, Pendleton Papers, SHC; Maggie Tucker to the Misses Munford, 1 January 1866, G.W. Munford Letters, Munford-Ellis Papers, Duke; Diary of Mary Washington (Cabell) Early, 19 April 1865, Early Family Papers, VHS. On thanksgiving see Henry A. Garrett Diary, 24 October 1865, pp. 177–18, John F.H. Claiborne Papers, Library of Congress, Washington, D.C.; Annie Snowden to A. Pamela Cunningham (copy), 1 October 1866, Mary A. Snowden Papers, SCL; E.T. Munford to G.W. Munford, 5 September 1865, G.W. Munford Letters, Munford-Ellis Papers, Duke; Jonathan E. Helmreich, "A Prayer for the Spirit of Acceptance: The Journal of Martha Wayles Robertson, 1860–66," *Historical Magazine of the Protestant Episcopal Church* 46 (December 1977): 407. For a more extensive and somewhat different discussion of the theological interpretation of defeat see Wilson, *Baptized in Blood*, pp. 58-78.

11. For an account of continued belief in independence see Miers, ed., *When the World Ended*, p. 95. Quotation is from Thomas Markham, Sermon, 20 August 1865, Markham Papers, LSU. See also letter of 15 May 1865 quoted in Peyton H. Hoge, *Moses Drury Hoge: Life and Letters* (Richmond: Presbyterian Committee of Publication, 1899), pp. 235–36; Fanny Downing, "The Land We Love," *Land We Love* 1 (July 1866): 161–62; Wm. Howard to Guy M. Bryan, 29 July 1867, Guy M. Bryan Papers, UTX; E. P. Alexander to Josiah Colston (copy) 22 April 1865 and J.A. Campbell to Anne Campbell, 22 June 1865, both in Campbell-Colston Papers, SHC; Emily to Bonnie Kell, 25 February 1866, John M. Kell Papers, Duke; "Dear Sir," 3 October 1866, Louis Bringier and Family Papers, LSU. For a reference to Romans 8:28 in this respect see C.C. Clay to Virginia Clay, 11 August 1865, Clay Papers, Duke.

12. Eva B. Jones to Mary Jones, 13 June 1865, in Myers, ed., *Children of Pride*, p. 1273; Andrews, *War-Time Journal*, pp. 367–68; John Bratton to Johnson, 20 November 1865, John Bratton Papers, SCL; Edward Turner to "Captain," 9 September 1865, Edward C. Wharton and Family Papers, LSU; George A. Mercer Diary, 11 June 1865, typescript vol. 5, part 1, pp. 229–31, SCH. See also Clement Eaton, *The Waning of the Old South Civilization* (New York: Pegasus, 1969; first published, 1968), pp. 111–37, and Dan T. Carter, "The Anatomy of Fear: The Christmas Day Insurrection Scare of 1865," *JSH* 42 (August 1976): 345–64.

13. Whitelaw Reid, *After the War: A Tour of the Southern States, 1865–1866*, C. Vann Woodward, ed. (New York: Harper & Row, 1965; first published 1866), pp. 295–99, *passim*. See also J.T. Trowbridge, *The South: A Tour of Its Battle-Fields and Ruined Cities . . .* (Hartford, Conn.: L. Stebbins, 1867), p. 589. For southerners waiting for another chance see *ibid.*, p. 71; Brooks Diary, 18 April 1865, AHS; W.C. Oates to E.P. Alexander, 25 August 1868, Edward Porter Alexander Papers, SHC; Wade Hampton III to _____, 10 May 1865, in Charles E. Cauthen, ed., *Family Letters of the Three Wade Hamptons, 1782–1901* (Columbia: University of South Carolina Press, 1953), p. 114. William B. Hesseltine, *Confederate Leaders in the New South* (Westport, Conn.: Greenwood Press, 1970; first published 1950), pp. 21–23. For lesser Confederates slow to settle down see journal of John B. Patrick, 25 December 1865, SCL; R.W. Waldrop Diary, vols. 2 and 3, Richard W. Waldrop Papers, SHC; Robert Y. Conrad to Charles F. Conrad, 2 August 1866, Conrad Papers, VHS; John A. Fite to Julian Mitchell, 10 January 1866, Julian Mitchell Papers, SCHS; Francis W. Dawson to Mother, 13 October 1865, Francis W. Dawson Papers, Duke. Robert A. Gilmour, "The Other Emancipation: Studies in the Society and Economy of Alabama Whites During Reconstruction" (Ph.D. diss., The Johns Hopkins University, 1972), pp. 43–54, provides evidence of migration in a statistical study of one state. For an interpretation that takes this period of flexibility more seriously see Hans L. Trefousse, "Andrew Johnson and the Failure of Reconstruction," in *Toward A New View of America: Essays in Honor of Arthur C. Cole*, Hans L. Trefousse, ed. (n.p.: Burt Franklin & Company, 1977), pp. 135–50. Trefousse's article disputes Michael Perman's emphasis on the South's "defiant optimism" after Appomattox. My approach agrees with Trefousse's analysis in that regard but goes further in stressing the need to acknowledge what the South did give up. See Perman, *Reunion Without Compromise: The South and Reconstruction, 1865–1868* (Cambridge: Cambridge University Press, 1973).

14. Andrews, *War-Time Journal*, p. 276; Sir Charles W. Dilke, *Greater Britain: A Record of Travel in English-Speaking Countries During 1866 and 1867* (New York: Harper & Brothers, Publishers, 1869), p. 18; Harris, "South in Defeat," pp. 176–80; Trowbridge, *South*, p. 71; Dennett, *South As It Is*, pp. 75–76; Herbert Quick, "A Good Old Rebel," *Collier's* 25 (4 April 1914): 20–21. Copies are also in scrapbook, Charles E.

Jones Papers, Duke; Scrapbook III, 1868–78, Clay Papers, Duke. The interpretation of defiance as more a psychological release than an important indication of southern sentiment differs from that of Eric L. McKitrick. See McKitrick, *Andrew Johnson and Reconstruction* (Chicago: University of Chicago Press, 1960), pp. 15–41.

15. Others have set up categories of response. Jack P. Maddex, Jr., mentions those who "withdrew," who "drift," who "fume and fuss" where "deprived of a social base from which to continue" resistance, and who "adapt" and lead the way to a new order. See *The Virginia Conservatives, 1867–1879: A Study in Reconstruction Politics* (Chapel Hill: University of North Carolina Press, 1970), pp. xii–xiii. James L. Roark, borrowing from Robert J. Lifton, identified three responses: transformationist, restorationist, and accommodationist; see *Masters Without Slaves*, p. 207.

16. A few members of the Confederate Navy who were at sea or abroad when the war ended did not return for fear of punishment. See, for example, John Grimball to Papa, 27 January 1866, John Berkley Grimball Papers, Duke; William Conway Whittle to Samuel Barron, 13 April 1866, Barron Family Papers, VHS.

17. There is no adequate history of the emigration movement as a whole. I have relied heavily on the following studies of individual countries and areas: Lawrence F. Hill, *The Confederate Exodus to Latin America* (n.p.: n.p., 1936); Andrew F. Rolle, *The Lost Cause: The Confederate Exodus to Mexico* (Norman: University of Oklahoma Press, 1965); W.C. Nunn, *Escape From Reconstruction* (Fort Worth: Texas Christian University, 1956); Douglas A. Grier, "Confederate Emigration to Brazil, 1865–1870" (Ph.D. diss., University of Michigan, 1968); Alfred J. and Kathryn Hanna, *Confederate Exiles in Venezuela* (Tuscaloosa: Confederate Publishing Company, 1960); George D. Harmon, "Confederate Migration to Mexico," *Hispanic American Historical Review* 17 (November 1937): 561–87; Carl C. Rister, "Carlota, A Confederate Colony in Mexico," *JSH* 11 (February 1945): 33–50; Alfred J. Hanna, "The Role of Matthew Fontaine Maury in the Mexican Empire," *Virginia Magazine of History and Biography* 55 (April 1947): 102–25; Blanche H.C. Weaver, "Confederate Emigration to Brazil," *JSH* 27 (February 1961): 33–53; Desmond Holdridge, "Toledo: A Tropical Refugee Settlement in British Honduras," *Geographical Review* 30 (July 1940): 376–93; B. Hayne, "Confederate Exiles in Canada West" (unpublished manuscript in VHS). The best introduction to the movement, unavailable when I wrote, is Daniel E. Sutherland, "Exiles, Emigrants, and Sojourners: The Post-Civil War Confederate Exodus in Perspective," *Civil War History* 31 (September 1985): 237–56, which differs from the interpretation here, especially in stressing economic motives for emigration and portraying southern emigration to the North and the West as essentially similar to that to foreign countries.

18. Robert Shalhope, in "Race, Class, Slavery, and the Antebellum Southern Mind," *JSH* 37 (November 1971): 562, also argues that émigrés to Mexico sought "to re-create as closely as possible the society they had left behind." "Utopian dream" is from George S. Barnsley (who went to Brazil himself), "Notes on Brazil during the years of 1867 to 1880," manuscript in George S. Barnsley Papers, SHC. On Maury's plan see M.F. Maury to wife (copy), 29 May and 11 June 1865, in vol. of copied letters, Richard L. Maury Papers, Duke, and Francis L. Williams, *Matthew Fontaine Maury: Scientist of the Sea* (New Brunswick, N.J.: Rutgers University Press, 1965), pp. 421–41.

19. On slavery and the attractiveness of Brazil, see F. Surget to Stephen Duncan, 14 June 1865, Stephen Duncan Papers, LSU; Thomas Tolson Gordon Reminiscences, typescript, pp. 5–16, UTX. Quotation is from J.D. Porter to John D. Templeton, 5 July 1867, James Denford Porter File, VHS.

20. Julia E. Ellis, "Fatal Cross of Stars: The Confederate Exiles in Mexico: A Study of Motives and Occupations" (M.A. thesis, Louisiana State University, 1974), p.

75, for instance, locates three different figures for the number of colonists in one place. Hill, Hanna, and Grier all accept the 10,000 total. Estimates of 2,500 in Mexico are accepted by Harmon, Hanna, and Nunn. Yet Nunn (using names collected by Hanna in addition to those he found) identified only 268 names of emigrants, and the newspaper considered to be the voice of the Confederate community in Mexico in January 1866 had only 137 subscribers. See Alfred J. Hanna, "A Confederate Newspaper in Mexico," *JSH* 12 (February 1946): 79–81. Brazil admitted only 3,585 southerners—a number considerably below the figure employed in reaching the 10,000 total. (From Alice Dugus, "Americans in Brazil," 1 October 1945, a typescript in the Vertical File, Louisiana Room, LSU. Dugus located and compiled these statistics from the archives in Rio de Janeiro. See Sara Mims, "Always a Grand Old Flag," article in Vertical File, Louisiana Room.) Dugus' figures are close to some provided by travelers in Brazil at the time. See Grier, "Emigration to Brazil," p. 30, and Jose A. Rios, "Assimilation of Emigrants from the Old South in Brazil," *Social Forces* 26 (December 1947): 146. If only 2,000 went to Mexico, 3,585 to Brazil, and 1,000 to Venzuela and British Honduras—probably a high estimate in each case—the total number of emigrants reached only 7,500. Percentages are given as percentage of white population of eleven Confederate states as of 1860. For comparison with emigration after the American Revolution see R.R. Palmer, *The Age of the Democratic Revolution: The Challenge*, 2 vols. (Princeton: Princeton University Press, 1959), 1: 188.

21. J.F. Grant to Joseph Jones, 1 August 1865, Jones Papers, Tulane; Lawrence Royster to Peter Wilson Roller, 6 August 1865, John S. Mosby Papers, VHS; John R. Baylor to Sister, 11 January 1866, Wharton Papers, LSU; E.B. Heyward to Jim, 22 January 1866, E.B. Heyward Papers, SCL; G.W.C. Lee to E.P. Alexander, 4 February 1866, Alexander Papers, SHC; Augusta McKinney to Uncle, 29 July and 4 December 1867, Jeptha McKinney Papers, LSU; John R. Baylor to Lou, 9 September 1868, Wharton Papers, LSU; John H. Moore, ed., *The Juhl Letters to the Charleston Courier: A View of the South, 1865–1871* (Athens: University of Georgia Press, 1974), pp. 81, 173, 178, 255. Roark, *Masters Without Slaves*, pp. 120–31, also points to the disparity between the number who went and many more who "longed" to join them. Quotations are from Jubal A. Early to Robert L. Dabney, 25 February, 29 November, and 14 March 1867, Robert L. Dabney Papers, UTSL. See also David H. Overy, "Robert Lewis Dabney: Apostle of the Old South" (Ph.D. diss., University of Wisconsin, 1967), pp. 157–60.

22. Discussion of the difficulties can be found in most of the secondary sources cited above. Quotation is from Frank to Moultrie and Margaret, 18 February 1867, William Moultrie Reid Papers, SCL.

23. On drinking see Mother to Fred, 25 January 1867, in Betsy Fleet, ed., *Green Mount After the War: The Correspondence of Maria Louisa Wacker Fleet and Her Family, 1865–1900* (Charlottesville: University Press of Virginia, 1978), p. 23; E.D. Cheney, "The Hope of the South," *Christian Examiner* 87 (September 1869): 244–45; A South Carolinian [Belton O'Neall Townsend], "South Carolina Morals," *Atlantic Monthly* 39 (April 1877): 469; Emily K. Abel, ed., "A Victorian Views Reconstruction: The American Diary of Samuel Augustus Barnett," *CWH* 20 (June 1974): 153–54; Robert Somers, *The Southern States Since the War, 1870–71*, Malcolm C. McMillan, ed. (University: University of Alabama Press, 1965), pp. 245–46. These observations have to be taken skeptically since they may well have been part of a general tendency to decry the sad state of the South. Remember, too, excessive drinking had been common in the Old South. See Bertram Wyatt-Brown, *Southern Honor: Ethics and Behavior in the Old South* (New York: Oxford University Press, 1982), pp. 278–81. On opium use see David T.

Courtwright, "The Hidden Epidemic: Opiate Addiction and Cocaine Use in the South, 1860–1920," *JSH* 49 (February 1983): 57–72, quotation on p. 66. Courtwright identified health care practices as the major factor.

24. Durkin, ed., *Dooley*, pp. 199–200, 209–16; Franklin Stringfellow to Jefferson Davis, 18 June 1880, Jefferson Davis Postwar Papers, Louisiana Historical Association Collection, Tulane. See also Moore, ed. *Juhl Letters*, p. 127. George A. Mercer Diary, typescript vol. "1860–1865," pp. 236–37.

25. William M. Browne to Howell Cobb, 28 March 1866, in Ulrich B. Phillips, ed., *The Correspondence of Robert Toombs, Alexander H. Stephens, and Howell Cobb*, in *Annual Report of the American Historical Association for the Year 1911* (Washington: American Historical Association, 1913), 2: 677–78; Wade Keyes to John Sanford, 5 June 1870, John W.A. Sanford Papers, Alabama Department of Archives and History, Montgomery. See also Jeptha McKinney to Ada McKinney, 15 May 1867, McKinney Papers, LSU; John Frazier to Marshal McGraw, 16 August 1867, Marshal McGraw Papers, SCL; Dennett, *South As It Is*, p. 224; Moore, ed., *Juhl Letters*, p. 107; A South Carolinian [Belton O'Neall Townsend], "The Political Condition of South Carolina," *Atlantic Monthly* 39 (January 1877): 180–81.

26. Donald H. Breese, "Politics in the Lower South During Presidential Reconstruction, April to November 1865" (Ph.D. diss., University of California at Los Angeles, 1963), Appendix B. Breese stresses the political activism, however, and attributes light voting to refusal to take the oath. On registration see Forrest G. Wood, "On Revising Reconstruction History: Negro Suffrage, White Disfranchisement, and Common Sense," *Journal of Negro History* 51 (April 1966): 98–113. Cf. William A. Russ, Jr., "Negro and White Disfranchisement Under Radical Reconstruction," *Mississippi Valley Historical Review* 19 (September 1934): 163–87. See also Paul H. Buck, *The Road to Reunion, 1865–1900* (Boston: Little, Brown and Company, 1937), pp. 35–37; Dan T. Carter, *When the War Was Over: The Failure of Self-Reconstruction in the South, 1865–1867* (Baton Rouge: Louisiana State University Press, 1985), pp. 270–71. Harris, "South in Defeat," pp. 259–60, sees withdrawal as a temporary phenomenon in 1865.

27. James A. Longstreet to E.P. Alexander, 9 August 1869, Alexander Papers, SHC; Longstreet to "My Dear General," 8 June 1867, James A. Longstreet Papers, Duke; William L. Richter, "James Longstreet: From Rebel to Scalawag," *Louisiana History* 11 (Summer 1970): 215–30.

28. Lloyd A. Hunter, "Missouri's Confederate Leaders After the War," *Missouri Historical Review* 67 (April 1973): 371–96; William B. Hesseltine and Larry Gara, "Mississippi's Confederate Leaders After the War," *Journal of Mississippi History* 13 (April 1951): 92–93; Carl N. Degler, *The Other South: Southern Dissenters in the Nineteenth Century* (New York: Harper & Row, Publishers, 1974), pp. 220–21; Mrs. Roger A. Pryor, *My Day: Reminiscences of a Long Life* (New York: Macmillan Company, 1909), pp. 325–29; Robert S. Holzman, *Adapt or Perish: The Life of General Roger A. Pryor, CSA* (Hamden, Conn.: Archon Books, 1976), pp. 88–89, *passim*; Mary A. Long, *High Time to Tell It* (Durham: Duke University Press, 1950), pp. 73–74, which also gives an indication of public hostility. On Alabama see William M. Cash, "Alabama Republicans During Reconstruction: Personal Characteristics, Motivations, and Political Activity of Party Activists, 1867–1880" (Ph.D. diss. University of Alabama, 1973). For citations to the large and growing literature on the social basis of southern Republicanism see Peter Kolchin, "Scalawags, Carpetbaggers, and Reconstruction: A Quantitative Look at Southern Congressional Politics, 1868–1872," *JSH* 45 (February 1979): 63.

29. Daniel E. Sutherland, "Former Confederates in the Post-Civil War North: An Unexplored Aspect of Reconstruction History," *JSH* 47 (August 1981): 393–410; Neal

C. Gillespie, *The Collapse of Orthodoxy: The Intellectual Ordeal of George Frederick Holmes* (Charlottesville: University of Virginia Press, 1972), p. 213, *passim*; Jack P. Maddex, Jr., *The Reconstruction of Edward A. Pollard: A Rebel's Conversion to Postbellum Unionism* (Chapel Hill: University of North Carolina Press, 1974); Jonathan M. Wiener, "Coming to Terms with Capitalism: The Postwar Thought of George Fitzhugh," *VMHB* 87 (October 1979): 438–47; but on Fitzhugh see also Robert D. Little, "The Ideology of the New South: A Study in the Development of Ideas, 1865–1900" (Ph.D. diss., University of Chicago, 1950), pp. 43–50.

30. M.F. Maury to R.L. Maury, 2 February 1867, R. L. Maury Papers, Duke; J.L.M. Curry, "Claims of the Hour on Young Men: Qualifications Necessary to Meet Them—The Spirit of a Gentleman and the Spirit of Religion," 16 March 1867, Jabez L.M. Curry Papers, LC.

31. On state conventions see McKitrick, *Andrew Johnson*, pp. 165–68. On 1868 election see R.E. Lee to W.S. Rosecrans (copy), 26 August 1868, Lee Letterbook, Lee Family Papers, VHS. For an extended discussion of a similar argument on acquiescence, see Carter, *When the War Was Over*, pp. 61–95. See also P.G.T. Beauregard to Mary E. Dickens, 25 March 1866, P.G.T. Beauregard Papers, LC. For travelers supporting this view see Martin Abbott, ed., "A Southerner Views the South, 1865: Letters of Harvey M. Watterson," *VMHB* 68 (October 1960): 480; Charles Nordhoff, *The Cotton States in the Spring and Summer of 1875* (New York: Burt Franklin, 1966; first published 1876), p. 10; William H. Dixon, *New America* (London: Hurst and Blackett, Publishers, 1869), pp. 431–32, 443–45. For more emphasis on the fact that acquiescence came only because it had to, see Reid, *After the War*, p. 409; Trowbridge, *South*, pp. 584–86; Charles F. Lee to Mary, 16 July 1865, Charles F. Lee Papers, SCL. For an opposing view see Dennett, *South as It Is*, pp. 357–62; Dilke, *Greater Britain*, pp. 19, 37–39.

32. Perman, *Reunion Without Compromise* stresses intransigence more than any other work. For efforts to eliminate black suffrage in border states see William Gillette, "Anatomy of a Failure: Federal Enforcement of the Right to Vote in the Border States During Reconstruction," in *Radicalism, Racism, and Party Realignment: The Border States During Reconstruction*, ed. Richard O. Curry (Baltimore: The Johns Hopkins University Press, 1969), pp. 265–304. Gillette does point out, however, that areas with heavy concentrations of ex-Confederates experienced the most violence. On equality's not being a war aim see C. Vann Woodward, "The Northern Crusade Against Slavery," *American Counterpoint: Slavery and Racism in North-South Dialogue* (Boston: Little, Brown and Company, 1971), pp. 140–62.

CHAPTER TWO.

AFTER APPOMATTOX:

THE SCARS OF DEFEAT

1. On repentance see Jeremiah Morton to John Perkins, 6 June 1866, John Perkins, Jr., Papers, SHC: Jonathan E. Helmreich, "A Prayer for the Spirit of Acceptance: The Journal of Martha Wayles Robertson, 1860–1866," *HMPEC* 46 (December 1977): 407–08; Sylvia Krebs, "Funeral Meats and Second Marriages: Alabama Churches in the Presidential Reconstruction Period," *Alabama Historical Quarterly* 37 (Fall 1975): 207–8. Several historians have documented how individuals and churches mixed a belief that God meant defeat for good with a call for better lives and greater personal piety. See Spain, *At Ease in Zion*, pp. 17–18; Ernest T. Thompson, *Presbyterians in the South*, 3 vols. (Richmond: John Knox Press, 1973), 2: 107; and Patrick, *The Fall of Richmond*, p. 99.

2. Quotations are from Horace Greeley, *Mr. Greeley's Letters from Texas and the Lower Mississippi* . . . (New York: Tribune Office, 1871), pp. 40–42; and R.M. Gray Reminiscences, typed copy, 1867, p. 3, SHC. See also Reid, *After the War*, pp. 379, 409; J. Ditzler, "The American Conflict," *LWL* 5 (June 1868): 136–56. For an exception see Solomon L.M. Conser, *Virginia After the War* (Indianapolis: Baker-Randolph Lith. & Eng. Company, 1891), p. 46.

3. For quotation and discussion of Congress's action see Thomas, *The Confederate Nation*, pp. 289–96. See also Robert F. Durden, *The Gray and the Black: The Confederate Debate on Emancipation* (Baton Rouge: Louisiana State University Press, 1972); Paul D. Escott, *After Secession: Jefferson Davis and the Failure of Confederate Nationalism* (Baton Rouge: Louisiana State University Press, 1978); Roark, *Masters Without Slaves*, pp. 85–108.

4. Untitled, undated, unattributed address in Survivors' Association Papers, SCHS; Jonathan T. Dorris, *Pardon and Amnesty Under Lincoln and Johnson: The Restoration of the Confederates to Their Rights and Privileges, 1861–1898* (Chapel Hill: University of North Carolina Press, 1953), p. 137; John E.H. Skinner, *After the Storm; Or, Jonathan and Its Neighbors in 1865–6*, 2 vols. (London: Richard Bentley, 1866), 2: 12–13; Francis W. Dawson to Father, 13 June 1865, Francis W. Dawson Papers, Duke.

5. Adele P. Allston used the word *acquiesce* twice in a March 1865 letter to Union commanders in her area; see J.H. Easterby, ed., *The South Carolina Rice Plantation as Revealed in the Papers of Robert F.W. Allston* (Chicago: University of Chicago Press, 1945), pp. 208–9. Historians interpret southern reaction in various ways. Stampp, "The Southern Road to Appomattox," pp. 246–69 and Carl N. Degler, *Place Over Time: The Continuity of Southern Distinctiveness* (Baton Rouge: Louisiana State University Press, 1977), pp. 106–7 both stress how readily southerners accepted abolition and how quickly they came to see it as a benefit. Degler also argues that the end of slavery "left few regrets upon the southern mind." My account more closely follows those of Roark, *Masters Without Slaves*, pp. 85–108; Litwack, *Been in the Storm So Long*, pp. 187–89; and Carter, *When the War Was Over*, pp. 82–95. All emphasize that the South accepted abolition, but that southerners displayed little guilt and continued to believe in the justness of the institution. First quotation is from A Southern Soldier, "The Late War: Its Causes and Results," *Christian Examiner* 86 (January 1869): 1; second from Annie E. Harper Manuscript, 1876, p. 49, MDAH. See also A South Carolinian [Belton O'Neall Townsend], "South Carolina Society," *Atlantic Monthly* 39 (June 1877): p. 684; Macrae, *The Americans at Home*, pp. 284–92; Conser, *Virginia*, p. 19; George A.H. Sala, *America Revisited: From the Bay of New York to the Gulf of Mexico, and from Lake Michigan to the Pacific* (London: Vizetelly & Company, 1885), pp. 199–200. It is interesting that these anti-slavery observations were usually made to visitors or were made well after the war. On Lyon see Rev. James A. Lyon Journal, pp. 102, 140–44, MDAH; Thompson, *Presbyterians*, 2: 195–96, and R. Milton Winter, "James A. Lyon: Southern Presbyterian Apostle of Progress," *Journal of Presbyterian History* 59 (Winter 1983): 314–35, which shows the continuity of his prewar views and his wartime Unionism. For other examples of the failure-of-stewardship argument see Avary, ed., *Recollections of Alexander H. Stephens*, p. 174; Spain, *At Ease in Zion*, pp. 18–19.

6. Ralph E. Morrow, *Northern Methodism and Reconstruction* (East Lansing: Michigan State University Press, 1956), pp. 101–7; Overy, "Robert Lewis Dabney," p. 192. For a snide comment by D.H. Hill on what little confession he did hear, see "Editorial," *LWL* 3 (May 1867): 85.

7. Quotations are from *Appleton's Annual Cyclopedia and Register of Important Events* (New York): 1865, p. 706; "Slavery," unattributed manuscript in Jubal A. Early

Papers, LC; Dennett, *The South as It Is*, pp. 18–22. For examples of southerners defending the morality of slavery see Jubal A. Early to Robert L. Dabney, 29 November 1867, Robert L. Dabney Papers, UTSL; William N. Pendleton to A. T. Irving, 27 January 1880, William Nelson Pendleton Papers, SHC; George Campbell, *White and Black: The Outcome of a Visit to the United States* (London: Chatto & Windus, 1879), pp. 296–97, 300; William Saunders, *Through the Light Continent; Or, The United States in 1877–8* (London: Cassell, Petter, and Galpin, 1879), p. 82; Joseph C. Carter, ed., *Magnolia Journey: A Union Veteran Revisits the Former Confederate States* (University: University of Alabama Press, 1974; first published 1869), pp. 104–5; Greeley, *Letters from Texas*, pp. 38–40. On compensation see Ella Gertrude Thomas Journal, 9 March 1871, Duke; W.C. Mitchell to Hugh, 9 January 1867, William Letcher Mitchell Papers, SHC; A South Carolinian [Belton O'Neall Townsend], "The Political Condition of South Carolina," p. 190; J. T. Trowbridge, *The South*, p. 390; Dennett, *South As It Is*, pp. 88–90, 184–85; and John E. Fisher, "Statesman of the Lost Cause: R.M.T. Hunter and the Sectional Controversy, 1847–1887" (Ph.D. diss., University of Virginia, 1968), p. 272.

8. On honor in the Old South see Charles S. Sydnor, "The Southerner and the Laws," *JSH* 6 (February 1940): 3–23; William J. Cooper, Jr., *The South and the Politics of Slavery, 1828–1856* (Baton Rouge: Louisiana State University Press, 1978), pp. 69–74 and *passim*; Wyatt-Brown, *Southern Honor*, quotation from p. xv; and Edward L. Ayers, *Vengeance and Justice: Crime and Punishment in the 19th-Century American South* (New York: Oxford University Press, 1984), which offers a helpful corrective on the importance of dignity as well as honor.

9. Untitled poem in James I. Metts Papers, SHC; Jubal A. Early to Hunter McGuire, 30 October 1865, Hunter Holmes McGuire Papers, UVA; Basil W. Duke, A *History of Morgan's Cavalry*, Cecil F. Holland, ed. (Bloomington: Indiana University Press, 1960; first published 1867), p. 9. See also J.B. Hood to S.D. Lee, 29 November 1865, Stephen D. Lee Papers, SHC. Richard M. Weaver, *The Southern Tradition at Bay: A History of Postbellum Thought*, George Core and M. E. Bradford, eds. (New Rochelle, N.Y.: Arlington House, 1968), p. 179, mentions this motive. Postwar magazines and memoirs are filled with feuds; two good examples can be found in "Controversy Deprecated," *Our Living and Our Dead* 1 (21 October 1873): 3, and John B. Hood, *Advance and Retreat: Personal Experiences in the United States and Confederate States Armies*, Richard N. Current, ed. (Bloomington: Indiana University Press, 1959; first published 1880), p. 68. Major feuds included those between Johnston and Davis, Early and Mosby, Early and Mahone, Johnston and Beauregard, Beauregard and Rhett, Beauregard and Davis. The Early-Mahone dispute involved honor and politics and very nearly resulted in a duel. See Robert E. Withers, *Autobiography of an Octogenarian* (Roanoke: The Stone Printing & Mfg. Co. Press, 1907), pp. 307–11. Durant, "The Gently Furled Banner," pp. 72–104, also discusses postwar feuds. On standards, see Wyatt-Brown, *Southern Honor*, pp. 34–43.

10. Quotation is from Wade Hampton III to John Parsons Carroll, 25 May 1866, in Cauthen, ed., *Family Letters of The Three Wade Hamptons*, pp. 120–21. See also Hampton's letter to the editor of *New York Day Book*, 15 July 1865, Wade Hampton Papers, SCL. For an overview of the controversy see Marion B. Lucas, *Sherman and the Burning of Columbia* (College Station: Texas A & M University Press, 1976). On Forrest see Basil W. Duke, *Reminiscences of General Basil W. Duke, C.S.A.* (Garden City, N.Y.: Doubleday, Page & Company, 1911), pp. 350–55.

11. Josiah Gorgas Journal, 22 August 1865, sec. 3, p. 51, SHC; Richmond politician quoted in Trowbridge, *South*, p. 194. See also Crabtree and Patton, eds.,

"Journal of a Secesh Lady:" The Diary of Catherine Ann Devereux Edmondston, 1860–1866, pp. 708–9, 714, 716; Robert Brown to Mrs. Virginia Clay, 1865, Clement C. Clay Papers, Duke; F.S. Surget to Stephen Duncan, 12 June 1865, Stephen Duncan Papers, LSU. Some southerners went to extremes to minimize the sense of dishonor or betrayal. See Overy, "Dabney," p. 155; Dabney H. Maury, *Recollections of A Virginian in the Mexican, Indian, and Civil Wars* (New York: Charles Scribner's Sons, 1894), p. 240. A copy of the oath in one scrapbook has the words "So Help Me God" scratched through. Miss E.F. Andrews Scrapbook, Andrews Papers, SHC. On importance of oath-taking, see Wyatt-Brown, *Southern Honor*, pp. 55–59.

12. Wyatt-Brown, *Southern Honor*, pp. 25–87; Anne Firor Scott, *The Southern Lady: From Pedestal to Politics, 1830–1930* (Chicago: University of Chicago Press, 1970), p. 101 and *passim*; Barbara Welter, "The Cult of True Womanhood: 1820–1860," *American Quarterly* 18 (Summer 1966): 151–74. For comments on "manhood" see N. Spring to S.G. French, 24 January 1866, Samuel G. French Papers, MDAH; George A. Mercer Diary, 17 December 1865, typescript vol. "1860–1865," p. 247; Jubal A. Early to Jefferson Davis, 5 September 1873, in Dunbar Rowland, ed., *Jefferson Davis, Constitutionalist: His Letters, Papers, and Speeches*, 10 vols. (Jackson: Mississippi Department of Archives and History, 1923), 7: 363–64; Joseph Shackford to Lou Fleet, 7 November 1872, in Fleet, ed., *Green Mount After the War*, pp. 85–86; and S. Milligan Dennison to Early, 27 June 1872, Early Papers, LC.

13. For discussion of the capture and the controversy that followed, see David R. Barbee, "The Capture of Jefferson Davis," *Tyler's Quarterly Historical and Genealogical Magazine* 29 (July 1947): 6–42; and Howard T. Dimick, "The Capture of Jefferson Davis," *JMH* 9 (October 1947): 238–54. "Arrest—Petticoat Lie," in Jefferson Davis File of the James D. and David R. Barbee Papers, LC, has copies of the cartoons and other information. On Barnum see John Muldowny, "Jefferson Davis: The Postwar Years," *Mississippi Quarterly* 23 (Winter 1969–70): 23; on the fight, Mrs. Davis to Jefferson Davis, 14 April 1866, Jefferson Davis Papers, Special Collections, Amelia Gayle Gorgas Library, University of Alabama, University; on the picture, Jefferson Davis to A. Dudley Mann, 19 April 1869, Davis Papers, UAL; on the cartoon incident, Eppes, *Through Some Eventful Years*, p. 321.

14. Hal M. LaGrange, "Fred Hammond: A Scout's Story," *OLOD* 1 (3 December 1873): 2 and 1 (10 December 1873): 1–2. For other explicit references to sexual abuse see "The Palmyra Massacre," *Southern Magazine* 10 (April 1872): 485–88; and Williamson S. Oldham, "Last Days of the Confederacy," p. 11, Williamson S. Oldham Papers, UTX. For an interesting account of sexual outrage, suspect because of its rather late publication, see A.R.H. Ranson, "Reminiscences of the Civil War by a Confederate Staff Officer: (Sixth Paper) Reconstruction Days in the South," *Sewanee Review* 23 (January 1915): 81–82.

15. Jubal Early to Hunter McGuire (copy), 30 October 1865, McGuire Papers, UVA; Thomas Journal, Monday night, October 1865, Duke. See also "Daughters of the South," by G.W.O., in P.G.T. Beauregard Papers, LSU; Benjamin M. Palmer to Anna, 16 May 1866, in Thomas Cary Johnson, ed., *The Life and Letters of Benjamin Morgan Palmer* (Richmond: Presbyterian Committee on Publication, 1906), p. 372; Thomas D. Clark, *The Southern Country Editor* (Indianapolis, Ind.: The Bobbs-Merrill Company, 1948), p. 97.

16. John Grimball Diary, 16 January 1865, typescript, p. 100, SHC; Raleigh E. Colston to Lou Colston, 20 October 1867, Raleigh E. Colston Papers, SHC; Maggie Tucker to Maggie Munford, 2 May 1868, G. W. Munford Letters, Munford-Ellis Papers; Duke; George W. Bagby, "*Sevantgalism* in Virginia," in *Selections from the Miscella-*

neous *Writings of Dr. George Bagby*, 2 vols. (Richmond: Whittet and Shepperson, 1884–1885), 1: 320–21. For a southern male praising young women for not depending on male support, however, see Garrett Diary, 27 August 1865, pp. 99–100, Claiborne Papers, LC.

17. H. Cassidy to O.J.E. Stuart, 23 August 1871, Oscar J. Stuart and Family Papers, MDAH; Robert L. Dabney, "The Duty of the Hour," copy in Robert L. Dabney Papers, UTSL. A fascinating hint of such fears appeared in a memoir published long after the war and is therefore suspect. James M. Morgan warned young men in 1914 to be wary of women who call for war, because they "would march off with the conqueror when he came, leaving their own men, the creatures of their fallacious teaching, prostrate under the heel of the victor, bereft of self-respect, property, and of all their good-looking young women." One cannot help wondering if Morgan spoke from his own feelings after the Civil War. See *Recollections of A Rebel Reefer*, p. 473.

18. S.H. Lockett to Wife, 2 May 1865 and Julia to S.H. Lockett, 4 May 1865, Samuel Henry Lockett Papers, SHC. See also Jefferson Davis to Wife, 23 April 1865 and Mrs. Davis to Davis, 28 April 1865, in Rowland, ed., *Jefferson Davis*, 6: 561, 566; Mrs. Eva B. Jones to Mrs. Mary Jones, 14 July 1865, Myers, ed., *The Children of Pride*, p. 1281.

19. Reid, *After the War*, p. 155; Abbie M. Brooks Diaries, 5 July 1865, AHS. See also John E. Hall to Laurie Hall, 1 July 1865, Bolling Hall Papers, ADAH; Grace Brown Elmore Diary, 4 July 1865, SCL; Sarah Morgan Dawson, *A Confederate Girl's Diary*, James I. Robertson, Jr., ed. (Bloomington: Indiana University Press, 1960; first published 1913), p. 403; Helen D. Longstreet, *Lee and Longstreet at High Tide: Gettysburg in Light of the Official Records* (Gainesville, Ga.: By the Author, 1905), p. 110.

20. Trowbridge, *South*, p. 160.

21. William H. Ellis Diary No. 2, 14 April 1865, LSU. The inconsistency between Evans's rhetoric and her behavior is drawn from information in, but not the interpretation of, William P. Fidler, *Augusta Evans Wilson, 1835–1909* (Birmingham: University of Alabama Press, 1951) and the following letters: Evans to J.H. Christman, 3 February 1866, Augusta Evans Wilson Papers, ADAH; Evans to Col. Seaver, 13 January 1867, Wilson Papers, UAL; Evans to P.G.T. Beauregard, 30 March 1867, Beauregard Papers, Duke. For examples of a change of heart when meeting Yankees see Mary B. Goodwin Diary, 3 May 1866, VSL; and Eppes, *Through Some Eventful Years*, pp. 308, 312. For examples of southern women socializing with northern soldiers see Jeannie Chew Young to Louisa Wharton, 16 January 1866, Edward Clifton Wharton and Family Papers, LSU; and John S. Wise, *The End of an Era*, Curtis C. Davis, ed. (New York: Thomas Yoseloff, 1965; first published 1899), pp. 460–61. For mention of marriage see C.C. Clay to Virginia Clay, 27 February 1867, Clay Papers, Duke; and Marjorie Howell Cook, "Restoration and Innovation: Alabamians Adjust to Defeat, 1865–1867" (Ph.D. diss., University of Alabama, 1968), p. 147. Paul B. Barringer, *The Natural Bent: The Memoirs of Dr. Paul B. Barringer* (Chapel Hill: University of North Carolina Press, 1949), pp. 108–9, suggests that Yankees often married factory girls.

22. Pearl Rivers, "True to the Gray," clipping in Scrapbook III, 1866–1878, C.C. Clay Papers, Duke. The hatred of southern women for the Yankees is generally accepted by scholars. See, for example, McKitrick, *Andrew Johnson*, pp. 39–40; Eaton, *The Waning of the Old South Civilization*, pp. 117–18; Buck, *Road to Reunion*, pp. 38–42. Many travelers' accounts refer to women's greater hostility. See, for example, Trowbridge, *South*, pp. 71, 186, 188; Dennett, *South As It Is*, pp. 75–76, 278–79; Emily K. Abel, ed., "A Victorian Views Reconstruction: The American Diary of Samuel Augustus Barnett," *CWH* 20 (June 1974): 135–56.

23. Cook, "Restoration and Innovation," p. 145; and Harris, "South in Defeat," pp. 191–92, both argue that women sometimes condemned southern men for surrendering or expressed hostility toward them. On the basis of the evidence presented above, I think reassurance the more common expression. Scott, *Southern Lady*, pp. 96–102, argues that postwar conditions "undermined the patriarchy." Marjorie S. Mendenhall, "Southern Women of a 'Lost Generation,'" *South Atlantic Quarterly* 33 (October 1934): 334–53, traced most of the same trends Scott did but still gave more emphasis to a continuity of role. John Carl Ruoff, "Southern Womanhood, 1865–1920: An Intellectual and Cultural Study" (Ph.D. diss., University of Illinois at Urbana-Champaign, 1976), pp. 135–83, does as well. Marriage statistics are from Gilmour, "Other Emancipation," pp. 181–88. (Gilmour also found a rise in the divorce rate. It would be tempting to relate it to the problems both sexes had with their roles after the war, but there is no evidence on which to do so. On divorces, see pp. 194–201.) On land and jobs see Frank J. Huffman, Jr., "Old South, New South: Continuity and Change in a Georgia County, 1850–1880" (Ph.D. diss., Yale University, 1974), p. 85; and Jonathan M. Wiener, "Female Planters and Planters' Wives in Civil War and Reconstruction Alabama, 1850–1870," *Alabama Review* 30 (April 1977): 140–41. On absence of a woman's movement see Massey, *Bonnet Brigades*, p. 358; Scott, *Southern Lady*, p. 170; and Kathryn R. Schuler, "Women in Louisiana During Reconstruction" (M.A. thesis, Louisiana State University, 1935), pp. 10–12, 54–64, 187–92. There were some people active in suffrage work in the South, though. For a similar argument for continuity in female roles see Jean E. Friedman, *The Enclosed Garden: Women and Community in the Evangelical South, 1830–1900* (Chapel Hill: University of North Carolina Press, 1985), pp. 92–109.

24. Glimour, "Other Emancipation," p. 188, mentions fear of blacks as a factor in marrying. On fear see Massey, *Bonnet Brigades*, p. 287. Harris, "South in Defeat," p. 184, suggests that women were less prepared for defeat. Buck, *Road to Reunion*, pp. 38–42, adds to women's burdens the pain of sacrifices made in vain and the fact that they had not met the enemy as individuals the way men had. See also Suzanne Lebsock, *The Free Women of Petersburg: Status and Culture in a Southern Town, 1784–1860* (New York: W.W. Norton and Company, 1984), pp. 237–49.

25. Elizabeth A. Meriwether, *Recollections of 92 Years: 1824–1916* (Nashville: The Tennessee Historical Commission, 1958), p. 162.

26. Quotations are from Harper Manuscript, pp. 45–46, MDAH; and Augusta Jane Evans to J.L.M. Curry, 7 October 1865, Wilson Papers, UAL. See also Schuler, "Women in Louisiana," pp. 36–37; and Massey, *Bonnet Brigades*, pp. 280–82, which calls the change a "domestic revolution." One indication of the impact of changing work patterns is that two out of six women asked in 1891 how the war had changed their lives mentioned changes in domestic occupations. See Wilbur F. Tillett, "Southern Womanhood as Affected by the War," *Century* 43 (November 1891): 9–16. On the Alabama woman see *Report of the Committee of the Senate Upon the Relations Between Labor and Capital and Testimony Taken by the Committee*, 5 vols. (Washington, D. C.: Government Printing Office, 1895), 4: 343–47.

27. Meriwether, *Recollections*, pp. 78–80; Margaret Muse Pennybacker Reminiscences, undated, pp. 7, 9, 12, 17, VSL; Frances A. Doughty, "Life in the Cotton Belt," *Lippincott's Monthly Magazine* 59 (May 1897): 693–94. See also Emma Wood Richardson Civil War Reminiscence, undated, p. 4, VSL; Mrs. W.J. Weeden, "Reminiscence of Mrs. Jno. D. Weeden, Daughter of Ex. Gov. R.M. Patton," in Mrs. Edward A. O'Neal Records, ADAH; Brooks Diary, 13 January 1870, AHS.

28. Quotation is from Albert T. Morgan, *Yazoo: Or, On the Picket Line of*

Freedom in the South. A Personal Narrative (Washington: By the Author, 1884), pp. 77–78. On attitudes toward Butler see Durant, "Gently Furled Banner," pp. 125–26. For examples of references to Yankee barbarity see Macrae, *Americans at Home*, pp. 147–54; and Carter, ed., *Magnolia Journey*, p. 30. For outrage stories with no mention of physical assault see B. Hood to Susan, 24 August 1865, B. Hood Papers, SCL; Harper Manuscript, MDAH; and Mary Olney Allan, *The New Virginians*, 2 vols. (Edinburgh: William Blackwood and Sons, 1880), 2: 205–22. For accounts that do mention physical abuse see Macrae, *Americans at Home*, p. 261; Miers, ed., *When the World Ended*, p. 80. Patrick, *Fall of Richmond*, p. 101, notes that people of that city felt that Yankees behaved well. In a careful study of another northern occupation, Marion B. Lucas discovered several accounts of such abuses as tearing off clothes, but no reports of rapes. A southern committee of investigation later concluded that there were six cases in which northern soldiers "insulted and outraged women." Lucas also observes, however, that most Columbia residents described the awful atrocities of the Yankees but added that the northerners with whom they had personal contact were relatively polite. Lucas, *Sherman and the Burning of Columbia*, pp. 157, 161. My impression is that the pattern Lucas noted holds true in other areas. Thomas Diary, 27 May 1865, Duke, suggests that some of the hostility toward northern soldiers resulted from their failure to treat ladies by southern standards of gentility.

29. Zillah H. Brandon Reminiscences, 4: 383–84, ADAH. Quotation is from Jennie to Jennie, 19 June 1865, G.W. Munford Letters, Ellis-Munford Papers, Duke. See also Florence F. Mosby, "The Times," 5 May 1865, John S. Mosby Papers, UVA.

30. For hostility see Macrae, *The Americans*, p. 404; Alex and Harris Rivington, *Reminiscences of America in 1869 by Two Englishmen*, 2d ed., (London: Sampson Law, Son, and Marston, 1870), p. 297; F.N. Boney, ed., *A Union Soldier in the Land of the Vanquished: The Diary of Sergeant Mathew Woodruff, June-December 1865* (University: University of Alabama Press, 1969), pp. 48–50; George Rose, *The Great Country; or Impressions of America* (London: Tinsley Brothers, 1868), pp. 150, 180; Charles Stearns, *The Black Man of the South and the Rebels* (New York: American News Company, 1872), pp. 66–71, 129–30, 256–65; Dennett, *The South As It Is*, pp. 273–75, 306–10, 312–43; and John W. De Forest, *A Union Officer in the Reconstruction*, James H. Croushore and David M. Potter, eds. (New Haven: Yale University Press, 1948), pp. 46, 196–98. But for more pleasant receptions see Sir John Henry Kennaway, *On Sherman's Track: Or, The South After the War* (London: Seeley, Jackson and Holliday, 1867), pp. 88–89 (but for mention of hostility, pp. 117–19, 131–37); Nathanial Holmes Bishop, *Voyage of the Paper Canoe: A Geographical Journey of 2,500 Miles* . . . (Edinburgh: David Douglas, 1878), pp. 213, 215; and Mrs. Ellen (McGowan) Biddle, *Reminiscences of a Soldier's Wife* (Philadelphia: J.B. Lippincott Co., 1907), pp. 23–43. For scholarly evaluations of receptions of northern visitors, see Anne Barber Harris, "The South as Seen by Travelers, 1865–1880" (Ph.D. diss., University of North Carolina, 1967), p. 127, *passim*; McKitrick, *Andrew Johnson and Reconstruction*, pp. 39–40; Perman, *Reunion Without Compromise*, pp. 13–24; and Lawrence N. Powell, *New Masters: Northern Planters During the Civil War and Reconstruction* (New Haven: Yale University Press, 1980), pp. 63–73. First quotation is from Gail Hamilton [Mary Abigail Dodge], *Wool-gathering* (Boston: Ticknor & Fields, 1867), pp. 273–74. For a southerner making the same point see C.S. Sussdorf letter in Elizabeth G. McPherson, ed., "Letters from North Carolina to President Johnson," *North Carolina Historical Review* 38 (July 1951): 363. Other quotations are from Trowbridge, *The South*, pp. 72, 328, 425, 568, and Anna to Marum Mary Dickinson, 30 April 1875, Anna E. Dickinson Papers, LC.

31. "Bill Arp Addresses Artemus Ward," 1 September 1865, reprinted in Charles

H. Smith, *Bill Arp, From the Uncivil War to Date, 1861–1903* (Atlanta: The Hudgins Publishing Company, 1903), pp. 84–88. Copies of the original column are in a scrapbook in Anne Bruin Papers, SHC, and E.F. Andrews Scrapbook, Garnett Andrews Papers, SHC. On southern response to the Ward letter see Anne M. Christie, "Bill Arp," *CWH* 2 (September 1956): 115–16. On Arp's general influence see Thomas D. Clark, *The Rural Press and the New South* (Baton Rouge: Louisiana State University Press, 1948), pp. 32–33. Salem Dutcher, "Bill Arp and Artemus Ward," *Scott's Monthly Magazine* 2 (June 1866): 473, said Arp "is doubtless, to-day, the most popular man in the South."

32. The importance of northern attitudes for southern honor during the antebellum period is stressed in Cooper, *Politics of Slavery*.

33. This discussion highlights a basic difference between the use of the term "honor" here and in other works on southern honor. Wyatt-Brown, *Southern Honor*, treats it as an exclusive value system. Ayers, *Vengeance and Justice*, sees a value system rooted in honor increasingly challenged by a competing one based on dignity and rooted in evangelical Protestantism. The treatment here assumes that southerners judged themselves both against what they considered God's standards (and therefore internalized Protestant values, which are part of what I take Ayers means by "dignity") and society's standards (part of what I take Wyatt-Brown to mean by "honor"). The conceptual disparity cannot be reconciled here, but postwar southerners certainly seemed concerned about both standards.

CHAPTER THREE.

CEREMONIAL BEREAVEMENT:

MEMORIAL ACTIVITIES

1. Copy of poem and biographical information by a friend are in Hannis Taylor, "Abram J. Ryan," *Library of Southern Literature*, 15 vols., Edwin A. Alderman and Joel Chandler Harris, eds. (Atlanta: The Martin & Hoyt Company, 1909), 10: 4623–44. For a better introduction to his life see Charles C. Boldrick, "Father Abram J. Ryan, 'The Poet-Priest of the Confederacy,'" *Filson Club Historical Quarterly* 46 (July 1972): 201–18; and Robert T. Adams, "A Study of the Life and Work of the Reverend Abram Joseph Ryan, Poet-Priest of the Confederacy," (M.A. thesis, Louisiana State University, 1964). The despair in Ryan's poem becomes especially clear when it is compared with a more positive version written by an Englishman in October 1865. See "Southern War Poetry," *OLOD* 1 (10 December 1873): 1.

2. Critic's quotation is from "Southern War Poetry," *Southern Review* 1 (April 1867): 284. Description of Ryan is from Cloy to Bonnie Kell, 9 January 1868, John McIntosh Kell Papers, Duke. "The Conquered Banner" was set to music by Theodore von Lahache in 1866; see Sheet Music Collection, Tulane.

3. On treatment of death in poetry in magazines, see Ray M. Atchison, "Southern Literary Magazines, 1865–1887" (Ph.D. diss., Duke University, 1956), pp. 77–78. For examples in private papers see Berry G. Benson Papers, SHC; James Metts Papers, SHC; Martin V. Moore Papers, SHC. Quotation is from Solomon L.M. Conser, *Virginia After the War*, p. 12. See also Lady Duffus Hardy, *Down South* (London: Chapman and Hall, Ltd., 1883), p. 14; Edward King, *The Great South*, W. Magruder Drake and Robert R. Jones, eds. (Baton Rouge: Louisiana State University Press, 1972; first published 1873–74), p. 35; and John Muir, *A Thousand-Mile Walk to the Gulf* (Boston: Houghton Mifflin Company, 1916), p. 84.

4. Anderson, ed., *Brokenburn*, p. 340. See also Elizabeth P. Allan, *The Life and Letters of Margaret Junkin Preston* (New York: Houghton, Mifflin, and Company, 1903),

pp. 207–8; Green, *The Journal of a Milledgeville Girl, 1861–1867*, pp. 75–76. For envy of dead or wish to die, see Chi to Julian Mitchell, 2 March 1866, Julian Mitchell Papers, SCHS; Fanny Downing, "Dixie," *LWL* 1 (October 1866): 381; Sarah A. Dorsey, *Recollections of Henry Watkins Allen, Brigadier-General Confederate States Army, Ex-Governor of Louisiana* (New York: M. Doolady, 1866), p. 285; Wade Hampton to Sister, 28 March 1867, Wade Hampton Papers, SCL; V., "What Time I Wore the Rebel Gray," *New Eclectic* 6 (March 1870): 380; Jos. Blythe Allston, "Stack Arms," Joseph Blyth Allston Papers, SCL; F. Barham Zincke, *Last Winter in the United States* (London: John Murray, 1868), p. 72; George A. Mercer Diary, 19–20 March 1865, 2: 76–81, SHC; and Grace Brown Elmore Diary, 4 July 1865, SCL.

5. Avery O. Craven, *Edmund Ruffin, Southerner: A Study in Secession* (Baton Rouge: Louisiana State University Press, 1932), pp. 256–59. Morton Keller, *Affairs of State: Public Life in Nineteenth Century America* (Cambridge: Harvard University Press, 1977), pp. 199–200, cites Ruffin and one other. Quotation is from Jubal A. Early to S.H. Early, 15 July 1867, Jubal A. Early Papers, LC.

6. Unless otherwise indicated, the account that follows of the activities of the memorial associations is based on the following sources: the histories of many LMAs published in Confederated Southern Memorial Association, *History of the Confederated Memorial Associations of the South* (New Orleans: The Graham Press, 1904) and several manuscript records: Records of the Memorial Society of the Ladies of the City of Petersburg, 1866–1912, VSL; Ladies' Memorial Association of Wake County, North Carolina Department of Archives and History, Raleigh; Young Ladies' Hospital Association, Columbia, SCL; Ladies' Memorial Association of Charleston, SCHS; Ladies' Memorial Association Records, AHS; Ladies' Memorial Association of Perote, Alabama, Minutes, 1874–1934, ADAH; and *First Annual Report of the Louisiana Benevolent Association of Louisiana*, in Memorial Association Papers, Louisiana Historical Association Collection, Tulane. On sources for Columbus and Winchester, see below.

7. For acknowledgement of Columbus's role see *HCMAS*, pp. 75–78, 88–90; on origin in wartime aid society, pp. 75, 84, 106, 107, 123, 171, 266, 294, 315. For leaders who lost relatives in war see *HCMAS*, pp. 113–14, 138–39; Mrs. George T. Fry, "The History of the Atlanta Memorial Association Told by Mrs. George T. Fry—Heroic Conduct of the Southern Ladies," clipping in Minute Book, LMA of Atlanta Records, AHS; and Mrs. Bettie A.C. Emerson, *Historic Southern Monuments: Representative Memorials of the Heroic Dead of the Southern Confederacy* (New York: The Neal Publishing Company, 1911), pp. 188–91.

8. Resolution by Ladies of Hollywood Memorial Association, 29 May 1866; Dawson to Mother, 17 June, 28 July, and 15 November 1866; N. Macfarland to Dawson, 8 November 1866—all in Francis W. Dawson Papers, Duke. On men presiding see LMA of Charleston Minutes, 14 May 1866, SCHS; Minutes of the LMA of Perote, Alabama, 27 April 1874, ADAH. For males joining see Minute Book Belonging to the Ladies' Memorial Association of Atlanta, Ga., 1884–1900, LMA of Atlanta Records, AHS. On financial support see P.F. Pescud, "A Sketch of the Ladies' Memorial Association of Raleigh, N.C.: Its Origin and History," 1882; List of Members, LMA of Wake County; LMA, Raleigh Minutes, 1866–1882—all in LMA of Wake County Records, NCDAH. Quotation is from *HCMAS*, p. 59. See also Circular, L.H. Pickins, "To the Patriotic Women of Edgefield County," Ladies' Memorial Association (Edgefield County), SCL; and "In Memoriam," *Southern Review* 19 (April 1876): 326–29. E. Merton Coulter, "The Confederate Monument in Athens, Georgia," *Georgia Historical Review* 40 (September 1956): 230–31, suggests that men "felt that it would be impolitic, if not a violation of the spirit of their paroles" to engage in such activity. I have found no evidence

to support that view. For mention of some memorial activity by men that apparently came to nothing, see Petersburg LMA Minutes, pp. 9, 11, 43, VSL; "Confederate Organizations in Mississippi," *Confederate Veteran* 2 (June 1894): 180; E. Kirby Smith to Jubal Early, 23 January 1872, Early Papers, LC; and P.G.T. Beauregard to E. Kirby Smith, 30 March 1872, Beauregard Papers, LC.

9. Figures were found in *HCMAS*, pp. 299–302 (Richmond), 168–72 (New Orleans), 107–11 (Augusta), 56–59 (Montgomery). On small towns (Romney, Virginia) see "First Confederate Monument," *CV* 19 (August 1911): 372–73; and clipping from *Alexandria Gazette* in Anne Bruin Scrapbook, SHC. In a very few instances states provided some money. See Coulter, "Confederate Monument," pp. 231–32; *HCMAS*, pp. 140–43.

10. LMA Petersburg Minutes, 6 May 1886, p. 1, VSL. On agents, see "Ladies' Memorial Association, Montgomery," manuscript in box #6, Thomas M. Owen Papers, ADAH. On other battlefields, see "Soldiers Monument," *Southern Historical Society Papers* 17 (1889): 388–403. On Gettysburg dead, see LMA of Charleston Minutes, 22 June 1870, SCHS; LMA Raleigh Minutes, 1866–1882, 3 May 1867, NCDAH; *New York Times*, 2 July 1873, p. 3.

11. On Winchester, see "Editorial Paragraphs," *SHSP* 7 (July 1879): 349–50; *New York Times*, 26 October 1866, p. 1; and *HCMAS*, pp. 314–18. On Resaca, see *HCMAS*, pp. 143–51.

12. "Something of Hollywood Cemetery," *CV* 1 (June 1893): 164; R.A.M. to G.S. Barnsley, 11 June [1866?], George S. Barnsley Papers, SHC; Myrta L. Avary, *Dixie After the War* (New York: Doubleday, Page & Company, 1906), pp. 405–6; quotation is from J.W. Waldrop Diary, 28 May 1866, 3:41, in Richard W. Waldrop Papers, SHC. On Raleigh, see *HCMAS*, pp. 227–30. Not all towns established Confederate cemeteries, of course. Northern and foreign visitors criticized the absence of Confederate cemeteries in some communities or belittled those in others. See Carter, ed., *Magnolia Journey*, pp. 11–12, 20, 31, 173; and Alex and Harris Rivington, *Reminiscences of America in 1869 by Two Englishmen* (London: Sampson, Low, Son and Marston, 1870), p. 305.

13. Hardy, *Down South*, p. 67; *HCMAS*, p. 149; Dolly B. Lamar, *When All Is Said and Done* (Athens: University of Georgia Press, 1952), p. 35.

14. For figures and sources on which the following discussion of monuments rests see Appendix 1. Similar observations on the types of monuments are made in John J. Winberry, "'Lest We Forget': The Confederate Monument and the Southern Townscape," *Southeastern Geographer* 23 (November 1983): 107–21; Stephen Davis, "Empty Eyes, Marble Hand: The Confederate Monument and the South," *Journal of Popular Culture* 16 (Winter 1982): 2–21.

15. *HCMAS*, pp. 91–92; A *Brief History of the Ladies' Memorial Association of Charleston, S.C.* (Charleston: H.P. Cooke & Co., Printers, 1880), pp. 8–9 (copy in Yates Snowden Papers, SCL).

16. Pictures of these and other monuments can be found in *HCMAS*; Emerson, *Historic Southern Monuments*; Ralph W. Widener, Jr., *Confederate Monuments: Enduring Symbols of the South and the War Between the States* (Washington: Andromedia Associates, 1982). On Victorian statuary see Edward Gillon, Jr., *Victorian Cemetery Art* (New York: Dover, 1972); David E. Stannard, *The Puritan Way of Death: A Study in Religion, Culture, and Social Change* (New York: Oxford University Press, 1977), pp. 171–88.

17. J.H. Hudson, Address Delivered by J.H. Hudson (LTC 26 SC Volunteers), at dedication of monument to Confederate Dead in Cheraw, S.C. 26 July 1867, in

Joshua H. Hudson Papers, SCL. See also Charles C. Jones, Jr., "Oration Delivered on the 31st of October, 1878, upon the Occasion of the unveiling and dedication of the Confederate Monument in Broad Street, Augusta, Georgia, . . . " in Charles C. Jones, Jr., Papers, Duke; and John S. Preston, "A Monumental Mystery," in John S. Preston Papers, SCL. An account of one is in Samuel P. Day, *Life and Society in America* (London: Newman and Company, 1880), pp. 190–92.

18. Boney, ed., *A Union Soldier in the Land of the Vanquished*, p. 45; *A History of the Origin of Memorial Day as Adopted by the Ladies' Memorial Association of Columbus, Georgia* (Columbus: Thos. Gilbert, Printer, 1898), and The Baroness Tautphoeus, *The Initials: A Story of Modern Life* (Philadelphia: J.B. Lippincott, 1903; first published 1853), pp. 247–49. For other claimants to being first, see Mary Hunt Affick, "Southern Aid Society, Harrodsburg, 1861–1865," CV 21 (January 1913): 30; Kate M. Power, "Where Was Decoration Day First Celebrated in the South?" clipping, 26 April 1908, United Sons of Confederate Veterans Papers, Louisiana Historical Association Collection, Tulane; Sue Adams Vaughn to Mrs. Gunn, 18 March 1907, and Vaughn to Miss Sallie, 4 April 1907, both in John L. Power Papers, MDAH; Mrs. J.E. Hopkins, "First Decorating of Graves," CV 15 (June 1907): 360–61; and *Minutes of Sixth Annual Meeting, United Daughters of the Confederacy*, 1899, p. 50. E. Merton Coulter, *The South During Reconstruction, 1865–1877* (Baton Rouge: Louisiana State University Press, 1947), p. 178, credits Columbus; Buck, *Road to Reunion*, p. 116, sees no point in trying to determine which was first.

19. In addition to sources already cited on variety in Memorial Day customs, see "In Memoriam," OLOD 1 (13 May 1874): 2; Mary W.D. to Lou, 1 June 1870, in Fleet, ed., *Green Mount After the War*, pp. 52–3; and McDonald Furman to Ma, 16 May 1884, Charles J. McDonald Furman Papers, SCL. "Memorial Day Orators," in LMA File, Memorial Association Papers, LHAC, Tulane, shows that from 1874 to 1887 New Orleans had orators only four times.

20. William Nelson Pendleton, "Speech on occasion of removing the remains of a number of Confederate Soldiers," in William N. Pendleton Papers, SHC; Henry D. Capers, *An Address Delivered Before the Ladies' Memorial Association of Putnam County, Georgia, April 28th, 1868* (Charleston: Walker, Evans & Cogswell, 1896). See also William C.P. Breckenridge, *Address in Memory of the Confederate Dead* (Lexington: Observer & Report Print., 1869); untitled speech by John Sanford, May 1869, John W. Sanford Papers, ADAH; "Address of Gen. R.E. Colston Before the Ladies' Memorial Association at Wilmington, N.C., May 10, 1870," in SHSP 21 (1893): 38–49; "Memorial Address of General Wade Hampton," SM 13 (August 1873): 225–32; Judge J.A.P. Campbell, "The Lost Cause," SHSP 16 (1888): 232–45; S.H. Lockett, "Address at Memorial Celebration, May 1st, 1875," Samuel H. Lockett Papers, SHC; "In Memoriam," SR 19 (April 1876): 328–33; Clipping, "Mr. Waddell's Address," 10 May 1879, scrapbook vol. 6, Alfred Moore Waddell Papers, SHC; A.M. Keiley, "Our Fallen Heroes," SHSP 7 (August 1879): 373–84; and R.T. Bennett, "The Confederate Soldier," SHSP 28 (1890): 272–75.

21. On common themes in Victorian-American society see Stannard, *Puritan Way of Death*, pp. 167–96; essays in Stannard, ed., "Death in America," *American Quarterly* 26 (December 1974); Stanley French, "The Cemetery as Cultural Institution: The Establishment of Mount Auburn and the 'Rural Cemetery' Movement," *American Quarterly* 26 (March 1974): 37–59; and James J. Farrell, *Inventing the American Way of Death, 1830–1920* (Philadelphia: Temple University Press, 1980). On Memorial Day adoption in the North, see Buck, *Road to Reunion*, pp. 116–21. The Grand Army of the

Republic had already formed and become active in the North: Mary R. Dearing, *Veterans in Politics; The Story of the Grand Army of the Republic* (Baton Rouge: Louisiana State University Press, 1952).

22. Walter L. Fleming, ed., *Documentary History of Reconstruction*, 2 vols. in 1 (New York: Peter Smith, 1950; first published 1906), 1: 211; S.G. French to T. Waring Mikell, 2 August 1866, T. Waring Mikell Papers, SCL; Moore, ed., *The Juhl Letters*, p. 115; "The Wearers of the Gray," clippings from *The Daily Picayune*, 20 July 1873, Edward C. Wharton and Family Papers, LSU; James R. Randall, "At Arlington," clipping in Thaddeus K. Oglesby Papers, Duke; Meriwether, *Recollections of 92 Years*, pp. 193–95; Mildred L. Rutherford, "Confederate Monuments and Cemeteries," CV 11 (January 1903): 17; James E. Sefton, *The United States Army and Reconstruction, 1865–1877* (Baton Rouge: Louisiana State University Press, 1967), pp. 97–98. For southern comments on giving in to the North, see Josiah Gorgas Journal, 3 February 1867, SHC; LMA of Charleston Minutes, 28 April 1867, SCHS; James Henry Gardner to Mary P. Florence, 1 June 1867, Gardner File, VHS. "The South Carolina Monument," CV 7 (May 1899): 231–32, tells of one instance in which politics did play a role in the decision about placement of a monument.

23. On widespread involvement see Francis B. Simkins and Robert H. Woody, *South Carolina During Reconstruction* (Chapel Hill: University of North Carolina Press, 1932), pp. 348–49; and Jerrell H. Shofner, *Nor Is It Over Yet: Florida in the Era of Reconstruction, 1863–1877* (Gainesville: The University Presses of Florida, 1974), pp. 141–42. Analysis of Charleston membership is based on a comparison of the members who joined between 1866 and 1879 as shown by the roll in the Charleston LMA Records, SCHS and Charleston city directories. Because of the difficulty of identifying single women in the directories (presumably, daughters of men who are listed) and married women who gave their own names when joining the LMA, conclusions about the backgrounds of female members are unusually tenuous. (Only 29 percent of the women were identified, compared with 82 percent of the men.) The names were also checked against a list of large planters in Chalmers Davidson, *The Last Foray: The South Carolina Planters of 1860: A Sociological Study* (Columbia: University of South Carolina Press, 1971). Only five planters were identified, although others less established than those in Davidson's sample may still have joined. But even if all the unidentified were planters, they would still be outnumbered by the twenty-six factors and commission merchants. Figures on the Charleston membership are as follows:

	Female	Male
Professional & high white-collar	56 (58.95%)	72 (87.80%)
Proprietary & low white-collar	35 (36.84%)	8 (9.76%)
Skilled craftsmen	4 (4.21%)	2 (2.44%)
Unskilled workers	—	—
Total identified	95	82
Unidentified	230	17

Except in two or three cases where the women themselves were employed, the females were categorized on the basis of their husbands' occupations. Here and throughout the study, I have relied on a modified form (I lump three unskilled classifications into one) of the occupation rating in Theodore Hershberg and Robert Dockhorn, "Occupational Classification," *Historical Methods Newsletter* 9 (March-June 1976): 59–98.

24. Anna to Mary Dickinson, 3 May 1875, Anna E. Dickinson Papers, LC; Hardy, *Down South*, pp. 257–61; Iza Duffus Hardy, *Between Two Oceans; Or, Sketches of American Travel* (London: Hurst and Blackett, 1884), pp. 318–20; Carter, ed., *Magnolia Journey*, pp. 93–94; *New York Times*, 3 June 1867, p. 8 and 5 June 1868, p. 8; southern comments in "Honored Heroes," clipping, 11 April 1874, Wharton Papers, LSU; Edward Clifford Anderson Diary, 26 April 1875, SHC; "In Memoriam," *OLOD* 1 (13 May 1874): 2; *HCMAS*, p. 172.

25. Peter Marris, *Loss and Change* (New York: Pantheon Books, 1974), pp. 23, 31 *passim*. Paul C. Rosenblatt, R. Patricia Walsh, and Douglas A. Jackson, *Grief and Mourning in Cross-Cultural Perspective* (n.p.: Human Relations Area Files, Incorporated, 1976), pp. 116–20, provides a critique of Marris.

26. Although infrequently made, the point that the dead had never surrendered can be seen in an 1871 speech by J.L. Girardeau in *A Brief History of the LMA of Charleston*, in Yates Snowden Papers, SCL; and in an untitled poem in Eliza Hall Parsley Papers, SHC.

27. Campbell, "The Lost Cause," pp. 244–45.

28. On blacks, see *HCMAS*, p. 103; "Subscription List to Bury the Confederate Dead in Virginia," Wharton Papers, LSU, which has a list of Louisiana Republicans, including P.B.S. Pinchback.

29. On early European beliefs, see Keith Thomas, *Religion and the Decline of Magic* (New York: Charles Scribner's Sons, 1971), pp. 587–606. For an introduction to those of other cultures see Rosenblatt, et al., *Grief and Mourning*. Also see Robert Blauner, "Death and Social Structure," *Passing: The Vision of Death in America*, Charles O. Jackson, ed., (Westport, Conn.: Greenwood Press, 1977), pp. 180–81, 191–92 *passim*. Phillipe Ariès, *Western Attitudes Toward Death: From the Middle Ages to the Present*, trans. Patricia M. Ranum (Baltimore: The Johns Hopkins University Press, 1974), pp. 78–79, mentions the importance of cults of the heroic dead in this period.

30. "Confederate Memorial Day Speech, Richmond, Virginia," n.d., John W. Daniel Papers, UVA; Charles C. Jones, *Addresses Delivered Before Confederate Survivor's Association of Augusta, Ga.*, 1880, p. 4. For southerners talking of dead as ghosts and/or claiming that the dead have influence on the living, see Zillah H. Brandon Reminiscences, 6 July 1865, 4: 375, ADAH; Thomas Markham, Sermon, 20 August 1865, Thomas R. Markham Papers, LSU; Sidney Lanier to Mrs. Clay, 6 August 1867, Clement Claiborne Clay Papers, Duke; Memoirs, p. 64, Benson Papers, SHS; Appleton Oaksmith, "The Lost Cause," *SM* 9 (October 1871): 449–52; and Mrs. Davis to "Own Precious Darling," 25 April 1880, Jefferson Davis Papers, UAL.

CHAPTER FOUR.

GHOST DANCE: THE FAILED REVITALIZATION MOVEMENT

OF THE VIRGINIANS

1. On the churches see Spain, *At Ease in Zion*; Hunter D. Farish, *The Circuit Rider Dismounts: A Social History of Southern Methodism, 1865–1900* (Richmond: The Dietz Press, 1938); Morrow, *Northern Methodism and Reconstruction*; Thompson, *Presbyterians in the South, Volume Two: 1861–1890*; Joseph B. Cheshire, Jr., *The Church in the Confederate States: A History of the Protestant Episcopal Church in the Confederate States* (London and New York: Longmans, Green, and Company, 1912); and Jack P. Maddex, Jr., "From Theocracy to Spirituality: The Southern Presbyterian Reversal on Church and State," *Journal of Presbyterian History* 54 (Winter 1976):

438–57. For a different view of the churches' role see Wilson, *Baptized in Blood*, pp. 34–35. Wilson does not demonstrate much institutional involvement, but rather rests his case on the activities of preachers outside the churches.

2. For one such academy see W. McKee Evans, *Ballots and Fence Rails: Reconstruction on the Lower Cape Fear* (New York: W.W. Norton & Company, 1966), p. 235. On the Confederate Home School, see "Editorial Paragraphs," *SHSP* 5 (May 1878): 254; and *Home for the Mothers, Widows and Daughters of Confederate Soldiers, Charleston, S.C., Annual Reports*. Quotation is from a speech by Major Theodore G. Baker in the 1871 report, p. 10. For attendance see "Statistics of the Confederate College of Charleston, founded 1867," in Confederate College of Charleston Papers, SCL. For a different view of the role of the educational institutions, one that discusses the same activities, see Wilson, *Baptized in Blood*, pp. 139–160.

3. Arthur B. Chitty, "Heir of Hopes: Historical Summary of the University of the South," *HMPEC* 23 (September 1954): 258–65; William W. Pusey, III, *The Interrupted Dream: The Educational Program at Washington College (Washington and Lee University), 1850–1880* (Washington and Lee University: Liberty Hall Press, 1976). On leaders as educators see Hesseltine, *Confederate Leaders in the New South*, pp. 78–88; and William W. White, *The Confederate Veteran* (Tuscaloosa, Alabama: Confederate Publishing Company, 1962), pp. 59–60.

4. On the KKK as the first stage of Confederate movement after the war see Wilson, *Baptized in Blood*, pp. 112–16; Hunter, "The Sacred South," pp. 78–79; and Osterweis, *Myth of the Lost Cause*, pp. 16–23. My interpretation of the Klan rests on information in Allen W. Trelease, *White Terror: The Ku Klux Klan Conspiracy and Southern Reconstruction* (New York: Harper & Row, Publishers, 1971). For another mention of Confederate ghosts see Evans, *Ballots and Fence Rails*, p. 100.

5. On the response to Pollard, see "Editorial Notes, etc." *DeBow's Review* 2 (November 1866): 558; Jubal A. Early to Edward A. Pollard (draft copy), 28 December 1866, Jubal A. Early Papers, LC; P.G.T. Beauregard, "Notes on E.A. Pollard's 'Lost Cause,'" *SM* 10 (January 1872): 55–64 and (February 1872): 163–71; Matthew C. Butler to D.H. Hill, 13 February 1868, and Paul H. Hayne to Hill, 17 October 1868, Daniel H. Hill Papers, NCDAH; Josiah Gorgas Journal, 26 November 1868, sec. 3, p. 123, SHC; "Editorial," *LWL*, 5 (July 1868): 281–85; and J. William Jones to William T. Walthall, 26 April 1878, William T. Walthall Papers, MDAH. On Pollard himself see Jack P. Maddex, Jr., *The Reconstruction of Edward A. Pollard: A Rebel's Conversion to Postbellum Unionism* (Chapel Hill: University of North Carolina Press, 1974). For a different view of his role see Osterweis, *Myth of the Lost Cause*, pp. 11–12.

6. Albert T. Bledsoe, *Is Davis a Traitor; Or was Secession a Constitutional Right Previous to the War of 1861?* (Baltimore: Printed for the author by Innes and Company, 1866); Robert L. Dabney, *A Defense of Virginia (and Through Her, of the South) In The Recent and Pending Contests against the Sectional Party* (New York: E.J. Hale & Son, 1867); Alexander H. Stephens, *A Constitutional View of the Late War Between the States: Its Causes, Character, Conduct and Results Presented in a Series of Colloquies at Liberty Hill*, 2 vols. (Philadelphia: National Publishing Company, 1868–70).

7. Atchison, "Southern Literary Magazines." Quotations are from D.H. Hill to S.D. Lee, 29 June 1866, Stephen Dill Lee Papers, SHC; "Editorial," *LWL* 5 (September 1868): 444–49. Also see Little, "The Ideology of the New South," pp. 52–60; and for another view of the *Southern Review*, Weaver, *The Southern Tradition At Bay*, pp. 135–38.

8. Rudolph Von Abele, *Alexander H. Stephens: A Biography* (New York: Alfred A. Knopf, 1946), p. 273: Overy, "Robert Lewis Dabney," p. 162; Theodrick Pryor to

Dabney, 4 June 1873, Robert L. Dabney Papers, UTSL; *SR* 8 (October 1870): 442 and 19 (January 1876): 252; "Editorial," *LWL* 5 (August 1868): 371; Jay B. Hubbell, *The South in American Literature* (Durham: Duke University Press, 1954), p. 721; "From Our Correspondents," *OLOD* 1 (15 October 1873): 3. Atchison, "Southern Literary Magazines," pp. 65–66, 241, speculates on the failure of such magazines. Durant, "Gently Furled Banner," pp. 13–71, in contrast, discusses their popularity.

    9. For early organizations see "Editorial Miscellanies," *DR* 1 (June 1866): 664–65; "The Washington Light Infantry, 1807–1861," *SHSP* 31 (1903): 1–11; "Notice of Meeting, HQ Association of Officers of 3d North Carolina Infantry," Raleigh E. Colston Papers, SHC; and "First Association of Confederate Veterans," *Confederate Veteran* 6 (June 1898): 265. On CSA see papers and pamphlets in Survivor's Association Papers, SCHS. On Memphis group see J. Harvey Mathes, *The Old Guard in Gray: Researches in the Annals of the Confederate Historical Association* (Memphis: Press of S.C. Toof & Co., 1897); and "Bivouac 18, CSA and Camp 28 UCV," *CV* 5 (November 1897): 566–67.

    10. On Confederates in New Orleans see Duke, *Reminiscences of General Basil W. Duke, CSA*, pp. 460–61. On SHS see Dabney H. Maury, "The Southern Historical Society: Its Origins and History," *SHSP* 18 (1890): 349–65; Maury, *Recollections*, pp. 251–52; and Beauregard to D.H. Hill, 1 July 1869, Beauregard Papers, LC.

    11. "The Southern Historical Society," *New Eclectic* 5 (October 1869): 443–46; Maury, "Historical Society," pp. 353–54. For evidence of widespread activity see "Official Circular," Southern Historical Society, in P.G.T. Beauregard and Family Papers, LSU; Wade Hampton to "Connor" (copy), 11 April 1869, Hampton Family Papers, SCL; Braxton Bragg to William Walthall, 28 June 1869, Walthall Papers, MDAH; B.M. Palmer to Edward McCrady, Jr., 7 July 1869, Survivors' Association Papers, SCHS; Joseph Jones to Ashbel Smith, 4 August 1869, Ashbel Smith Papers, UTX; C.M. Wilcox to S.H. Lockett, 19 November 1869, Samuel H. Lockett Papers, SHC; and Edwin W. Pettus to John Sanford, 29 November 1869, John W.A. Sanford Papers, ADAH. Also see *New York Times*, 23 March 1870, p. 4; Historicus, "The Relic of the First Revolution," *NE* 5 (December 1869): 68–69; "The Green Table," *NE* 6 (January 1870): 118–19; and Joseph Jones to Braxton Bragg, 20 November 1869, Joseph Jones Papers, LSU.

    12. On Lee as a symbol, see Buck, *Road to Reunion*, pp. 250–54; Hesseltine, *Confederate Leaders*, pp. 27–39; Marshall W. Fishwick, *Lee After the War* (New York: Dodd, Mead & Company, 1963), pp. 42–43; and Allen W. Moger, "Letters to General Lee After the War," *VMHB* 64 (January 1956): 69. Quotation on sadness is in Macrae, *The Americans at Home*, pp. 200–1. See also Cornelia McDonald, *A Diary With Reminiscences of the War and Refugee Life in the Shenandoah Valley, 1860–65* (Nashville: Cullom and Ghertner, 1935), p. 272. On the unwritten book, see Douglas S. Freeman, *The South to Posterity: An Introduction to the Writing of Confederate History* (New York: Charles Scribner's Sons, 1939), pp. 42–43; and Allen W. Moger, "General Lee's Unwritten History of the Army of Northern Virginia," *VMHB* 71 (July 1963): 341–63. Neither offers the interpretation given here. On not reading war books, see Lee to Edward A. Pollard, 24 January 1867, and Lee to A.T. Bledsoe, 28 October 1867. Both copies are in Lee Letterbook, Lee Family Papers, VHS.

    13. On Lee's attitude toward activities, see Freeman, *R.E. Lee*, 4: 436–37; and Lee to Thos. L. Rosser, 13 December 1866, R.E. Lee Letterbook, Lee Family Papers, VHS. Quotation is from R.E. Lee, Circular letter (copy), 31 July 1865, Hampton Papers, SCL. On encouragement, see Lee to Early (copy), 15 October 1866, Early Papers, LC; Lee to R.L. Dabney, 13 July 1866, Lee Letterbook, Lee Family Papers, VHS; and Lee

to A.T. Bledsoe, 8 October 1866, Albert T. Bledsoe Papers, UVA. On numbers see Lee to Walter Taylor, 31 July 1865; Lee to Joseph L. Topham, 26 August 1865; and Lee to Early, 22 November 1865 and 15 March 1866—all in Lee Letterbook, Lee Family Papers, VHS.

14. On doubts about Lee see A.H. Mason to P.G.T. Beauregard, 4 September 1865, John R. Peacock Papers, SHC; Gorgas Journal, 19 April 1867, 3: 86, SHC; and Beauregard to Thomas Jordan, [n.d.] December 1868, Beauregard Papers, LC. On hero status see Miers, ed., *When the World Ended*, pp. 95–96; Henry A. Garrett Diary, 22 August 1865, John F.H. Claiborne Papers, LC; Reid, *After the War*, p. 300; Macrae, *Americans at Home*, pp. 162–70; Moger, "Letters to Lee," pp. 30–69; and R. Barnwell Rhett, "The Destroyers of the Late Confederacy," *SM* 15 (August 1874): 149. Rhett also criticizes other men for climbing on Lee's reputation for their own purposes. On travels see George Blow to Eliza Waller Pegram, 2 December 1867, Pegram Family Papers, VHS; Perceval Reniers, *The Springs of Virginia: Life, Love, and Death at the Waters, 1775–1900* (Chapel Hill: University of North Carolina Press, 1941), p. 206; and Freeman, *Lee*, 4: 444–67. Quotation is from Fanny Downing, "Perfect Through Suffering," *LWL* 4 (January 1868): 194–95.

15. First quotation is from Abbie M. Brooks Diary, 13 October 1870, AHS. Also see Walthall Diaries, 15 October 1870, Walthall Papers, MDAH; "Tributes to General Lee," *SM* 8 (January 1871): 1–46; Edward C. Anderson Diary, 13 and 15 October 1871, vol. 7, SHC; Mary S. Mallard to Joseph Jones, 20 October 1870, Jones Papers, LSU. Other quotations are from Johnson, *The Life and Letters of Benjamin Morgan Palmer*, pp. 347–52; and *Proceedings of Survivors' Association of South Carolina, 2d Annual Meeting*, p. 18.

16. Beauregard to W.N. Pendleton, 4 November 1870, Beauregard Papers, LC; Beauregard to Early, 29 November 1870, Early Papers, LC; Robert E. Lee Monumental Association of New Orleans, Circular Letter, 1870, Joseph Jones Papers, Tulane.

17. Susan Pendleton Lee, *Memoirs of William Nelson Pendleton, D.D. . . .* (Philadelphia: J.B. Lippincott, 1893), pp. 454–63; Pendleton to S.D. Lee, 5 November 1870, Thomas G. Jones to Pendleton, 24 January 1871, Circular—all in Pendleton Papers, SHC. For more on this and the groups discussed below, but with a different interpretation, see Thomas L. Connelly, *The Marble Man: Robert E. Lee and His Image in American Society* (New York: Alfred A. Knopf, 1977), pp. 27–61.

18. Early to Pendleton, 13 October 1870, Pendleton Papers, SHC; *New York Times*, 28 October 1870, p. 2; Early to Pendleton, 24 October 1870, Pendleton Papers, SHC; Dabney Maury to Early, 26 October 1870, Early Papers, LC.

19. Bradley T. Johnson to Early, 25 October 1870, Early Papers, LC.

20. Johnson to Early, 30 October 1870, Early Papers, LC; "The Monument to General Robert E. Lee," *SHSP* 17 (1889): 187–93; "Sketch of Lee Memorial Association," *SHSP* 11 (August-September 1883): 388–406; Pendleton to Wife, 3 November 1870, Pendleton Papers, SHC; W. Allen to Early, 25 October 1870, Early Papers, LC.

21. Early to Edward McCrady, Jr., 1 December 1870, Survivors' Association Papers, SCHS; Fitz Lee to Early, 6 May 1871, Early Papers, LC; Ledger and Minutes of the Virginia Division of the Association of the Army of Northern Virginia, 1871–1894, 7 November 1871, in Items from Cooper's Old Book Store, Richmond, UVA.

22. Wm. Preston Johnston to Pendleton, 19 November 1870, Pendleton Papers, SHC; W. Allen to Early, 16 December 1870 and W.P. Johnston to Early, 16 December 1870, Early Papers, LC; B.T. Johnson to Early, 20 December 1870; J.B. Gordon to Early, 26 December 1870, Early Papers, LC. First quotation is from Early to Pendleton, 8 December 1870, Pendleton Papers, SHC. Also see Pendleton to S.D. Lee, 10 February

1871, Lee Papers, SHC; Jubal A. Early, "The Lee Monumental Fund—A Caution," clipping, 17 February 1871, and Early to Pendleton, 20 February 1871, Pendleton Papers, SHC; W.P. Johnston to Early, 9 December 1871 and 4 January 1872, Early Papers, LC; and untitled resolution, 1872, Pendleton Papers, SHC; Minutes of AANVA, 3 October 1872, Cooper Book Store, UVA. Second quotation is from Early to Pendleton, 13 February 1873, Pendleton Papers, SHC.

23. On SHS and New Orleans, see Dabney H. Maury to Early, 29 July 1871, Early Papers, LC; fragment of speech in Hampton Family Papers, SCL; on reorganization, see John W. Caldwell to Early, 13 October 1871, 27 May 1873, and 10 June 1873, Early Papers, LC; Early to Pendleton, 19 July 1873, Pendleton Papers, SHC; *The Proceedings of the Southern Historical Convention, Which Assembled at the Montgomery White Sulphur Springs, Va. on the 14th of August, 1873, and of the Southern Historical Society, as Reorganized, with the Address by Gen. Jubal A. Early, delivered before the Convention on the First day of its session* (Baltimore: Turnbull Brothers, n.d.). Quotation is from "Southern Historical Society," *OLOD* 1 (20 August 1873): 3. See also King, *The Great South*, p. 677. On the springs see Reniers, *Springs of Virginia*.

24. "Transactions of the Southern Historical Society," *SM* 14 (January 1874); *Proceedings of Southern Historical Convention*, p. 17; George W. Munford to Thomas T. Munford, 22 November 1873, G.W. Munford Letters, Munford-Ellis Papers, Duke; "The Southern Historical Society: Its Origins and History," *SHSP* 18 (1890): 363–65; "Southern Historical Society, Second Annual Meeting," *SM* 15 (December 1874): 208–18; "The Southern Historical Society," *SHSP* 1 (January 1876): 44; "The Green Table," *SM* 8 (November 1873): 633.

25. "Editorial Paragraphs," *SHSP* 3 (March 1877): 159–60; "Editorial Paragraphs," *SHSP* 2 (November 1876): 252; Fitz Lee to Early, 15 September 1874, Early Papers, LC; Ledger and Minutes of AANVA, 29 October 1874, Cooper Book Store, UVA.

26. Millard K. Bushong, *Old Jube: A Biography of General Jubal A. Early* (Boyce, Va.: Carr Publishing Company, 1955); William D. Hoyt, Jr., "New Light on General Jubal A. Early After Appomattox," *JSH* 9 (February 1943): 113–17; Early to S.H. Early, 27 July 1868, Early Papers, LC; Martin F. Schmitt, ed., "An Interview with General Jubal A. Early in 1889," *JSH* 11 (November 1945): 547–63. Quotation is from Bushong, *Old Jube*, p. 297. See also fragment of letter probably by J.R. Bryan, November 1884, Bryan Family Papers, VSL.

27. "Porcupine" is from J.L.M. Curry to Children, 7 August 1879, Jabez L.M. Curry Papers, Duke. For example of his defensiveness see Early, "Card from General Early," clipping from *Richmond Whig*, 25 January 1870, Early Papers, LC. On voice and appearance, see Wise, *The End of an Era*, p. 228. Other observations are from Schmitt, ed., "Interview"; and Withers, *Autobiography*, pp. 526–27. Interestingly, Early may not have had a strong Christian faith to offer him solace; see J. Wm. Jones to Early, 24 February 1884, Early Papers, LC; and Rich McIlwaine to John W. Daniel, 11 October 1906, John W. Daniel Papers, UVA.

28. For biographical information see Harry W. Readnour, "General Fitzhugh Lee, 1835–1905: A Biographical Study" (Ph.D. diss., University of Virginia, 1971); Lee, *Memoirs of Lee*; Maury, *Recollections*; and Wilson, *Baptized in Blood*, pp. 119–38 (on Jones). On Virginia politics and for occasional references to some of these men see Maddex, *The Virginia Conservatives*, and James T. Moore, *Two Paths to the New South: The Virginia Debt Controversy, 1870–1883* (Lexington: The University of Kentucky Press, 1974).

29. Richard B. Doss, "John Warwick Daniel: A Study in the Virginia Democracy" (Ph.D. diss., University of Virginia, 1955), pp. 62–63, sees a connection between

the Conservatives and the Confederacy. Connelly, *Marble Man*, pp. 26–61, offers a more psychological interpretation but one that also stresses these men's own military shortcomings.

30. Observations are based on Richmond members on the roll for 1873–74 in Ledger and Minutes of AANVA, Cooper Book Store, UVA. Numbers below are based on identification of these names in Richmond city directories:

Professional & high white-collar	42 (53.85%)
Proprietary & low white-collar	31 (39.74%)
Skilled craftsmen	5 (6.41%)
Unskilled workers	—
Total identified	78
Unidentified	18
Total number of members from Richmond	96

31. Quotations from *New York Times*, 8 September 1873, p. 5; Bradley T. Johnson, "The Maryland Conf. Monument at Gettysburg," *SHSP* 14 (1886): 433; and "Address to the People of Georgia by the State Agent of the Society," clipping, 16 January 1874, in Scrapbook, 1872–75, p. 70, John Emory Bryant Papers, Duke. See also Henry Eubank, "A Duty of the Hour," *SM* 12 (May 1873): 606–10. For conscious use of history see Robert L. Dabney to D.H. Hill, 1 December 1873, Daniel H. Hill Papers, SHC. In retrospect Johnson said that the associations helped bring about the return of white Democratic rule. Undoubtedly, they may have had some indirect influence, but there is little evidence of direct involvement or of consideration of this goal when forming the groups. After all, native conservatives had already regained control in Virginia by the time the SHS reorganized. A hostile observer, probably John Emory Bryant, considered the SHS a conspiracy by the landed aristocracy to fix the status of laborers. See *New York Times*, 6 July 1875, p. 2; J.E. Bryant to Benjamin Harrison, 8 February and 1 March 1889, Bryant Papers, Duke. Wiener, *Social Origins of the New South*, pp. 196–200, 215–21, implies much the same thing. It is not clear that Wiener had the groups discussed here in mind. Although the Virginians' general defense of the social order probably helped planters, there is little evidence that such a goal influenced these men or that they had close ties to the planter elite—although a few did have landholdings.

32. Anthony F.C. Wallace, "Revitalization Movements," *American Anthropologist* 58 (1956): 264–81; "Nativism and Revivalism," *International Encyclopedia of Social Sciences*, David L. Sills, ed., 18 vols. (New York: The Macmillan Company and the Free Press, 1968), 11: 75–80, quotation from p. 75; and Ralph Linton, "Nativistic Movements," *American Anthropologist* 45 (April-June 1943): 230–40, quotation from p. 233.

33. The historical vision comes from *SHSP*, *OLOD*, and the papers of the individuals involved. I will not always cite all of the articles on any topic. On the POW issue see J. Wm. Jones to Hunter McGuire, 2 October 1888, Colston Papers, SHC; "Editorial Paragraphs," *SHSP* 1 (Feburary 1876): 109–10.

34. Early is quoted in *Proceedings of Southern Historical Convention*, p. 27. The interpretation here resembles that of Thomas J. Pressly, *Americans Interpret Their Civil War* (New York: The Free Press, 1962), pp. 81–126.

35. For an introduction to the literature of the controversy see Theodore H. Jabbs, "The Lost Cause: Some Southern Opinion Between 1865 and 1900 About Why the Confederacy Lost the Civil War" (M.A. thesis, University of North Carolina-Chapel Hill, 1967). Variations on both explanations can be found in manuscript sources as well.

See, for examples, Virginia J. Mosby Diary, 9 April 1866, John S. Mosby Papers, UVA; Beauregard to Augusta J. Evans, 17 March 1866, Beauregard Papers, LC; John W. Daniel to L.Q. Washington, 5 October 1868, Daniel Papers, UVA. On numbers argument see "Book Notices," *SHSP* 1 (January 1876): 47; William Allen, "Review of Books; Battle of Gettysburg," *SHSP* 1 (May 1876): 365–70; "Resources of the Confederacy," *SHSP* 2 (July 1876): 56–63, (August 1876): 85–105, (September 1876): 113–28. Quotation is from "What We Expect to Show," *OLOD* 1 (2 July 1873): 2.

36. For surveys of the controversy, see Connelly, *Marble Man*, pp. 83–90; and Donald B. Sanger and Thomas R. Hay, *James Longstreet* (Baton Rouge: Louisiana State University Press, 1952), pp. 410–36. On coordination see Fitz Lee to Early, 24 April 1876 and J. Wm. Jones to Early, 2 May 1878, Early Papers, LC. But cf. *SHSP* 4 (December 1877): 241. On those unconvinced by the Virginians, see Dabney H. Maury to Jefferson Davis, 2 November 1877, in Rowland, ed., *Jefferson Davis*, 8: 39–40; D.H. Hill to Longstreet, 5 February 1887, James Longstreet Papers, Duke; Thomas P. Goree to Longstreet (copy), 17 May 1875, Longstreet Papers, SHC; Henry T. Owen to Miss Boyson, 5 August 1886, Henry T. Owen Papers, VSL; Rebecca L. Felton, "*My Memoirs of Georgia Politics*" (Atlanta: The Index Printing Company, 1911), pp. 625–29; and William A. Fletcher, *Rebel Private: Front and Rear*, Bell I. Wiley, ed. (Austin: University of Texas Press, 1954; first published 1908), p. 63. For two they did convince, see W.W. Taylor to Longstreet (copy), 28 April 1875, James Longstreet Papers, Emory University; Taylor to Early, 2 May 1876, Early Papers, LC; Charles Marshall to Longstreet, 7 May 1875, Longstreet Papers, Emory; and Marshall to Early, 13 March 1878, Early Papers, LC. See also Wade Hampton to Early, 27 March 1876, Early Family Papers, VHS.

37. For Longstreet's criticizing Lee see Gorgas Journal, 12 August 1865, 3: 80, SHC; "Colston's Recollections," 1907, in Edward P. Alexander Papers, SHC. See also Longstreet, *Lee and Longstreet at High Tide*, pp. 82–83. For Early's claiming that he only replied, see J.A. Early, "Reply to General Longstreet's Second Paper," *SHSP* 5 (June 1878): 287; Early to Davis, 30 May 1877, in Rowland, ed. *Jefferson Davis*, 7: 545. For a suggestion that Longstreet should be ignored see T.H.B. Randolph to Pendleton, 11 March 1878, Pendleton Papers, SHC. Also see Fitz Lee, "A Review of the First Two Days' Operation at Gettysburg and a Reply to General Longstreet," *SHSP* 5 (April 1878): 176–77; Charles Marshall to Early, 26 March 1877 and J. Wm. Jones to Early, 23 March 1876, in Early Papers, LC; and Pendleton to Longstreet (copy), [nd] April 1875, Pendleton Papers, SHC. The Early Papers also make it clear that Early would defend Davis, Jackson, and other Confederates as well as Lee.

38. A. Dudley Mann to Davis, 30 August 1872, in John P. Moore, ed., "*My Ever Dearest Friend:" The Letters of A. Dudley Mann to Jefferson Davis, 1869–1889* (Tuscaloosa: Confederate Publishing Company, 1960), pp. 34–35; Lee, "A Review," p. 162; "'Within a Stone's Throw of Independence' at Gettysburg," *SHSP* 12 (March 1884): 111–12; Edmund Pendleton to Early, 20 March 1876, Early Papers, LC.

39. Richmond (Va.) *Daily Dispatch*, 24 February 1883.

40. "Chancellorsville," *SR* 2 (October 1867): 462–85; Edward A. Pollard, "Stonewall Jackson—An Historical Study," *Putnam's Magazine* 2 (December 1868): 733–40; R.L. Dabney, "Stonewall Jackson," *SHSP* 11 (April-May 1883): 144–58; Duke, *Reminiscences*, pp. 416–17; Edward M. Daniel, comp., *Speeches and Orations of John Warwick Daniel* (Lynchburg, Va.: J.P. Bell Company, 1911), pp. 41–61. On monument see "The Green Table," *SM* 17 (June 1875): 763–64; "Oration by Rev. Moses Hoge at Unveiling of Stonewall Jackson's Statue—October 26, 1875," *SHSP* 13 (1885): 314–32. Connelly, *Marble Man*, p. 25, argues that Jackson was the more important hero than Lee

at first, and that the Virginians then moved Lee into the top position. Connelly, it seems to me, overestimates Jackson's position vis-à-vis Lee early and underestimates it later.

41. Literature on Lee is too extensive to cite. Quotation is from Robert Stiles, "Address Delivered Before Washington and Lee University," *SM* 16 (March 1875): 42.

42. Early's speech is in J. William Jones, *Personal Reminiscences, Anecdotes, and Letters of Gen. Robert E. Lee* (New York: D. Appleton and Company, 1875), pp. 43, 49. See also Early to W.P. Johnson, 1 January 1872, Albert Sidney and William Preston Johnson Papers, Tulane.

43. My assertions on the general reputation of the private soldier are based on comments in letters, memoirs of the war, and observations by travelers. It is also interesting that only 24 percent of the statues erected before 1885 featured the Confederate soldier, compared with 62 percent in the period 1885–1899 and 80 percent in 1900–12. See Appendix 1. Durant, "The Gently Furled Banner," pp. 82–84, comments on observations about the lack of discipline. For a very different view see Guy Stephen Davis, "Johnny Reb in Perspective: The Confederate Soldier's Image in Southern Arts" (Ph.D. diss., Emory University, 1979), pp. 81–83.

44. In addition to historical interpretations cited above see Carlton McCarthy, "Camp Fires of the Boys in Gray," *SHSP* 1 (February 1876): 86, who said, "The acquirement of subordination certainly is a useful one, and that the soldier perforce has."

45. Ledger and Minutes of the AANVA, Cooper Book Store, UVA; "Cause of Confederates in Maryland," *CV* 1 (February 1893): 39. On the operation of the New Orleans group see Association of the Army of Northern Virginia Papers, Louisiana Historical Association Collection Papers, Tulane. On the importance of the tomb, see Minute Book, 1878–1884, vol. 14, 8 January 1881. For mention of other early groups see Harold B. Simpson, *Hood's Texas Brigade in Reunion and Memory* (Hillsboro, Tx.: Hill Junior College Press, 1974); and White, *Confederate Veteran*, pp. 9–25. On Hampton's efforts see Wade Hampton to James Conner, 7 November 1873, Conner Collection, SCHS; Hampton to Early, 18 November 1873, Early Papers, LC. On other efforts, see "Editorial Paragraphs," *SHSP* 5 (April 1878): 208; and Southern Historical Society Records, VHS. On SHS groups elsewhere see M.C. Butler to Early, 24 September 1873, Early Papers, LC; *OLOD, passim*; and "An Atlanta Gentleman Makes a Good Speech," clipping *Daily Constitution*, 23 April 1874, in Scrapbook, 1872–74, Bryant Papers, Duke. Subscription numbers are given in "Annual Meeting of the Southern Historical Society," *SHSP* 2 (November 1876): 246–47.

46. *New York Times*, 22 February 1872, p. 5. The article does not make it clear whether the figures were for Richmond or Lexington. See also Pendleton to W.J. Walters (copy), 27 December 1880, Pendleton Papers, SHC; and "Recumbent Figure of Gen. R.E. Lee," *CV* 7 (November 1899): 513. The women's group in Richmond did better than either of the other two. See Sarah N. Randolph to Fitz Lee, 15 April 1873, Early Papers, LC. Figures on local memorial groups are from Chapter 3.

47. On trouble with agents see Southern Historical Society Records, VHS; J. Wm. Jones to Early, 1 December 1877 and 28 July 1878, Early Papers, LC.

CHAPTER FIVE.

TOWARD A UNITED NATION:

SIGNS OF RECONCILIATION

1. For examples see Charles Ellis to Mrs. E.T. Munford, 24 July 1866, G.W. Munford Letters, Munford-Ellis Family Papers, Duke; George Rose, *The Great Country*;

Or, *Impressions of America* (London: Tinsley Brothers, 1868), p. 182; and "The Character of the Late War," *Southern Review* 11 (October 1872): 438–74. Quotation is from Charles H. Smith, *Bill Arp's Peace Papers* (New York: G.W. Carleton & Co., Publishers, 1873), p. 14.

2. George C. Rable, "Southern Interests and the Election of 1876: A Reappraisal," *CWH* 26 (December 1980): 348; Jabez L.M. Curry Diary, 8 November 1876, Curry Papers, LC; Richmond (Va.) *Daily Dispatch*, 9 November 1876.

3. Curry Diary, 20 November 1876, LC.

4. Fitzhugh Lee to B.T. Johnson, 18 and 28 December 1876, Bradley T. Johnson Papers, Duke; Wm. Preston Johnson to Early, 18 December 1876, Jubal A. Early Papers, LC; Early to Johnson, 5 January 1877, Johnson Papers, Duke; Fitz Lee to Early, 8 January 1877, Early Papers, LC; William H. Payne to Johnson, 12 January 1877, Johnson Papers, Duke.

5. Johnson to Early, 8 January 1877, Early Papers, LC. Of the Virginians, Johnson played the more public role. See Richmond (Va.) *Daily Dispatch*, 6 December 1876 and 9 January 1877.

6. Michael Les Benedict, "Southern Democrats in the Crisis of 1876–1877: A Reconsideration of *Reunion and Reaction*," *JSH* 46 (November 1980): 489–524.

7. "Reagan on the Electoral Commission of 1876," copy of 27 March speech in Palestine, Texas, vol. 3, John H. Reagan Papers, UTX. See also Reagan to James W. Truett, 14 May 1877, Reagan Papers; Ben H. Procter, *Not Without Honor: The Life of John H. Reagan* (Austin: University of Texas Press, 1962), pp. 214–16. For similar evaluations see Withers, *Autobiography*, pp. 350–59; John Goode, *Recollections of a Lifetime* (New York: The Neale Publishing Company, 1906), p. 156.

8. Payne to Early, 5 March 1877, Early Papers, LC.

9. Richmond (Va.) *Daily Dispatch*, 2 December 1876, 15 and 18 January and 14 and 19 February 1877, quotation is from 15 January; Johnson to Early, 8 January 1877, Early Papers, LC. See also Josiah Gorgas Journal, 1 January 1877, sec. 3, pp. 146–47, SHC; "Resolution on Electoral Commission," in box 17, John W. Daniel Papers, UVA; C. Vann Woodward, *Reunion and Reaction: The Compromise of 1877 and the End of Reconstruction*, 2d rev. ed. (Garden City, N.Y.: Doubleday & Company, 1956), pp. 33–35; Charles F. Ritter, "The Press in Florida, Louisiana, and South' Carolina and the End of Reconstruction, 1865–1877: Southern Men with Northern Interests" (Ph.D. diss., Catholic University, 1976), pp. 249–62. But cf. David Fleet to Sis Bess, 31 December 1876, in Fleet, ed., *Green Mount After the War*, p. 150.

10. On concrete southern gains see C. Vann Woodward, "Yes, There Was a Compromise of 1877," *Journal of American History* 60 (June 1973): 215–23. William Gillette, *Retreat From Reconstruction, 1869–1879* (Baton Rouge: Louisiana State University Press, 1979).

11. Annie E. Harper Manuscript, p. 75, MDAH; Vincent P. De Santis, *Republicans Face the Southern Question: The New Departure Years, 1877–1897* (New York: Greenwood Press, 1969; first published 1959); Stanley P. Hirshson, *Farewell to the Bloody Shirt: Northern Republicans and the Southern Negro, 1877–1893* (Bloomington: Indiana University Press, 1962); Peyton H. Hoge, *Moses Drury Hoge: Life and Letters* (Richmond: Presbyterian Committee of Publication, 1899), pp. 314–18, quotation on p. 318. On Garfield's death see also E.T. Munford to Husband, 29 August 1881, G.W. Munford Letters, Munford-Ellis Papers, Duke; John E. Buser, "After Half a Generation: The South of the 1880s" (Ph.D. diss., University of Texas-Austin, 1968), pp. 93–95; and Buck, *Road to Reunion*, pp. 141–42.

12. Quotations are from John T. Morgan to Mrs. Clay, 2 January 1885, Clement

C. Clay Papers, Duke; Curry to R.C. Winthrop, 13 November 1884, Curry Papers, LC; Jones to John S.H. Fogg, 21 August 1884, Charles C. Jones, Jr., Papers, Duke. See also Curry Diary, 18 November 1884, LC; Jones to Henry T. Donne, 10 November 1884, and Jones to J.A. Maxwell, 12 November 1884, Jones Papers, Duke; C.J.M. Furman Diary, 1885–1903, 6 March 1885, Charles J.M. Furman Papers, SCL; John L. Johnson, *Autobiographical Notes* (n.p.: Privately printed, 1958), pp. 242–43; Charles Dudley Warner, *Studies in the South and West, With Comments on Canada* (New York: Harper & Brothers, 1889), p. 4; Edwin Mims, "Autobiography—A Frontier Community," p. 15, in Edwin Mims Papers, Joint Universities Library, Nashville, Tenn.; and Mims, "The Passing of Two Great Americans," *SAQ* 7 (October 1908): 325.

13. Buck, *Road to Reunion*, pp. 236–40; Wade Hall, *The Smiling Phoenix: Southern Humor From 1865 to 1914* (Gainesville: University of Florida Press, 1965), p. 134; Joe Gray Taylor, *Louisiana Reconstructed, 1863–1877* (Baton Rouge: Louisiana State University Press, 1974), p. 67. Herman Hattaway, "The United Confederate Veterans in Louisiana," *Louisiana History* 16 (Winter 1975): 19–20, dissents. For contemporary views see Daniel Thompson to Cyrus Woodman, 11 April 1866, in C.J. Marquette, ed., "Letters of a Yankee Sugar Planter," *JSH* 6 (November 1940): 524; J.T. Trowbridge, *A Picture of the Desolated States and the Work of Restoration* (Hartford, Conn.: L. Stebbins, 1868), p. 188; and Ellen Biddle, *Reminiscences of a Soldier's Wife* (Philadelphia: J.B. Lippincott Co., 1907), p. 26. Joyce Appleby, "Reconciliation and the Northern Novelist, 1865–1880," *CWH* 10 (June 1964): 126–27, found that northern novelists developed this theme very early. For political comparisons see "Editorial," *LWL* 3 (June 1867): 177–78; and Richard Taylor, *Destruction and Reconstruction: Personal Experiences of the Late War*, Richard B. Harwell, ed. (New York: Longmans, Green and Co., 1955; first published 1878), pp. 181–82.

14. Dearing, *Veterans in Politics*, pp. 86–87, and *passim*.

15. On role of prewar friendship see James Longstreet, *From Manassas to Appomattox: Memoirs of the Civil War in America* (Philadelphia: J.B. Lippincott Company, 1896), pp. 632–34; Withers, *Autobiography*, pp. 390–91; Henry Heth, *The Memoirs of Henry Heth*, James L. Morrison, Jr., ed. (Westport, Conn.: Greenwood Press, 1974), pp. 198–235; and Lynwood M. Holland, *Pierce M.B. Young: The Warwick of the South* (Athens: University of Georgia Press, 1964), pp. 113, 128. My interpretation of the role of memory relies heavily on Cruce Stark, "Brothers At/In War: One Phase of Post-Civil War Reconciliation," *Canadian Review of American Studies* 6 (Fall 1975): 174–81; Thomas C. Leonard, *Above the Battle: War-Making in America From Appomattox to Versailles* (New York: Oxford University Press, 1978), pp. 7–39; and Maddex, *Virginia Conservatives*, pp. 123–25.

16. John F. Cowan, *A New Invasion of the South. Being A Narrative of the Expedition of the Seventy-First Infantry, National Guard Through the Southern States, to New Orleans, February 24–March 7, 1881* (New York: Board of Officers of the Seventy-First Infantry, 1881). Quotation is from clipping, 4 March 1881, in Reunions File, Association of the Army of Northern Virginia Papers, LHAC, Tulane. On latter visits see "Editorial Paragraphs," *SHSP* 9 (May 1881): 239–40; and Louis C. Gosson, *Post-Bellum Campaigns of the Blue and Gray, 1881–1882* (Trenton: Naar, Day & Naar Printers, 1882).

17. "Ex-Confederates in New Jersey," *SHSP* 10 (May 1882): 233–35; Gosson, *Campaigns*; George L. Kilmer, "A Note of Peace," *Century* 36 (July 1888): 440–42; C.H. Benson, *"Yank and Reb:" A History of a Fraternal Visit Paid by Lincoln Post, No. 11, GAR of Newark, NJ* (Newark: M. H. Neuhut, Printer, 1884). On Gettysburg in 1887 and 1888 see Scrapbook, Charles T. Loehr Papers, VHS; Circular with letter, J.F. Rocken to

E.P. Reeve, 5 August 1887, William R. Aylett to Reeve, 22 May 1888, undated and untitled history of movement for a monument—all in Edward P. Reeve Papers, SHC; C.C. Jones to George L. Christian, 22 and 25 May 1888, C.C. Jones, Jr., Papers, Duke; and Raleigh Colston, "Gettysburg Twenty-Five Years After," clipping, Raleigh E. Colston Papers, SHC.

18. Joseph E. Roy, *Pilgrim's Letters. Bits of Current History Picked Up in the West and the South, During the Last Thirty Years, for the Independent, the Congregationalist, and the Advance* (Boston: Congregational Sundayschool and Publishing Society, 1888), pp. 206–7; Warner, *Studies on the South*, p. 9; Special Committee Report, 10 May 1883, Association of the Army of the Tennessee Papers, LHAC, Tulane. Quotation is from Mrs. E.C. Minor to Pres., Ladies' Memorial Association of Atlanta, 2 May 1887, in Minute Book Belonging to the Ladies' Memorial Association of Atlanta, Ga., 1884–1900, in Ladies' Memorial Association of Atlanta Records, AHS. See also Buser, "After Half A Generation," p. 96.

19. Dearing, *Veterans in Politics*, pp. 328–405; George J. Lankevich, "The Grand Army of the Republic in New York State, 1865–1898" (Ph.D. diss., Columbia University, 1967), pp. 212–28; Elmer E. Noyes, "A History of the Grand Army of the Republic in Ohio from 1866 to 1900" (Ph.D. diss., Ohio State University, 1945), pp. 125–63, 220–29.

20. On southern demand for equal treatment, see E.P. Reeve to editor of Richmond (Va.) *Whig*, clipping 31 July 1888, Reeve Papers, SHC; "Editorial Paragraphs," *SHSP* 9 (February 1881): 96.

21. Appleby, "Northern Novelists;" Anne Rowe, *The Enchanted Country: Northern Writers in the South, 1865–1910* (Baton Rouge: Louisiana State University Press, 1978); Rayburn S. Moore, "Southern Writers and Northern Literary Magazines, 1865–1900" (Ph.D. diss., Duke University, 1956), pp. 353–66; L. Moffitt Cecil, "William Dean Howells and the South," *Mississippi Quarterly* 20 (Winter 1966–67): 13–24; Osterweis, *Myth of the Lost Cause*, pp. 30–41.

22. On series as a whole see Stephen Davis, "'A Matter of Sensational Interest': The Century 'Battles and Leaders' Series,'" *CWH* 27 (December 1981): 338–49. First quotation is from "Topics of the Time: Battles and Leaders of the Civil War," *The Century* 28 (October 1884): 943–44. Second is from Davis, p. 341.

23. Robert Underwood Johnson, *Remembered Yesterdays* (Boston: Little, Brown and Company, 1923), p. 194; editor of *Century Magazine* to Jubal Early, 23 April 1884, Early Papers, LC. See also *Battles and Leaders of the Civil War* (New York: The Century Company, 1884–1887), 1: ix; and C.C. Buel to Berry Benson, 3 January 1887, Berry G. Benson Papers, SHC.

24. Johnson, *Remembered Yesterdays*, p. 194. Buck, *Road to Reunion* and Osterweis, *Myth of the Lost Cause*—following an idea first suggested by Albion Tourgée—imply the South somehow won with the pen what it lost on the battlefield. On this idea see also Michael C.C. Adams, *Our Masters the Rebels: A Speculation on Union Military Failure in the East, 1861–1865* (Cambridge, Mass.: Harvard University Press, 1978), pp. 179–87.

25. Huber W. Ellingsworth, "Southern Reconciliation Orators in the North, 1868–1899" (Ph.D. diss., Florida State University, 1955); "Conquered Nations," in Edward M. Daniel, comp., *Speeches and Orations of John Warwick Daniel* (Lynchburg, Va.: J.P. Bell Company, Inc., 1911), pp. 105–58. Hill quoted in "Reunion of the Virginia Division, Army of Northern Virginia," *SHSP* 13 (1885): 275–76; McCrady in "Address Before the Virginia Division of Army of Northern Virginia at Their Reunion on the Evening of Oct. 21, 1886," *SHSP* 14 (1886): 218. See also Walter S. Towns,

"Ceremonial Speaking and the Reinforcing of American Nationalism in the South, 1875–1890" (Ph.D. diss., University of Florida, 1972).

26. Sir George Campbell, *White and Black*, pp. 31–32; Orra Langhorne, *Southern Sketches from Virginia, 1881–1901*, Charles E. Wynes, ed. (Charlottesville: The University Press of Virginia, 1964), p. 19; Alexander K. McClure, *The South: Its Industrial, Financial, and Political Condition* (Philadelphia: J. B. Lippincott Company, 1886), pp. 32–33. See also Warner, *Studies in the South*, p. 7; and Charles H. Levermore, "Impressions of a Yankee Visitor in the South," *New England Magazine* n.s. 3 (November 1890): 312.

27. Frank Robinson, "Claims of the People on the Rising Generation," 23 June 1880, in Jeptha McKinney Papers, LSU. McClure, *The South*, p. 32, credits the younger generation in the South with leading the way toward reconciliation. But in the eighties, most people active in public life had not come of age since Appomattox. For other thoughts on age and reconciliation see Maddex, *Virginia Conservatives*, pp. 287–92; and William B. Hesseltine and Henry L. Ewbank, Jr., "Old Voices in the New South," *Quarterly Journal of Speech* 39 (December 1953): 458.

28. L.Q.C. Lamar to C.C. Clay, 5 September 1874, Clay Papers, Duke. See also James B. Murphy, *L.Q.C. Lamar: Pragmatic Patriot* (Baton Rouge: Louisiana State University Press, 1973), pp. 112–20.

29. Untitled speech at fair in Lynchburg, 24 October 1877, in Scrapbook, Curry Papers, LC; Curry to Manly Curry, 12 August 1886, Curry Papers, LC. In the late 1870s and early 1880s southerners seemed almost to be looking for an excuse to embrace reconciliation; for two examples see Carol Ann Cole, "George William Bagby: Reconciling the New South and the Old Dominion" (M. A. thesis, University of Virginia, 1971); Joseph L. King, Jr., *Dr. George William Bagby: A Study of Virginian Literature, 1850–1880* (New York: Columbia University Press, 1927), pp. 183–84; and Wilson, *Baptized in Blood*, p. 59 (on Father Ryan).

30. J.A. Early to Davis, 16 February 1878, in Rowland, ed., *Jefferson Davis*, 8: 81–82.

31. Moore, ed., *"My Ever Dearest Friend."* Quotation is from pp. 67–69. See Northrop letters in Rowland, ed., *Jefferson Davis*, 9: 179–81, 468–70.

32. Quotation is from David H. Overy, "When the Wicked Beareth Rule: A Southern Critique of Industrial America," *Journal of Presbyterian History* 48 (Summer 1970): 134. On his life see Overy, "Robert Lewis Dabney."

33. Quotations are from William H. Payne to M.J. Wright, 27 August 1886, Marcus J. Wright Papers, SHC; H.B. McClellan to Payne, 16 September 1886 and summary of Payne's response on back, William H. Payne Papers, VSL. See also Payne to Early, 10 July 1887 and 3 May 1893, Early Papers, LC; Payne to Johnson, 9 December 1897, B.T. Johnson Papers, Duke.

34. On Davis after the war see Hudson Strode, *Jefferson Davis, Tragic Hero: The Last Twenty-Five Years, 1864–1889* (New York: Harcourt Brace, & World, Inc., 1964); John Muldowny, "Jefferson Davis: The Postwar Years," *MQ* 23 (Winter 1969–70): 17–33; and Marilyn Miller Thompson, "Jefferson Davis, the Reluctant Orator: A Study of His Postwar Speaking" (M.A. thesis, Louisiana State University, 1974).

35. Jefferson Davis, *The Rise and Fall of the Confederate Government*, 2 vols. (New York: D. Appleton and Company, 1881). Quotations are from I: 439, II: 5, 279.

36. McClure, *The South*, pp. 231–38.

37. Particularly interesting letters can be found in Rowland, ed., *Jefferson Davis*, 7: 425, 426–27, 434–40, 478–87; 9: 593; Davis to Crafts J. Wright, 10 January 1878, Jefferson Davis Papers (microfilm), MDAH; and Davis to B.M. Blackburn, 4 July 1881,

Davis Papers, UAL. Quotation from Rowland, ed., *Jefferson Davis*, 10: 47–48. Thompson, "Davis," pp. 61–63, argues that Davis became reconciled "at least to a point." Muldowny, "Davis," tends toward the same conclusion but suggests we will never know for sure.

38. On Jones as irreconcilable see John Donald Wade, "Old Wine in A New Bottle," *Virginia Quarterly Review* 11 (April 1935): 244; Woodward, *Origins*, pp. 173–74. For an introduction to his life, see James C. Bonner, "Charles Colcock Jones: Macaulay of the South," *GHQ* 27 (December 1943): 324–38. My conclusions are based on my reading of Charles C. Jones, Jr., Papers, Duke; quotation is from Jones to Charles E. Whitehead, 3 June 1880; on West Point appointment see Jones to Alexander H. Stephens, 21 January 1880; Obituary to Grady, 23 December 1889—all in C.C. Jones, Jr., Papers, Duke.

39. Grace King to Brevard, 29 November 1885, Grace King Papers, LSU; Stuart McGuire, "Sketch of the Life of Hunter Holmes McGuire, MD, LLD," in Hunter Holmes McGuire Papers, VHS.

40. Howard M. Lovett, "A Study in Gray—Miss M.A.H. Gay," *CV* 16 (December 1908): 633–35; Mary Ann Harris Gay, *Life in Dixie During the War* (Atlanta: Foote & Davis, 1894).

41. Wade, "Old Wine;" Weaver, *The Southern Tradition at Bay*. But cf. Woodward, *Origins*, pp. 173–74.

CHAPTER SIX.

TOWARD A NEW SOUTH:

SOCIAL TENSIONS

1. For an introduction to the historiographical debate see James T. Moore, "Redeemers Reconsidered: Change and Continuity in the Democratic South, 1870–1920," *JSH* 44 (August 1978): 357–378; and Harold D. Woodman, "Sequel to Slavery: The New History Views the Postbellum South," *JSH* 43 (November 1977): 523–54.

2. Comparisons are derived from Donald B. Dodd and Wynella S. Dodd, comps., *Historical Statistics of the South, 1790–1970* (University: The University of Alabama Press, 1973), pp. 2–73. See also Woodward, *Origins*, pp. 107–41; Broadus Mitchell, *The Rise of Cotton Mills in the South* (New York: Da Capo Press, 1968; first published 1921); Harold D. Woodman, *King Cotton & His Retainers: Financing & Marketing the Cotton Crop of the South, 1800–1925* (Lexington: University of Kentucky Press, 1968), pp. 314–59; David L. Carlton, *Mill and Town in South Carolina, 1880–1920* (Baton Rouge: Louisiana State University Press, 1982); Randolph D. Werner, "Hegemony and Conflict: The Political Economy of a Southern Region, Augusta, Georgia, 1865–1895" (Ph.D. diss., University of Virginia, 1977); and Steven Hahn, *The Roots of Southern Populism: Yeoman Farmers and the Transformation of the Georgia Upcountry, 1850–1890* (New York: Oxford University Press, 1983).

3. Quotation is from Woodman, *King Cotton*, p. 328. See Woodward, *Origins*, pp. 123–24, 145–46; John F. Stover, *The Railroads of the South, 1865–1900: A Study in Finance and Control* (Chapel Hill: University of North Carolina Press, 1955), pp. 186–209; and William W. White, "A Community Portrait From Postal Records: Byway, Mississippi, 1881–1900," *JMH* 25 (January 1963): 33–37.

4. Paul M. Gaston, *The New South Creed: A Study in Southern Mythmaking* (New York: Alfred A. Knopf, 1970); Little, "The Ideology of the New South." On

expositions, see John S. Ezell, *The South Since 1865*, 2d ed. (New York: Macmillan Publishing Co., 1975), pp. 331–33.

5. Henry Grady, *The New South: Writings and Speeches of Henry Grady*, Mills Lane, ed. (Savannah, Ga.: The Beehive Press, 1971), pp. 107–8 and *passim*; W.I. Kimball to Jefferson Davis, 14 December 1881, Davis Postwar Papers, LHAC, Tulane; C.C. Jones to H.I. Kimball, 27 May 1881, C.C. Jones, Jr., Papers, Duke; Rayburn S. Moore, *Paul Hamilton Hayne* (New York: Twayne Publishers Co., 1972), pp. 127–28; "The Southern Exposition," *Southern Bivouac* 3 (September 1884): 47. See also Gaston, *New South Creed*, pp. 153–86.

6. Moore, *Hayne*, pp. 127–28; H. I. Kimball, *International Cotton Exposition (Atlanta, Georgia, 1881)—Report of the Director General* (New York: D. Appleton and Company, 1882), pp. 252–56; Edward Atkinson, "Significant Aspects of the Atlanta Cotton Exposition," *Century Magazine* 23 (February 1882): 565–69.

7. Henry Watterson, "Oddities of Southern Life," *Century* 23 (April 1882): 884–95; Watterson, *The Compromises of Life, and Other Lectures and Addresses, Including Some Observations on Certain Downward Tendencies of Modern Society* (New York: Fox, Duffield, & Company, 1903), pp. 288–93.

8. Walter Hines Page, "Study of an Old Southern Borough," *Atlantic Monthly* 47 (May 1881): 648–58; W.H.P., "Our New York Letter," Raleigh (N.C.) *State Chronicle*, 4 February 1886. See also John M. Cooper, Jr., *Walter Hines Page: The Southerner as American, 1855–1918* (Chapel Hill: University of North Carolina Press, 1977), pp. 76–81. For others critical of the Old South see Sarah M. Howell, "The Editorials of Arthur S. Colyar, Nashville Prophet of the New South," *Tennessee Historical Quarterly* 27 (Fall 1968): 264; and E. Merton Coulter, "The New South: Benjamin H. Hill's Speech Before the Alumni of the University of Georgia, 1871," *GHQ* 57 (Summer 1973): 179–99.

9. C.R. Vaughan, ed., *Discussions by Robert L. Dabney, D.D., LL.D.*, 4 vols. (Mexico, Mo.: Crescent Book House, 1897), 4: 1–24.

10. Hoge, *Moses Drury Hoge*, pp. 403–5.

11. "The Address," clipping, 10 May 1887, vol. 6, Alfred Moore Waddell Papers, SHC; W.H. Payne to Early, 19 March 1887, and Bradley T. Johnson to Early, 18 May 1887, Jubal A. Early Papers, LC. See also Walter S. Bragg to Bolling Hall, 15 May 1888, Bolling Hall Papers, ADAH; and Holmes Conrad to Early, 27 June 1889, Early Papers.

12. Quotation is from Jones to Gordon, 7 March 1887. See also Jones to Gordon, 12, 14, 17 March 1887. All in C.C. Jones, Jr., Papers, Duke. For a somewhat different treatment of these events see Michael M. Cass, "Charles C. Jones, Jr., and the 'Lost Cause,'" *GHQ* 55 (Summer 1971): 222–33.

13. *Addresses Delivered Before the Confederate Survivors' Association in Augusta, Georgia, at its Annual Meetings on Memorial Day, 1879–1897*, 1887, pp. 6–18.

14. Jones to Gordon, 28 April and 16 May 1887. See also Jones to Simon Gratz, 13 April 1889; and Jones to W.H. Payne, 1 April 1887. All in C.C. Jones, Jr., Papers, Duke.

15. C.C. Jones, Jr., *"Georgians During the War Between the States:" An Address Delivered Before the Confederate Survivors' Association in Augusta, Ga., April 26, 1889* (Augusta: Chronicle Publishing Co., 1889).

16. Jones to John S.H. Fogg, 18 June 1889, C.C. Jones, Jr., Papers, Duke; Gordon to Jones, 6 June 1889, John B. Gordon Papers, Duke; William E. Boggs to Jones, 10 June 1889 and Clement A. Evans to Jones, 12 June 1889, C.C. Jones, Jr., Papers, Duke; Beauregard to Jones, 1 July 1889, P.G.T. Beauregard Papers, Duke.

17. Geo. A. Mercer to Jones, 30 May 1889, and W.H. King to Jones, 22 June 1889, C.C. Jones, Jr., Papers, Duke. See also Geo. W. Rains to Jones, 28 May 1889, C.C. Jones, Jr., Papers, Duke; and J.M. Kell to Jones, 5 June 1889, John M. Kell Papers, Duke.

18. S.D. Lee to Jones, 30 July 1889, C.C. Jones, Jr., Papers, Duke. On Lee and New South see Herman Hattaway, *General Stephen D. Lee* (Jackson: University Press of Mississippi, 1976), p. 160.

19. Arlin Turner, ed., *The Negro Question: A Selection of Writings on Civil Rights in the South by George W. Cable* (Garden City, N.Y.: Doubleday & Company, 1958) contains of Cable's attacks.

20. For overviews of the controversy see Louis D. Rubin, Jr., *George W. Cable: The Life and Times of a Southern Heretic* (New York: Pegasus, 1969), pp. 178–84; and George M. Fredrickson, *The Black Image in the White Mind: The Debate on Afro-American Character and Destiny, 1817–1914* (New York: Harper & Row, 1971), pp. 216–27. Quotations are from Wirt Adams to Walthall, 25 November 1884, William T. Walthall Papers, MDAH; and Robert L. Dabney, "George W. Cable in the Century Magazine," *SHSP* 13 (1885): 148–53.

21. Turner, ed., *Negro Question*, pp. 85–87, 126.

22. On farmers' revolt I have relied on Robert C. McMath, Jr., *Populist Vanguard: A History of the Southern Farmers' Alliance* (Chapel Hill: University of North Carolina Press, 1975); Lawrence Goodwyn, *Democratic Promise: The Populist Moment in America* (New York: Oxford University Press, 1976); and Bruce Palmer, *"Man Over Money": The Southern Populist Critique of American Capitalism* (Chapel Hill: University of North Carolina Press, 1980).

23. James P. Sullivan, "Louisville and Her Southern Alliance, 1865–1890" (Ph.D. diss., University of Kentucky, 1965), pp. 287–96; Markham Memorandum Book, 10 September 1881, Thomas R. Markham Papers, LSU; Leslie S. Hough, "Discontent in a Southern Tobacco Town: Lynchburg, Virginia, Workers in the 1880s" (M.A. thesis, University of Virginia, 1973); Harold J. Goldstein, "Labor Unrest in the Birmingham District, 1871–1894" (M.A. thesis, University of Alabama, 1951); Melton A. McLaurin, *The Knights of Labor in the South* (Westport, Conn.: Greenwood Press, 1978); Peter Jay Rachleff, "Black, White, and Gray: Working Class Activism in Richmond, Virginia, 1865–1890" (Ph.D. diss., University of Pittsburgh, 1981); Leon Fink, *Workingmen's Democracy: The Knights of Labor and American Politics* (Urbana: University of Illinois Press, 1983), pp. 28–29, 149–78.

24. Jas. Wood Davidson to John P. Thomas, 14 January 1889, John P. Thomas Papers, SCL. See also Maury, *Recollections*, p. 252; Hoge, *Hoge*, pp. 292–93; Taylor, *Destruction and Reconstruction*, pp. 329–31; *Addresses Delivered Before*, CSA, Augusta, Ga., 1882, p. 4; D.H. Hill to Son, 24 August 1886, Daniel Harvey Hill Papers, NCDAH; and Jabez L.M. Curry to R.C. Winthrop, 18 January and 4 July 1887, Jabez L.M. Curry Papers, LC.

25. Early to Jones, 9 August 1889, Jubal A. Early Papers, Duke.

CHAPTER SEVEN.

THE CONFEDERATE TRADITION IN TRANSITION:

DEVELOPMENTS IN THE EIGHTIES

1. Strode, *Jefferson Davis, Tragic Hero*, pp. 461–66.

2. "Unveiling of Valentine's Recumbent Figure of Lee at Lexington, Va., June 28, 1883," *SHSP* 11 (August-September 1883): 337–88; "Sketch of the Lee Memorial

Association," *SHSP* 11 (August-September 1883): 391–413; Doss, "John Warwick Daniel," pp. 63–68. On the statue itself see Melissa Moss, "Edward Valentine, A Southern Artist" M.A. thesis, School of Art of Virginia Commonwealth University, 1969), pp. 44–51.

3. Quotation is from "Confederate Survivors' Association," clipping, *Chronicle and Sentinel*, 1 May 1878. See "Confederate Survivors," clipping, *Augusta Evening News*, 1 May 1878; "Confederate Survivors," clipping, *Chronicle and Sentinel*, 4 May 1878; "Confederate Survivors," clipping, *Chronicle and Sentinel*, 10 May 1878—all in Scrapbook, Antiquities of Georgia, 1877–1878. *Constitution of the Confederate Survivors' Association, Augusta, Georgia* (Augusta: Jowitt & Shavers Printing House, 1878), in Scrapbook. All of the above are in Charles C. Jones, Jr., Papers, Duke. C.E. Jones, "The Confederate Survivors' Association," clipping, November 1910, Charles E. Jones Papers, Duke, mentions an early veterans' group in Augusta that merged with the CSA. For some aid to needy see Jones to Charles H. Phinzy, 8 September 1880; Jones to De Saussure Ford, 3 May 1884; Jones to K.C. Stiles, 8 May 1884—all in C.C. Jones, Jr., Papers, Duke.

4. *Addresses Delivered Before Confederate Survivors' Association, Augusta, Georgia*, 1882, p. 6; 1884, pp. 4–5; 1887, pp. 3–4; Jones to CSA of Augusta, [January 1884]; and Jones to John B. Gordon, 7 and 12 March 1887, C.C. Jones, Jr., Papers, Duke. Membership statistics are compiled from Confederate Survivors' Association Roster, 1898–1909, Charles E. Jones Papers, Duke.

5. *Southern Bivouac* 1 (September 1882): 1; "Soldier's Record," *SB* 3 (February 1885): 284–86; Basil W. Duke to Early, 7 September 1886, Early Papers, LC; "To Our Subscribers," *SB* 3 (May 1885): 423–26; Atchison, "Southern Literary Magazines," pp. 237–53; Rayburn S. Moore, "A Distinctively Southern Magazine: *The Southern Bivouac*," *Southern Literary Journal* 2 (Spring 1970): 51–65. William C. Davis, *The Orphan Brigade: The Kentucky Confederates Who Couldn't Go Home* (Garden City, N.Y.: Doubleday & Company, 1980), pp. 268–69, gives a slightly different interpretation of the origins of the *Bivouac*. On themes see "Editorial," 3 (April 1885): 339; "Editorial," 3 (January 1885): 238; Caleb Rose, "The Destruction of Louisville," n.s. 2 (June 1886): 49–58; "The Editor's Table," n.s. 2 (June 1886): 68–69; and "The Editor's Table," n.s. 2 (January 1887): 518—all in *SB*.

6. "General Fitzhugh Lee's Second Tour in Behalf of the Southern Historical Society," *SHSP* 11 (April-May 1883): 231; Association of the Army of Northern Virginia Papers and Association of the Army of Tennessee Papers, LHAC, Tulane.

7. "Historical Sketch of the R.E. Lee Monumental Association of New Orleans," *SHSP* 14 (1886): 96–99; "Ceremonies Connected with the Unveiling of the Statue of General Robert E. Lee at Lee Circle, New Orleans, February 22, 1884," *SHSP* 14 (1886): 62–96; Edward J. Cocke, *Monumental New Orleans* (New Orleans: La Fayette Publishers, 1968), pp. 4–5. On invitations see the letters of rejection in Lee Monument Association File, Memorial Association Papers, LHAC, Tulane.

8. P.H. Boyle to Wm. Miller Owen, 11 February 1884, Memorial Association Papers, LHAC, Tulane.

9. J. William Jones to Early, 26 July 1877 and 7 October 1879, Early Papers, LC; "Editorial Paragraphs," *SHSP* 7 (March 1879): 159–60; "Editorial Paragraphs," *SHSP* 7 (May 1879): 253–54; "Editorial Paragraphs," *SHSP* 8 (June–July 1880): 324; "Meeting at White Sulphur Springs," *SHSP* 7 (October 1879): 449; "Editorial Paragraphs," *SHSP* 9 (July–August 1881): 382; Jones to Early, 30 November 1881, Early Papers, LC; "Annual Meeting of the SHS," *SHSP* 11 (December 1883): 532; Strode,

Davis, Tragic Hero, pp. 457–58; "A Grand Meeting in New Orleans on the 25th of April in Behalf of the Southern Historical Society," *SHSP* 10 (May 1882): 223–33; "Editorial Paragraphs," *SHSP* 11 (June 1882): 254–55; "Editorial Paragraphs," *SHSP* 11 (January 1883): 44–48; Dabney H. Maury to Early, 31 December 1882, Early Papers, LC; "General Fitzhugh Lee's Second Tour in Behalf of the Southern Historical Society," *SHSP* 11 (April–May 1883): 228–38.

10. Record, v. 1, 5 April 1883, Lee Camp Records, VHS; "Editorial Paragraphs," *SHSP* 12 (March 1884): 141–42; "The Soldiers' Home, Richmond, Va.," *SHSP* 20 (1892): 315–24.

11. Analysis here is based on comparison of list of charter members in R.E. Lee Camp, No. 1, Roster—18 April 1883–8 March 1918, VSL with AANVA membership list of 1873–74. Lee Camp officers and organizational committee were found in Record, v. 1, 5 April 1883, Lee Camp Records, VHS. Because of the absence of membership records for AANVA from 1874–84 some of the Lee Camp organizers could at some time have been members of the AANVA. The 1884 list of AANVA members was a list of those paying dues and would have included any who joined in that time who did not quit before 1884. Occupations are from Richmond city directories.

12. Table below is based on Lee Camp members who joined in 1883–84, from Roster cited above, who could be identified in Richmond city directories. For comparison with AANVA, see footnote 30, Chapter 4.

Professional & high white-collar	68 (26.98%)
Proprietary & low white-collar	112 (44.44%)
Skilled craftsmen	54 (21.43%)
Unskilled workers	18 (7.14%)
Total identified	252
Unidentified	50
Total	302

13. Richmond *Daily Dispatch*, 19 and 20 April 1883. Only in 1892, and at the request of the Grand Camp of Virginia, did Lee Camp appoint an historical committee. See Record, v. 3, 29 July 1892, Lee Camp Records, VHS.

14. Record, v. 1, 27 April, 29 May, 12 October 1883, Lee Camp Records, VHS; Resolution, filed August 1885, R.E. Lee Camp, No. 1, Board of Visitors Papers, VSL; "Editorial," *SB* 2 (June 1884): 479; J.B. Gordon to Dear Sir, 7 April 1884 and other clippings and correspondence in 1884 File, Board of Visitors Papers, VHS.

15. Record, v. 1, 1 June 1883, v. 2, 4 September and 9 October 1885, 3 December 1886, Lee Camp Records, VHS; James H. Patton to Early (copy), 18 November 1884, Early Family Papers, VHS.

16. Figures are from a list in Ledger, AANVA. See also Ledger, 15 January 1886 and December 1891, Cooper Store, UVA; and Thomas Ellett to T.T. Munford, 1 February 1892, T.T. Munford Division, Munford-Ellis Papers, Duke.

17. Dabney Maury to Early, 1 November 1884 and 28 August 1883, Early Papers, LC; R.A. Brock to Munford, 4 February 1888, T.T. Munford Division, Munford-Ellis Papers, Duke; Early to Davis, 4 May 1889, in Rowland, ed., *Jefferson Davis,* 10: 112; Jones to D.H. Hill, 8 February 1887, Daniel H. Hill Papers, NCDAH. On Brock see "Editorial," *SHSP* 39 (1914): 213–17.

18. On Davis's reputation see Duke, *Reminiscences,* pp. 339–44; Clark, *The*

Southern Country Editor, pp. 178–83; and Clement Eaton, *Jefferson Davis* (New York: The Free Press, 1977), p. 262. Harris, "The South in Defeat: 1865," p. 200, argues that Davis became the representative man right after his imprisonment. On his tour see Strode, *Davis, Tragic Hero*, pp. 478–87; and Raymond B. Nixon, *Henry W. Grady: Spokesman of the New South* (New York: Alfred A. Knopf, 1943), pp. 226–31. James G. Towery, "The Georgia Gubernatorial Campaign of 1886" (M.A. thesis, Emory University, 1945), pp. 13–16, argues that the roles of both Davis and Gordon had nothing to do with the election.

19. *Atlanta Constitution*, 22 and 27 April and 1 May 1886. Felton, "*My Memoirs of Georgia Politics*," pp. 624–25, argues that Davis later came to resent the way he had been manipulated for Gordon's benefit, but she is far from a dispassionate observer on anything concerning Gordon.

20. "Address of J.C.C. Black, at the Unveiling of the Hill Statue, Atlanta, Georgia, May 1, 1886," *SHSP* 14 (1886): 163–79. Grady is quoted in Nixon, *Grady*, pp. 228–31.

21. Buser, "After Half A Generation," p. 139; Mother to Daughters, 30 April and 4 May 1886, Louisa B. and Mary B. Poppenheim Papers, Duke; D.H. Hill to Joe, 3 May 1886, Daniel H. Hill Papers, NCDAH; *Atlanta Constitution*, 3 May 1886. See also F.W. Dawson, clipping, Charleston *News and Courier*, in Scrapbook, Thaddeus K. Oglesby Papers, Duke; "The Editor's Table," *SB*, n.s. 2 (June 1886): 70.

22. *Atlanta Constitution*, 1 May 1886; *New York Times*, 22 September 1886, p. 1; "Address Before the Virginia Division of Army of Northern Virginia, at their Reunion on the Evening of Oct. 21, 1886," *SHSP* 14 (1886): 181–82; Strode, *Davis, Tragic Hero*, pp. 492–94; E. Merton Coulter, "Jefferson Davis and the Northeast Georgia Fair," *GHQ* 50 (September 1966): 253–75; "Record of N.B. Forrest Camp, No. 4, UCV," *Confederate Veteran* 13 (September 1905): 394.

23. Quotation is from *New York Times*, 22 September 1886, p. 1. See also unidentified clipping, Varina Davis Scrapbook, Davis Papers, LHAC, Tulane; and Chiles C. Ferrell, "The Daughter of the Confederacy: Her Life, Character and Writings," *Publications of the Mississippi Historical Society* 2 (1899): 74. On the other daughter's resentment see Mrs. M.J.D. Hayes to Mrs. Kimbrough, 15 November 1906, Jefferson Davis Papers (microfilm), MDAH. She did, however, sometimes elicit her own warm reception. See *Minutes of the Annual Meetings and Reunions of the United Confederate Veterans*, 1900, p. 77; 1907, pp. 58–59.

24. Clippings, v. 3, George Moorman Scrapbooks, Tulane; *New York Times*, 30 October 1887, p. 2; Strode, *Davis, Tragic Hero*, pp. 517–24; Markham Memorandum Books, 11 December 1889, Thomas R. Markham Papers, LSU; Stella Bringier to Browse, 7 December 1889, Louis Bringier Papers, LSU; C.J. McDonald Furman Diary, 1885–1903, 31 December 1889, C.J. McDonald Furman Papers, SCL; J.L.M. Curry to Manly Curry, 18 December 1889 and Curry to My Dear Child, 18 December 1889, Jabez L.M. Curry Papers, Duke; Curry to Winthrop, 16 December 1889, Curry Papers, LC.

25. "The Lee Equestrian Statue," clipping, November 1877, Lee Equestrian Statue Clipping File; Clippings, Monuments-Richmond, Lee, Vertical File. All in Valentine Museum. *New York Times*, 20 November 1877, p. 5; "The Monument to General Robert E. Lee: History of the Movement From Its Existence," *SHSP* 17 (1889): 195–201; Readnour, "General Fitzhugh Lee," pp. 172–73; "The Monument to Lee," clipping, Richmond *Times*, 25 May 1890, Monuments—Richmond, Lee Vertical File, Valentine Museum; Sarah N. Randolph to Fitzhugh Lee, 16 April 1886, Fitzhugh Lee Governor's Papers, VSL.

26. Randolph to Lee, 6 August 1886 and Early to Lee, 27 March 1886, Lee Governor's Papers; Wm. Preston Johnson to Edward Valentine, 24 August 1887, Lee Equestrian Statue Letter File, Valentine Papers, Valentine Museum; Moss, "Valentine," p. 76. On Lee and Virginians see Lee to Early, 9 May 1875; William H. Payne to Early, 16 May 1875; and Lee to Early, 1 April 1878—all in Early Papers, LC.

27. *New York Times*, 23 June 1886, p. 1; Curry to Manly Curry, 4 April 1889, Curry Papers, Duke; Record, v. 2, 29 July and 21 October 1887, Lee Camp Records, VHS; Fitzhugh Lee to Early, 9 and 18 August 1887, Early Papers, LC; "The Monument to Gen. Robert E. Lee," *SHSP* 17 (1889): 208–27.

28. Lee to Early, 25 April, 15 June, and 30 July 1889, Early Papers, LC; Record, v. 3, 19 July 1889, Lee Camp Records, VHS; "Letter From General Early," clipping, 26 July 1889, Monuments—Richmond, Lee, Vertical File, Valentine Museum; R.A.M. Viney to Early, 19 March 1890, Early Papers, LC; Morton Marke to Early, 28 April 1890, Early Family Papers, VHS; Record, v. 3, 17 and 24 January 1890, Lee Camp Records, VHS.

29. "Removal of the Statue from the Richmond, Fredericksburg and Potomac Railroad, May 7th, 1890," *SHSP* 17 (1889): 248–62.

30. "The Unveiling of the Statue of General Robert E. Lee, at Richmond, Va., May 29th, 1890," *SHSP* 17 (1889): 262–335.

31. "The Unveiling," pp. 262–335. Anderson's speech on pp. 312–35.

32. Archer Anderson to John W. Daniel, 4 June 1890, John W. Daniel Papers, Duke; Cameron to J.W. Pegram, 6 June 1890, Pegram Family Papers, VHS; "Washington Artillery," offprint from *Daily Picayune*, 20 June 1890, William H. Ellis Papers, LSU. See also J.Y. Gilmore to Wife, 29 May 1890, J.Y. Gilmore Papers, LSU; Jones to F.E. Eve, 6 June 1890, C.C. Jones, Jr., Papers, Duke; J. Taylor Wood to J.W. Pegram, 7 June 1890, Pegram Family Papers, VHS; H. Dudley Coleman to Wm. H. Ellis, 23 July 1890, Ellis Papers, LSU.

33. "The Unveiling of the Lee Statue," *Public Opinion* 9 (7 June 1890): 189–92. Northern papers surveyed in this article did not all agree; some condemned the ceremonies as teaching treason. For a different view see Michael B. Chesson, *Richmond After the War, 1865–1890* (Richmond: Virginia State Library, 1981), p. 205.

CHAPTER EIGHT.
THE CONFEDERATE CELEBRATION:
ITS ORGANIZATIONAL STRUCTURE

1. Increase is clear from a variety of sources, including articles in the *Southern Historical Society Papers* and *Confederate Veteran*, which are too numerous to cite. On Lee Camp's role see Record, v. 2, 21 September 1888; v. 3, 21 March 1890, UCV, R.E. Lee Camp No. 1 Records, VHS; V.S. Hilliard to Jefferson Davis, 21 July 1887, in Rowland, ed., *Jefferson Davis*, 10: 584. On the CSA of Augusta's role see several letters in Charles C. Jones, Jr., Papers, Duke. See also, on formation of camps in this period, *Roster and Historical Sketch of A.P. Hill Camp, CV, No. 6, Va.* (Petersburg, Va.: n.p., n.d.), pp. 4–6; United Confederate Veterans, Camp Hampton, Richland County, 1887–1894, Records, SCL; Minutes, December 23, 1889–May 10, 1906, Jefferson Davis Memorial Association, SCL. On Florida camp and its call see *By-Laws and Rules of Order of Florida Camp No. 1 of Confederate Veterans, Adopted June 10, 1885* (Jacksonville, Fla.: Chas. W. DaCosta, 1885); Minutes, v. 3, 13 December 1887 and

Report of Executive Committee, 13 December 1887, Association of the Army of Tennessee Papers, LHAC, Tulane; Minutes, 21 November 1887, Association of the Army of Northern Virginia Papers, LHAC, Tulane; and Camp Hampton Records, 1887–1897, 7 November 1888, SCL. On state associations see Record, v. 2, 4 and 11 November, 9 December 1887 and 20, 27 January 1888, Lee Camp Records, VHS; *Proceedings of the Grand Camp Confederate Veterans, Department of Virginia*, 1894, pp. 3–4; *Charter, Constitution and Laws of the Association of Confederate Soldiers, Tennessee Division, Governing State and Local Bivouacs of the Organization* (Nashville: Foster & Webb Printers, 1888); "Wearers of the Gray," clipping, *Nashville Daily American*, 26 February 1889, v. 5, George Moorman Scrapbooks, Tulane; "Beginning of Tennessee Bivouac," CV 13 (October 1905): 457; Jones to John F. Dillon, 17 September 1888, Jones to A.W.C. Duncan, 9 September 1889, Jones to A. McDuncan, 9 October 1889— all in C.C. Jones, Jr., Papers, Duke; and *Proceedings of the Convention of the Confederate Survivors' Association of the State of Georgia, held at Atlanta, Ga. Aug. 15, 1889*, copy in John M. Kell Papers, Duke.

2. *Charter and By-Laws, Social, Benevolent and Historical Association, Veteran Confederate States Cavalry* (New Orleans: Brandao, Gill, 1889); *Proceedings of the Great Reunion of the Veterans of the Confederate States Cavalry, Held in The City of New Orleans, La. In Washington Artillery Arsenal, On Monday, February 13th, 1888*, copy in Veteran Confederate States Cavalry Papers, LHAC, Tulane.

3. Leon Jastremski, "The Organization of the UCV," CV 12 (September 1904): 425; Fred A. Ober to Comrades, Army of Northern Virginia, 10 June 1890, AANVA Papers, LHAC, Tulane; J.A. Chalaron, et al., to President, 11 March 1889 and Minutes, v. 3, 12 February 1889, AAT Papers, LHAC, Tulane; Minutes, v.15, February to June 1889, AANVA Papers, LHAC, Tulane.

4. Clipping, 11 June 1889, Letter File Book, Joseph Jones Papers, LSU; *Proceedings of the Convention for Organization and Adoption of the Constitution of the United Confederate Veterans, June 10th, 1889* (New Orleans: Hopkins Printing Office, 1891). For a more thorough discussion of the organizational structure of the UCV see White, *The Confederate Veteran*, pp. 27–33.

5. *Minutes of the Annual Meetings and Reunions of the United Confederate Veterans*, 1890, pp. 6–7; 1891, pp. 4–5; Record, v. 3, 13 and 20 June, 4 and 11 July 1890, Lee Camp Records, VHS. Because of difficulties presented by the Grand Camp constitution, Lee Camp did not officially join the UCV until 1892. See Record, v. 3, 17 June and 1 July 1892. On Moorman's selection see George Moorman to Joseph Jones, 12 June 1891, Joseph Jones Papers, Tulane; Moorman to Gordon, 4 July 1891, Adjutant General, Letterpress Book, United Confederate Veterans' Association Papers, LSU. Quotations are from Fred L. Robertson to W.E. Mickle, 6 October 1903, William E. Mickle Papers, Duke; "Gen. George Moorman Died in Harness," CV 11 (January 1903): 8; S.D. Lee to Wm. E. Mickle, 4 April 1897, United Confederate Veterans Papers, Special Collections, University of Georgia Library. See also *UCV Minutes*, 1899, pp. 76–77; 1892, pp. 11, 84–85. Generalizations on Moorman's techniques rest on evidence in his letterpress books for early years in UCVA Papers, LSU. On use of name see Moorman to Jas. C. Tappan, 15 August 1891. For examples of camps acting with little or no urging, see Minutes, 24 June 1893, Jefferson Davis Memorial Association Papers, SCL; Minutes, 25 July and 8 September 1893, Camp Hampton Records, SCL; Vol. 1893–1899, 4 February 1895, United Confederate Veterans, Abner Perrin Camp (Edgefield), SCL.

6. Clipping, "The United Confederate Veteran," UCV Letter File Box, Jones ·
Papers, LSU; Reda C. Goff, "The *Confederate Veteran* Magazine," *Tennessee Historical*

Quarterly 31 (Spring 1972): 45–60; CV 1 (May 1893): 144; but cf. "About the Term New South," CV 15 (December 1907): 538. On the standing of the magazine see Cunningham, "Camps That Indorse the Veteran," CV 2 (May 1894): 155–56; Moorman to Cunningham, 18 December 1893 and 2 September 1895, AG Lpb, UCVA Papers, LSU. A series of letters from Moorman in AG Lpb v. 4, makes it clear Moorman was giving support not only to the *Veteran* but to other magazines as well. Cunningham to Moorman, 11 February 1898, Adjutant General's Letter Box, UCVA Papers, LSU. See also CV 1 (August 1893): 232; "Birmingham Reunion Reports," CV 2 (May 1894): 131.

7. The price went up in January 1894. "The Veteran Seven Years Old," CV 7 (December 1899): 544; "Published by Order of P.O. Department," CV 20 (November 1912): 499; "Where the Veteran Goes," CV 8 (March 1900): 126–27; and Colyer Meriwether, "Southern Historical Societies," in *The South in the Building of the Nation*, v. 7, *History of the Literary and Intellectual Life of the South*, John Bell Henneman, ed (Richmond: Southern History Publication Society, 1909), p. 516. Some copies went to UCV and UDC chapters, and many members had access to them. Some individual subscribers shared their copies with others as well. See, for example, CV 10 (November 1902): 492. "Extracts from Recent Letters," CV 11 (April 1903): 226–27, suggests that some of the subscribers were from the lower classes.

8. *UCV Minutes*, 1896, p. 52; 1904, p. 28. In 1904, only a little under half the camps had paid dues, but the next year 1,474 camps were listed as "alive." 1905, p. 55. To find geographical distribution within states, the locations of camps were plotted on state maps. Virginia was under-represented in part because many camps in Grand Camp, Virginia, never joined the UCV. The following tables summarize the findings on the distribution of UCV camps.

Comparison of the Percentage of UCV Camps by State with the Percentage of Veteran Population in Each State in 1890

State	Percentage of Camps	Percentage of Veterans
Alabama	7.98	7.88
Arkansas	6.26	6.18
Florida	2.89	1.89
Georgia	10.02	10.92
Kentucky	4.69	2.57
Louisiana	4.85	3.69
Maryland	0.9	—
Mississippi	6.18	6.16
Missouri	6.10	4.08
North Carolina	4.69	8.96
South Carolina	10.25	5.46
Tennessee	6.06	7.42
Texas	18.95	15.50
Virginia	3.68	11.28

Percentage of camps is from UCV Minutes, 1900, p. 84. Percentage of veterans is from "Soldiers and Widows," *Compendium of the Eleventh Census: 1890*, pt. 3, *Population . . .* (Washington: Government Printing Office, 1897), p. 575. Maryland had no more than 8,000 Confederate veterans and was not listed in the census.

Percentage of Counties with UCV Camps by State

State	Percentage of Counties with Camps
Alabama	96.96
Arkansas	81.33
Florida	86.66
Georgia	88.32
Kentucky	48.73
Louisiana	76.27
Maryland	37.5
Mississippi	90.66
Missouri	52.17
North Carolina	70.83
South Carolina	100.0
Tennessee	66.6
Texas	70.9
Virginia	61.3

Counties were counted on the basis of 1890; camps were all formed by 1912. The use of a later year for counties, and hence a larger number, would not have made much difference. Some of the camps were in new counties, but they were counted as multiple camps in an 1890 county.

9. Computations from figures on dues in UCV *Minutes*, 1902, p. 48, yeild a total of 35,198 members. Herman Hattaway, "United Confederate Veterans," *The Encyclopedia of Southern History*, David C. Roller and Robert W. Twyman, eds. (Baton Rouge: Louisiana State University Press, 1979), p. 1262, places the figure at 160,000. White, *Confederate Veteran*, pp. 34–35, puts it at from 80,000 to 85,000. *Atlanta Constitution*, 17 May 1903. "Soldiers and Widows," *Compendium of the Eleventh Census: 1890*, pt. 3, *Population* . . . (Washington: Government Printing Office, 1897), p. 573, reported that 428,747 white Confederates survived. Ruoff, "Southern Womanhood, 1865–1920," pp. 97–98, estimates from white survival rates that 31 percent of the veterans alive in 1890 had died by 1900. I therefore used a figure of 290,000 for the number of veterans surviving in 1903. The *Constitution*, however, reported that only 100,000 survived that year. White, without explaining or providing his source, gives a figure of one in three for the number of living veterans who joined the UCV.

10. White, *Confederate Veteran*, p. 24; Resolution, 9 April 1887 and secretaries' reports, particularly for 1890, AANVA Papers, LHAC, Tulane; Report of the Executive Committee, ca. 3 February 1890, AAT Papers, LHAC, Tulane; Minute Book, 19 January 1891, Urquahart-Gillette Camp, UCV (Franklin, Va.) Records, VHS; Minutes, 3 July 1894, Camp Hampton Records, SCL; Minute Book, 6 July 1888, Record of Frank Cheatham Bivouac, 1887–1906 and Minutes of Fred Ault Camp No. 5, UCV, Knoxville, Knoxville Co., Tenn., 1889–1915, 12 February 1894, in United Confederate Veterans, Tennessee Division, Bivouac Records, TSL; Philip H. Hall to W.E. Mickle, 9 September 1904, Mickle Papers, Duke; C.D.W. McNeill to Mickle, 11 January 1906, AG Lb, UCVA Papers, LSU; Chapter By-laws and Rules of Order of Cabell-Graves Camp of CV, of Danville, Va., copy in box 3, UCVA Papers, LSU; A.L. Scott to Moorman, 26 March 1897, Berry L. Danehero to Moorman, 20 April 1897, W.S. Chilton to Moorman, 21 April 1897, J.D. Garvis to Moorman, 19 June 1897, J.L. Burke to Moorman, 22 June 1898, E.G. Williams to Moorman, 4 February 1898—all in AG

Lbs, UCVA Papers, LSU. On membership in the three urban camps see Appendix 2. Several letters suggested that the UCV had little success among cotton mill workers. See Thomas W. Collery to Moorman, 15 June 1898, J.O. Jenkins to Moorman, 19 February 1898, and W.F. Smith to Moorman, 24 December 1907—all in AG Lbs, UCVA Papers, LSU. According to the 1890 census, only 725 Confederate veterans had become cotton mill workers. See *Compendium*, 1890, p. 581.

11. Record, v. 2, 15 May and 22 June 1888, v. 3, 30 August 1889, 13 March, 24 April, 23 October 1891, v. 4, 6 January 1893, 10 November 1894, Lee Camp Records, VHS; *Minutes of the Annual Meetings of the United Daughters of the Confederacy*, 1896, pp. 3–4; Patricia F. Climer, "Protectors of the Past: The United Daughters of the Confederacy, Tennessee Division, and the Lost Cause" (M.A. thesis, Vanderbilt University, 1973), p. 10; "A Wife of a Veteran," to W.P. Smith, 22 June 1892 and Commander's Report with Minutes of 1892, Grand Camp Confederate Veterans, Department of Virginia Records, VSL; Minutes, March 1893, Records of the Memorial Society of the Ladies of the City of Petersburg, 1866–1912, VSL; Minutes of the Ault Camp, 25 September 1896, UCV, Tennessee Division, Bivouac Records, TSL; Homer Richey, *Memorial History of the John Bowie Strange Camp, United Confederate Veterans* (Charlottesville: Michie Company, 1920), p. 13; *UDC Minutes*, 1894; Mrs. Raines, "United Daughters of the Confederacy," CV 6 (October 1898): 451; M.M. Harrison, "Founder of United Daughters of the Confederacy," clipping, Scrapbook 1908–1913, Mrs. D. Mitchell Cox Scrapbooks, AHS; Mrs. Roy Weeks McKinney, "Origin," in *The History of the United Daughters of the Confederacy*, Mary B. Poppenheim, et al. (Raleigh: Edwards & Broughton Company, 1925), pp. 1–12. Interestingly, the UDC's account says little of early male involvement. A group in Missouri called the "Daughters of the Confederacy" formed in 1891, but it had no influence on the development of the regional organization. See *UDC Minutes*, 1897, p. 30, for help of UCV.

12. Minutes, v. 3, 12 March 1889, AAT Papers, LHAC, Tulane; Records, v. 3, 23 February 1889, 7 March 1890, Lee Camp Records, VHS; Jones to F.M. Stovall, 4 June 1891, C.C. Jones, Jr., Papers, Duke: *Addresses Before the CSA Augusta, Ga.*, 1891, pp. 8–9, 1892, p. 5; Minutes, 7 May 1889, Camp Hampton Records, SCL; *UCV Minutes*, 1890, pp. 2–5; "United Sons, Confederate Veterans," CV 4 (August 1896): 258–59; "A Call for a General Organization of Sons of Confederate Veterans by R.E. Lee Camp No. 1, SCV, Richmond, Virginia," in the United Sons of Confederate Veterans' Papers, LHAC, Tulane; *Atlanta Constitution*, 1 July 1896; *Minutes of the Annual Reunion, United Sons of Confederate Veterans*, 1908, pp. 119–20. The abbreviation SCV will be used throughout in the text.

13. Moorman to J.B. Gordon, 20 June 1892, AG Lpb; "Memorandum, Baltimore, April 1894," filed with Winnifield Peters to Moorman, 3 April 1894, AG Lb; Moorman to Chas. E. Hooker, 7 and 14 February 1900, AG Lpb. All in UCVA Papers, LSU. Quotations are from Bradley Johnson to T.T. Munford, 29 December 1894, T.T. Munford Division, Munford-Ellis Papers, Duke; and William H. Payne to Marcus J. Wright, 11 July 1895, Marcus J. Wright Papers, Duke. Early was feuding with Gordon in the late eighties over events at Cedar Creek, and the feud may have contributed to his reluctance to support the UCV. On participation see William H. Payne to James W. Peagram, 26 February 1894, R.E. Lee Camp Board of Visitor Papers, VSL; Record, v. 4, 3 March and 13 June 1893, 13 September and 27 November 1895, Lee Camp Records, VHS.

14. Record, v. 3, 25 March 1892, Lee Camp Records, VHS; Moorman to Jones, 25 February 1896, AG Lpb, UCVA Papers, LSU.

15. Information on these men is from the following sources: "Gen. J.F. Shipp,"

CV 18 (May 1910): 206; Edward Pinkowski, *Pills, Pen and Politics: The Story of General Leon Jastremski, 1843–1907* (Wilmington, Del.: Captain Stanislaus Mlotkowski Memorial Brigade Society, 1974); *Official Journal of the House of Representatives* (Baton Rouge: Leon Jastremski State Printing, 1888); "Fred A. Ober Dies," *The Daily Picayune*, 5 March 1913, p. 6; "Funeral Service Held," clipping in J.A. Chalaron Scrapbook 7, USCV Papers, and Chalaron Papers, LHAC, Tulane.

16. "Gen. Moorman Dies," pp. 8–11; Moorman Scrapbooks, Tulane; E. Russ Williams, Jr., "Louisiana's Public and Private Immigration Endeavors: 1866–1893," *Louisiana History* 15 (Spring 1974): 163–64.

17. "Sumner Archibald Cunningham," CV 22 (January 1914): 6–10; Goff, *"Confederate Veteran,"* pp. 45–60; Rebecca Cameron to J.G. de R. Hamilton, 28 June 1911, J.G. de Roulhac Hamilton Papers, SHC.

18. Felton, *"My Memoirs of Georgia Politics,"* pp. 478–546; Curry to Manly Curry, 22 November 1890, J.L.M. Curry Papers, Duke. See Ralph C. Eckert, "John Brown Gordon: Soldier, Southerner, American" (Ph.D. diss., Louisiana State University, 1983); Allen P. Tankersley, *John B. Gordon: A Study in Gallantry* (Atlanta: The Whitehall Press, 1955); and Howard Dorgan, "A Case Study in Reconciliation: General John B. Gordon and the 'Last Days of the Confederacy,'" *Quarterly Journal of Speech* 60 (February 1974): 88–90.

19. Eckert, "Gordon;" Tankersley, *Gordon*; William Anderson, "The Resignation of John B. Gordon from the United States Senate in 1880," *Georgia Historical Quarterly* 52 (December 1968): 438–42.

20. Clement A. Evans, "General Gordon and General Longstreet," *Independent* 56 (February 1904): 314; Lamar, *When All Is Said and Done*, p. 70; Toombs quoted in James G. Towery, "The Georgia Gubernatorial Campaign of 1886" (M.A. thesis, Emory University, 1945), p. 80; *Proceedings of the Convention for Organization . . . of the UCV*, pp. 7–8; Florence Barlow, "Lieut. Gen'l. J.B. Gordon," *The Lost Cause* 10 (January 1904): 88. See also *UCV Minutes*, 1901, p. 21; "Underwood Sues the Veteran for $50,000," CV 7 (August 1899): 345. See Mary L. and Louisa A. Mayo, "Veterans of the Confederacy," *Munsey's Magazine* 18 (February 1898): 753–62, for a quick summary of which general had what scars. Gordon had the most, though not the most severe.

21. Nixon, *Henry W. Grady*, pp. 106, 161, 294–95; Werner, "Hegemony and Conflict," pp. 225–34; J.B. Gordon to J. Madison Drake, 27 May 1889, John B. Gordon Papers, Duke.

22. See especially Ledger and Minutes of the Virginia Division, Association of the Army of Northern Virginia, 1871–1894, 3 October 1872, in Items from Cooper's Old Book Store, Richmond, UVA; Frank Gordon to Joseph Jones, 15 May 1876, Southern Historical Society Records, VHS. On Gordon's popularity see "The Louisville Reunion," CV 8 (June 1900): 243; and *UCV Minutes*, 1891, pp. 13–14.

23. Figures were compiled from R.E. Lee Camp No. 1, Roster, April 18, 1883–March 8, 1918, VSL; and *Compendium of Census*, 1890, p. 573. But for an interesting though dissimilar analysis of lynching that does see the veteran generation interested in "educating" the rising generation, see David Herbert Donald, "A Generation of Defeat," in Walter J. Frazer, Jr. and Winfred B. Moore, Jr., eds. *From the Old South to the New: Essays on the Transitional South* (Westport, Conn.: Greenwood Press, 1981), pp. 3–20.

24. "The Last Roll," CV 5 (March 1897): 107; Minute Book, 1 June 1888, Records of Frank Cheatham Bivouac, UCV, Tennessee Division, Bivouac Records, TSL; several copies of Constitution and By-laws of individual camps in box 3, UCVA Papers, LSU; Record, v. 3, 19 February 1892, Lee Camp Records, VHS; "Burial Service

Suggested," *CV* 2 (July 1894): 212; Moorman to Will Lambert, 8 June 1893, AG Lpb, UCVA Papers, LSU; *General Orders, UCV,* v. 1, #212, 1 May 1899; *UCV Minutes,* 1899, p. 170. Quotation is from S.D. Lee to Wm. E. Mickle, 4 April 1897, United Confederate Veterans Papers, UGA.

25. Frank H. Heck, *The Civil War Veteran in Minnesota Life and Politics* (Oxford, Ohio: The Mississippi Valley Press, 1941), p. 257; Dearing, *Veterans in Politics,* pp. 275–77 and *passim;* Lankevich, "The Grand Army of the Republic in New York State," pp. 254–55 and *passim;* Noyes, "A History of the Grand Army of the Republic in Ohio," p. 156 and *passim.*

26. Wallace E. Davies, *Patriotism on Parade: The Story of Veterans' and Hereditary Organizations in America, 1783–1900* (Cambridge: Harvard University Press, 1955); Arthur M. Schlesinger, "Biography of a Nation of Joiners," *Paths to the Present* (Boston: Houghton Mifflin Company, 1964), p. 43; William S. Powell, *Paradise Preserved* (Chapel Hill: University of North Carolina Press, 1965); Lyon G. Tyler, "Preservation of Virginia History," *NCHR* 3 (October 1926): 537–38; Eric Hobsbawm and Terrence Ranger, eds., *The Invention of Tradition* (Cambridge: Cambridge University Press, 1983).

27. On recession see Ayers, *Vengeance and Justice,* pp. 250–51. See also Keller, *Affairs of State,* pp. 440–41.

28. Quotation is from Roger and Sara Pryor to Virginia Clopton, 27 October 1908, C.C. Clay Papers, Duke. For another reference to scars see F.W. Dawson quoted in E. Culpepper Clark, "Henry Grady's New South: A Rebuttal from Charleston," *Southern Speech Communication Journal* 41 (Summer 1976): 354; to bruises, J.H. Steinmyer to Ellison Capers, 16 June 1900, Ellison Capers Papers, Duke; to pain, Wm. Preston Johnston to T.T. Munford, 19 January 1894, T.T. Munford Division, Munford-Ellis Papers, Duke.

CHAPTER NINE.

THE CONFEDERATE CELEBRATION:

ITS INTERPRETATION OF THE WAR

1. Quotations are from An Ex-Officer of Lee's Army, *Counsel for Old Confederates,* 1903, leaflet in United Confederate Veterans Papers, LHAC, Tulane. The same attack was also made in J.T. James to J.B. Gordon, 17 February 1903, AG Lb, UCVA Papers, LSU. For mention of a similar sermon see T.K. Oglesby, "A Plea for the Truth of History," clipping, *Atlanta Journal,* 9 May 1909, in Thaddeus K. Oglesby Papers, Duke.

2. Felton, "*My Memoirs of Georgia Politics,*" pp. 5–9, 26–46.

3. Other scholars have also sketched the South's view of its past. See especially Herman Hattaway, "Clio's Southern Soldiers: The United Confederate Veterans and History," *Louisiana History* 12 (Summer 1971): 213–42; Dorgan, "Southern Apologetic Themes"; Durant, "The Gently Furled Banner."

4. Hattaway, "Clio's Southern Soldiers"; *UCV Minutes,* 1896, pp. 29–48; Mrs. St. John Alison Lawton, et al., "Historical Work," *The History of the United Daughters of the Confederacy,* Mary B. Poppenheim, et al. (Raleigh: Edwards & Broughton, Company, 1925), pp. 135–41; *UDC Minutes,* 1904, pp. 196–205; *Proceedings of the Grand Camp Confederate Veterans, Department of Virginia,* 1898, pp. 20–23; 1906, pp. 26–29; "Memorable Reunion at Owensboro," *Confederate Veteran* 10 (August 1902): 342–45; "Hearty Tributes to Laura Gault," *CV* 10 (October 1902): 437; "Laura Gault

Honored in Far West," *CV* 11 (January 1903): 5–6; "Georgia State Reunion," *CV* 11 (December 1903): 532; *UDC Minutes*, 1903, p. 109; "Delightful Reunion at Nashville," *CV* 4 (November 1896): 364; "Yankee History," clipping, scrapbook v. 8, United Confederate Veterans' Papers, LHAC, Tulane; *UCV Minutes*, 1905, pp. 34–35; 1899, pp. 151–52; Minutes of the Meeting of Fred Ault Camp No. 5, UCV, 14 October 1895, United Confederate Veterans, Tennessee Division, Bivouac Records, TSL; *UDC Minutes*, 1897, p. 13; Camp Hampton Records, 8 December 1899, United Confederate Veterans, Camp Hampton Records, SCL; Helen De Berneire Wills to J.Y. Joyner, undated, and Joyner to Wills, 3 March 1904, in scrapbook v. 20, Elvira E. Moffitt Papers, SHC; "Texas Confederate Veterans Gather," *CV* 16 (October 1908): 503; Bessie L. Pierce, *Public Opinion and The Teaching of History in the United States* (New York: Alfred A. Knopf, 1926), pp. 39–40, 45–47, 66–67, 163. For another account of the battle over textbooks see Hunter, "The Sacred South," pp. 224–31.

    5. "Relics in Atlanta Exposition," *CV* 3 (September 1895): 282; "Confederate Relics at the Exposition," *CV* 5 (October 1897): 498; *HCMAS*, pp. 198–201; "Act of Incorporation and By-laws of the Louisiana Historical Association, New Orleans." Figures are from Minutes, 5 April 1900, 2 April 1902, April 1903, April 1906, 3 April 1907, but cf. with lower totals in Visitor's Registers—all in Louisiana Historical Association, Administrative Papers, LHAC, Tulane. On White House see "The South's Museum," *SHSP* 23 (1895): 354–81. For a description by a famous visitor see Henry James, *The American Scene* (London: Chapman and Hall, 1907), pp. 383–89. On Battle Abbey see "A Confederate Westminster," *CV* 1 (July 1893): 207; Camille Williams, "The South's Great Battle Abbey," *CV* 1 (December 1893): 361; *UCV Minutes*, 1895, pp. 56–60; "About the South's Battle Abbey," *CV* 4 (March 1896): 67–68; and "Charles Broadway Rouss,". clipping, scrapbook v. 5, United Confederate Veteran Scrapbooks, LSU.

    6. *UCV Minutes*, 1896, p. 46.

    7. *UCV Minutes*, 1897, p. 48; "Gen Bennett Young at Cave Hill Cemetery," *CV* 20 (August 1912): 372–73. See also "The Causes of the War," *CV* 1 (July 1893): 200–5; J.H. McNeilly, "By Graves of Confederate Dead," *CV* 2 (September 1894): 264–65; "Confederate Monument at Franklin," *CV* 8 (January 1900): 5–10; and Porter McFerrin, "View of the War Issues by a Student," *CV* 20 (July 1912): 332–33. The theme of vindication receives much more extensive treatment in Howard Dorgan, "The Doctrine of Victorious Defeat in the Rhetoric of Confederate Veterans," *Southern Speech Communication Journal* 38 (Winter 1972): 119–30, and in his dissertation cited above.

    8. Clement A. Evans to J.L.M. Curry, 25 July 1896, Jabez L.M. Curry Papers, LC; *UCV Minutes*, 1896, p. 46. See also B.B. Munford, "The Vindication of the South," *SHSP* 27 (1899): 60–84; *UCV Minutes*, 1900, pp. 26–34; W.R. Hammond, "Was the Confederate Soldier a Rebel?" *SHSP* 28 (1900): 247–50; George L. Christian, "Official Report of the History Committee of the Grand Camp Confederate Veterans, Department of Virginia," *SHSP* 28 (1900): 169–96; J.H. Fowles, "Last Days of The Great War," *CV* 14 (March 1906): 124–27. Durant, "The Gently Furled Banner," pp. 282–84, sees a shift in this period in the cause fought for by southerners from the "compact theory and state rights to constitutional liberty and the right of local self-government."

    9. For examples of use of these terms during and after the war see Davis, "Johnny Reb in Perspective," pp. 14, 18–19; Kennaway, *On Sherman's Track*, p. 89; Henry Latham, *Black and White: A Journal of a Three Month's Tour in the United States* (London: Macmillan and Company, 1867), p. 110; A.H. Mason to P.G.T. Beauregard, 4 September 1865, John R. Peacock Papers, SHC; "Editorial," *LWL* 2 (January 1867): 227; Ella Gertrude Thomas Journal, 31 March 1871, Duke; "In Memoriam," *Southern Review* 19 (April 1876): 326; C.C. Jones to W.L. Baringer, 10 June 1878, Charles C.

Jones, Jr., Papers, Duke; Charles T. O'Ferrall, *Forty Years of Active Service* (New York: Neale Publishing Company, 1904), pp. 151–52; *UCV Minutes*, 1898, p. 38; "Julian S. Carr's Address at Lexington, Va., June 3, 1916," Julian Shakespeare Carr Papers, SHC; Editorial, *CV* 2 (May 1894): 145; "Call Me a Rebel," *CV* 2 (August 1894): 230. Quotation is from "The Name of the War," *CV* 2 (June 1894): 174.

10. Berry Benson to John McElroy, 15 February 1913, Berry G. Benson Papers, SHC; *UCV Minutes*, 1898, pp. 44–52; *UDC Minutes*, 1910, p. 13; Adjutant General, Sons of Confederate Veterans, [probably of Nathan Bedford Forrest Camp], circular letter, n.d., United Sons of Confederate Veterans' Papers, LHAC, Tulane; *USCV Minutes*, 1903, p. 36. See also John L. Johnson, *Autobiographical Notes* (n.p.: Privately printed, 1958), p. 259; Richard H. Wilmer, *The Recent Past From a Southern Standpoint; Reminiscences of a Grandfather* (New York: Thomas Whittaker, 1887), p. 201. In a 1908 prologue to her wartime diary, Eliza F. Andrews wrote, "the word 'rebel,' now so bitterly resented as casting a stigma on the Southern cause, is used throughout the diary as a term of pride and affectionate endearment." *The War–time Journal of a Georgia Girl*, p. 3. But the sentiment was not universal. During the 1909 UCV reunion someone used the term, and "Then pandemonium broke loose. It was difficult to tell whether the majority favored her sentiments or opposed them. Cheers were mingled with cat calls and hisses, and above all reverberated the ear–splitting rebel yell." *Atlanta Constitution*, 10 June 1909.

11. "The late unpleasantness" was used much less often than folklore suggests, but for examples see "Literary Notes," *SHSP* 10 (October–November 1882): 527; C.K. Marshall to Senator George, 27 January 1886, John J. Hood Papers, MDAH; Camp Hampton Records, 21 November 1893, SCL. "The Name of Our War," *CV* 2 (April 1894): 112; *UCV Minutes*, 1898, p. 87, says the UCV adopted a resolution to call it the "civil war between the states," but that may have been a mistake. See Wm. I. DeRosset to Moorman, 12 August 1898, AG Letterbox, UCVA Papers, LSU. See also *UCV Minutes*, 1900, pp. 78, 80; *UDC Minutes*, 1899, pp. 72–74; 1912, 315–16; 1915, 250–52. Everyone still did not agree or conform. See, for examples, address of Mrs. Thomas B. Pugh in *Minutes of the Sixth Annual Convention of the Louisiana Division, United Daughters of the Confederacy*, p. 5, copy in United Daughters of the Confederacy Papers, LHAC, Tulane; and V. Clay–Clopton to Bishop Peterkin (copy), 28 March 1911, Clement C. Clay Papers, Duke. J.J. Shaffer used the term "Civil War" in his speeches between 1905 and 1915; see William A. Shaffer Papers, SHC.

12. *UCV Minutes*, 1892, pp. 30–31; 1896, pp. 26–29; *Proceedings of Grand Camp*, 1899, p. 22. See also "Unveiling of the Monument to the Richmond Howitzers," *SHSP* 20 (1892): 259–95; *UCV Minutes*, 1898, pp. 28–40; Hugh B. Hammett, *Hilary Abner Herbert: A Southerner Returns to the Union* (Philadelphia: American Philosophical Society, 1976), pp. 35–38.

13. W.P. DuBose to Mrs. Hoges, 5 March 1898, Habersham Elliott Papers, SHC; *UCV Minutes*, 1898, p. 38. See also "Causes of the War," *CV* 1 (July 1893): 205; George L. Christian, "Official Report of the History Committee of the Grand Camp, CV, Department of Virginia," *SHSP* 28 (1900): 196–98; *UCV Minutes*, 1906, p. 70; 1910, p. 72; and "Address of Hon. John Lamb to Neff-Rice Camp, UCV, 19 August 1910," *SHSP* 38 (1910): 299.

14. *UCV Minutes*, 1904, p. 15; O'Ferrall, *Forty Years*, pp. 47–48. There was some discussion and dispute, of course. See "Periodical Literature," *Publications of the Southern History Association* 7 (September 1903): 409; "Notes and News," *PSHA* 7 (January 1903): 63–64; W.G. Lee, "Armies of North And South," *CV* 17 (March 1909): 125; R.T. Bean, "Numerical Strength of the Confederate Army," *CV* 22 (August 1914):

339. See especially an interesting interchange in Duncan Rose, "Why the Confederacy Failed," *Century* 53 (November 1896): 33–38, and replies by S.D. Lee, Joseph Wheeler, E.P. Alexander, E.M. Law, *Century* 53 (February 1897): 626–33, for the continued power of the numbers argument.

15. On the state of the controversy see Robert M. Stribling, "The Gettysburg Failure," *SHSP* 25 (1897): 60–67; Isaac R. Trimble, "The Battle and Campaign of Gettysburg," *SHSP* 26 (1898): 116–28; and David G. McIntosh, "Review of the Gettysburg Campaign," *SHSP* 37 (1909): 74–143. My observations on shift in emphasis to Pickett's charge are based on impressions of frequency of its discussion in *CV*, *SHSP*, and other sources too numerous to cite. Durant argues that the charge was the single most frequently discussed incident of the war, but without any mention of its being more often recounted in any one period. See "Gently Furled Banner," p. 246. On renewal of Longstreet controversy see Longstreet, *From Manassas to Appomattox*, pp. 334–432; John B. Gordon, *Reminiscences of the Civil War* (New York: Charles Scribner's Sons, 1903), pp. 153–61; Longstreet, *Lee and Longstreet at High Tide*; Chas. S. Arnall to Jed Hotchkiss, (copy), 22 January 1896, and W.H. Taylor to Jed Hotchkiss, 23 June 1898, Hunter Holmes McGuire Papers, VHS; E.P. Alexander to Frederick Colston, 9 February 1904, Campbell-Colston Papers, SHC; and J. Coleman Anderson, "Lee and Longstreet at Gettysburg," *CV* 12 (October 1904): 488.

16. J.D. Shewalter to S.D. Lee, 29 May 1905 and Shewalter to Mickle, 8 June 1905, AG Lb, UCVA Papers, LSU; Longstreet to T.J. Goree, 11 September 1894, T.J. Goree Papers, LSU; Sanger and Hay, *James Longstreet*, pp. 404–409, 440; Edward Augier, "Biographical Sketch of General James Longstreet," in Edward C. Wharton and Family Papers, LSU; Longstreet, *Lee and Longstreet*, pp. 116–17, 119–22; *UCV Minutes*, 1892, pp. 19, 47; Longstreet to Thos. B. O'Brien, 14 January 1890, AANVA Papers, LHAC, Tulane; Minutes, 1 April 1891, Louisiana Historical Association, Administrative Papers, LHAC, Tulane; "William H. Ellis," clipping, William H. Ellis Papers, LSU; Eugene Alvarez, "The Death of the 'Old War Horse' Longstreet," *GHQ* 52 (March 1968): 70–77; Longstreet, *Lee and Longstreet*, pp. 93–94, 272–330; Connelly, *The Marble Man*, p. 64; *Atlanta Constitution*, 26 May 1907; "Monument to Pay Tribute to Memory of General Longstreet," *CV* 21 (June 1913): 280. For a variety of sentiments on Longstreet see R.J. Hancock to Daniel, 27 January 1904, Daniel Papers, UVA; Jos. W. Bidgood to T.T. Munford, 23 May 1913, Thomas T. Munford Division, Munford-Ellis Papers, Duke; James I. Metts, "The Charge of Longstreet," clipping, *Charlotte Daily Observer*, 16 June 1901, UCV Scrapbooks, LSU; Will H. Thompson, "Who Lost Gettysburg?" *CV* 23 (June 1915): 257; and especially the ambivalence of Clement A. Evans, "General Gordon and General Longstreet," *Independent* 56 (February 1904): 311–16; and W.H. Edwards, "A Comrade's Tribute to General Longstreet," and Florence Barlow, "Lieut. Genl. J.A. Longstreet," both in *Lost Cause* 10 (January 1904): 86–89.

17. *UCV Minutes*, 1905, p. 19; 1903, p. 61; "Innisfallen—Newry, SC," *CV* 10 (November 1902): 514–15; *UDC Minutes*, 1908, p. 99; 1910, p. 344; "Pictures of Jefferson Davis and R.E. Lee," *CV* 16 (July 1908): 363; *Minutes of the Annual Convention, Confederated Southern Memorial Association*, 1908, pp. 5–6, 8–9. Walter Hines Page, *The Southerner, A Novel; being the Autobiography of Nicholas Worth* [pseud] (New York: Doubleday, Page & Company, 1909), pp. 146–48, has some interesting observations on pictures in schools. On Hampton see Emerson, *Historic Southern Monuments*, pp. 269–73; and John A. Rice, *I Came Out of the Eighteenth Century* (New York: Harper and Brothers Publishers, 1942), pp. 90–91. Hampton owed much of his

reputation to his role in restoring home rule in South Carolina. See "Wade Hampton: A Tribute," *CV* 12 (May 1904): 213–14.

18. Street, *American Adventures*, pp. 258–59; "Lee Namesakes," *Lost Cause* 3 (February 1900): 116 and (May 1900): 185; *New York Times*, 21 January 1874, p. 1; D. H. Maury to Jefferson Davis, 19 January 1876, in Rowland, ed., *Jefferson Davis*, 7: 487; "Robert Edward Lee," *SHSP* 18 (1890): 133–58; "The Nineteenth of January, Lee's Birthday," *SHSP* 19 (1891): 389–406; "Celebrating Lee's Birthday," *CV* 6 (February 1898): 81–82; "The Natal Day of General Robert Edward Lee—1901," *SHSP* 28 (1900): 228–40; "The Celebration of Lee's Natal Day," *CV* 9 (February 1901): 58–59; "Notes and News," *PSHA* 11 (January 1907): 75; Kate Mason Rowland, "Red Letter Days in Dixie," *CV* 12 (February 1904): 78. The states that declared Lee's birthday a legal holiday were Virginia, North Carolina, South Carolina, and Georgia. On themes see Collins Denny, "Robert E. Lee, The Flower of the South," *SHSP* 41 (1916): 3–13; address by George L. Petrie, in Homer Richey, *Memorial History of the John Bowie Strange Camp, United Confederate Veterans* (Charlottesville, Va.: Michie Company, 1920), pp. 250–56; "Silliness and Shame of Swearing," *CV* 12 (July 1904): 336; *CV* 5 (March 1897): 112; Albert W. Gaines, "Washington and Lee Inseparable," *CV* 18 (August 1910): 373. On Lee as a national hero see Connelly, *Marble Man*, pp. 99–122; Dixon Wecter, *The Hero in America* (Ann Arbor: University of Michigan Press, 1963; first published 1941), pp. 273–306.

19. Richey, *Memorial History*, p. 247. See also John S. Williams, "Advance from Appomattox," *SHSP* 34 (1906): 336–52.

20. Richey, *Memorial History*, pp. 182–83; J. Wm. Jones, "The Career of General Jackson," *SHSP* 35 (1907): 98; Dabney H. Maury, "General T.J. (Stonewall) Jackson," *SHSP* 25 (1897): 309–16; Gordon, *Reminiscences*, pp. 95–99. Quotation is from R.P. Chew to T.T. Munford, 5 March 1912, T.T. Munford Division, Munford-Ellis Papers, Duke. See also Hunter McGuire, "Gen. T.J. ('Stonewall') Jackson CSA, His Career and Character," *SHSP* 25 (1897): 91–112; J. Wm. Jones, "Worked His Way Through: How a Poor Orphan Boy Became One of the Immortals," *CV* 9 (December 1901): 535–37; Randolph Barton, "Stonewall Jackson," *SHSP* 38 (1910): 272–73; D.H. Hill, "The Real Stonewall Jackson," *Century* 47 (February 1894): 623–38; Stonewall Jackson Calendar, 1912, issued by Stonewall Jackson Chapter, UDC, Clarksburg, West Virginia, in UDC Papers, LHAC, Tulane; and William A. Anderson, "Stonewall Jackson," *SHSP* 40 (1915): 160.

21. John A. Simpson, "The Cult of the 'Lost Cause,'" *THQ* 34 (Winter 1975): 355–56; *UCV Minutes*, 1890, pp. 4–5; 1895, p. 61; *HCMAS*, pp. 186–89; Rowland, "Red Letter Days," p. 78. The states that made Davis's birthday a legal holiday were Virginia, South Carolina, Georgia, Florida, Tennessee, and Louisiana. On celebrations see "The Ninety-Third Anniversary of the Birth of Pres. Jefferson Davis," *SHSP* 29 (1901): 1–33; "Birthday Anniversary of Jefferson Davis," in George W. Littlefield Papers, UTX; *UCV General Orders*, v. 2, #80, 23 April 1908; #4, 14 November 1908. On Davis's character see *HCMAS*, pp. 9–15; John J. Watkins, "Jefferson Davis," 1889, in LMA of Wake County Records, NCDAH. Quotations are from John W. Daniel, "Jefferson Davis," in Edward M. Daniel, comp., *Speeches and Orations of John Warwick Daniel* (Lynchburg, Va.: J.P. Bell Company, 1911), pp. 295–332; Charles M. Blackford, "The Trials and Trial of Jefferson Davis," *SHSP* 29 (1901): 75. See also Edmonda A. Nickerson, "The Women of the Confederacy," *CV* 10 (October 1902): 446–47; John W. Akin, "The Uncrowned King," *CV* 16 (March 1908): 116–19; C.C. Cummings, "Story of R.E. Lee Camp, Fort Worth, Tex.," *CV* 17 (December 1909): 585; and especially

"The Laying of the Corner-Stone of the Monument to President Jefferson Davis, in Monroe Park at Richmond, Virginia, Thursday, July 2, 1896 with Oration of General Stephen D. Lee," *SHSP* 24 (1896): 368–74. For a picture of the temple see *Atlanta Constitution*, 1 July 1896. The emphasis on the role and attitudes of the man may explain why Davis seems to be the only one of the three heroes of the Confederate celebration not to have sustained his status. See Frank E. Vandiver, "Jefferson Davis—Leader Without Legend," *JSH* 43 (February 1977): 3–18.

22. William H. Stewart, "The Private Infantryman: The Typical Hero of the South," *SHSP* 20 (1892): 312.

23. "Daughters in Arkansas," *CV* 4 (July 1896): 203; Mrs. D. Giraud Wright, "Maryland and the South," *SHSP* 31 (1903): 214; James A.B. Scherer, "Crusades of the Sixties," clipping, *The News and Courier*, 9 May 1905, in Ulysses R. Brooks Papers, Duke. Durant, "Gently Furled Banner," p. 199, mentions the use of knightly imagery, but most of the quotes refer to officers. Quotation is from speech, Mt. Airy, 3 June 1911, Carr Papers, SHC. Davis, "Johnny Reb," develops the image of the private soldier as a man of "courage, endurance, devotion."

24. Speech, Tarboro, 29 October 1904, Carr Papers, SHC; J. Bennett, "The Private Soldier," LMA of Wake County Records, NCDAH; G.B. Baskette, "Typical Confederate Soldier," *CV* 1 (December 1893): 367; "Memphis," *Lost Cause* 4 (January 1901): 90; "Dedicating a Monument in Tennessee," *CV* 9 (February 1901): 60–61; Undated speech to James B. Gordon, UDC Chapter, Alfred M. Waddell Papers, SHC; O'Ferrall, *Forty Years of Service*, pp. 161–69; Gordon, *Reminiscences*, p. 136; Robert Q. Mallard, *Montevideo-Maybank: Some Memoirs of a Southern Christian Household in Olden Time* (Richmond: Presbyterian Committee of Publication, 1898), pp. 66–68. Some disagreed; see Duke, *Reminiscenses*, pp. 227–79; W.A. Smith, untitled speech February 1906, Smith Papers, Duke, specifically rejects the machine image. Davis, "Johnny Reb," pp. 168–70, argues that the soldier is portrayed with lack of discipline; Durant, "Gently Furled Banner," pp. 220–32, says the magazines tried to make the soldier an intelligent individual, not "just a cog in a war machine." Yet her interesting analysis of the frequent accounts of charges—"This moment when each man was on his own and yet in union with his leaders and his buddies captured the spirit of the war," (p. 245)—evokes an image of the soldier not unlike what is set up here. Leonard, *Above The Battle*, p. 15, mentions that people felt the war had helped enhance discipline. Much of the historiography of the Civil War suggests that in fact the Confederate soldier was anything but well disciplined. Here and throughout I do not attempt to judge the celebration's interpretation against the actual historical record.

25. W.A. Smith to "The Anson Guards," 23 March 1901, Smith Papers, Duke; F.E. Daniel, *Recollections of a Rebel Surgeon (And Other Sketches) Or In The Doctor's Sappy Days* (Austin, Tx.: Von Boeckmann, Schutze & Co., 1899), pp. 71–72, 120–22. Quotation is from John Lamb, "The Character & Services of the Confederate Soldier," *SHSP* 40 (1915): 233. For examples of accounts of destruction see "General Lee's Chambersburg Order," *CV* 21 (July 1913): 356; "Why General Sherman's Name Is Detested," *CV* 14 (July 1906): 295–98; T.T. Munford, fragment of speech to Garland Rhodes Camp, in T.T. Munford Division, Munford-Ellis Papers, Duke; Gordon, *Reminiscences*, pp. 301–6; A.C. Quisenberry, "Morgan's Men in Ohio," *SHSP* 39 (1914): 91–99; Untitled brochure in clippings file, T.T. Munford Division, Munford-Ellis Papers, Duke.

26. John S. Mosby to H.C. Jordan, 23 August 1909, Bryan Family Papers, VSL.

27. *UCV Minutes*, 1895, pp. 9–11; "Confederate Monument at Albany, Ga.," *CV* 10 (January 1902): 28; *Proceedings of Grand Camp*, 1896, p. 25. See also Waddell,

speech to James B. Gordon UDC Chapter, Waddell Papers, SHC; M.C. Butler, "Southern Genius: How War Developed It in an Industrial and Military Way," *SHSP* 16 (1888): 281–96; "Monument Dedicated at Lebanon, Tenn.," *CV* 7 (August 1899): 343–44; *UCV Minutes*, 1900, pp. 48–57; "Confederate Monument Unveiled Last Saturday," typescript of newspaper account, in Confederate Monument File, Thomas M. Owen Papers, ADAH.

28. "Confederate Monument at Gallatin, Tenn.," *CV* 12 (April 1904): 152; "Eulogy on Confederate Women by J.L. Underwood delivered in 1896," in J.L. Underwood, *The Women of the Confederacy* (n.p.: By the author, 1906), p. 65. See also "Texas Confederate Veterans Gather," *CV* 16 (October 1908): 501–2; Unidentified speech, 1897, John L. Power Papers, MDAH.

29. Moorman to Clement Evans, 19 November 1895, Adjutant General's Letterpress book, UCVA Papers, LSU. For an interesting and earlier discussion of the irrelevance of the issues of the war in veterans' activity see Peagram's Battalion Association Minute Book, 18 August 1885, VSL.

CHAPTER TEN.

THE CONFEDERATE CELEBRATION:

ITS RITUAL ACTIVITIES

1. Minute Book Belonging to the Ladies' Memorial Association of Atlanta, Ga., 1884–1900, 16 October 1884, Ladies' Memorial Association of Atlanta Records, AHS; *UDC Minutes*, 1907, appendix, p. 18; "Confederate Affairs in Arkansas," *Confederate Veteran* 2 (September 1894): 270; "Graves of Our Dead at Resaca," *CV* 2 (February 1894): 54; "Confederate Dead at Fredericksburg," *CV* 4 (July 1896): 230; *Minutes of the Annual Convention, Confederated Southern Memorial Association*, 1906, p. 9; Minutes, 1866–1899, 29 September 1898, Ladies' Memorial Association of Wake County, NCDAH; Circular from R.E. Lee Camp, No. 1, UCV, 8 April 1887, in Minute Book, LMA of Atlanta Records, AHS; Minutes, 3 May 1887, Ladies' Memorial Association of Charleston (Minutes, 1866–1915), SCHS.

2. Charles E. Jones, "Lines on Memorial Day," April 1889, Charles E. Jones Papers, Duke. See also Clement A. Evans, "Our Confederate Memorial Day," *CV* 4 (July 1896): 222–28.

3. W.S. Primrose to Moffitt, 13 May 1903, Mrs. Elvira Moffitt Papers, SHC; "The Confederate Dead in Stonewall Cemetery, Winchester, Va.," *SHSP* 22 (1894): 41–48; *HCMAS*, pp. 98–99, 138; "How Atlanta Observed Memorial Day," *CV* 17 (July 1909): 341; "Radford (Va.) Memorial Services," *CV* 20 (July 1912): 333; Mrs. A. Jefferson Nelson, "Decoration Day Dances," *CV* 21 (April 1913): 220.

4. For examples of various fund-raising drives see *HCMAS*, pp. 71–72; "Confederate Monument at Clarksville," *CV* 1 (November 1893): 328; "Murfreesboro Confederate Monument," *CV* 9 (November 1901): 494; G.W. Tyler, "Patriotism in a Tennessee County," *CV* 6 (March 1898): 125–28; T.C. Kelley, "'Eastern Shore of Virginia Confederates," *CV* 16 (December 1908): 628–29. Sometimes governments aided these projects, but rarely. In a few instances individuals gave the monument to the town; see "Charles C. Hemming," *SHSP* 27 (1899): 129–31; "Benefactions of Comrade," *CV* 2 (December 1894): 376–77.

5. See Appendix 1.

6. Clarence Poe to Benjamin Sledd (copy), 21 September 1915, Clarence Poe Papers, NCDAH; William A. Percy, *Laterns on the Levee: Recollections of a Planter's Son*

(New York: Alfred A. Knopf, 1941), pp. 11–12. For other criticisms, see "Eulogy on Confederate Women by J.L. Underwood Delivered in 1896," in Underwood, *The Women of the Confederacy*, p. 51; and especially *UCV Minutes*, 1910, p. 8–9. There were, of course, exceptions in which a more romantic design was chosen.

7. Hoge, *Moses Drury Hoge*, pp. 460–61; *UCV Minutes*, 1906, p. 32. See also "Daughters at Franklin," *CV* 8 (April 1900): 172–73; J.S. Carr, speech in Tarboro, 29 October 1904, Julian S. Carr Papers, SHC; Lizzie G. Henderson, "Appeal for Monuments and Markers," *CV* 14 (April 1906): 164–65; Emerson, *Historic Monuments*, pp. 355–57; and *UCV Minutes*, 1911, appendix, pp. 52–53.

8. "Unveiling of the Soldiers' and Sailors' Monument, At Richmond, 30 May 1894," *SHSP* 22 (1894): 336–80; "Honoring the Private Soldier," *CV* 2 (June 1894): 162–64.

9. Discussion here is based primarily on the numerous accounts of unveilings in the *SHSP* and *CV*. There are too many to cite individually.

10. My account here owes much to the insights in Victor W. Turner, *The Ritual Process: Structure and Anti-Structure* (London: Routledge & Kegan Paul, 1969), pp. 131–72.

11. On relief activities see records of Association of the Army of Northern Virginia and Association of the Army of Tennessee, both in LHAC, Tulane; Minute Book, Record of Frank Cheatham Bivouac, 1887–1906, UCV, Tennessee Division, Bivouac Records, TSL; R.E. Lee Camp No. 1, Records, VHS. See also Minutes, 4 September 1896, UCV, Camp Hampton, Richland County, 1887–1894, Records, SCL; "Model Camp in South Carolina," *CV* 7 (September 1899): 409–10; C.C. Cummings, "Story of R.E. Lee Camp, Fort Worth, Tex.," *CV* 17 (December 1909): 585–86; and especially *Proceedings of Grand Camp Confederate Veterans, Department of Virginia*, 1900, p. 23; 1901, p. 22. For the survey, see "Circular #3, UCV," in Joseph Jones Papers, Tulane. Of 98 camps responding, 73 had given out no money in a year, 8 had given $50 or less; 9 had given more than $50; and 8 wrote unclear responses. On state aid see "The Southern States and Their Veteran Soldiers," *SHSP* 19 (1891): 336–37; William G. Glasson, "The South's Care for Her Confederate Veterans," *Review of Reviews* 36 (July 1907): 40–47; Glasson, "The South's Pension and Relief Provisions for the Soldiers of the Confederacy," *Proceedings of the Eighteenth Annual Session of the State Literary and Historical Association of North Carolina*, Bulletin No. 23, Publications of the North Carolina Historical Commission (Raleigh: Edwards & Broughton Printing Company, 1918), pp. 61–71; "Visiting Confederate Soldiers' Homes," *CV* 16 (April 1908): 180–82; Thomas L. Miller, "Texas Land Grants to Confederate Veterans and Widows," *Southwestern Historical Quarterly* 69 (July 1965): 59–65; and especially a chart in Tommy G. Lashley, "Oklahoma's Confederate Veterans Home," *Chronicles of Oklahoma* 55 (Spring 1977): 44. On lobbying see Minutes of the Meetings of Fred Ault Camp No. 5, UCV, 12 January 1891, in UCV, Tennessee Division, Bivouac Records, TSL; Minute Book, 13 July 1891, Urquhart–Gillette Camp No. 1611, UCV (Franklin, Va.), Records, VHS; Robert L. Rodgers, untitled report, 1892, in Sons of Confederate Veterans Collection, AHS; "Record of N.B. Forrest Camp, No. 4, UCV," *CV* 13 (September 1905): 395, 397; Record, v. 6, 5 September 1902, Lee Camp Records, VHS; Camp Hampton Records, 1 November 1888, 1 September 1891, 7 February 1896, 5 April 1901, 2 January 1903, SCL; Thomas E. Partlow, ed., *Minutes, United Confederate Veterans Camp #941, Wilson County, Tennessee* (Baltimore: Gateway Press, 1975), pp. 20–21; and *Atlanta Constitution*, 13 May 1899.

12. Resolution, 9 July 1889 and circular, 9 September 1889, filed in Minutes, v.

3, AAT Papers, LHAC, Tulane; Minute Book, 1885–1898, 23 February 1892, AANVA Papers, LHAC, Tulane; Minutes of Ault Camp, 13 October 1890 and *passim*, UCV Papers, TSL; Record, v. 4, 2 February 1894 and *passim*, Lee Camp Records, VHS; Partlow, ed., *Minutes of UCV Camp #941, passim*; Minute Book of Tom McKiethen Camp, UCV, Robinson Springs, Ala., in Bolling Hall Papers, ADAH; Robert L. Rodgers, untitled report, 1898, Confederate Veterans' Association of Atlanta, in SCV Collection, AHS; Minutes of the Clarke County Confederate Veterans' Association, 1891–1920 (copy), in Military Records, ADAH; "The Raw Confederates of April 1861," *SHSP* 21 (1893): 346–47; George S. Bernard, comp., *War Talks of Confederate Veterans* (Petersburg, Va.: Fenn, 1892). On the centrality of the reunion see Moorman to John Boyd, 14 April 1896, Adjutant General's Letterpress book, United Confederate Veterans' Association Papers, LSU; Fred L. Robertson to Mickle, 6 October 1903, William E. Mickle Papers, Duke; Minutes, Patrons Union Camp, UCV, 1902–24, MDAH; and Minute Book, Tom McKiethen Camp, in Hall Papers, ADAH.

13. Minute Book, 13 July 1891, Urquhart–Gillette Camp Records, VHS; Records, Hampton Camp, SCL; Minute Book, 1892–1930, UCV, L.A. Armistead Camp No. 26 (Meklenburg Co., Va.), VHS; programs of Braxton Bragg Camp UCV reunions, in v. 34, William A. Shaffer Papers, SHC; "Reunion at Hawkinsville, Ga.," *CV* 2 (August 1894): 244; "Hart's Famous Battery," *CV* 2 (October 1894): 291; *CV* 9 (October 1901): 461. Quotation is from W.H. Woods, "The Reunion at Fisher's Hill," *CV* 6 (September 1898): 429–30. On state reunions see "Annual State Reunions of U.C.V.," *CV* 17 (November 1909): 545–46; Will Lambert, "The Texas Reunion at Houston," *CV* 1 (May 1893): 154; "Delightful Reunion at Nashville," *CV* 4 (November 1896): 363–66; "Gathering of Old Soldiers Exceeds all Expectations," clipping, 1901, Hampton Family Papers, SCL; *Minutes of the Eighth Annual Meeting of the Association of Confederate Soldiers, Tennessee Division*, 1895, copy in Other Veterans' Organizations Papers, LHAC, Tulane; and *CV* 10 (May 1902): 196.

14. N.T.N. Robinson to Henry Wise Garnett, 7 April 1892, N.T.N. Robinson Papers, Tulane; *Atlanta Constitution*, 8 April 1892; *UCV General Orders*, v. 1, #99, 1 July 1893; #103, 2 August 1893; #108, 16 September 1893; *Atlanta Constitution*, 25 and 26 April 1894.

15. On planning a reunion see Lamar, *When All Is Said and Done*, pp. 144–47; and Katherine Du Pre Lumpkin, *The Making of a Southerner* (New York: Alfred A. Knopf, 1947), pp. 114–16. On cost, see *Atlanta Constitution*, 22 June 1897; "To the Finance Committee of the Common Council of the City of Richmond, Virginia," 6 December 1906 and Bennett H. Young to John W. Gordon, 20 July 1906, Reunion File, 1907, Lee Camp Records, VHS. On halls see *Atlanta Constitution*, 30 June 1896, 18 July 1898; Thomas Kane & Co. to Peyton Wise, 5 May 1896, Grand Camp Confederate Veterans, Department of Virginia, Papers, VSL; Jerry E. Henderson, "A History of the Ryman Auditorium in Nashville, Tennessee: 1892–1920" (Ph.D. diss., Louisiana State University, 1962), pp. 84–95; Editorial, *Lost Cause* 3 (January 1900): 96; and General Order #9, General Headquarters, USCV, 5 May 1903, SCV Papers, LHAC, Tulane. On crowds see *Atlanta Constitution*, 1 July 1896, 22 and 24 July 1898, 10 and 11 May 1899, 17 May 1903. Quotation is from 2 July 1896.

16. On poor, see "Christmas Spirit at Reunions," *CV* 16 (June 1908): 252; J.W. Richardson to W.R. Smoot, 27 May 1896 and R.W. Smith to Peyton Wise, 31 May 1896, Grand Camp Papers, VSL; C.M. Stigleman to Maury, 15 and 24 June 1896, Richard L. Maury Papers, Duke; "Reunion Notes," *Lost Cause* 3 (April 1900): 167; C.B. Morgan to Ellyson, 7 July 1905, and Peter J. White to Ellyson, 20 April 1909, J. Taylor

Ellyson Papers, UVA; John W. Gordon to Edward Bourne, 8 May 1907, Reunion File, 1907, Lee Camp Records, VHS; D.A. Brown, Jr., to Comrades, 18 April 1907, John W. Daniel Papers, UVA; J. Van Ness to Commander, Anson Camp UCV, 31 January and 26 July 1909, William A. Smith Papers, Duke; J.F. Maull to Berry Benson, 7 October 1900, Berry G. Benson Papers, SHC; *UCV Minutes*, 1900, p. 7; W.H. Sanders to W.A. Smith, 19 May 1907, Smith Papers, Duke; Minutes, 22 June 1903, Stonewall Jackson Camp No. 72, New Orleans, in United Daughters of the Confederacy Papers, LHAC, Tulane. See *Atlanta Constitution*, 24 April 1902 for number of veterans compared to nonveterans. Some vets did not feel that the entire crowd came for the reunion. "It is estimated that over one hundred and fifty thousand persons visited Memphis during the three days, and it is safe to say that one hundred and forty-five thousand of them were people who took advantage of a cheap rate to witness the sights. In other words, Confederate reunions have been turned into gatherings of Country people, who so crowd the streets, and places for holding our meetings, that old soldiers are unable to find each other, or to legislate for the good of their distressed comrades." James Dinkins, Report on Reunion, 11 June 1901, AAT Papers, LHAC, Tulane.

17. R.D. Rugely to B.W. Partridge, 16 June 1895, Benjamin W. Partridge Papers, Duke; Geo. A. McGehee to Moorman, 31 March 1897, Adjutant General's Letterbox, UCVA Papers, LSU; "Stenographic Report—Proceedings of the Investigation Committee, Grand Camp, C.V., Dept. of Va., Richmond, Va.," December 9 & 10, 1897, in Grand Camp Papers, VSL; *Atlanta Constitution*, 22 July 1898; E.G. Williams to William E. Mickle, 2 October 1906, AG Lb, UCVA Papers, LSU; *UCV Minutes*, 1907, pp. 14–16; "There's Life in the Old Land Yet," *CV* 22 (January 1914): 248; John W. Lyles to John McMahan, 2 April 1915, John J. McMahan Papers, SCL. Quotations are from Pearl Witt to Mickle, 28 July 1908, AG Lb, UCVA Papers, LSU; "The Reunion," *CV* 11 (March 1903): 108; and "Address and Report of Major General Leon Jastremski, Commanding La. Div., UCV at the Annual Convention, at Memorial Hall, August 6th, 1902," in UCV Papers, LHAC, Tulane.

18. *UCV Minutes, passim.*

19. On sense of festivity see R.M. Cary to Walthall, 12 August 1896, William T. Walthall Papers, MDAH; Polk Miller, "Jolly Side of Life at Louisville Reunion," *CV* 8 (June 1900): 289; Bennett H. Young to Mickle, 23 February 1907, AG Lb, UCVA Papers, LSU; and Bennett H. Young, "Work of United Confederate Veterans," *CV* 20 (June 1912): 259–60. On lack of sectionalism see W.W. Farabaugh, "Issues of the War," *CV* 9 (September 1901): 414–16; Belle Kearney, *A Slaveholder's Daughter* (New York: Abby Press, 1900), pp. 222–23; *Atlanta Constitution*, 2 July 1896 and 19 May 1903; and *UCV Minutes*, 1894, pp. 12–13. But some did protest: see Circular, Camp Pelham, UCV, 1 June 1897, UCV Papers, LHAC, Tulane; Minutes, 8 June 1897, AAT Papers, LHAC, Tulane; and Editorial, *CV* 5 (June 1897): 256. On recreation of wartime see *UCV Minutes*, 1892, p. 14 and *passim*; "Reunion Souvenir Songs," and "Songsheet, State Reunion, Monroe, Louisiana," UCV Papers, LHAC, Tulane; and *Atlanta Constitution*, 8 April 1892, 17 April 1894. On blacks see R.E. Bland to Tom, 14 June 1896 and J.M. Gollehorn to Thos. Ellett, 16 June 1896, Grand Camp Papers, VSL; *Atlanta Constitution*, 23 July 1898 and 17 May 1899; *UCV Minutes*, 1910, p. 10; 1912, pp. 26–28; and Kearney, *Slaveholder's Daughter*, p. 222.

20. A.G. Peterson, "Union Veteran at Confederate Reunion," *CV* 21 (July 1913): 364; Moorman to Gordon, 21 June 1898, AG Lpb, UCVA Papers, LSU; *UCV General Orders*, v. 2, #60, 8 January 1907; *Atlanta Constitution*, 27 April 1894; "Birmingham Reunion Reports," *CV* 2 (May 1894): 131; section A, Lily McGee Papers,

Duke. On characteristics of sponsors see W.T. Cadro to Moorman, 19 May 1900, AG Lb, UCVA Papers, LSU; Moorman to W.H. Jackson, 9 February 1894, AG Lpb, UCVA Papers, LSU; W.L. Landon to W.A. Smith, 28 March 1903, Smith Papers, Duke; Moorman to C. Irvine Walker, 8 May 1900, AG Lpb, UCVA Papers, LSU; and *UCV Minutes*, 1914, p. 88. See also sketches in *Atlanta Constitution*, 28 June 1896. On presentation see *Atlanta Constitution*, 22 July 1898.

21. *UCV Minutes*, 1898, p. 86. This was not the only time Gordon was kissed. *Atlanta Constitution*, 20 May 1903.

22. Quotation is from "Miss Lumpkin to Georgia Veterans," *CV* 12 (February 1904): 69–70. See *UCV Minutes*, 1905, p. 42; *Proceedings of Grand Camp*, 1905, p. 41; "Hampton and Gordon, and a Young Woman Orator," clipping, *The State*, 9 May 1901, Hampton Family Papers, SCL; and Lumpkin, *Making of a Southerner*.

23. "Tributes to Miss Winnie Davis," *CV* 6 (October 1898): 467–68.

24. Moorman to W.L. Cabell, 21 March 1892, AG Lpb, UCVA Papers, LSU. Quotation is from *Atlanta Constitution*, 22 July 1898. For similar sentiments see "Address to guests of Garland-Rhodes Camp, UCV at Lynchburg by General Munford," undated, T.T. Munford Division, Munford-Ellis Papers, Duke. On popularity of sponsors among veterans see Moorman to Clement Evans, 25 June 1898, AG Lpb, UCVA Papers, LSU ("I don't see how it is that you old Veterans have such a sweet tooth for these pretty young girls, and try and gobble up all the beauty and talent in the country."); "Devoted South Carolina Confederates," *CV* 8 (January 1900): 28; Fred Robertson to Mickle, 20 April 1904, Mickle Papers, Duke; and *UCV Minutes*, 1912, p. 22.

25. Quotations are from "The Parade," *Lost Cause* 6 (April 1902): 142; Lamar, *When All Is Said*, pp. 148–49; and *Atlanta Constitution*, 27 April 1894. See also Moorman to Bennett Young, 20 February 1900, AG Lpb, UCVA Papers, LSU; *Atlanta Constitution*, 15 July 1898; *UCV Minutes*, 1900, p. 89; *Atlanta Constitution*, 3 June 1900; "The Parade," *Lost Cause* 3 (June 1900): 209; Geo. W. Gordon to Mickle, 11 July 1900, Mickle Papers, Duke; and Mickle to Lee, 3 May 1906, William E. Mickle Letterbook, UTX. Some people tried to abolish the parade as the veterans became older, but they never succeeded.

26. *Atlanta Constitution*, 3 July 1896, 25 June 1897, 23 July 1898, 31 May 1901, 17 and 23 May 1903, 12 June 1908.

27. *Atlanta Constitution*, 27 April 1894; J.W. Wilcox to Mickle, 4 May 1906, AG Lb, UCVA Papers, LSU. See also L.H. Harris, "The Confederate Veteran," *Independent* 53 (October 1901): 2358; Albert S. Morton, "Two Great Reunions," *CV* 4 (October 1896): 333–35; and *Atlanta Constitution*, 23 May 1903.

28. There is no direct evidence for this interpretation of the leaders' being on horseback. On at least one occasion reunion planners talked of mounting all cavalrymen, but they found there were too few horses to go around. See *Atlanta Constitution*, 17 May 1903. However, for an association of high prestige and an equestrian statue, see J.W. Daniel to Mrs. Janet H. Randolph, 30 January 1906, Fitzhugh Lee Monumental Association Papers, VHS. Quotation is from Clement A. Evans to Moorman, 24 June 1898, AG Lb, UCVA Papers, LSU.

29. *Atlanta Constitution*, 27 April 1894; Raymond Firth, *Symbols: Public and Private* (Ithaca, N. Y.: Cornell University Press, 1973), pp. 328–67. For more on role of Confederate flags see Hunter, "The Sacred South," pp. 133–40.

30. *USCV Minutes*, 1903, p. 38.

31. "White People and Negroes," *CV* 13 (September 1905): 421–23. On

disfranchisement see Jno. N. Wells to Moorman, 23 May 1900, AG Lb, UCVA Papers, LSU; Tennant S. McWilliams, *Hannis Taylor: The New Southerner As An American* (University: University of Alabama Press, 1978), pp. 60–61. On *Confederate Veteran Magazine* see Durant, "The Gently Furled Banner," pp. 153–57.

32. By-laws of the Joe Kendall Camp No. 1747, Of the Straight Democratic Confederate Veterans, in box 3, UCVA Papers, LSU; Moorman quoted in *Atlanta Constitution*, 2 July 1896; Thomas P. Clinton to Owen, 6 August 1899, Thomas M. Owen Papers, ADAH; Wm. L. DeRosset to Moorman, 15 September and 24 December 1900, and B.W. Foster to Moorman, 20 November 1902—all in AG Lb, UCVA Papers, LSU; Carr to "My Dear Comrades," 30 April 1904, Julian S. Carr Papers, SHC; Thomas S. Martin to Daniel, 20 March 1905, John W. Daniel Papers, Duke; J.S. Mosby to H.C. Jordan, 23 August 1909, Bryan Family Papers, VSL; Lynwood M. Holland, *Pierce M.B. Young: The Warwick of the South* (Athens: University of Georgia Press, 1964), p. 215.

33. Geo. Tupper to Moorman, 12 April 1894; John H. Carter to Moorman, 20 November 1900; B.H. Young to Moorman, 10 May 1900—all in AG Lb, UCVA Papers, LSU. Quotation is from "Daughters at Franklin," CV 8 (April 1900): 172–73. See also *Atlanta Constitution*, 4 June 1907; R.D.W. Conner, "Alfred Moore Scales," LMA of Wake County Records, NCDAH. There is a surprising lack in the celebration of anti–Populist rhetoric and even of references to the party.

34. Unidentified speech, Henry Askew Papers, UTX. See also Circular on book by Col. Wm. Henry Steward, George S. Bernard Papers, SHC; J.J. Shaffer, speech to Braxton Bragg Camp, 1 March 1906, v. 34, William A. Shaffer Papers, SHC.

35. *UCV Minutes*, 1894, p. 20; Harry M. Edmunds, "The Thin Gray Line," clipping, Askew Papers, UTX.

36. *Charter, By-Laws, Rules of Order and List of Officers and Members of R.E. Lee Camp No. 1, Confederate Veterans, Adopted, August 1890*, copy in box 3, UCVA Papers, LSU. Other camp constitutions in this box also carry the same clause. See also unidentified speech by J.L.M. Curry, Curry Papers, LC; W.C. Clovis to J.A. Chalaron, et al., 6 April [?], AAT Papers, LHAC, Tulane; John L. Watkins, "Jefferson Davis," 1889, Ladies' Memorial Association of Wake County Papers, NCDAH.

37. My argument here is influenced by Clifford Geertz, *Negara: The Theatre State in Nineteenth-Century Bali* (Princeton: Princeton University Press, 1980). See also Quentin Skinner, "The World As a Stage," *New York Review of Books* 28 (16 April 1981): 35–36.

38. Only two monuments (that I know of) are memorials to an enlisted man: one to Sam Davis in Tennessee and another to Henry Wyatt in Raleigh, North Carolina. On rank see A.G. Peterson, "Union Veteran at Confederate Reunion," CV 21 (July 1913): 364.

39. "Reunion of Texas Veterans at Waco," CV 2 (April 1894): 122–23; *Congressional Record*, 53d Cong., 2 sess., 1894, pp. 4564–65, 7240–41; *UCV Minutes*, 1897, p. 58; *New York Times*, 15 July 1894, p. 1.

40. *UCV Minutes*, 1895, pp. 33–35; J. Wm. Jones, "The National Flag," CV 4 (August 1896): 260–61; CV 2 (July 1894): 209. For similar direct use of the Confederate tradition in the cause of order see *UCV Minutes*, 1896, pp. 73–74; 1899, pp. 156–57; "Address of Hon. R.T. Bennett—At Laying of the Corner-Stone of the Confederate Monument at Raleigh, N.C., May 22, 1894," SHSP 22 (1898): 85–86; *Address of Hon. Joseph R. Lamar of Augusta, Georgia, Delivered on Memorial Day, April 1902, at Athens Georgia*, pamphlet in John H. Claiborne Papers, UVA; M.B. McSweeney to M.C. Butler, 20 November 1902, Matthew C. Butler Papers, SCL; and *UCV Minutes*, 1905, Appendix, p. 29; 1913, p. 134.

CHAPTER ELEVEN.

THE SOUTH VINDICATED:

THE SPANISH-AMERICAN WAR AND ITS AFTERMATH

1. Huber W. Ellingsworth, "Southern Reconciliation Orators in the North, 1868–1899" (Ph.D. diss., Florida State University, 1955), p. 76, with Gordon quoted on p. 77. File 7896, 1891, Records of the Adjutant General's Office, RG 94, National Archives. Second quotation is from R.S. Lewis to Secretary of War, 11 April 1891. See also J. Alexander Karlin, "The Italo-American Incident of 1891 and the Road to Reunion," *JSH* 8 (May 1942): 242–46.

2. Gen. Clement A. Evans, "Contributions of the South to the Greatness of the American Union," *SHSP* 23 (1895): 23; McWilliams, *Hannis Taylor*, pp. 20–33; Gerald G. Eggert, "Our Man in Havana: Fitzhugh Lee," *Hispanic American Historical Review* 47 (November 1967): 463–85.

3. Quotation is from J.A. Boyman to "My Dear Kins-woman," 16 March 1897, Clement C. Clay Papers, Duke. On attitudes toward involvement see W.C. Gregory to Joseph Wheeler, 17 April 1898, Joseph Wheeler Papers, ADAH; W.L. Wilson to J.L.M. Curry, 19 April 1898, Jabez L.M. Curry Papers, LC; William J. Schellings, "Florida and the Cuban Revolution, 1895–1898," *Florida Historical Quarterly* 39 (October 1960): 175–86; Schellings, "The Advent of the Spanish–American War in Florida," *FHQ* 39 (April 1960): 311–29; Bertha Davidson, "Arkansas in the Spanish-American War," *Arkansas Historical Quarterly* 5 (Fall 1946): 208–10; Donald B. Kelley, "Mississippi and 'The Splendid Little War' of 1898," *JMH* 26 (May 1964): 123–34; Joseph C. Kiger, "Social Thought as Voiced in Rural Middle Tennessee Newspapers, 1878–1898," *THQ* 9 (June 1950): 153–54; W. Harrison Daniel, "Virginia Baptists and the Myth of the Southern Mind, 1865–1900," *SAQ* 73 (Winter 1974): 91–92; George H. Gibson, "Attitudes in North Carolina Regarding the Independence of Cuba, 1868–1898," *NCHR* 44 (January 1966): 43–65; and Gerald F. Linderman, *The Mirror of War: American Society and the Spanish-American War* (Ann Arbor: University of Michigan Press, 1974), p. 129.

4. Moorman to John B. Gordon, 21 April 1898, AG Lpb; S.D. Lee to Gordon, 23 April 1898, AG Lb. Both in UCVA Papers, LSU.

5. Quotation is from M.B. Shaw to Moorman, 28 March 1898, AG Lb, UCVA Papers, LSU; "About Enlisting in the Spanish War," *CV* 10 (May 1902): 205; Claude Gentry, *Private John Allen: Gentleman-Statesman-Sage-Prophet* (n.p.: The Author, 1951), p. 100; Editorial, *CV* 6 (July 1898): 304. For other southern expressions of opposition to the war see Washington Taylor to Thomas Ellett, 5 April 1898, Grand Camp Confederate Veterans, Department of Virginia Papers, VSL; W.P. Campbell to Wheeler, 20 April 1898, Wheeler Papers, ADAH; Nannie E. Stone to R.L. Maury, 27 April 1898, Richard L. Maury Papers, Duke; Wade Hampton to B.T. Johnson, 3 March 1899, Bradley T. Johnson Papers, Duke; and Wm. Preston Johnston to Mrs. Davis, 18 April 1899, Jefferson Davis Papers, UAL.

6. *Atlanta Constitution*, 18 May 1898, p. 4; Moorman to President, 2 May 1898, AG Lpb, UCVA Papers, LSU; Thomas L. Rosser to John W. Daniel, 20 April, 25 and 27 May, 10 and 11 June, 18 July 1898, John W. Daniel Papers, Duke; T.T. Munford to Russell A. Alger, 16 June 1898, T.T. Munford Division, Munford-Ellis Papers, Duke; J.M. Porter to S.G. French, 16 April 1898, Samuel G. French Papers, MDAH; A.R. Bates to Wheeler, 18 April 1898 and Fred S. Ferguson to Wheeler, 12 April 1898, Wheeler Papers, ADAH; R.A. Broadus to Moorman, 26 March 1898, AG Lb, UCVA Papers, LSU; Moorman to Gordon, 4 May 1898, AG Lpb, UCVA Papers, LSU; John P.

Dyer, *Fight'n Joe Wheeler* (Baton Rouge: Louisiana State University Press, 1941), pp. 333–34. Quotation is from John J. Williams to Thomas Ellett, 14 May 1898, Grand Camp Papers, VSL. For other examples of southerners who had reservations about the war but still urged enlistment see Wade Hampton to Alfred Hampton, 7 May 1898, Hampton Family Papers, SCL; "Col. Mosby Opposed to War," clipping in scrapbook 5, United Confederate Veteran Scrapbooks, LSU; Stephen M. White to John S. Mosby, 2 July 1898 and telegrams Mosby to Miles, 4 and 6 May 1898, in Mosby Family Papers, UVA; and Maury Klein, *Edward Porter Alexander* (Athens: University of Georgia Press, 1971), p. 208. On Carr see "A Distinguished Son of Dixie," clipping, *The Boston Traveler*, 21 September 1898, Julian Shakespeare Carr Papers, SHC. For benediction see untitled clipping by William Banks, 25 July 1898 in John M. Bateman Scrapbook, SCL.

      7. For mentions of "Dixie," and so on see *Atlanta Constitution*, 1 June 1898, p. 3; Joseph F. Steelman, *North Carolina's Role in the Spanish-American War* (Raleigh: N.C. Department of Cultural Resources, Division of Archives and History, 1975), pp. 5, 19; "Our Boys at Chickamauga," 11 July 1898 clipping, Bateman Sb, SCL; George F. Garnett File, Spanish-American War Archive, Military History Institute, Carlisle Barracks, Pa. Quotations are from *Atlanta Constitution*, 25 April 1898, p. 5; "Mr. Moorman's Patriotism," 4 July 1898 clipping, Bateman Sb, SCL; G.E. Allen to Joseph Wheeler, 4 April 1898, Joseph Wheeler Papers, ADAH; and *Atlanta Constitution*, 24 July 1898, p. 6. For other evidence of southern surety of victory see *Atlanta Constitution*, 5 April 1898, p. 4; Norman C. Delaney, "John McIntosh Kell: A Confederate Veteran in Politics," *GHQ* 57 (Fall 1973): 384; and Mary Alves Long, *High Time to Tell It* (Durham: Duke University Press, 1950), pp. 290–91.

      8. *UCV Minutes*, 1898, pp. 25–27, 55–56; *Atlanta Constitution*, 24 July 1898. Moorman, however, thought the UCV slighted in appointments in the federal army. Moorman to S.D. Lee, 17 June 1898, AG Lpb, UCVA Papers, LSU.

      9. W.S. Thorington to Joseph Wheeler, 1 May 1898; George W. McKinney to Wheeler, 5 April 1898; G.E. Allen to Wheeler, 4 April 1898. All in Joseph Wheeler Papers, ADAH.

      10. Tennant S. McWilliams, "The Lure of Empire: Southern Interest in the Caribbean, 1877–1900," *MQ* 29 (Winter 1975–76): 59; "Confederates Commanding U.S. Regiments," *CV* 6 (August 1898): 365; Scrapbooks 5 and 6, UCV Scrapbooks, LSU; "Patriotic Confederate Veterans," *Independent* 52 (July 1900): 1629; Clark, *The Southern Country Editor*, p. 186. On Hobson see Wm. T. Sampson, "Naval Battle Near Santiago Cuba," *Lost Cause* 1 (Augusta 1898): 45–50; Steelman, *N.C. Role in Spanish–American War*, p. 34; William G. Brown, "A New Hero of an Old Type," in *The Lower South in American History* (New York: The Macmillan Company, 1903), pp. 229–44; *Atlanta Constitution*, 5 June 1898, p. 3.

      11. *Atlanta Constitution*, 23 July 1898, p. 1; 12 June 1898, p. 16; 19 June 1898, p. 16; E.P. Alexander to Wheeler, 19 August 1898, M.J. Kernaehan to Wheeler, 4 February 1899, and B.W. Griffin to Wheeler, 31 October 1900, all in Wheeler Papers, ADAH. See also "Lieutenant Blue of South Carolina," clipping, *Atlanta Constitution*, 27 June 1898, Thaddeus K. Oglesby Papers, Duke; "The Unbroken Chain of Heroism," *CV* 8 (August 1900): 339; "Gen. Joseph Wheeler," *SHSP* 26 (1898): 291–305; Mrs. Carry A. Folk, "The Soldier of 1861–1898," *CV* 9 (July 1901): 310–11.

      12. John T. Morgan to Mrs. Clopton, 31 March 1895, C.C. Clay Papers, Duke; *The Congressional Record*, 57 Cong., 1 sess., 1902, p. 6085. See also O. Lawrence Burnette, Jr., "John Tyler Morgan and Expansionist Sentiment in the New South," *Alabama Review* 18 (July 1965): 163–82. For an attitude similar to Morgan's see Gordon,

Reminiscences of the Civil War, pp. 464–65; and *UCV Minutes*, 1904, appendix. For other southerners in support of expansion see M.C. Butler to John T. Morgan, 27 October 1898, Matthew C. Butler Papers, SCL; William Alexander MacCorkle, "The Attitude of the Progressive South," in *Some Southern Questions* (New York: G.P. Putnam's Sons, 1908), p. 123; Thomas L. Rosser to John W. Daniel, 31 July 1898, John W. Daniel Papers, Duke; Emmet O'Neal to Wheeler, 6 February 1899, Wheeler Papers, ADAH; and McWilliams, "Lure of Empire." A New York *Herald* survey found the South the only region where a majority of newspapers opposed expansion, but only by 64 to 55. See "Various Topics," *Public Opinion* 25 (December 1898): 810.

13. For the vote and the importance of the Bacon Resolution see Edwina C. Smith, "Southerners on Empire: Southern Senators and Imperialism, 1898–1899," *MQ* 31 (Winter 1977–78): 88–107. The following discussion rests primarily on my reading of the debates and votes on the Philippines in the *Congressional Record*, 1898–1902.

14. Quotations are from *Congressional Record*, 57 Cong., 1 sess., 1902, p. 5102; 55 Cong., 3 sess., 1899, p. 1298; and 57 Cong., 1 sess., 1902, p. 4718.

15. *Congressional Record*, 55 Cong., 3 sess., 1899, p. 837. See also Christopher Lasch, "The Anti–Imperialists, the Philippines, and the Inequality of Man," *JSH* 24 (August 1958): 319–31.

16. *Congressional Record*, 55 Cong., 3 sess., 1899, p. 1431; *Atlanta Constitution*, 6 February 1899, p. 4; *Congressional Record*, 57 Cong., 1 sess., 1902, pp. 5739, 6096.

17. See Richard E. Welch, Jr., *Response to Imperialism: The United States and the Philippine-American War, 1899–1902* (Chapel Hill: University of North Carolina Press, 1979), p. 71 and *passim*. On southern hesitancy to volunteer, see clipping "South Against War," in Sb 7, UCV Sbs, LSU. Southern states were well below their quotas for volunteers, but the quotas were based on the number of blacks as well as whites of militia age. But only 8 percent of the volunteers were permitted to be black (two out of the twenty-five regiments were recruited among blacks). The fact that those southern states (with the exception of Georgia) that had the highest black population tended to be the ones that were furtherest from filling their quotas supports the idea that the built–in discrimination against blacks explains the low southern enlistments. That southerners constituted around 17.2 percent of the volunteers while southern whites were only 15.6 percent of the nation's militia-age population does, too (although undoubtedly some of the 17.2 percent were black). See *Annual Report of Adjutant-General to Major General Commanding the Army*, in *Annual Report of the War Department for Fiscal Year Ending June 30, 1899* (Washington: Government Printing Office, 1899), p. 375, for enlistments. See *Abstract of Twelfth Census of the United States, 1900* (Washington: Government Printing Office, 1902), p. 69, for militia-age population by race.

18. John L. Jordan to Mother, 18 May 1900, copy from Tennessee State Library collection in 38th Infantry File, Spanish-American War Archive, MHI; James H. Donegan to Wheeler, 13 December 1902, Wheeler Papers, ADAH; "Maj. W.J. Whitthorne," CV 9 (June 1901): 260–61; B.N. Coffman to Alexander, 14 January 1908, Edward P. Alexander Papers, SHC.

19. On Tillman's attitude toward Confederate history see William J. Cooper, Jr., *The Conservative Regime: South Carolina, 1877–1890* (Baltimore: Johns Hopkins University Press, 1968), pp. 147, 205–6; *Congressional Record*, 56 Cong., 1 sess., 1900, pp. 5683–84. Quotation is from P. Donan to Virginia Clay-Clopton, 24 December 1900, Clay Papers, Duke. Other letters in this collection show Donan's irreconcilability. See also B.F. Armstrong to Mrs. Kell, 17 April 1902 and 4 May 1903, John M. Kell Papers,

Duke; John N. Lyle to B.T. Johnson, 8 July 1899, Johnson Papers, Duke; Berkeley Minor, "The South and the Union," *SHSP* 30 (1902): 336; and George C. McEderry to J.W. DuBose, 17 March 1897, John W. DuBose Papers, ADAH.

    20. *UCV Minutes*, 1899, p. 145.

    21. *Speeches and Addresses of William McKinley, From March 1, 1897 to May 30, 1900* (New York: Doubleday & McLure Co., 1900), pp. 158–59; Elizabeth Marshall, "Atlanta Peace Jubilee," *GHQ* 50 (September 1966): 276–82; Linderman, *Mirror of War*, pp. 35, 70.

    22. G.I. Wilson to B.T. Johnson, 18 May 1898, Johnson Papers, Duke; Charles C. Ivey to Moorman, 16 December 1898, AG Lb, UCVA Papers, LSU; "National Dignity and Confederate Heroes," *CV* 6 (December 1898): 546; *UCV Minutes*, 1899, pp. 34–35, 158–66; *Atlanta Constitution*, 11, 12, 13 May 1899.

    23. "Confederate Dead Buried in the Cemetery at Arlington," *SHSP* 29 (1901): 354–56; *Congressional Record*, 56 Cong., 1 sess., 1900, p. 5309; Mrs. W.J. Behan to J.S. Richard, 5 May 1901, Tomb Committee Reports and Resolution, 14 May 1901, AAT Papers, LHAC; Behan to Elihu Root, 10 April 1901; J.B. Gordon to Behan, 14 May 1901; W.W. Herod to Behan, 14 May 1901, all in Confederated Southern Memorial Association Papers, Memorial Association Papers, LHAC, Tulane. See also *New York Times*, 7 June 1903, p. 1.

    24. *Congressional Record*, 55 Cong., 3 sess., 1899, pp. 1152, 1964; *UCV Minutes*, 1901, p. 75; Katie W. Behan to Mrs. Jones, 7 June 1902, Ladies' Memorial Association of Wake County Records, NCDAH; *Congressional Record*, 57 Cong., 2 sess., 1902, pp. 95, 1062, 1171, 1346; 58 Cong., 1 sess., 1903, p. 524; 58 Cong., 2 sess., 1903, pp. 313, 1109–10, 1229; *UCV Minutes*, 1904, pp. 35–36; 1905, pp. 47–48; Samuel E. Lewis to William E. Mickle, 1, 10, 19 December 1904, William E. Mickle Papers, Duke; *Congressional Record*, 59 Cong., 1 sess., 1906, pp. 270, 622, 711, 900, 980, 3245–46, 3254, 3365, 3437, 3368, 3426.

    25. *Congressional Record*, 58 Cong., 3 sess., 1905, pp. 2381, 2874, 3007, 3131, 3627; 59 Cong., 1 sess., 1906, pp. 1859, 2393, 2554, 2589, 9723; *New York Times*, 26 April 1905, pp. 2–3; but cf. 26 February 1905, p. 4; "Returned Confederate States' Flags," *SHSP* 33 (1905): 297–305. For the origin of the idea of returning the battle flags during the Spanish-American War, see *Atlanta Constitution*, 20 May 1898, p. 4; W.S. Rice to Wheeler, 19 March 1899, Wheeler Papers, ADAH.

    26. "Restoration of the Name of Jefferson Davis to the Cabin John Bridge, Washington, D.C.," *SHSP* 38 (1910): 41–155; Mrs. J. Enders Robinson to S.E. Lewis, 16 July 1909, Mrs. Behan to Lewis, 14 July and 30 March 1909, postcard, all in Behan File, Lee Camp Records, VHS. Also see postcard in scrapbook, 1865–1904, Thomas R. Markham Papers, LSU.

    27. Connelly, *The Marble Man*, pp. 116–20; Charles Francis Adams, "Shall Cromwell Have a Statue?," *SHSP* 30 (1902): 1–32; Samuel Chiles Mitchell, "An Aftermath of Appomattox: A Memoir," pp. 148–49, copy in Samuel C. Mitchell Papers, SHC; R.T. Barton to T.T. Munford, 11 October 1911, T.T. Munford Division, Munford-Ellis Papers, Duke; Charles E. Stowe, "Honest Confession Good for the Country," *CV* 19 (July 1911): 326–27; Jim Anderson, "Let the 'Conquered Banner' Wave," *CV* 19 (March 1911): 103.

    28. "Julian S. Carr's Address at Lexington, Va., June 3, 1916," Julian S. Carr Papers, SHC.

    29. "Notes and Queries," *Publications of the Southern History Association* 1 (April 1897): 156–57; J. Alleine Brown to Mickle, 26 March 1911, AG Lb, UCVA Papers, LSU; *UDC Minutes*, 1907, pp. 58–59; 1910, p. 33; *UCV Minutes*, 1908, pp.

101–102; Clipping UDC, Charles Clark Chapter Scrapbook, 1912, MDAH; but cf. *UCV General Orders*, v. 2, #6, 30 July 1910; Circular Letter, United States Ex-Slave Owners Registration Bureau, 1896, French Papers, MDAH; E.H. Lively, "Payment for Slaves Suggested," *CV* 18 (March 1910): 120; "Minutes of the Annual Meeting," 7 November 1899, United Daughters of the Confederacy, Grand Division of Virginia Records, VHS. The last item reveals the division of opinion over the matter of compensation for slaves. The Georgia UDC division approved of a request for compensation, but the Virginia Daughters did not. For examples of celebrations of slavery see Charles L.C. Minor, "The Old System of Slavery," *SHSP* 30 (1903): 125–29; Cornelia Branch Stone, "Vivid Reminiscences of the Old Plantation," *CV* 20 (December 1912): 568–69; and Julian S. Carr, "Befo' De War," undated, Carr Papers, SHC. Not all agreed, however. See *UCV Minutes*, 1911, pp. 107–10; Anderson, ed., *Brokenburn*, p. 8; Fielding A. Coakley to B.W. Jones, 27 July 1912, Benjamin W. Jones Papers, UVA; and Minutes of Ault Camp, UCV, 11 May 1908, United Confederate Veterans, Tennessee Division, Bivouac Records, TSL.

30. Mildred Rutherford, "The Historian General's Page," *CV* 23 (April 1915): 159; *UDC Minutes*, 1901, pp. 147–49; 1900, pp. 114–17; Mrs. W.C.N. Merchant, "The Southern Cross of Honor," in *The History of the United Daughters of the Confederacy*, Mary B. Poppenheim, et al. (Raleigh: Edwards & Broughton Company, 1925), pp. 145–54. In 1908, the UDC began to award the Cross to descendants. *UDC Minutes*, 1908, p. 44. See also Sallie M. Owen to Nicholas Cuny, 20 May 1902, United Daughters of the Confederacy Papers, LHAC, Tulane; *Minutes of the Grand Division of Virginia, United Daughters of the Confederacy*, 1902, p. 9; and *UDC Minutes*, 1905, pp. 156–57; 1908, p. 230.

31. Unidentified speeches, v. 34, (microfilm), William A. Shaffer Papers, SHC. See also unidentified speech, UDC Papers, LHAC, Tulane.

32. For figures on monuments see Appendix 1. See *HCMAS*, pp. 162–64; and Emerson, *Historic Southern Monuments*, p. 57. Quotation is from "Arkansas Confederate Monument," *CV* 13 (August 1905): 350–57. See also "Daughters at Franklin," *CV* 8 (April 1900): 172–73; Emerson, *Historic Monuments*, pp. 184, 197–99, 241, but cf. p. 80.

33. John H. Moore, "The Jefferson Davis Monument," *Virginia Cavalcade* 10 (Spring 1961): 29–34, quotation is on p. 32; Confederate Monument and Davis Monument, Vertical File, Valentine Museum; "Davis' Statue Hauled by Children," *CV* 15 (May 1907): 199.

34. *UCV Minutes*, 1907, pp. 118–56; *Atlanta Constitution*, 26 and 31 May, 1 and 4 June 1907; William G. Glasson, "The South's Care For Her Confederate Veterans," *Review of Reviews* 36 (July 1907): 40–42.

CHAPTER TWELVE.

CHANGES IN THE CELEBRATION:

THE DECLINING IMPORTANCE OF THE CONFEDERATE TRADITION

1. Moorman to Gordon, 26 September 1899, AG Lpb, UCVA Papers, LSU.

2. *UCV Minutes*, 1900, pp. 111–13.

3. *Atlanta Constitution*, 21 July 1900; *New York Times*, 20 July 1900, p. 3; 21 July 1900, p. 7.

4. "Shall the History Be Perpetuated?," *CV* 8 (July 1900): 297; Minutes, 14 August 1900 and undated resolution, AAT Papers, LHAC, Tulane; Clippings, scrapbook

8, UCV Scrapbooks, LSU. The resolution also condemned Gordon's acceptance of an invitation to a GAR Reunion, but that issue remained secondary.

5. *New York Times*, 21 August 1900, p. 9; J.B. Gordon to CVA, Army of Tennessee, 21 August 1900 and Resolution, 11 September 1900, AAT Papers, LHAC, Tulane.

6. "A Plea Against Intersectional Reunions," *Lost Cause* 4 (August 1900): 6; "Crisp Resolutions Adopted in Virginia," *CV* 8 (September 1900): 396. There are several letters of endorsement in United Confederate Veterans Papers, LHAC, Tulane. See *CV* 8 (September 1900): 394; S.D. Lee to Moorman, 4 September 1900, AG Lb and Moorman to Lee, 3 September 1900, AG Lpb, UCVA Papers, LSU. Lee himself seemed to have reservations about Blue-Gray reunions.

7. "About Inviting the President to Memphis," *CV* 9 (January 1901): 6; Minutes, 8 January 1901, AAT Papers, LHAC, Tulane; Gordon to Moorman, 17 and 18 January 1901, AG Lb, UCVA Papers, LSU; Circular Letter, No. 140, UCV, 20 February 1901, UCV Papers, LHAC, Tulane. This collection also contains several letters of protest by individuals. See Alex P. Stewart to J.A. Chalaron, 26 April 1901 and P.D. Stephenson to Chalaron, 9 February 1901, J.A. Chalaron Papers, LHAC, Tulane. See also George Gordon to Moorman, 10 March 1901 and S.D. Lee to Moorman, 26 March 1901, AG Lb, UCVA Papers, LSU.

8. M.R. Tunno to Gordon, 1 July 1901, UCV Papers, UGA; Gordon to Moorman, 13 July, 24 August, 1 September 1901, Frank Gordon to Moorman, 7 November 1901, Clement Evans to Moorman, 20 October 1901—all in AG Lb, UCVA Papers, LSU; "Suggestions about the Dallas Reunion," *CV* 11 (August 1901): 344; *UCV Minutes*, 1901, p. 72; 1902, p. 82; Minutes, 14 June 1901, AAT Papers, LHAC, Tulane; "Tennessee Vets Refuse to Secede," clipping, 12 July 1905, scrapbook #7, UCV Papers, LHAC, Tulane.

9. First quotation is from George McCormick to J.A. Harral, 19 November 1901, J.A. Harral Papers, LHAC, Tulane. See also J.D. Gaines to Moorman, 14 May 1901, AG Lb, UCVA Papers, LSU; George L. Christian to John W. Daniel, 31 August and 21 September 1906, John W. Daniel Papers, UVA; James R. Randall to T.K. Oglesby, 5 April 1907, Oglesby Papers, Duke; and Samuel White, "Jefferson Davis Vindicated," *CV* 19 (October 1911): 479–81. Quotation from Pinckney is in Gustavus M. Pinckney to Yates Snowden, 11 November 1904, but see also 24 June 1903, 16 January and 15 November 1904. All in Yates Snowden Papers, SCL. Also see Pinckney, *The Coming Crisis; Three Ideas: A Work in Two Parts* (Charleston: Walker, Evans, & Cogswell, 1905). For information on Pinckney, see "A Believer in Ideals," clipping, *The State*, 15 December 1912, Snowden Papers. For other examples from the postwar generation see Walter Allen Watson Diary, VHS; W.C. Gorgas to Mother, 3 May 1901 and 29 December 1903, William C. Gorgas Papers, UAL.

10. Moorman to Gordon, 9 August 1900, AG Lpb and S.D. Lee to Moorman, 26 March 1901, AG Lb, UCVA Papers, LSU; but cf. Duke, *Reminiscences*, pp. 466–67; *USCV Minutes*, 1908, pp. 120–22; Street, *American Adventures*, pp. 193–4.

11. On Rouss and Battle Abbey see Chapter 9. On feuding see Minute Book, 6 September, 5 December 1895; 1898; 7 July 1899, Record of Frank Cheatham Bivouac, United Confederate Veterans, Tennessee Division, Bivouac Records, TSL; "Memphis Wants the Abbey," *CV* 4 (March 1896): 88; *UCV Minutes*, 1898, pp. 53–54, 57–58; Minutes and clipping, 8 February 1898, Association of the Army of Tennessee Papers, LHAC, Tulane; "What of the Atlanta Reunion?," *CV* 6 (August 1898): 355; "Tennesseans Want Their Money Returned," *CV* 8 (October 1900): 437; *CV* 7 (June 1899): 257–58; Chas. Lantonia to Robert White, 7 October 1899 and John C. Underwood to

J.S. Richards, 18 January 1901, Financial Committee Correspondence, AAT Papers, LHAC, Tulane; "Underwood Sues the Veteran for $50,000," *CV* 7 (August 1899): 345–54; "United States Court of Appeals," *CV* 10 (June 1902): 249–53; *UCV Minutes,* 1903, pp. 77–78; 1905, pp. 36–40; and "Dedication of the South's Battle Abbey," *CV* 29 (June 1921): 204. The fight over the Battle Abbey became intertwined briefly with that over reconciliation when New Orleans vets objected to the committee's solicitation of northern contributions. See also John A. Simpson, "The Cult of the 'Lost Cause,'" *THQ* 34 (Winter 1975): 356.

12. Resolution, 14 March 1907, United Confederate Veterans' Papers, LHAC, Tulane; Wm. C. Harrison to Moorman, 7 February 1900, AG Lb, UCVA Papers, LSU; The Adjutant General's Letterpress book, 1900 and AG Lb, 1905 also contain a good bit of material on feuding in California. On Tennessee and Louisiana see Mickle to Lee, 7 April 1906, William E. Mickle Letterbook, UTX; John W. Morton to Mickle, 7 March 1903 and Tomlinson Fort to Mickle, 12 May 1905, in AG Lb, UCVA Papers, LSU; Army of Northern Virginia Association to J. Alphonse Prudhomme, 19 June 1907 and Prudhomme to O'Brien, 23 June 1907, Association of the Army of Northern Virginia Papers, LHAC, Tulane; Clippings, September 1910, Scrapbook #9, UCV Papers, LHAC, Tulane; and T.W. Castleman to C. Irvine Walker, 11 April 1911, A.B. Booth to W.D. Gooch, 3 April 1909, T.W. Castleman, "Secession of Two Camps from the La. Division, UCV," 12 March 1914, all in manila boxes, UCVA Papers, LSU.

13. "Adj. Gen. William E. Mickle," *CV* 11 (February 1903): 51; Mickle to Lee, 18 July 1906; Mickle to Young, 8 and 30 June 1904. All in Mickle Letterbook, UTX; S.D. Lee to J.A. Chalaron, 29 June 1904, UCV Papers, LHAC, Tulane; Young to Lee, 24 December 1904, AG Lb, UCVA Papers, LSU; Mickle to S.E. Lewis, 30 September 1909, Mickle File, Lee Camp Records, VHS.

14. Hattaway, *General Stephen D. Lee,* pp. 196–99; *UCV Minutes,* 1904, p. 38; 1905, p. 49; 1908, pp. 127–29; 1909, pp. 84–85; 1910, pp. 148–51; C. Irvine Walker to T.W. Castleman, 29 April 1912, and Castleman to Walker, 3 May 1912, cardboard box labeled AG Correspondence, UCVA Papers, LSU; "Confederates Should Remain United," *CV* 22 (August 1912): 358; Henry Askew to J.J. Hall, 14 May 1912, and Askew to K.M. Van Zandt, undated, Henry Askew Papers, UTX; *UCV Minutes,* 1913, pp. 170–71; Young to Mickle, 23 August 1915, cardboard box, UCVA Papers, LSU.

15. Herman Hattaway, "The United Confederate Veterans in Louisiana," *Louisiana History* 16 (Winter 1975): 26, agrees that the 1900–10 period was the last strong decade. For slightly different observations on veteran survival see Ruoff, "Southern Womanhood, 1865–1920," pp. 97–98. On camps and delegates see *UCV Minutes,* 1900–1910. Subscriptions to the CV reached 20,000 in 1899 and remained at that level in 1912. See "The Veteran Seven Years Old," *CV* 7 (December 1899): 544; "Published by Order of PO Department," *CV* 20 (November 1912): 499. S.D. Lee to J.A. Chalaron, 29 June 1904, UCV Papers, LHAC, Tulane, did suggest that enthusiasm had waned.

16. *UDC Minutes,* 1911, p. 325; 1912, p. 92; 1915, pp. 56–57, 67; UDC, Black Oak Chapter Minutes, March 1912, Duke. On early use in advertising, see Coulter, *The South During Reconstruction,* pp. 180–81. On offers to Daughters see "To the Daughters of the Confederacy," *CV* 17 (April 1909): 187; ad, *CV* 18 (December 1910): 600. On agents see "Monument Work During the Summer," *CV* 18 (September 1910): 424; clipping, UDC, Charles Clark Chapter Scrapbook, MDAH; and Black Oak Chapter Minutes, 2 February and 2 March 1911, Duke. For the fountain see "Confederate Memorial Drinking Fountain: Combine Art, Sentiment, and Utility," *CV* 24 (September 1916): 432. For a very different interpretation of memorial drinking fountains see Wilson, *Baptized in Blood,* p. 29. Others have pointed to the commercialization of the monument

movement. See E. Merton Coulter, "The Confederate Monument in Athens, Georgia," *GHQ* 40 (September 1956): 247; and Davis, "Johnny Reb in Perspective," pp. 142–44.

17. Ebb F. Stephenson to Will, 3 July 1909, William A. Smith Papers, Duke; T.W. Castleman to Walker, 18 January 1912, unnumbered cardboard box, and Young to Mickle, 14 January 1911, AG Lb, UCVA Papers, LSU; *UCV Minutes*, 1911, pp. 123–26; *Atlanta Constitution*, 7, 8, 10 May 1912; J.R. Gibbons, "Expense of Confederate Reunions," *CV* 23 (November 1915): 517.

18. Back Cover, *CV* 9 (October 1901); R.W. Crabb to Moorman, 1 November 1902, AG Lb, UCVA Papers, LSU; *CV* 4 (August 1896): 282; *CV* 10 (April 1902): 149. Such advertising was not new, but at this time it did seem to be accepted and exploited more than it had before by the celebrants themselves.

19. *CV* 16 (December 1908): 671.

20. Robert Chilsom to Lillie McGee, 13 June 1893, Lily McGee Papers, Duke; *Atlanta Constitution*, 30 June 1896; 24 June 1897; 19 July 1898; 27 and 31 May, 2 June 1900; 26 and 28 May 1901; 22, 23, 25 April 1902; 17 May 1903.

21. *UCV Minutes*, 1906, pp. 7–8.

22. R.B. Paddock, "Reunion Management Criticized," *CV* 14 (June 1906): 272–73; George H. Levy, "Treatment of Veterans at Reunions," *CV* 18 (February 1910): 55; Lee to Mickle, 6 February 1905, UCV Papers, UGA; Annie to Mrs. Clopton and Humes, 8 June 1913, Clement C. Clay Papers, Duke. Some complaints were voiced as early as 1897. See B.H. Teague, "Suggestions About the Reunion," *CV* 5 (April 1897): 161–62; and "What of the Atlanta Reunion?," *CV* 6 (August 1898): 354. They became common after 1900, however. See S.D. Lee to George Moorman, 26 November 1901, AG Lb, UCVA Papers, LSU; "Suggestions Concerning Reunions," *CV* 10 (February 1902): 52; Robert E. Houston to Mickle, 9 February 1903, AG Lb, UCVA Papers, LSU; Samuel E. Lewis to Mickle, undated draft but after June 1905, Arlington Monument File, R.E. Lee Camp Records, VHS; W.G. Hamilton to J.A. Chalaron, 18 July 1905, J.A. Chalaron Papers, LHAC, Tulane; E.W. Anderson, Resolution of Rouss Camp, 23 April 1906, Reunion, New Orleans File, Lee Camp Records, VHS; A.P. Evans, "Veterans Somewhat Neglected at Reunions," *CV* 16 (March 1908): 115; "About Neglect of Veterans at Reunions," *CV* 16 (April 1908): 203; and Mrs. Willie G. Quinn, "Private Soldiers at Reunion," *CV* 18 (May 1910): 207. In addition, after 1900 a few veterans complained that the social activities included "sinful" dancing. See, for example, A.T. Goodloe, "Reunion Suggestions and Comments," *CV* 9 (July 1901): 293.

23. Programs existed to subsidize the participation of poor veterans but not their families' and friends'.

24. See Appendix 3 for membership comparisons. The comparison also suggests a significant drop in upper–class participation; this might indicate a fall in prestige, but more likely reflects the fact that the relative young Sons had not yet become fully established. Quotation is from *USCV Minutes*, 1905, pp. 14–15.

25. For examples of difficulties in becoming a chapter, see letters to Mrs. Mary Gilmore Harnett during 1908 in J.Y. Gilmore Papers, LSU. Quotations are from A.M. Raines to Parsley, 10 February 1896 and 1 November 1894, Eliza H. Parsley Papers, SHC; *UDC Minutes*, 1907, p. 87. On applications see "Extracts from Constitution and By Laws of Cape Fear Chapter," Parsley Papers, SHC. Records that allow comparisons between UCV camps and UDC chapters similar to the ones made between UCV and SCV camps were unavailable. (The UDC "Bylaws prohibit our making membership available to anyone," Marion H. Giannasi, Office Manager, UDC, to author, 22 March 1983, author's possession.) Observations on class bias of the UDC are therefore

speculative, but Ruoff, "Southern Womanhood," p. 100, reaches the same conclusion. The only evidence I have found that points to any other conclusion is J.C. Norman, "Model Work of a Chapter of UDC," *CV* 11 (January 1903): 30.

26. Minutes of the Meetings of Fred Ault Camp No. 5, UCV, 8 November 1897, UCV Papers, TSL; *Proceedings of Grand Camp Confederate Veterans, Department of Virginia*, 1910, p. 45. Examples of hostility between the UCV and SCV are found in *USCV Minutes*, 1906, pp. 111–12; and Thomas M. Owen to Mickle, 26 March 1910, AG Lb, UCVA Papers, LSU. On plan see *UCV Minutes*, 1903, pp. 85–86; and *Atlanta Constitution*, 14 June 1904.

27. *USCV Minutes*, 1903, p. 101; 1908, p. 103; General order #5, Louisiana Division, USCV, 13 March 1903, SCV Papers, LHAC, Tulane; *USCV Minutes*, 1905, pp. 34–35, 48; 1907, p. 77. See also Register of Visiting Sons: Fourteenth Annual Reunion of United Sons of Confederate Veterans, Memphis, Tenn., 1909, in Scrapbook #7, SCV Papers, LHAC, Tulane; *USCV Minutes*, 1907, pp. 173–74. Quotation is from Owen to Ralston F. Green, 18 April 1907, SCV Papers, LHAC, Tulane. See also Moorman to V.Y. Cook, 28 January 1898, AG Lpb, UCVA Papers, LSU; Homer D. Wade to Mickle, 20 January 1903, AG Lb, UCVA Papers, LSU; *USCV Minutes*, 1905, pp. 9, 13; "Notes and News," *Publications of the Southern History Association* 9 (September 1905): 350–51; W.P. Renwick to Ralston T. Green, 19 November 1906, J. Renwick to G.K. Renaud, 2 and 6 September 1909, SCV Papers, Tulane; Hanson-Bellows Company to Franklin Riley, 13 August 1914, Franklin L. Riley Papers, SHC.

28. *UDC Minutes*, 1912, p. 250. This material on UDC activities is based on records of individual chapters, division reports in *UDC Minutes*, and Poppenheim, et al., *The History of the United Daughters of the Confederacy*. On Children of the Confederacy see Mrs. Robert Downs Wright, "Children of the Confederacy," in *History of UDC*, pp. 181–89; and "Children of the Confederacy," *CV* 4 (July 1896): 201. There are only scattered references to the childrens' work in the *UDC Minutes*, and the national organization did not seem to give much emphasis to it.

29. *UDC Minutes*, 1910, p. 272; Mary B. Poppenheim, "Education," in *History of UDC*, pp. 95–127. The Georgia and Tennessee Divisions also supported dorms for women at colleges. See *UDC Minutes*, 1897, pp. 34–36; and Martha S. Gielow, "Daughters of the Confederacy: Confederate Veterans and People of the South, A Message to Friends and Compatriots," and "To the United Daughters of the Confederacy, Replying to Mrs. Lizzie George Henderson's Letter of May 1906," Mrs. Marion Butler Papers, SHC. For support of the school see "Raben Gap Industrial School," clipping, Cox Scrapbooks, AHS; and *UDC Minutes*, 1906, p. 244.

30. For an example see *UDC Minutes*, 1910, pp. 44–45. Quotation is from 1899, p. 49.

31. "A Novel and Unique Reception," *CV* 5 (October 1897): 504.

32. Adelia A. Dunovant to Mrs. Clay-Clopton, 8 August 1904, Clay Papers, Duke; Lizzie George Henderson, "United Daughters of Confederacy," *CV* 15 (August 1907): 349.

33. For examples of the variety of attitudes on suffrage see Scott, *The Southern Lady*, p. 180; Mrs. T.L. Kennedy to Virginia Clay-Clopton, 5 July and 4 September 1898, Clay Papers, Duke; untitled fragment, Lillie V. Archbell Papers, SHC; Lloyd C. Taylor, Jr., "Lila Meade Valentine: The FFV as Reformer," *VMHB* 70 (October 1962): 482; and Margaret N. Price, "The Development of Leadership by Southern Women Through Clubs and Organizations" (M.A. thesis, University of North Carolina, 1945), pp. 84–85. Contrast with traditional roles for women is seen clearly in two poems read to

the annual meeting. See *UDC Minutes*, 1898, pp. 96–98, and 1906, pp. 42–44. Mrs. T.J. Latham, "Evolution of the Women of the South," *CV* 11 (May 1903): 217–18, celebrates the passing of the home-bound southern woman. Members still performed homemaking duties within the celebration. See, for example, *Grand Division of Virginia Minutes*, 1900, p. 32; and Georgiette Clarke Holmes to Mr. Barham, 13 November 1913, Benjamin W. Jones Papers, UVA. Quotation is from *UDC Minutes*, 1913, p. 20. See also Mrs. Elizabeth Lumpkin Glenn, "The Land of Our Desire," *CV* 14 (November 1906): 494–96. Ruoff, "Southern Womanhood," pp. 77–106, following Price, "Development of Leadership," pp. 90–91, labels the UDC a transitional organization. Although his interpretation stresses many of the themes developed above, mine puts more emphasis on the divisions within the movement and less on its function in transforming the role of southern women.

34. Owen to Comrade, 18 April 1907, SCV Papers, LHAC, Tulane.

35. *UDC Minutes*, 1900, p. 127; 1899, pp. 65–67. At the request of the UDC, the CSMA later joined the efforts for the Davis Memorial. Behan to S.D. Lee, 20 July 1905, UDC Papers, LHAC, Tulane.

36. *USCV Minutes*, 1903, pp. 31–33; *UDC Minutes*, 1905, pp. 263–64. First quotation is from T.A. Hamilton, "Words for 'Dixie,'" *CV* 11 (November 1903): 486–87; second, "Reunion of Missouri Confederates," *CV* 11 (November 1903): 491. See also A.W. Riecke, "'Dixie,'" *CV* 12 (January 1904): 39; and Mrs. Dowdell, "Shall the Words of Dixie Be Changed?," *CV* 12 (May 1904): 215–16. John A. Simpson interprets the UDC move as an attempt to achieve southern vindication. Simpson, "Shall We Change the Words of 'Dixie'?" *Southern Folklore Quarterly*, 45 (1981): 19–40.

37. *UCV Minutes*, 1904, pp. 58–61; 1905, pp. 44–45; *UDC Minutes*, 1904, p. 153; 1909, pp. 105–6; "How Shall We Sing 'Dixie'?," *CV* 23 (October 1915): 438; "How Shall We Sing 'Dixie'?," *CV* 23 (September 1915): 422–23.

38. *UCV Minutes*, 1896, pp. 128–30; 1900, 42–44; *UDC Minutes*, 1902, pp. 123–24; *UCV Minutes*, 1903, pp. 73–74; 1904, pp. 47–48, 49–50; *USCV Minutes*, 1903, pp. 21–24; 1905, pp. 42–46; *UDC Minutes*, 1906, p. 54; *USCV Minutes*, 1907, pp. 82–104; "Gen. C.I. Walker," *CV* 36 (May 1928): 176–77.

39. "Monument to Southern Women," *CV* 3 (January 1895): 22; *UDC Minutes*, 1897, pp. 36–37; "Living Monument to Southern Women," *CV* 5 (August 1897): 420; Mrs. W.L. Merchant–Chatham to Andrews, 23 April 1901, Garnett Andrews Papers, SHC; Martha S. Gielow to Thomas M. Owen and endorsement by Clay-Clopton, 27 March 1906 and Gielow to Clay-Clopton, 17 June 1906, Clay Papers, Duke; Clay-Clopton to Confederate Veterans, undated but convention of 1906, box 3, UCVA Papers, LSU; Thomas M. Owen to C.I. Walker, 24 August 1905, Owen Papers, ADAH; *USCV Minutes*, 1906, pp. 78–87; 1907, pp. 86–87; Sallie S. Hunt, "Women Want Building for Monument," *CV* 17 (April 1909): 181; Sara R. Richmond, "The Southern Mothers' Scholarship," *CV* 15 (August 1907): 351.

40. "Monument to Confederate Women," *CV* 17 (April 1909): 152; H.M. Hamill, "Confederate Woman's Monument," *CV* 17 (April 1909): 150; Archibald Young, "Suitable Monuments—Southern Women," *CV* 18 (October 1910): 457–58; "Review of Memphis Reunion," *CV* 17 (July 1909): 316; "Southern Woman's Monument," *CV* 17 (July 1909): 312.

41. *UDC Minutes*, 1910, pp. 107–8. Quotation is from Mrs. George H. Tichenor, undated circular letter to the UCV Camps; T.W. Castleman to Charles Scott, 2 April 1912; W.P. Renwick to Castleman, 22 March 1912—all in unnumbered cardboard box, UCVA Papers, LSU; Mrs. George Tichenor to Mickle, 6 February 1911, AG Lb, UCVA Papers, LSU. This fight may also have been caught up in the internal

UCV squabbles in Louisiana mentioned earlier in this chapter. See Castleman to Walker, 18 May 1912, unnumbered cardboard box, UCVA Papers, LSU.

42. Several other towns put up monuments to women but used different designs. See Widener, *Confederate Monuments*.

CHAPTER THIRTEEN.
ACADEMIC MISSIONARIES:
THE CHALLENGE OF THE PROFESSIONALS

1. On professionalization of history in the South see James W. Webb, "Historical Activity in the South: 1880–1890" (M.A. thesis, Louisiana State University, 1963); David D. Van Tassel, "The American Historical Association and the South, 1884–1913," *JSH* 23 (November 1957): 465–82; Joseph J. Mathews, "The Study of History in the South," *JSH* 31 (February 1965): 3–20; Randall G. Patterson, "Writing Southern Literary History: A Study of Selected Critics and Historians of the Literature of the South, 1890–1910" (Ph.D. diss., University of North Carolina-Chapel Hill, 1976); Frederick W. Moore, et al., "The Teaching of History in the South: A Report," *School Review* 11 (February 1903): 107–22; Moore, "The Status of History in Southern Colleges," *SAQ* 2 (April 1903): 169–71; E.C. Barker, "Southern History in Southern State Universities," in Barker-Littlefield Correspondence, Littlefield Holding Collection, UTX; William K. Boyd, "Southern History in American Universities," *SAQ* 1 (July 1902): 241; Henry N. Snyder, "The Reconstruction of Southern Literary Thought," *SAQ* 1 (April 1902): 153–54; paper filed with Daniel C. Gilman to Curry, 19 August 1899 (giving number of JHU graduates teaching in the South), J.L.M. Curry Papers, LC; *USCV Minutes*, 1901, pp. 176–81; and Robert R. Simpson, "The Origin of State Departments of Archives and History in the South" (Ph.D. diss., University of Mississippi, 1971).

2. Yates Snowden Papers, SCL; Mims to Clara Puryear, 11 July 1897, in Michael O'Brien, ed., "'To Seek a Newer World': Selected Correspondence of Edwin Mims" (M.A. thesis, Vanderbilt University, 1973), pp. 236, 127–28, 133, 230–31; Samuel C. Mitchell, "An Aftermath of Appomattox: A Memoir," p. 22, copy in Samuel C. Mitchell Papers, SHC; John S. Bassett to Mims, 17 October 1907 and 4 September 1910, Edwin Mims Papers, JUL; and William E. Dodd, "History and Patriotism," *SAQ* 12 (April 1913): 109–21.

3. This analysis is based generally on my reading of some of their papers and publications. Not all agreed on every point; Dodd, for instance, had doubts about industrialization. For a similar analysis of this generation see Bruce Clayton, *The Savage Ideal: Intolerance and Intellectual Leadership in the South, 1890–1914* (Baltimore: Johns Hopkins University Press, 1972); Michael O'Brien, *The Idea of the American South: 1920–1941* (Baltimore: Johns Hopkins University Press, 1979), pp. 3–14. See also James P. Hendrix, Jr., "From Romance to Scholarship: Southern History at the Take-Off Point," *Mississippi Quarterly* 30 (Spring 1977): 192–211. On the need for a critical study of the past see Wendell Holmes Stephenson, *Southern History in the Making: Pioneer Historians of the South* (Baton Rouge: Louisiana State University Press, 1964), pp. 101–2; Alderman, "Lecture on Teaching History," 1886, Edwin A. Alderman Papers, UVA; William P. Trent, "The Study of Southern History," *Vanderbilt Southern Historical Society Publications*, 1: 4–5; Snyder, "Reconstruction," p. 152; Mims to Clara Puryear, 8 November 1896, in O'Brien, "Mims," p. 190; Trent to Mims, 28 December 1905, Mims Papers, JUL; Bassett to Dodd, 28 April 1907, William E. Dodd Papers, LC;

Mims, "The Function of Criticism in the South," *SAQ* 2 (October 1903): 334–45; and William P. Trent, "Tendencies of Higher Life in the South," *Atlantic Monthly* 79 (June 1897): 771. Even the more conservative of them came to agree on the need for freedom of thought. Fleming, for example, at first defended the UDC and took a traditional stance, but soon expressed his doubts. See Fleming to Miss Cozart, 27 April 1902 and 16 April 1909, Walter L. Fleming Papers, ADAH; Fleming to Franklin L. Riley, 13 September 1910, Franklin L. Riley Papers, SHC. Even Hamilton found himself in confrontation with accepted views. See Kate Mason Rowland to Hamilton, 14 July 1909; Berkeley Minor to Hamilton, 19 July 1909; Hamilton to Minor (copy), 7 August 1909. All in J.G. de Roulhac Hamilton Papers, SHC.

4. William Dodd, "The Status of History in Southern Education," *Nation* 75 (August 1902): 109–11; Dodd, "Some Difficulties of the History Teacher in the South," *SAQ* 3 (April 1904): 117–22; Moore, "Teaching of History," p. 106, 116–19. See also Snyder, "Reconstruction," pp. 154–55; William K. Boyd, "Southern History," pp. 238–46; "Notes and News," *Publications of the Southern History Association* 6 (March 1902): 192–94.

5. J.H.T. McPherson to Adams, 4 October and 11 November 1891, in W. Stull Holt, ed., *Historical Scholarship in the United States, 1876–1901: As Revealed in the Correspondence of Herbert B. Adams*, John Hopkins University Studies in Historical and Political Science, vol. 56, no. 4 (Baltimore: Johns Hopkins University Press, 1938), pp. 167–68, 170; Stephens, *Southern History*, pp. 167–68; Franklin T. Walker, "William Peterfield Trent—A Critical Biography" (Ph.D. diss., George Peabody College for Teachers, 1943), pp. 125–43; William P. Trent, *William Gilmore Simms* (Boston: Houghton Mifflin Company, 1892), pp. vi., 39, 274, 287, *passim*. See also John McCardell, "Trent's *Simms*: The Making of a Biography," *A Master's Due: Essays in Honor of David Herbert Donald*, William J. Cooper, Jr., Michael F. Holt, and John McCardell, eds. (Baton Rouge: Louisiana State University Press, 1985), pp. 177–203.

6. Walker, "Trent," pp. 134–57, 483–93; C.T. Quintard to Charles W. Kent, 29 June 1892 and Trent to Kent, 2 November 1893, Tucker-Harrison-Smith Family Papers, UVA; William C. Miller to Yates Snowden, 17 September 1913, Yates Snowden Papers, SCL. See also Clayton, *Savage Ideal*, pp. 68–72. Trent's very next book, *Southern Statesmen of the Old Regime*, also raised the ire of some. See *UDC Minutes*, 1898, pp. 37–38.

7. First quotation is from Walker, "Trent," pp. 208–210. Trent, *Robert E. Lee* (Boston: Small, Maynard & Company, 1899), second quotation from p. 130. Trent's views on the South continued to moderate. See George H. Sass to Snowden, 8 December 1904 and Trent to Snowden, 6 May 1913 and 23 May 1915, Snowden Papers, SCL.

8. Circular filed in 1902, AG Lb, UCVA Papers, LSU; Minute Book, 2 February 1902, Record, Frank Cheatham Bivouac, United Confederate Veterans, Tennessee Division, Bivouac Records, TSL; *UCV Minutes*, 1902, pp. 53–54; Gilbert E. Govan and James W. Livingood, *The University of Chattanooga: Sixty Years* (Chattanooga: University of Chattanooga Press, 1947); John S. Bassett, "Stirring up the Fires of Race Antipathy," *SAQ* 2 (October 1903): 297–305. For a convenient overview of the affair, see Clayton, *Savage Ideal*, pp. 84–99.

9. Articles on Lee appeared in the *SAQ* 4 (January 1905): 63–70; 4 (October 1905): 305–15; 6 (January 1907): 1–26; 8 (October 1908): 359–69; 10 (January 1911): 23–30; 10 (April 1911): 103–18; 10 (July 1911): 232–47; 10 (October 1911): 301–13; 12 (October 1913): 291–301. On participation in the celebration see *USCV Minutes*, 1907, p. 112; Sassie J. Dossner to Smith, 17 June 1910, C. Alphonso Smith Papers, UVA; Mary Z. Payne to Mitchell, 21 August 1911 and Yates Snowden to Mitchell, 9 March 1912,

Mitchell Papers, LC; Carrie L. Robins to Dodd, 13 June 1913, Dodd Papers, LC; "Diary of Maj. Kincloch Falconer," *CV* 9 (September 1901): 408; S.P. Patterson, "Longstreet and the War Between the States," *Sewanee Review* 4 (May 1896): 326–33; Frederick W. Moore, "The Functions of State History," *Ibid.* 9 (April 1901): 204–14; Celina E. Means, "The Reminiscences of Four Southern Women," *Ibid.* 13 (October 1905): 474–95; J.R. Ormond, "Review of *Reminiscences of the Civil War* by General John B. Gordon," *SAQ* 3 (April 1904): 187–88; "Review of *Lee and Longstreet at High Tide: Gettysburg in the Light of Official Records* by Helen D. Longstreet," *SAQ* 4 (January 1905): 92–93; Sara A. Pryor to Dodd, 21 March 1910, Dodd Papers, LC; Thomas Owen to Comrades, 4 April 1907, Sons of Confederate Veterans Papers, Tulane; Riley to Ruth B. Hawes, 2 April 1910, Riley Papers, SHC.

10. Owen to E.A. Smith, 27 November 1895, Thomas M. Owen Papers, ADAH; "Historical Sketch of the Association," *PSHA* 1 (January 1897): 1–8; "List of Members of the Southern History Association," *PSHA* 8 (September 1904): 427–35; "The Southern History Association: Membership Roll," in Colyer Meriwether Papers, SCL. See also *PSHA, passim.*

11. Gaines M. Foster, "Mirage in the Sahara of the Bozart: *The Library of Southern Literature,*" *MQ* 28 (Winter 1974–75): 3–19; Rines to Mitchell and contract attached, 29 April 1908, Mitchell Papers, LC; Rines to Smith, 11 January 1909, C. Alphonso Smith Papers, UVA; College endorsements filed in Library of Southern Literature File, 1905–07, Tucker-Harrison-Smith Papers, UVA.

12. Foster, "Mirage in the Sahara."

13. Quotation is from George E. Rines to Louisa B. Poppenheim, 15 March 1909, Louisa B. and Mary B. Poppenheim Papers, Duke. For essays see Julian A.C. Chandler, et al., eds., *The South in The Building of the Nation,* 12 vols. (Richmond: Southern Historical Publication Society, 1909–1913), 1: xvii; 4:383–422, 442–86.

14. On slavery see Trent, "Study of Southern History," pp. 8–9; Mitchell, "Aftermath of Appomattox," p. 35, copy in Mitchell Papers, SHC; Kent to Ellen Kent, 12 March 1887, Tucker-Harrison-Smith Papers, UVA. On generals see Walker, "Trent," p. 100. The professionals did, however, try to broaden interest to periods of southern history other than the Civil War. On this point see Page, *The Southerner,* pp. 149–50. Dodd probably did more of this than the others.

15. Walker, "Trent," pp. 223–31; Trent to Adams, 8 January 1898, in Holt, ed., *Historical Scholarship,* pp. 249–50; Stephenson, *Southern History in the Making,* p. 131; Dodd to Wife, 12 April 1908 and Dodd to McClaughlin, 16 April 1908, Dodd Papers, LC. Professional ambition may have influenced historians' decision to move out of the South, too. See Bassett to Hamilton, 27 May 1908, Hamilton Papers, SHC.

16. John Bell Heneman to Mims, 18 May 1908, Mims Papers, JUL; Ad, *CV* 14 (February 1906): 87; Fleming to Mickle, 20 September and 2 October 1905, Arthur Clark Co. to Mickle, 7 December 1906, AG Lb, UCVA Papers, LSU; Fleming to E.C. Barker, 30 December 1912, Barker-Littlefield Correspondence, Littlefield Holding Collection, UTX; Riley to Hamilton, 24 April 1913, Hamilton Papers, SHC; Riley to J. Powell Riley, 11 December 1912, Riley Papers, SHC. Scholars may also have been careful not to offend because they needed the help of the leaders of the celebration in getting access to historical materials. See, for examples, Fleming to Mrs. Clay-Clopton, 28 June 1907, Clement C. Clay Papers, Duke; Fleming to Mrs. W.J. Behan, 9 November 1907, Ladies' Memorial Association, Memorial Association Papers, LHAC, Tulane; and [?] to Mrs. W.J. Behan, 12 August 1910, Sons of Confederate Veterans Papers, LHAC, Tulane.

17. Observations on backgrounds are based on data on the following more important of the missionary academics: John S. Bassett, Franklin L. Riley, William E.

Dodd, Frederick W. Moore, Julian A.C. Chandler, William K. Boyd, Walter L. Fleming, J.G. de Roulhac Hamilton, Edwin A. Alderman, Samuel Chiles Mitchell, William P. Trent, Colyer Meriwether, Henry Nelson Snyder, Charles W. Kent, C. Alphonso Smith, Thomas M. Owen, and Stephen B. Weeks. For other historians in the South at this time see list in J.G. de Roulhac Hamilton, "History in the South—A Retrospect of Half a Century," *NCHR* 31 (April 1954): 173–8; and "Alphabetical List of Teachers in Southern Colleges," Library of Southern Literature File, 1905–07, Tucker-Harrison-Smith Papers, UVA. See Henry N. Snyder, *An Educational Odyssey* (Nashville and New York: Abingdon–Cokesbury Press, 1947), pp. 14–15; Trent to Mims, 2 May 1903, Mims Papers, JUL; and Houghton–Mifflin Company to Kent, 7 December 1900, Tucker-Harrison-Smith Papers, UVA.

18. *UCV Minutes*, 1901, p. 62; 1903, pp. 62–63; 1906, pp. 62–75; 1899, p. 147; 1905, p. 32; *USCV Minutes*, 1906, p. 259; 1908, pp. 60–65; *UDC Minutes*, 1905, p. 237; Simpson, "Origin of State Archives," pp. 100–2.

19. Christine Boyson, "Robert E. Lee—A Present Estimate," CV 16 (December 1908): 657–60; Mrs. Livingston Rowe Schuyler to Smith, 25 February 1909, Smith Papers, UVA; Minutes, 6 February 1909, United Confederate Veterans, Camp Hampton, Richland County, Records, SCL; "That Prize Essay Criticized," CV 17 (February 1909): 56; Adelia A. Dunovant, "That Columbia College Prize Essay," CV 20 (July 1912): 341–44; clippings in Daybook, George H. Tichenor Papers, LSU; Scrapbook 7, Camp Beauregard, SCV Papers, LHAC, Tulane; "Daughters of Confederacy Here Adopt Resolutions," clipping with Celica P. McGowan to Smith, 15 February 1909 and Mrs. George B. Ketchum to Smith, 8 February 1909, Smith Papers, UVA; L. Virginia Tate to Col. Green, 14 March 1909 and C.N. Kessore to W.J. Green, 15 March 1909, Adeline E.B. Green Papers, Duke; Raleigh (N.C.) *News and Observer*, 31 January 1909; Mary Louisa Pace to Smith, 29 January 1909, Smith Papers, UVA.

20. F.P. Gamble to Smith, 24 February 1909, Smith Papers, UVA; "Open Letter of President E.A. Alderman to Mrs. Norman V. Randolph," clipping Richmond (Va.) *News Leader*, 4 February 1909, Alderman Papers, UVA.

21. *News and Observer*, 3 February 1909.

22. Chapel Hill UDC Resolution, 2 February 1909; Sallie Yate Faison to Smith, 3 February 1909; Mrs. Wm. B. Nix to Smith, 16 February 1909; Rebecca Cameron to Smith, 2 March 1909; Lionara R. Schuyler to Smith, 15 December 1908. All in Smith Papers, UVA. See Mrs. L.R. Schuyler, "That Teacher's College Prize Essay," CV 17 (January 1909): 39; "The Prize Essay, Columbia University," CV 17 (March 1909): 100–3, 106–9; "Last Words About The Prize Essay," CV 17 (April 1909): 157; *UDC Minutes*, 1909, pp. 57–58; Board of Visitors Minutes, University of Virginia, 23 March 1909, v. 8, p. 228, UVA; John H. Latane to Smith, 30 March 1909, Mims to Smith, 4 February 1909, Walter A. Montgomery to Smith, 17 February 1909, R.W.D. Connor to Smith, 3 February 1909, J.B. Crenshaw to Smith, 7 February 1909, E.L. Stephens to Smith, 12 February 1909—all in Smith Papers, UVA.

23. Enoch M. Banks, "A Semi-Centennial View of Secession," *Independent* 70 (February 1911): 299–303; "Free Speech Supprest," *Independent* 70 (April 1911): 807–8; *UDC Minutes*, 1911, pp. 323–24; James W. Garner, "The Dismissal of Professor Banks," *Independent* 70 (April 1911): 900.

24. William E. Eisenberg, *The First Hundred Years: Roanoke College, 1842–1942* (Salem, Va.: Trustees of Roanoke College, 1942), pp. 259–89; *New York Times*, 28 February 1911, pp. 1, 55; "Elson's Book: Slavery and Secession," clipping in Thaddeus K. Oglesby Papers, Duke; "Judge W.W. Moffett's Letter to the Public," CV 19 (June 1911): 273–75; "Daughters of the Confederacy at the College," CV 19 (August

1911): 365; "Salem (Va.) Daughters on Objectionable History," *CV* 20 (February 1912): 57.

25. Eisenberg, *First Hundred Years*, pp. 281–82, 285–88 contains the faculty's and president's statements. See also "Faculty of Roanoke College 'Defended,'" *CV* 19 (May 1911): 194–96; J.A. Morehead, "A Problem in Southern Education," *CV* 19 (July 1911): 317–19; and "Prof. Elson's Defense," offprint from New York, Boston, Philadelphia, and Chicago papers, in 1911, AG Lb, UCVA Papers, LSU.

26. "Defended," p. 195; "Judge Moffett Replies to Elson's Letter," *CV* 19 (September 1911): 413–14; "Roanoke College—The Elson Book," *CV* 19 (August 1911): 365; B.F. Grady, "Dealing with the Elson History," *CV* 19 (December 1911): 576; "North Carolinians on Elson History," *CV* 19 (August 1911): 404; "Reunion at Hinton, West Virginia," *CV* 19 (November 1911): 517; "Hypocrisy of the 'Elson History,'" *CV* 20 (March 1912): 103; Y.R.L. Monnier, "Duty of the Hour," 12 October 1911, in Association of the Army of Tennessee Papers, LHAC, Tulane; *UCV Minutes*, 1912, pp. 158–59, 1911, Appendix, pp. 11–14; *UDC Minutes*, 1911, pp. 28–31; *Minutes of the Annual Convention, Confederated Southern Memorial Association*, 1911, p. 17; *Proceedings of the Grand Camp Confederate Veterans, Department of Virginia*, 1911, pp. 37–38.

27. *UDC Minutes*, 1911, pp. 350–51; Rebecca Cameron to Hamilton, 13 and 28 June and 4 September 1911, Hamilton Papers, SHC; Hariet P. Lynch to Yates Snowden, 1 May 1911, Yates Snowden Papers, SCL. In unintended commentary on the entire affair, Lynch wrote: "I am curious to see Elson's history and I would be very glad to pay one of those poor boys you speak of, for his copy of the book when it is discarded." E.C. Barker to President S.E. Mezes (copy), 12 April 1911, Eugene C. Barker Letters, Archives Collection, UTX; *UDC Minutes*, 1911, p. 371.

28. George W. Littlefield to Barker, 15 April 1911, and Barker to Littlefield, 17 April 1911, Barker Letters, UTX; Barker to Littlefield, 5 December 1912, rough draft of letter clipped to the above, Barker to Littlefield, 28 April, 24 March, 1 April, 16 May 1914, 5 January 1916 (copy)—all in Barker-Littlefield Correspondence, Littlefield Holding Collection, UTX; "Resolution of Appreciation," *CV* 22 (July 1914): 332.

CONCLUSION

1. *Atlanta Constitution*, 16, 18, 19 May 1911.

2. Edwin A. Alderman to Woodrow Wilson, 22 November 1910, Edwin A. Alderman Papers, UVA; George B. Tindall, *The Emergence of the New South, 1913–1945* (Baton Rouge: Louisiana State University Press, 1967), pp. 1–3.

3. C. Irvine Walker, "Gray and Blue to Join Hands on the Field of Gettysburg," offprint, Charleston (S.C.) *The Sunday News*, 24 March 1912, in unnumbered cardboard box, United Confederate Veterans Association Papers, LSU; *UCV Minutes*, 1913, pp. 139–44; "Gettysburg, Gettysburg," *Confederate Veteran* 21 (August 1913): 377–86; Capt. McCulloch, "The High Tide at Gettysburg—By One of Pickett's Men," in *Reminiscences of the Women of Missouri During the Sixties*, comp. Missouri Division, United Daughters of the Confederacy (Jefferson City, Mo.: Hugh Stephens Printing Co., n.d.), pp. 298–308. See also W.H. Frazier, "The Aftermath of Gettysburg," in Mrs. Agatha (Abney) Woodson Papers, Duke; S.A. Cunningham, "Blue and Gray," *CV* 21 (February 1913): 54; Cunningham, "The South and the Veterans of Both Armies," *CV* 21 (October 1913): 472; "Fraternity Between Veterans," *CV* 21 (November 1913): 522, 556; John A. Simpson, "The Cult of the 'Lost Cause,'" *THQ* 34 (Winter 1975): 358–59. In 1914 a monument to the Confederate dead was unveiled in Arlington National Cemetery.

4. Joel Williamson, *The Crucible of Race: Black-White Relations in the American South Since Emancipation* (New York: Oxford University Press, 1984), p. 206; John E. White, *"My Old Confederate,"* pamphlet in Sons of Confederate Veterans Papers, AHS.

5. Reid Mitchell, "The Creation of Confederate Loyalties," in *New Perspectives on Race and Slavery in America: Essays in Honor of Kenneth M. Stampp*, Robert H. Abzug and Stephen E. Maizlisch, ed. (Lexington: The University of Kentucky Press, forthcoming); James R. Green, *Grass-Roots Socialism: Radical Movements in the Southwest, 1895–1943* (Baton Rouge: Louisiana State University Press, 1978), p. 146; Felton, *"My Memoirs of Georgia Politics,"* p. 169.

6. Lawrence Goodwyn, *The Populist Moment: A Short History of the Agrarian Revolt in America* (New York: Oxford University Press, 1978), p. 99. On what he calls the "great man" theory, see Melton A. McLaurin, *Paternalism and Protest: Southern Cotton Mill Workers and Organized Labor, 1875–1905* (Westport, Conn.: Greenwood Publishing Co., 1971), *passim*, but especially p. 55.

7. For treatments that seem to portray the Lost Cause as a trick or a delusion, see Evans, *Ballots and Fence Rails*, pp. 213–16; and Goodwyn, *Populist Moment*. Goodwyn, however, emphasizes the Lost Cause's cultural roots in the loss of the war in "Hierarchy and Democracy: The Paradox of the Southern Experience," in *From the Old South to the New: Essays on the Transitional South* (Westport, Conn.: Greenwood Press, 1981), pp. 226–39.

8. Chas. H. Scott to Jos. Bryan, 11 April 1908, Bryan Family Papers, VSL; *UDC Minutes*, 1911, pp. 313–14; Special Orders, No. 4 Louisiana Division, UCV, 22 April 1905, Adjutant General's Letterbox, UCVA Papers, LSU.

9. David Spence Hill, "Personification of Ideals by Urban Children," *Journal of Social Psychology* 1 (August 1930): 385; Raven I. McDavid, Jr., and Virginia G. McDavid, "The Late Unpleasantness: Folk Names for the Civil War," *Southern Speech Journal* 34 (Spring 1969): 194–204; Virginius Dabney, *The Last Review: The Confederate Reunion, Richmond, 1932* (Chapel Hill, N.C.: Algonquin Books, 1984); Thomas L. Connelly and Barbara L. Bellows, *God and General Longstreet: The Lost Cause and the Southern Mind* (Baton Rouge: Louisiana State University Press, 1982), pp. 113–17 (Connelly and Bellows, however, still think the memory of defeat important); John Shelton Reed, *Southerners: The Social Psychology of Sectionalism* (Chapel Hill: University of North Carolina Press, 1983), pp. 85–91.

10. Jack Temple Kirby, *Media-Made Dixie: The South in the American Imagination* (Baton Rouge: Louisiana State University Press, 1978); Edward D.C. Campbell, Jr., *The Celluloid South: Hollywood and the Southern Myth* (Knoxville: University of Tennessee Press, 1981); Fred C. Hobson, Jr., *Serpent in Eden: H.L. Mencken and the South* (Chapel Hill: University of North Carolina Press, 1974); Tindall, *Emergence*, pp. 210–18. Reed, *Southerners*, pp. 70–84 has an excellent discussion of continued defensiveness.

11. James McBride Dabbs, *The Southern Heritage* (New York: Alfred A. Knopf, 1958); C. Vann Woodward, *The Burden of Southern History* (New York: Random House, 1960). On conservative uses see Davis, "Johnny Reb in Perspective." Weaver, *The Southern Tradition at Bay*, is an attempt at using the tradition in the cause of a fundamentally conservative view of the modern world. See also Gerald DeMaio, "Richard Weaver, Southerner: The Paradox of American Conservatism," *Canadian Review of American Studies* 7 (Fall 1976): 179–96.

Appendix 1

Confederate Monuments Erected in the South, 1865–1912

Date of Dedication	Cemetery			In Town			Unknown			Total
	Funereal	Soldier	Unknown	Funereal	Soldier	Unknown	Funereal	Soldier	Unknown	
1865 to 1885	46	15	3	19	7	—	3	—	1	94
1886 to 1899	28	23	2	8	34	2	—	2	1	100
1900 to 1912	19	18	1	37	192	12	2	16	9	306
Unknown	4	2	3	—	16	3	1	1	14	44

The above statistics do not include statues to individuals, to southern women (all of which came after 1895), or those in the form of drinking fountains (also all of which came after 1895). In compiling the list I tried not to include plaques or boulders sometimes referred to as monuments, because they did not really seem to me to be public statuary or of equal importance as cultural artifacts. Since I found no complete list of Confederate monuments, I have compiled my own. It is surely incomplete, but I have no reason to suspect any particular bias in it. It was compiled from the following sources: all mention of monuments in the *Southern Historical Society Papers*, the *Confederate Veteran* magazine, and the United Daughters of the Confederacy minutes; books that offered pictures and information on Confederate monuments: Confederated Southern Memorial Association, *History of the Confederated Memorial Associations of the South* (New Orleans: Graham Press, 1904); Bettie A.C. Emerson, *Historic Southern Monuments: Representing Memorials of the Heroic Dead of the Southern Confederacy* (New York: Neale Publishing Company, 1911); and Ralph W. Widener, Jr., *Confederate Monuments: Enduring Symbols of the South and the War Between the States* (Washington: Andromedia, 1982); lists compiled by Confederate organizations: responses to a questionnaire on monuments, April 1, 1902, in AG Letterbox #5, United Confederate Veterans' Association Papers, LSU; Report of the Monument Committee, 11th Annual Reunion, United Sons of Confederate Veterans, 1906, in United Confederate Veterans' Papers, LHAC, Tulane; "Report of the Historian," *Minutes of the Annual Conventions, Confederated Southern Memorial Association*, 1914, pp. 19–21; and several state lists: *Proceedings of the Grand Camp Confederate Veterans, Department of Virginia*, 1906, pp. 31–32; "Confederate Monuments File," in box 7, Thomas M. Owen Papers, ADAH; "List of Monuments in Texas, (Incomplete)," in May Williams Pennington Papers, UTX; Richard W. Jones, "Confederate Cemeteries and Monuments in Mississippi," *Publications of the Mississippi Historical Society* 8 (1904): 87–119; "Confederate Monuments and Markers in South Carolina," compiled by Mrs. James Stuart Land under the auspices of the United Daughters of the Confederacy of South Carolina, 1955–58, SCL; Patricia F. Climer, "Protectors of the Past: The United Daughters of the Confederacy, Tennessee Division, and the Lost Cause" (M.A. thesis, Vanderbilt University, 1973), pp. 111–13.

Appendix 2

Occupational Structure of Selected Groups of Veterans

Category	Army of Tennessee Assn., New Orleans, La.[1]		Cheatham Bivouac, Nashville, Tenn.[2]		Lee Camp, Richmond, Va.[3]		Total veterans South, 1890[4]	
	Number	Percentage	Number	Percentage	Number	Percentage	Number	Percentage
Professional & high white-collar	96	20.38	140	30.7	137	24.08	33,474	28.47
Proprietary & low white-collar	224	47.56	174	38.16	248	43.59	25,117	21.36
Skilled craftsmen	117	24.84	110	24.12	136	23.90	41,741	35.50
Unskilled workers	34	7.22	32	7.02	48	8.44	17,236	14.66
Total non-farm (basis for percentage)	471	100.00	456	100.00	569	100.01[5]	117,568	99.99[5]
Agricultural sector	21	—	101	—	—	—	264,521	—
Unidentified	33	—	51	—	165	—	—	—
Total	525	—	608	—	734	—	382,089	—

[1] Compiled from Membership Applications, Association of the Army of Tennessee, LHAC, Tulane.

[2] Compiled from Membership Applications, Frank Cheatham Bivouac, United Confederate Veterans, Tennessee Division, Bivouac Records, TSL.

[3] Compiled by finding names from R.E. Lee Camp No. 1, Roster—April 1883–8 March 1918, Virginia State Library (only members who joined from 1884 to 1895 were identified) in Richmond city directories. Occupational ratings followed the tables in Theodore Hershberg and Robert Dockhorn, "Occupational Classification," *Historical Methods Newsletter* 9 (March–June 1976): 59–98. The agricultural sector was left out in all cases because of the difficulty of ranking types of farmers and planters when the camp records in both cases gave no more information than that. There were 16 planters and 5 farmers in the AAT records, 3 planters and 98 farmers in the Cheatham Records. (In addition, in the AAT 7 members listed "planter" along with some other occupation and were counted under the other occupation.)

[4] Compiled from "Soldiers and Widows," *Compendium of the Eleventh Census: 1890*, pt. 3, *Population* . . . (Washington: Government Printing Office, 1897), pp. 580–82.

[5] Percentage totals do not equal 100 due to rounding.

Appendix 3

Occupational Structure of Selected Groups of Sons of Confederate Veterans

Category	Army of Tennessee Assn., New Orleans, La. [1]			Frank Cheatham Bivouac, Nashville, Tenn. [2]			Camp Beauregard, New Orleans, La. [3]	
	Number	Percentage	(Percentage in Veterans)	Number	Percentage	(Percentage in Veterans)	Number	Percentage
Professional & high white-collar	14	12.39	(20.38)	3	10.00	(30.7)	87	21.01
Proprietary & low white-collar	83	73.45	(47.56)	21	70.00	(38.16)	259	62.56
Skilled craftsmen	13	11.50	(24.84)	5	16.67	(24.12)	63	15.22
Unskilled workers	3	2.66	(7.22)	1	3.33	(7.02)	5	1.21
Total non-farm (basis of percentage)	113	100.00	—	30	100.00	—	414	100.00
Agricultural sector	3	—	—	1	—	—	2	—
Students	14	—	—	6	—	—	39	—
Unidentified	3	—	—	7	—	—	18	—
Total	133			44			473	

[1] Compiled from membership applications, Sons of Confederate Veterans, Association of the Army of Tennessee Papers, LHAC, Tulane. Parent Camp percentages taken from Appendix 2.

[2] Compiled from membership applications, Frank Cheatham Camp, Sons of Confederate Veterans, Frank Cheatham Bivouac, United Confederate Veterans, Tennessee Division, Bivouac Records, TSL. Parent Camp percentages taken from Appendix 2.

[3] Compiled from membership applications, Camp Beauregard, Sons of Confederate Veterans Papers, LHAC, Tulane. There was no corresponding camp of veterans in this instance. Occupational ratings followed those used in Appendix 2. The agricultural sector was omitted to make closer comparison with the figures for the Veterans. However, in each camp the number of farmers and planters was dramatically lower than in the Veterans groups. Students were also not counted in the percentages because it is impossible to tell what sort of occupation they would eventually enter. A major classification problem that did not arise often with the Veterans undermines the reliability of the figures of the Sons. Many of them listed their occupation as "clerk," and I consistently treated it as a proprietary & low white-collar occupation. However, that decision is debatable. See Clyde Griffin, "Occupational Mobility in Nineteenth-Century America: Problems and Possibilities," *Journal of Social History* 5 (Spring 1972): 311.

Selected Bibliography

PRIMARY SOURCES

Manuscript Collections
The following list includes only those collections consulted in their entirety for the period 1865–1913; it excludes those used merely for individual letters or for a few items located through finding aids.
Alabama Department of Archives and History. Montgomery, Ala. (ADAH)
        Zillah (Haynie) Brandon Papers
        William Cooper Papers
        Walter L. Fleming Papers
        Bolling Hall Papers
        Julia L. Keyes Papers
        Ladies' Memorial Association of Perote, Minutes
        Mrs. Edward A. O'Neal Papers
        Thomas M. Owen Papers
Special Collections, University of Alabama Library. University, Ala. (UAL)
        Jefferson Davis Papers
        Augusta Evans Wilson Papers
Atlanta Historical Society. Atlanta, Ga. (AHS)
        Myrta Lockett Avary Papers
        Abbie M. Brooks Diaries
        Children of the Confederacy Records
        Ladies' Memorial Association Records
        Sons of Confederate Veterans Collection
        United Confederate Veterans Papers
Manuscript Department, William R. Perkins Library, Duke University. Durham, N.C. (Duke)
        P.G.T. Beauregard Papers
        Ulysses R. Brooks Papers
        Ellison Capers Papers
        Clement Claiborne Clay Papers

John Esten Cooke Papers
J.L.M. Curry Papers
John W. Daniel Papers
Jubal A. Early Papers
John A. Elder Papers
Clement A. Evans Papers
James L. Fleming Papers
John B. Gordon Papers
Adeline E.B. Davis Green Papers
John Berkley Grimball Papers
Daniel H. Hill Papers
Bradley T. Johnson Papers
Charles C. Jones, Jr., Papers
Charles Edgeworth Jones Papers
John McIntosh Kell Papers
James Longstreet Papers
William G. McCabe Papers
Lily McGee Papers
Dabney H. Maury Papers
Richard L. Maury Papers
William E. Mickle, Sr., Papers
Munford-Ellis Family Papers
Thaddeus K. Oglesby Papers
Benjamin W. Partridge Papers
Louisa B. and Mary B. Poppenheim Papers
Ella Gertrude Thomas Journal
United Confederate Veterans Papers
UDC, S.C. Division, Black Oak Chapter Minute Book, 1910–1915
UDC, S.C. Division, Edgefield Chapter Papers
Benjamin S. Williams Papers
Mrs. Agatha (Abney) Woodson Papers
Special Collections, University of Georgia Library. Athens, Ga. (GA)
United Confederate Veterans Papers
Joint Universities Library, Vanderbilt University. Nashville, Tenn. (JUL)
Frederick W. Moore Papers
Library of Congress. Washington, D.C. (LC)
James D. and David R. Barbee Papers
P.G.T. Beauregard Papers
Jabez L.M. Curry Papers
Jefferson Davis Papers (microfilm)
William E. Dodd Papers
Jubal A. Early Papers
Hampton Family Papers
Samuel Chiles Mitchell Papers
John S. Mosby Papers
Alfred Roman Papers
Manuscript Department, Hill Memorial Library, Louisiana State University. Baton Rouge, La. (LSU)
P.G.T. Beauregard Papers
Louis Bringier and Family Papers

Stephen Duncan Papers
William H. Ellis Papers
J.Y. Gilmore Papers
T.J. Goree Papers
Hennen-Jennings Papers
Andrew Hero, Jr., and George Hero Papers
Joseph Jones Papers
Jeptha McKinney Papers
Thomas R. Markham Papers
William M. and Allison Owen Papers
W.S. Rosecrans Selected Correspondence
William and Walter Stewart Papers
George H. Tichenor Diaries
United Confederate Veterans Association Papers (UCVA Records, boxes 1–10;
    Adjutant General's Letter Boxes, 1895–1912; Adjutant General's Letterpress
    Books, 1895–1904)
United Confederate Veterans Papers
United Confederate Veterans Scrapbooks
Edward C. Wharton and Family Papers

Mississippi Department of Archives and History. Jackson, Miss. (MDAH)
Anonymous Diary
Daughters of Confederate Veterans Papers
Jefferson Davis Papers (microfilm)
Samuel G. French Papers
Annie E. Harper Manuscript
Stephen D. Lee Papers
Lowry (Robert) -Jayne (J.M.) Family Papers
Robert Lowry Papers
Rev. James A. Lyon Journal
William H. McCardle Papers
Patrons Union Camp, UCV Papers
John L. Power Papers
Alfred Holt Stone Papers
Oscar J. Stuart and Family Papers
UCV Minutes, William Barksdale Camp #445, Kosciusko, Miss.
United Daughters of the Confederacy Papers
UDC, Charles Clark Chapter Scrapbook
UDC, Nathan Bedford Forrest Chapter
UDC, W.D. Holder Chapter
UDC, Frank M. Montgomery Chapter
William T. Walthall Papers

North Carolina Department of Archives and History. Raleigh, N.C. (NCDAH)
Ladies' Memorial Association of Wake County, General Records
Daniel H. Hill Papers
Lewis McDaniel Papers
United Confederate Veterans. Records of Richmond County Camp #830 and of
    W.F. Martin Camp #1590
United Daughters of the Confederacy. General James Johnston Pettigrew
    Chapter, Raleigh.

South Carolina Historical Society. Charleston, S.C. (SCHS)

    Julian Mitchell Papers

    Ladies' Memorial Association of Charleston (Minutes, 1866–1916)

    Survivors' Association Papers

South Caroliniana Library, University of South Carolina. Columbia, S.C. (SCL)

    David W. Aiken Papers

    Matthew C. Butler Papers

    Records of Camp Henry Buist, Sons of Confederate Veterans, Charleston, S.C.

    Ellison Capers Papers

    Confederate Monuments and Markers in South Carolina, Complied by Mrs. James Stuart Land under the auspices of the UDC of South Carolina, 1955–58

    Hampton Family Papers

    Paul H. Hayne Papers

    Joshua H. Hudson Papers

    Jefferson Davis Memorial Association, Fort Mill, Records.

    Ellison S. Keitt Papers

    McGrady Family Papers

    Marshal McGraw Papers

    Colyer Meriwether Papers

    Jane Mikell Papers

    T. Waring Mikell Papers

    Peter J. Shand Papers

    Mary A. Snowden Papers

    Yates Snowden Papers

    UCV, Camp Hampton, Richland County, 1887–1894 Records

    UCV, Richard Kirkland Camp, Camden, Records

    UCV, Abner Perrin Camp (Edgefield, S.C.) Records

    United Confederate Veterans, S.C. Division, Charleston, General and Special Orders, 1895–1902

    UDC, Marion Chapter Record Book

    Thomas S. Waring Papers

    George A. Wauchope Papers

    Young Ladies' Hospital Association, Columbia, Records

Southern Historical Collection, University of North Carolina Library. Chapel Hill, N.C. (SHC)

    Edward P. Alexander Papers

    Edward C. Anderson Diary

    Garnett Andrews Papers

    Lillie V. Archbell Papers

    Alphonso C. Avery Papers

    George S. Barnsley Papers

    Berry G. Benson Papers

    George S. Bernard Papers

    Annie L. (Harris) Broidrick Recollections

    Anne Bruin Scrapbook

    Catherine B. Broun Diary

    Armistead Burwell Papers

    Mrs. Marion Butler Papers

    Campbell-Colston Papers

    John L.P. Cantwell Papers

Julian Shakespeare Carr Papers
Laura Comer Diary
Confederate Sketches
Sumner Archibald Cunningham Papers
Charles W. Dabney Papers
William Porcher DuBose Reminiscences
Habersham Elliott Papers
John R. Ficklen Papers
Josiah Gorgas Journal
R.M. Gray Reminiscences
John Berkley Grimball Diary
Journal of Meta Morris Grimball
Daniel H. Hill Papers
Bartlett S. Johnston Papers
Ladies' Memorial Association Papers
Stephen D. Lee Papers
Walter H. Lee Scrapbooks
Samuel H. Lockett Papers
James Longstreet Papers
Stephen R. Mallory Papers
George A. Martin Papers
George A. Mercer Diary
James I. Metts Papers
Samuel Chiles Mitchell Papers
Elvira E. Moffitt Papers
Martin V. Moore Papers
John R. Peacock Papers
William Nelson Pendleton Papers
John Perkins Papers
John A. Ramsay Papers
Edward P. Reeve Papers (microfilm)
Franklin L. Riley Papers
William A. Shaffer Papers
Alfred Moore Waddell Papers
Richard W. Waldrop Diary
Marcus J. Wright Papers
Tennessee State Library. Nashville, Tenn. (TSL)
Collins D. Elliot Papers
UCV, Tennessee Division, Bivouac Records
Archives Collection, University of Texas. Austin, Tex. (UTX)
Henry G. Askew Papers
Guy M. Bryan Papers
Eugene C. Barker Letters
Barker-Littlefield Correspondence, Littlefield Holding Collection
Thomas T. Gordon Reminiscences
William W. Heartstill Diary
George W. Littlefield Papers
John B. Long Papers
William E. Mickle Letterbook

      Williamson S. Oldham Papers
      May Williams Pennington Papers
      John H. Reagan Papers
      UDC, Austin's Albert Sidney Johnston Chapter, 1904–1914
Manucript Department, Howard-Tilton Memorial Library, Tulane University. New Orleans, La. (Tulane)
      Behan Family Papers
      Daisy Hodgson Papers
      Joseph Jones Papers
Louisiana Historical Association Collection
      Association of the Army of Northern Virginia Papers
      Association of the Army of Tennessee Papers
      J.A. Chalaron Papers
      J.A. Harral Papers
      Memorial Association Papers
      Other Veterans' Organizations Papers
      United Confederate Veterans' Papers
      United Daughters of the Confederacy Papers
      United Sons of Confederate Veterans' Papers
      Veteran Confederate States Cavalry Association Papers
      George Moorman Scrapbooks
Union Theological Seminary Library. Richmond, Va. (UTSL)
      Robert L. Dabney Correspondence
      Moses D. Hoge Correspondence
U.S. Army Military History Institute. Carlisle Barracks, Pa. (MHI)
      Spanish-American War Archive (southern units)
Manucripts Department, Alderman Library, University of Virginia. Charlottesville, Va. (UVA)
      Edwin A. Alderman Papers
      Albert T. Bledsoe Papers
      John H. Claiborne Papers
      John W. Daniel Papers
      J. Taylor Ellyson Papers
      Benjamin W. Jones Papers
      Ledger and Minutes of the Virginia Division of the Association of the Army of Northern Virginia, 1871–1894, in Items from Cooper's Old Book Store, Richmond
      John S. Mosby Papers
Virginia Historical Society. Richmond, Va. (VHS)
      Barron Family Papers
      Confederate Memorial Association of Spotsylvania County, Va.
      Holmes Conrad Papers
      Early Family Papers
      Fitzhugh Lee Monumental Association
      Garnett Family Papers
      Basil B. Gordon Papers
      Gregory Family Papers
      Eppa Hunton Papers
      Alexander C. Jones Papers

Robert Edward Lee Letterbook, Lee Family Papers
Henry B. McClellan Papers
Hunter Holmes McGuire Papers
John S. Mosby Papers
Pegram Family Papers
Charles Pickett Papers
R.E. Lee Camp No. 1, Records, UCV, Richmond (Minutes, 1884–1915; Reunion File, 1907)
Southern Historical Society Records
Talcott Family Papers
UCV, L.A. Armistead Camp No. 26, (Meklenburg Co., Va.) Minute Book
UCV, Urquhart-Gillette Camp No. 1611 (Franklin, Va.) Records
UDC, Grand Division of Virginia, Minutes
UDC, Virginia Division, Minutes
Walter A. Watson Papers

Virginia State Library. Richmond, Va. (VSL)
Cornelius H. Carlton Diary
Confederate Records from the Battle Abbey
Mary B. Goodwin Diary and Papers
Grand Camp Confederate Veterans, Department of Virginia Records
J. William Jones Papers
Henry T. Owen Papers
William H. Payne Papers
Peagram Battalion Association, City of Richmond, Minute Book
Margaret M. Pennybacker Reminiscences
Mrs. Archibald Campbell Pryor Recollections
R.E. Lee Camp No. 1, Roster
Records of the Memorial Society of the Ladies of the City of Petersburg, 1866–1912
Emma Wood Richardson, Civil War Reminiscence

Published Letters, Diaries, and Speeches

Abbott, Martin, ed. "A Southerner Views the South, 1865: Letters of Harvey M. Watterson." *Virginia Magazine of History and Biography* 68 (October 1960): 478–89.

Anderson, John Q., ed. *Brokenburn: The Journal of Kate Stone, 1861–1868.* Baton Rouge: Louisiana State University Press, 1972.

Avary, Myrta L., ed. *Recollections of Alexander H. Stephens: His Diary Kept When a Prisoner at Fort Warren, Boston Harbor, 1865. . . .* New York: Doubleday, Page & Company, 1910.

Daniel, Edward M., comp. *Speeches and Orations of John Warwick Daniel.* Lynchburg, Va.: J.P. Bell Company, 1911.

Dawson, Sarah Morgan. *A Confederate Girl's Diary.* James I. Robertson, Jr., ed. Bloomington: Indiana University Press, 1960.

Durkin, Joseph T., ed. *John Dooley, Confederate Soldier: His War Journal.* Washington: Georgetown University Press, 1945.

Eppes, Susan Bradford. *Through Some Eventful Years.* Macon: J.W. Burke Company, 1926.

Fleet, Betsy, ed. *Green Mount After the War: The Correspondence of Maria Louisa*

Wacker Fleet and Her Family, 1865–1900. Charlottesville: University Press of Virginia, 1978.

Green, Anna Maria. *The Journal of a Milledgeville Girl, 1861–1867.* James C. Bonner, ed. Athens: University of Georgia Press, 1964.

Hoge, Peyton H. *Moses Drury Hoge: Life and Letters.* Richmond, Va.: Presbyterian Committee of Publication, 1899.

Holt, W. Stull, ed. *Historical Scholarship in the United States, 1876–1901: As Revealed in the Correspondence of Herbert B. Adams. Studies in Historical and Political Science.* Vol. 56, No. 4. Baltimore: The Johns Hopkins University Press, 1938.

Johnson, Thomas Cary. *The Life and Letters of Benjamin Morgan Palmer.* Richmond: Presbyterian Committee of Publication, 1906.

LeConte, Emma. *When the World Ended: The Diary of Emma LeConte.* Earl S. Miers, ed. New York: Oxford University Press, 1957.

Moger, Allen W., ed. "Letters to General Lee After the War." *Virginia Magazine of History and Biography* 64 (January 1956): 30–69.

Moore, John P., ed. *"My Ever Dearest Friend:" The Letters of A. Dudley Mann to Jefferson Davis, 1869–1889.* Tuscaloosa: Confederate Publishing Company, 1960.

Rowland, Dunbar, ed. *Jefferson Davis: Constitutionalist: His Letters, Papers, and Speeches.* Jackson: Mississippi Department of Archives and History, 1923.

Shurter, Edwin D., ed. *Oratory of the South: From the Civil War to the Present Time.* New York: Neale Publishing Company, 1908.

Strode, Hudson, ed. *Jefferson Davis: Private Letters, 1823–1889.* New York: Harcourt, Brace, & World, 1966.

Watterson, Henry. *The Compromises of Life, and Other Lectures and Addresses, Including Some Observations on Certain Downward Tendencies of Modern Society.* New York: Fox, Duffield, & Company, 1903.

Minutes of Organizations

Addresses Delivered Before the Confederate Survivors' Association in Augusta, Georgia, at its Annual Meetings on Memorial Day. 1878–1897.

Minutes of the Annual Convention, Confederated Southern Memorial Association. 1900–1914.

Minutes of the Annual Meetings and Reunions of the United Confederate Veterans. 1891–1915.

Minutes of the Annual Meetings of the United Daughters of the Confederacy. 1895–1915.

Minutes of the Annual Meetings of the United Sons of Confederate Veterans. 1903, 1905–1908.

Minutes, United Confederate Veterans Camp #941, Wilson County, Tennessee. Thomas E. Partlow, ed. Baltimore: Gateway Press, 1975.

Orders, U.C.V., General and Special. William E. Mickle, ed. 2 vols. New Orleans: United Confederate Veterans, 1911–12.

Proceedings of the Grand Camp Confederate Veterans, Department of Virginia. 1894–1915.

The Proceedings of the Southern Historical Convention, Which Assembled at the Montgomery White Sulphur Springs, Va. on the 14th of August, 1873, and of the Southern Historical Society, as Reorganized, with the Address by Gen. Jubal A. Early, delivered before the Convention on the First Day of its Session. Baltimore: Turnbull Brothers, n.d.

Memorial Volumes

Benson, C.H. *"Yank and Reb,"* A History of a Fraternal Visit Paid by Lincoln Post, No. 11, GAR of Newark, N.J. Newark: M.H. Neuhut, Printer, 1884.

Confederated Southern Memorial Association. *History of the Confederated Memorial Associations of the South.* New Orleans: Graham Press, 1904.

Cowan, John F. *A New Invasion of the South. Being a Narrative of the Expedition of the Seventy-First Infantry, National Guard, Through the Southern States, to New Orleans, February 24-March 7, 1881.* New York: Board of Officers, Seventy-First Infantry, 1881.

Emerson, Mrs. Bettie A.C. *Historic Southern Monuments. Representative Memorials of the Heroic Dead of the Southern Confederacy.* New York: Neale Publishing Company, 1911.

Gosson, Louis C. *Post-Bellum Campaigns of the Blue and Gray, 1881–1882.* Trenton: Naar, Day & Naar, Printers, 1882.

A History of the Origin of Memorial Day as Adopted by the Ladies' Memorial Association of Columbus, Georgia. Columbus: Thos. Gilbert, Printer & Manufacturing Stationeer, 1898.

Jones, J. William. *Personal Reminiscences, Anecdotes, and Letters of Gen. Robert E. Lee.* New York: D. Appleton and Company, 1875.

Mathes, J. Harvey. *The Old Guard in Gray: Researches in the Annals of the Confederate Historical Association.* Memphis: Press of S.C. Toof & Co., 1897.

Poppenheim, Mary B., et al. *The History of the United Daughters of the Confederacy.* Raleigh, N.C.: Edwards and Broughton, 1925.

Richey, Homer, ed. *Memorial History of the John Bowie Strange Camp, United Confederate Veterans.* Charlottesville, Va.: Michie Company, 1920.

Roster and Historical Sketch of A.P. Hill Camp, CV, No. 6, Va. Petersburg, Va.: N.p., 1914 [?].

Underwood, J.L. *The Women of the Confederacy.* N.p.: By the author, n.d.

Memoirs

Alexander, John B. *Reminiscences of the Past Sixty Years.* Charlotte: Ray Printing, 1908.

Andrews, Eliza F. *The War-Time Journal of a Georgia Girl, 1864–1865.* Spencer B. King, Jr., ed. Macon: Ardivan Press, 1960.

Andrews, Mrs. Marietta M. *Memoirs of a Poor Relation.* New York: E.P. Dutton and Company, 1927.

Barringer, Paul B. *The Natural Bent: The Memoirs of Dr. Paul B. Barringer.* Chapel Hill: University of North Carolina Press, 1949.

Clay-Clopton, Virginia. *A Belle of the Fifties.* New York: Doubleday, Page & Company, 1905.

Daniel, F.E. *Recollections of a Rebel Surgeon (And Other Sketches) Or, In the Doctor's Sappy Days.* Austin, Tex.: Von Boeckmann, Schutze, & Co., 1899.

Duke, Basil W. *A History of Morgan's Cavalry.* Edited by Cecil F. Holland. Bloomington: Indiana University Press, 1960.

_____. *Reminiscences of General Basil W. Duke, CSA.* Garden City, N.Y.: Doubleday, Page & Company, 1911.

Early, Jubal A. *A Memoir of the Last Year of the War for Independence of the Confederate States of America.* New Orleans: Blelock and Co., 1867.

Early, R.H., ed. *Lieutenant General Jubal Anderson Early, C.S.A.: Autobiographical*

    Sketch and Narrative of the War Between the States. Philadelphia: J.B. Lippincott Company, 1912.

Felton, Rebecca L. *"My Memoirs of Georgia Politics."* Atlanta: Index Printing Company, 1911.

Fletcher, William A. *Rebel Private: Front and Rear*. Bell I. Wiley, ed. Austin, Tex.: University of Texas Press, 1954.

Gordon, John B. *Reminiscences of the Civil War*. New York: Charles Scribner's Sons, 1903.

Green, Wharton J. *Recollections and Reflections: An Autobiography of Half a Century and More*. Raleigh, N.C.: Edwards and Broughton Printing Company, 1906.

Harrison, Mrs. Burton. *Recollections Grave and Gay*. New York: Charles Scribner's Sons, 1911.

Heth, Henry. *The Memoirs of Henry Heth*. James L. Morrison, Jr., ed. Westport, Conn.: Greenwood Press, 1974.

Hood, John B. *Advance and Retreat: Personal Experiences in the United and Confederate State Armies*. Richard N. Current, ed. Bloomington: Indiana University Press, 1959.

Kearney, Belle. *A Slaveholder's Daughter*. New York: Abbey Press, 1900.

Lamar, Dolly Blount. *When All Is Said and Done*. Athens: University of Georgia Press, 1952.

Lee, Susan Pendleton. *Memoirs of William Nelson Pendleton, D.D.* Philadelphia: J.B. Lippincott, 1893.

Lewisohn, Ludwig. *Up Stream, An American Chronicle*. New York: Boni and Liveright, 1922.

Longstreet, Helen D. *Lee and Longstreet at High Tide: Gettysburg in Light of the Official Records*. Gainesville, Ga.: By the Author, 1905.

Longstreet, James. *From Manassas to Appomattox: Memoirs of the Civil War in America*. Philadelphia: J.B. Lippincott Company, 1896.

Lumpkin, Katharine Du Pre. *The Making of a Southerner*. New York: Alfred A. Knopf, 1947.

McDonald, Cornelia. *A Diary with Reminiscences of the War and Refugee Life In the Shenandoah Valley, 1860–65*. Nashville, Tenn.: Cullom and Ghertner, 1935.

Maury, Dabney H. *Recollections of a Virginian in the Mexican, Indian and Civil Wars*. New York: Charles Scribner's Sons, 1894.

Meriwether, Elizabeth A. *Recollections of 92 Years: 1824–1916*. Nashville: Tennessee Historical Commission, 1958.

Merrick, Caroline E. *Old Times in Dixie Land: A Southern Matron's Memories*. New York: Grafton Press, 1901.

Missouri Division, UDC., comp. *Reminiscences of the Women of Missouri During the Sixties*. Jefferson City, Mo.: Hugh Stephens Printing Co., n.d.

Montgomery, Frank A. *Reminiscences of a Mississippian in Peace and War*. Cincinnati: Robert Clarke Company, 1901.

Morgan, James M. *Recollections of a Rebel Reefer*. Boston: Houghton Mifflin Company, 1917.

O'Ferrall, Charles T. *Forty Years of Active Service*. New York: Neale Publishing Company, 1904.

Pember, Phoebe Y. *A Southern Woman's Story*. New York: G.W. Carlton & Company, 1879.

Percy, William Alexander. *Lanterns on the Levee: Recollections of a Planter's Son*. New York: Alfred A. Knopf, 1941.

Pryor, Sara. *Reminiscences of Peace and War.* New York: Macmillan Company, 1904.

Reagan, John H. *Memoirs With Special Reference to Secession and the Civil War.* Austin and New York: Pamberton Press, 1968.

Rice, John A. *I Came Out of the Eighteenth Century.* New York: Harper and Brothers, 1942.

Richardson, Simon P. *The Lights and Shadows of Itinerant Life: An Autobiography.* Nashville, Tenn.: Publishing House, Methodist Episcopal Church, South, 1901.

Snyder, Henry Nelson. *An Educational Odyssey.* Nashville, Tenn.: Abingdon-Cokesbury Press, 1947.

Taylor, Richard. *Destruction and Reconstruction: Personal Experiences of the Late War.* Richard B. Harwell, ed. New York: Longmans, Green, and Company, 1955.

Watterson, Henry. *"Marse Henry," An Autobiography.* 2 vols. New York: George H. Doran Company, 1919.

Williams, Jim C. *Civil War Records and a Trip to Macon, Ga.* Lewisville, Tex.: Enterprise Job Department, n.d.

Wilmer, Richard H. *The Recent Past from a Southern Standpoint, Reminiscences of a Grandfather.* New York: Thomas Whittaker, 1887.

Wise, John S. *The End of an Era.* Curtis C. Davis, ed. New York: Thomas Yoseloff, 1965.

Withers, Robert E. *Autobiography of an Octogenarian.* Roanoke, Va.: Stone Printing & Manufacturing Company, 1907.

Contemporary Commentaries and Histories

Avary, Myrta L. *Dixie After the War.* New York: Doubleday, Page & Company, 1906.

Bledsoe, Albert Taylor. *Is Davis a Traitor: Or was Secession a Constitutional Right Previous to the War of 1861?* Baltimore: For the author by Innes & Company, 1866.

Cockerill, John A. [Hampton, Randolph G.]. *The Major in Washington City: A Series of Timely Letters from a Strict Southern Standpoint.* New York: Morning Advertiser, 1893.

Cussons, John. [A Confederate Soldier]. *United States 'History' as the Yankee Makes and Takes It.* Glen Allen, Va.: Cussons, May, & Company, 1900.

Dabney, Robert L. *A Defense of Virginia, (And Through Her, of the South) in Recent and Pending Contests Against the Sectional Party.* New York: E.J. Hale & Son, 1867.

Davis, Jefferson. *The Rise and Fall of the Confederate Government.* 2 vols. New York: D. Appleton and Company, 1881.

Grady, Henry. *The New South: Writings and Speeches of Henry Grady.* Edited by Mills Lane. Savannah, Ga.: Beehive Press, 1971.

Langhorne, Orra. *Southern Sketches from Virginia, 1881–1901.* Charles E. Wynes, ed. Charlottesville: University Press of Virginia, 1964.

Moore, John H., ed. *The Juhl Letters to the Charleston Courier: A View of the South, 1865–1871.* Athens: University of Georgia Press, 1974.

Newton, John C.C. *The New South and the Methodist Episcopal Church.* Baltimore: King Brothers, 1887.

Page, Walter Hines. *The Southerner; A Novel; Being the Autobiography of Nicholas Worth [pseud.].* New York: Doubleday, Page, & Company, 1909.

Pollard, Edward A. *The Lost Cause: A New Southern History of the War of the Confederates.* New York: E.B. Treat, 1866.

Smith, Charles H. *Bill Arp: From the Uncivil War to Date, 1861–1903.* Memorial Edition. Atlanta: Hudgins Publishing Company, 1903.

———. *Bill Arp's Peace Papers.* New York: G.W. Carleton & Co., 1873.

———. *Bill Arp's Scrap Book: Humor and Philosophy.* Atlanta: Jas. P. Harrison & Co., 1884.

Stephens, Alexander H. *A Constitutional View of the Late War Between the States: Its Causes, Character, Conduct and Results Presented in a Series of Colloquies at Liberty Hill.* 2 vols. Philadelphia: National Publishing Company, 1868–70.

Steel, S.A. *The South Was Right.* Columbia, S.C.: R.L. Bryan Company, 1914.

Trent, William P. *William Gilmore Simms.* Boston: Houghton Mifflin Company, 1892.

Turner, Arlin, ed. *The Negro Question: A Selection of Writings on Civil Rights in the South by George W. Cable.* Garden City, N.Y.: Doubleday and Company, 1958.

Travelers' Accounts

Abel, Emily K., ed. "A Victorian Views Reconstruction: The American Diary of Samuel Augustus Barnett." *Civil War History* 20 (June 1974): 135–56.

Campbell, Sir George. *White and Black: The Outcome of a Visit to the United States.* London: Chatto & Windus, 1879.

Carter, Joseph C., ed. *Magnolia Journey: A Union Veteran Revisits the Former Confederate States. Arranged from Letters of Correspondent Russell H. Conwell to the Daily Evening Traveller (Boston, 1869).* University: University of Alabama Press, 1974.

Conser, Solomon L.M. *Virginia After the War. An Account of Three Years' Experience in Reorganizing the Methodist Episcopal Church in Virginia at the Close of the Civil War.* Indianapolis: Baker-Randolph Litho. & Eng., 1891.

De Forest, John W. *A Union Officer in the Reconstruction.* James H. Croushore and David M. Potter, eds. New Haven: Yale University Press, 1948.

Dennett, John R. *The South As It Is: 1865–1866.* Henry M. Christman, ed. New York: Viking Press, 1965.

Greeley, Horace. *Mr. Greeley's Letters from Texas and the Lower Mississippi. . . .* New York: Tribune Office, 1871.

Hardy, Lady Duffus. *Down South.* London: Chapman and Hall, 1883.

Hart, Albert Bushnell. *The Southern South.* New York: D. Appleton and Company, 1910.

James, Henry. *The American Scene.* London: Chapman and Hall, 1907.

Kennaway, Sir John H. *On Sherman's Track; or, the South after the War.* London: Seeley, Jackson, and Halliday, 1867.

King, Edward. *The Great South.* W. Magruder Drake and Robert R. Jones, eds. Baton Rouge: Louisiana State University Press, 1972.

McClure, Alexander K. *The South: Its Industrial, Financial, and Political Condition.* Philadelphia: J.B. Lippincott, 1886.

Macrae, David. *The Americans at Home.* New York: E.P. Dutton, 1952.

———. *America Revisited and Men I Have Met.* Glasgow: J. Smith & Son, 1908.

Morgan, Albert T. *Yazoo: Or, On the Picket Line of Freedom in the South. A Personal Narrative.* Washington: Published by the author, 1884.

Muir, John. *A Thousand-Mile Walk to the Gulf.* Boston: Houghton Mifflin Company, 1916.

Nordhoff, Charles. *The Cotton States in the Spring and Summer of 1875.* New York: Burt Franklin, 1966.

Prentis, Noble L. *Southern Letters*. Topeka, Kans.: George W. Martin, Kansas
    Publishing House, 1881.
Ralph, Julian: *Dixie, Or, Southern Scenes and Sketches*. New York: Harper & Brothers,
    1896.
Sherman, Ernest A. *Dedicating in Dixie*. Cedar Rapids, Ia.: Record Printing Company,
    1907.
Somers, Robert. *The Southern States Since the War, 1870–1871*. Malcolm C. McMil-
    lan, ed. University: University of Alabama Press, 1965.
Street, Julian L. *American Adventures: A Second Trip "Abroad at Home."* New York:
    Century Company, 1917.
Stearns, Charles. *The Black Man of the South and the Rebels*. New York: American News
    Company, 1872.
Trowbridge, J.T. *The South: A Tour of its Battle-Fields and Ruined Cities, A Journey
    Through the Desolated States, and Talks With the People*. Hartford, Conn.: L.
    Stebbins, 1866.
Warner, Charles Dudley. *Studies in the South and West, With Comments on Canada*.
    New York: Harper and Brothers, 1889.

Magazines and Articles
Confederate Veteran, Nashville, 1893–1915.
The Land We Love, Charlotte, N.C., 1866–1869.
Our Living and Our Dead, New Bern, N.C., 1873–1874; n.s., Raleigh, 1874–1876.
Publications of the Southern History Association, Washington, D.C., 1897–1907.
The Sewanee Review, Nashville, 1892–1915.
The South Atlantic Quarterly, Durham, N.C., 1902–1915.
The Southern Bivouac, Louisville, 1882–1885; n.s., 1885–1887.
Southern Historical Society Papers, Richmond, 1876–1915.
The Southern Magazine, Baltimore, 1871–1875.
The Southern Review, Baltimore, 1867–1881.
Atkinson, Edward. "Significant Aspects of the Atlanta Cotton Exposition." *Century
    Magazine* 23 (February 1882): 563–74.
Banks, Enoch M. "A Semi-Centennial View of Secession." *Independent* 70 (April 1911):
    299–303.
Dodd, William E. "The Status of History in Southern Education." *Nation* 75 (August
    1902): 109–11.
Doughty, Frances A. "Life in the Cotton Belt." *Lippincott's Monthly Magazine* 59 (May
    1897): 687–94.
Evans, Clement A. "General Gordon and General Longstreet." *Independent* 56 (Febru-
    ary 1904): 311–16.
Ferrell, Chiles C. "The Daughter of the Confederacy: Her Life, Character and Writings."
    Publications of the Mississippi Historical Society 2 (1899): 69–84.
Glasson, William G. "The South's Care for Her Confederate Veterans." *Review of
    Reviews* 36 (July 1907): 40–47.
———. "The South's Pension and Relief Provisions for the Soldiers of the Confederacy."
    *Proceedings of the Eighteenth Annual Session of the State Literary and Historical
    Association of North Carolina*. Bulletin of the N.C. Historical Commission. No.
    23. Raleigh: Edwards & Broughton, 1918.
Harris, Mrs. L.H. "The Confederate Veteran." *Independent* 53 (October 1901): 2357–58.
Hill, D.H. "The Real Stonewall Jackson." *Century* 47 (February 1894): 623–28.
Kilmer, George L. "A Note of Peace." *Century* 36 (July 1888): 440–42.

Moore, Frederick W., et al. "The Teaching of History in the South: A Report." *School Review* 11 (February 1903): 107–22.

Owen, Edward. "The Confederate Veterans' Camp of New York." *National Magazine* 16 (August 1892) 455, 480.

Page, Walter Hines. "The Rebuilding of Old Commonwealths." *Atlantic Monthly* 89 (May 1902): 651–61.

_____. "Study of an Old Southern Borough." *Atlantic Monthly* 47 (May 1881): 648–58.

Pollard, Edward A. "Stonewall Jackson—An Historical Study." *Putnam's Magazine* 2 (December 1868): 733–40.

Riley, Franklin L. "Is State History Worth While?" *History Teachers' Magazine* 2 (March 1911): 156–57.

Rose, Duncan. "Why the Confederacy Failed." *Century* 53 (November 1896): 33–38.

A South Carolinian [Townsend, Belton O'Neall]. "The Political Condition of South Carolina." *Atlantic Monthly* 39 (January 1877): 177–94.

_____. "South Carolina Morals." *Atlantic Monthly* 39 (April 1877): 467–75.

_____. "South Carolina Society." *Atlantic Monthly* 39 (June 1877): 670–84.

Tillett, Wilbur F. "Southern Womanhood as Affected by the War." *Century* 43 (November 1891): 9–16.

Trent, William P. "Dominant Forces in Southern Life." *Atlantic Monthly* 79 (January 1897): 42–53.

_____. "Notes on Recent Work in Southern History." *Collections of the Virginia Historical Society* n. s. 11 (1892): 49–59.

_____. "Tendencies of Higher Life in the South." *Atlantic Monthly* 79 (June 1897): 766–78.

"The Unveiling of the Lee Statue." *Public Opinion* 9 (June 1890): 189–92.

Watterson, Henry. "Oddities of Southern Life." *Century* 23 (April 1882): 884–95.

Weems, Albert G. "Work of the United Daughters of the Confederacy." *Publications of the Mississippi Historical Society* 4 (1901): 73–78.

SECONDARY SOURCES

Books

Alderman, Edwin A. and Gordon, Armistead C. *J.L.M. Curry: A Biography*. New York: Macmillan Company, 1911.

Braden, Waldo W., ed. *Oratory in the New South*. Baton Rouge: Louisiana State University Press, 1979.

Buck, Paul H. *The Road to Reunion, 1865–1900*. Boston: Little, Brown and Company, 1937.

Bushong, Millard K. *Old Jube: A Biography of General Jubal A. Early*. Boyce, Va.: Carr Publishing Company, 1955.

Carlton, David L. *Mill and Town in South Carolina, 1880–1920*. Baton Rouge: Louisiana State University Press, 1982.

Clark, Thomas D. *The Rural Press and the New South*. Baton Rouge: Louisiana State University Press, 1948.

_____. *The Southern Country Editor*. Indianapolis: Bobbs-Merrill Company, 1948.

Clayton, Bruce. *The Savage Ideal: Intolerance and Intellectual Leadership in the South, 1890–1914*. Baltimore: The Johns Hopkins University Press, 1972.

Connelly, Thomas L. *The Marble Man: Robert E. Lee and His Image in American Society*. New York: Alfred A. Knopf, 1977.

Cooper, John M., Jr. *Walter Hines Page: The Southerner as American, 1855–1918.* Chapel Hill: University of North Carolina Press, 1977.

Cooper, William J., Jr. *The Conservative Regime: South Carolina, 1877–1890.* Baltimore: The Johns Hopkins University Press, 1968.

Dallek, Robert. *Democrat and Diplomat: The Life of William E. Dodd.* New York: Oxford University Press, 1968.

Davies, Wallace E. *Patriotism on Parade: The Story of Veterans' and Hereditary Organizations in America, 1783–1900.* Cambridge: Harvard University Press, 1955.

Davis, Michael. *The Image of Lincoln in the South.* Knoxville: University of Tennessee Press, 1971.

Dearing, Mary R. *Veterans in Politics: The Story of the G.A.R.* Baton Rouge: Louisiana State University Press, 1952.

Dyer, John P. *"Fightin' Joe" Wheeler.* Baton Rouge: Louisiana State University Press, 1941.

Evans, W. McKee. *Ballots and Fence Rails: Reconstruction on the Lower Cape Fear.* New York: W.W. Norton and Company, 1966.

Farish, Hunter D. *The Circuit Rider Dismounts: A Social History of Southern Methodism, 1865–1900.* Richmond: Dietz Press, 1938.

Fishwick, Marshall W. *Lee After the War.* New York: Dodd, Mead, & Company, 1963.

Freeman, Douglas Southall. *R.E. Lee: A Biography.* Vol. 4. New York: Charles Scribner's Sons, 1935.

———. *The South to Posterity: An Introduction to the Writing of Confederate History.* New York: Charles Scribner's Sons, 1939.

Gaston, Paul M. *The New South Creed: A Study in Southern Mythmaking.* New York: Alfred A. Knopf, 1970.

Gillette, William. *Retreat from Reconstruction, 1869–1879.* Baton Rouge: Louisiana State University Press, 1979.

Goodwyn, Lawrence. *Democratic Promise: The Populist Moment in America.* New York: Oxford University Press, 1976.

Hair, William I. *Bourbonism and Agrarian Protest: Louisiana Politics, 1877–1906.* Baton Rouge: Louisiana State University Press, 1969.

Hall, Wade. *The Smiling Phoenix: Southern Humor From 1865 to 1914.* Gainesville: University of Flordia Press, 1965.

Hammett, Hugh B. *Hilary Abner Herbert: A Southerner Returns to the Union.* Philadelphia: American Philosophical Society, 1976.

Hanna, Alfred J. and Kathryn Hanna. *Confederate Exiles in Venezuela.* Tuscaloosa: Confederate Publishing Company, 1960.

Hattaway, Herman. *General Stephen D. Lee.* Jackson: University Press of Mississippi, 1976.

Heck, Frank H. *The Civil War Veteran in Minnesota Life and Politics.* Oxford, Ohio: Mississippi Valley Press, 1941.

Hesseltine, William B. *Confederate Leaders in the New South.* Westport, Conn.: Greenwood Press, 1970.

Hesseltine, William B., and Hazel C. Wolf. *The Blue and the Gray on the Nile.* Chicago: University of Chicago Press, 1961.

Hill, Lawrence F. *The Confederate Exodus to Latin America.* N.p.: n.p., 1936.

Hobson, Fred. *Tell About the South: The Southern Rage to Explain.* Baton Rouge: Louisiana State University Press, 1983.

Holman, C. Hugh. *The Immoderate Past: The Southern Writer and History.* Athens: University of Georgia Press, 1977.

Holzman, Robert S. *Adapt or Perish: The Life of General Roger A. Pryor, CSA.* Hamden, Conn.: Archon Books, 1976.

Keller, Morton. *Affairs of State: Public Life in Late Nineteenth Century America.* Cambridge: Belknap Press of Harvard University Press, 1977.

Klein, Maury. *Edward Porter Alexander.* Athens: University of Georgia Press, 1971.

Leonard, Thomas C. *Above the Battle: War-Making in America from Appomattox to Versailles.* New York: Oxford University Press, 1978.

Linenthal, Edward T. *Changing Images of the Warrior Hero in America: A History of Popular Symbolism.* New York: The Edwin Mellen Press, 1982.

Lucas, Marion B. *Sherman and the Burning of Columbia.* College Station: Texas A & M University Press, 1976.

MacKethan, Mrs. Edwin R. *Chapter Histories, North Carolina Divison, United Daughters of the Confederacy, 1897–1947.* Raleigh: Edwards and Broughton, 1947.

McLaurin, Melton A. *The Knights of Labor in the South.* Westport, Conn.: Greenwood Press, 1978.

_____. *Paternalism and Protest: Southern Cotton Mill Workers and Organized Labor, 1875–1905.* Westport, Conn.: Greenwood Press, 1971.

McMath, Robert C., Jr. *Populist Vanguard: A History of the Southern Farmers' Alliance.* Chapel Hill: University of North Carolina Press, 1975.

McWilliams, Tennant S. *Hannis Taylor: The New Southerner as an American.* University: University of Alabama Press, 1978.

Maddex, Jack P., Jr. *The Reconstruction of Edward A. Pollard: A Rebel's Conversion to Postbellum Unionism.* Chapel Hill: University of North Carolina Press, 1974.

_____. *The Virginia Conservatives, 1867–1879: A Study in Reconstruction Politics.* Chapel Hill: University of North Carolina Press, 1970.

Malone, Dumas. *Edwin A. Alderman: A Biography.* New York: Doubleday, Doran and Company, 1940.

Moore, James Tice. *Two Paths to the New South: The Virginia Debt Controversy, 1870–1883.* Lexington: University Press of Kentucky, 1974.

Moorhead, James H. *American Apocalypse: Yankee Protestants and the Civil War, 1860–1869.* New Haven: Yale University Press, 1978.

Morrow, Ralph E. *Northern Methodism and Reconstruction.* East Lansing: Michigan State University Press, 1956.

Mulder, John M. *Woodrow Wilson: The Years of Preparation.* Princeton: Princeton University Press, 1978.

Murphy, James B. *L.Q.C. Lamar: Pragmatic Patriot.* Baton Rouge: Louisiana State University Press, 1973.

Nixon, Raymond B. *Henry W. Grady: Spokesman of the New South.* New York: Alfred A. Knopf, 1943.

Nunn, W.C. *Escape From Reconstruction.* Fort Worth: Texas Christian University, 1956.

O'Brien, Michael. *The Idea of the American South: 1920–1941.* Baltimore: The Johns Hopkins University Press, 1979.

Osterweis, Rollin G. *The Myth of the Lost Cause, 1865–1900.* Hamden, Conn.: Archon Books, 1973.

Palmer, Bruce. *"Man Over Money:" The Southern Populist Critique of American Capitalism.* Chapel Hill: University of North Carolina Press, 1980.

Pierce, Bessie L. *Public Opinion and the Teaching of History in the United States.* New York: Alfred A. Knopf, 1926.

Pinkowski, Edward. *Pills, Pen, and Politics: The Story of General Leon Jastremski,*

1843–1907. Wilmington, Del.: Captain Stanislaus Mlotkowski Memorial Brigade Society, 1974.

Polakoff, Keith. *The Politics of Inertia: The Election of 1876 and the End of Reconstruction*. Baton Rouge: Louisiana State University Press, 1973.

Pressly, Thomas J. *Americans Interpret Their Civil War*. New York: Free Press, 1962.

Procter, Ben H. *Not Without Honor: The Life of John H. Reagan*. Austin: University of Texas Press, 1962.

Pulley, Raymond H. *Old Virginia Restored: An Interpretation of the Progressive Impulse, 1870–1930*. Charlottesville: University Press of Virginia, 1968.

Rice, Jessie P. *J.L.M. Curry: Southerner, Statesman, and Educator*. New York: King's Crown Press, 1949.

Roark, James L. *Masters Without Slaves: Southern Planters in the Civil War and Reconstruction*. New York: W.W. Norton and Company, 1977.

Rolle, Andrew F. *The Lost Cause: The Confederate Exodus to Mexico*. Norman: University of Oklahoma Press, 1965.

Ross, Ishbel. *First Lady of the South: The Life of Mrs. Jefferson Davis*. New York: Harper & Brothers, 1958.

Sanger, Donald B., and Thomas R. Hay. *James Longstreet*. Baton Rouge: Louisiana State University Press, 1952.

Scott, Anne Firor. *The Southern Lady: From Pedestal to Politics, 1830–1930*. Chicago: University of Chicago Press, 1970.

Shofner, Jerrell H. *Nor Is It Over Yet: Florida in the Era of Reconstruction, 1863–1877*. Gainesville: University Presses of Florida, 1974.

Simkins, Francis B., and Robert H. Woody. *South Carolina During Reconstruction*. Chapel Hill: University of North Carolina Press, 1932.

Simpson, Harold B. *Hood's Texas Brigade in Reunion and Memory*. Hillsboro, Tex.: Hill Junior College Press, 1974.

Spain, Rufus B. *At Ease in Zion: Social History of Southern Baptists, 1865–1900*. Nashville: Vanderbilt University Press, 1961.

Stephenson, Wendell H. *The South Lives in History: Southern Historians and Their Legacy*. Baton Rouge: Louisiana State University Press, 1955.

———. *Southern History in the Making: Pioneer Historians of the South*. Baton Rouge: Louisiana State University Press, 1964.

Strode, Hudson. *Jefferson Davis: Tragic Hero; The Last Twenty-five Years, 1865–1889*. New York: Harcourt, Brace & World, 1964.

Taylor, Joe Gray. *Louisiana Reconstructed, 1863–1877*. Baton Rouge: Louisiana State University Press, 1974.

Tankersley, Allen P. *John B. Gordon: A Study in Gallantry*. Atlanta: Whitehall Press, 1955.

Thompson, Ernest T. *Presbyterians in the South*. Volumes 2 and 3. Richmond: John Knox Press, 1973.

Tindall, George B. *The Emergence of the New South, 1913–1945*. A History of the South, Vol. 10. Baton Rouge: Louisiana State University Press, 1967.

Wall, Joseph F. *Henry Watterson, Reconstructed Rebel*. New York: Oxford University Press, 1956.

Warren, Robert Penn. *The Legacy of the Civil War: Meditations on the Centennial*. New York: Random House, 1961.

Weaver, Richard M. *The Southern Tradition at Bay: A History of Postbellum Thought*. George Core and M. E. Bradford, eds. New Rochelle, N.Y.: Arlington House, 1968.

Wecter, Dixon. *When Johnny Comes Marching Home.* Cambridge: Houghton Mifflin, 1944.

White, William W. *The Confederate Veteran.* Tuscaloosa, Ala.: Confederate Publishing Company, 1962.

Wilson, Charles R. *Baptized in Blood: The Religion of the Lost Cause, 1865–1920.* Athens: University of Georgia Press, 1980.

Wilson, Edmund. *Patriotic Gore: Studies in the Literature of the American Civil War.* New York: Oxford University Press, 1962.

Woodward, C. Vann. *The Burden of Southern History.* New York: Vintage, 1960.

_____. *Origins of the New South, 1877–1913.* A History of the South, Vol. 9. Baton Rouge: Louisiana State University Press, 1951.

_____. *Reunion and Reaction: The Compromise of 1877 and the End of Reconstruction.* Second edition, revised. Garden City, N.Y.: Doubleday and Company, 1956.

Wyatt-Brown, Bertram. *Southern Honor: Ethics and Behavior in the Old South.* New York: Oxford University Press, 1982.

Articles

Alvarez, Eugene. "The Death of the 'Old War Horse' Longstreet." *Georgia Historical Quarterly* 52 (March 1968): 70–77.

Appleby, Joyce. "Reconciliation and the Northern Novelist, 1865–1880." *Civil War History* 10 (June 1964): 117–29.

Barbee, David R. "The Capture of Jefferson Davis." *Tyler's Quarterly Historical and Genealogical Magazine* 29 (July 1947): 6–42.

Boldrick, Charles C. "Father Abram J. Ryan, 'The Poet-Priest of the Confederacy.'" *Filson Club Historical Quarterly* 46 (July 1972): 201–18.

Bonner, James C. "Charles Colcock Jones: Macaulay of the South." *Georgia Historical Quarterly* 28 (December 1943): 324–38.

Bush, Robert. "Dr. Alderman's Symposium on the South." *Mississippi Quarterly* 27 (Winter 1973–74): 3–19.

Carter, Dan T. "The Anatomy of Fear: The Christmas Day Insurrection Scare of 1865." *Journal of Southern History* 42 (August 1976): 345–64.

Cass, Michael M. "Charles C. Jones, Jr., and the 'Lost Cause.'" *Georgia Historical Quarterly* 55 (Summer 1971): 222–33.

Cecil, L. Moffitt. "William Dean Howells and the South." *Mississippi Quarterly* 20 (Winter 1966–67): 13–24.

Chitty, Arthur B. "Heir of Hopes: Historical Summary of the University of the South." *Historical Magazine of the Protestant Episcopal Church* 23 (September 1954): 258–65.

Christie, Anne M. "Bill Arp." *Civil War History* 2 (September 1956): 103–19.

Clebsch, William A. "Christian Interpretations of the Civil War." *Church History* 30 (June 1961): 212–22.

Cook, Charles O. "The Glory of the Old South and the Greatness of the New: Reform and the Divided Mind of Charles Hillman Brough." *Arkansas Historical Quarterly* 34 (Autumn 1975): 227–41.

Coulter, E. Merton. "The Confederate Monument in Athens, Georgia." *Georgia Historical Quarterly* 40 (September 1956): 230–47.

_____. "Jefferson Davis and the Northeast Georgia Fair." *Georgia Historical Quarterly* 50 (September 1966): 253–75.

_____. "The New South: Benjamin H. Hill's Speech Before the Alumni of the University of Georgia." *Georgia Historical Quarterly* 57 (Summer 1973): 179–99.

———. "What the South Has Done About Its History." *Journal of Southern History* 2 (February 1936): 3–28.

Cresap, Bernan. "The *Confederate Veteran*." *Alabama Review* 12 (October 1959): 243–57.

Davis, Steve. "John Esten Cooke and Confederate Defeat." *Civil War History* 24 (March 1978): 66–83.

Dimick, Howard T. "The Capture of Jefferson Davis." *Journal of Mississippi History* 9 (October 1947): 238–54.

Dorgan, Howard. "A Case Study in Reconciliation: General John B. Gordon and the 'Last Days of the Confederacy.'" *Quarterly Journal of Speech* 60 (February 1974): 83–91.

Doster, James F. "Thomas McAdory Owen, Sr.," in *Keepers of the Past.* Clifford L. Lord, ed. Chapel Hill: University of North Carolina Press, 1965.

Eaton, Clement. "The Role of Honor in Southern Society." *Southern Humanities Review* 10 (Bicentennial Issue 1976): 47–58.

Franklin, John Hope. "A Century of Civil War Observances." *Journal of Negro History* 47 (April 1962): 97–107.

Gass, W. Conrad. "Franklin L. Riley and the Historical Renaissance in Mississippi, 1897–1914." *Journal of Mississippi History* 32 (August 1970): 195–227.

———. "Kemp Plummer Battle and the Development of Historical Instruction at the University of North Carolina." *North Carolina Historical Review* 45 (January 1968): 1–22.

Ginther, James E. "Charles Henry Smith, Alias 'Bill Arp.'" *Georgia Review* 4 (Winter 1950): 313–21.

Goff, Reda C. "The *Confederate Veteran* Magazine." *Tennessee Historical Quarterly* 31 (Spring 1972): 45–60.

Hamilton, J.G. de Roulhac. "History in the South—A Retrospect of Half a Century." *North Carolina Historical Review* 31 (April 1954): 173–81.

Hattaway, Herman. "Clio's Southern Soldiers: The United Confederate Veterans and History." *Louisiana History* 12 (Summer 1971): 213–42.

———. "The United Confederate Veterans in Louisiana." *Louisiana History* 16 (Winter 1975): 5–37.

Hardacre, Paul H. "History and Historians at Vanderbilt, 1875–1918." *Tennessee Historical Quarterly* 25 (Spring 1966): 22–31.

Hendrix, James P., Jr. "From Romance to Scholarship: Southern History at the Take-Off Point." *Mississippi Quarterly* 30 (Spring 1977): 192–211.

Hesseltine, William B., and Henry L. Ewbank, Jr. "Old Voices in the New South." *Quarterly Journal of Speech* 39 (December 1953): 451–58.

Hollis, Daniel W. "Samuel Chiles Mitchell, Social Reformer in Blease's South Carolina." *South Carolina Historical Magazine* 70 (January 1969): 20–37.

Hunter, Lloyd A. "Missouri's Confederate Leaders after the War." *Missouri Historical Review* 67 (April 1973): 371–96.

Jones, H.G. "Stephen Beauregard Weeks: North Carolina's First 'Professional' Historian." *North Carolina Historical Review* 42 (October 1965): 410–23.

Karlin, J. Alexander. "The Italo-American Incident of 1891 and the Road to Reunion." *Journal of Southern History* 8 (May 1942): 242–46.

Kiger, Joseph C. "Social Thought as Voiced in Rural Middle Tennessee Newspapers, 1878–1898." *Tennessee Historical Quarterly* 9 (June 1950): 131–54.

Kondert, Nancy T. "The Romance and Reality of Defeat: Southern Women in 1865." *Journal of Mississippi History* 35 (May 1973): 141–52.

Lashley, Tommy G. "Oklahoma's Confederate Veterans Home." *Chronicles of Oklahoma* 55 (Spring 1977): 34–45.

Livingood, James W. "Chickamauga and Chattanooga National Military Park." *Tennessee Historical Quarterly* 23 (March 1964): 3–23.

McDavid, Raven I., Jr., and Virginia G. McDavid. "The Late Unpleasantness: Folk Names for the Civil War." *Southern Speech Journal* 34 (Spring 1969): 194–204.

McWilliams, Tennant S. "The Lure of Empire: Southern Interest in the Caribbean, 1877–1900." *Mississippi Quarterly* 29 (Winter 1975–76): 43–63.

Marshall, Elizabeth. "'Atlanta Peace Jubilee.'" *Georgia Historical Quarterly* 50 (September 1966): 276–82.

Mathews, Joseph J. "The Study of History in the South." *Journal of Southern History* 31 (February 1965): 3–20.

Meanders, Margaret I. "Postscript to Appomattox: My Grandpa and Decoration Day." *Georgia Review* 24 (Fall 1970): 297–304.

Mendenhall, Marjorie S. "Southern Women of a 'Lost Generation.'" *South Atlantic Quarterly* 33 (October 1934): 334–53.

Miller, Thomas L. "Texas Land Grants to Confederate Veterans and Widows." *Southwestern Historical Quarterly* 69 (July 1965): 59–65.

Moore, John H. "The Jefferson Davis Monument." *Virginia Cavalcade* 10 (Spring 1961): 29–34.

Mounger, Dwyn M. "History as Interpreted by Stephen Elliott." *Historical Magazine of the Protestant Episcopal Church* 44 (June 1975): 285–317.

Muldowny, John. "Jefferson Davis: The Postwar Years." *Mississippi Quarterly* 23 (Winter 1969–70): 17–33.

O'Brien, Michael. "Edwin Mims: An Aspect of the Mind of the New South Considered; Parts I and II." *South Atlantic Quarterly* 73 (Spring 1974): 199–212 and 73 (Summer 1974): 323–34.

Overy, David H. "When the Wicked Beareth Rule: A Southern Critique of Industrial America." *Journal of Presbyterian History* 48 (Summer 1970): 130–42.

Parrish, William E. "Jefferson Davis Comes to Missouri." *Missouri Historical Review* 57 (July 1963): 344–56.

Rable, George C. "Southern Interests and the Election of 1876: A Reappraisal." *Civil War History* 26 (December 1980): 347–61.

Reilly, Timothy F. "Benjamin M. Palmer: Secessionist Becomes Nationalist." *Louisiana History* 18 (Summer 1977): 287–301.

Richter, William L. "James Longstreet: From Rebel to Scalawag." *Louisiana History* 11 (Summer 1970): 215–30.

Russ, William A., Jr. "Was There Danger of a Second Civil War During Reconstruction?" *Mississippi Valley Historical Review* 25 (June 1938): 39–58.

Rutman, Darrett B. "Philip Alexander Bruce: A Divided Mind of the South." *Virginia Magazine of History and Biography* 58 (October 1960): 387–407.

Schellings, William J. "The Advent of the Spanish-American War in Florida." *Florida Historical Quarterly* 39 (April 1960): 311–29.

———. "Florida and the Cuban Revolution, 1895–1898." *Florida Historical Quarterly* 39 (October 1960): 175–86.

Simms, L. Moody, Jr. "A Virginia Sculptor." *Virginia Cavalcade* 20 (Summer 1970): 20–27.

Simpson, John A. "The Cult of the 'Lost Cause.'" *Tennessee Historical Quarterly* 34 (Winter 1975): 350–61.

Smiley, David L. "The Quest for the Central Theme in Southern History." *South Atlantic Quarterly* 77 (Summer 1972): 307–25.

Smith, Edwina C. "Southerners on Empire: Southern Senators and Imperialism, 1898–1899." *Mississippi Quarterly* 31 (Winter 1977–78): 89–107.

Smith, John David. "An Old Creed for the New South: Southern Historians and the Revival of the Proslavery Argument, 1890–1920." *Southern Studies* 18 (Spring 1979): 75–87.

Stampp, Kenneth M. "The Southern Road to Appomattox." *The Imperiled Union: Essays on the Background of the Civil War.* New York: Oxford University Press, 1980, pp. 246–69.

Stark, Cruce. "Brothers At/in War: One Phase of Post-Civil War Reconciliation." *Canadian Review of American Studies* 6 (Fall 1975): 174–81.

Tindall, George B. "Mythology: A New Frontier in Southern History." *The Idea of the South: Pursuit of a Central Theme.* Edited by Frank E. Vandiver. Chicago: University of Chicago Press, 1964, pp. 1–15.

Van Tassel, David D. "The American Historical Association and the South." *Journal of Southern History* 23 (November 1957): 465–82.

Vandiver, Frank E. "The Confederacy and the American Tradition." *Journal of Southern History* 28 (August 1962): 277–86.

——— "Jefferson Davis—Leader Without Legend." *Journal of Southern History* 43 (February 1977): 3–18.

Wade, John Donald. "Old Wine in a New Bottle." *Virginia Quarterly Review* 11 (April 1935): 239–52.

——— "What the South Figured: 1865–1914." *Southern Review* 3 (1937–38): 360–67.

Weaver, Blanche H.C. "Confederate Emigration to Brazil." *Journal of Southern History* 27 (February 1961): 33–53.

Wiener, Jonathan M. "Female Planters and Planters' Wives in Civil War and Reconstruction: Alabama 1850–1870." *Alabama Review* 30 (April 1977): 135–49.

Wyatt-Brown, Bertram. "The Antebellum South as a 'Culture of Courage.'" *Southern Studies* 20 (Fall 1981): 328–46.

Unpublished Theses and Dissertations

Adams, Robert T. "A Study of the Life and Work of the Reverend Abram J. Ryan, Poet-Priest of the Confederacy." M.A. thesis, Louisiana State University, 1964.

Atchison, Ray M. "Southern Literary Magazines, 1865–1887." Ph.D. dissertation, Duke University, 1956.

Bennett, John B. "Albert Taylor Bledsoe: Social and Religious Controversialist of the Old South." Ph.D. dissertation, Duke University, 1942.

Buchanan, Raymond W., Jr. "The Epideictic Speaking of Robert Love Taylor Between 1891 and 1906." Ph.D. dissertation, Louisiana State University, 1970.

Buser, John E. "After Half a Generation: The South of the 1880's." Ph.D. dissertation, University of Texas at Austin, 1968.

Cash, William M. "Alabama Republicans During Reconstruction: Personal Characteristics, Motivations, and Political Activity of Party Activists, 1867–1880." Ph.D. dissertation, University of Alabama, 1973.

Climer, Patricia Faye. "Protectors of the Past: The United Daughters of the Confederacy, Tennessee Divison, and the Lost Cause." M.A. thesis, Vanderbilt University, 1973.

Cole, Carol A. "George William Bagby: Reconciling the New South and the Old Dominion." M.A. thesis, University of Virginia, 1971.

Cook, Marjorie Howell. "Restoration and Innovation: Alabamians Adjust to Defeat, 1865–1867." Ph.D. dissertation, University of Alabama, 1968.

Davis, Guy Stephen. "Johnny Reb in Perspective: The Confederate Soldier's Image in Southern Arts." Ph.D. dissertation, Emory University, 1979.

Dorgan, Howard. "Southern Apologetic Themes, as Expressed in Selected Ceremonial Speaking of Confederate Veterans, 1889–1900." Ph.D. dissertation, Louisiana State University, 1971.

Doss, Richard B. "John Warwick Daniel: A Study in the Virginia Democracy." Ph.D. dissertation, University of Virginia, 1955.

Durant, Susan S. "The Gently Furled Banner: The Development of the Myth of the Lost Cause." Ph.D. dissertation, University of North Carolina, 1972.

Ellingsworth, Huber W. "Southern Reconciliation Orators in the North, 1869–1899." Ph.D. dissertation, Florida State University, 1955.

Eubank, Wayne C. "Benjamin Morgan Palmer: A Southern Divine." Ph.D. dissertation, Louisiana State University, 1943.

Flusche, Michael A. "The Private Plantation: Versions of the Old South Myth, 1880–1914." Ph.D. dissertation, The Johns Hopkins University, 1973.

Gilmour, Robert A. "The Other Emancipation: Studies in the Society and Economy of Alabama Whites During Reconstruction." Ph.D. dissertation, The Johns Hopkins University, 1972.

Grier, Douglas A. "Confederate Emigration to Brazil, 1865–1870." Ph.D. dissertation, University of Michigan, 1968.

Hannum, Sharon E. "Confederate Cavaliers: The Myth in War and Defeat." Ph.D. dissertation, Rice University, 1965.

Harris, Anne Barber. "The South as Seen by Travelers, 1865–1880." Ph.D. dissertation, University of North Carolina, 1967.

Harris, Robert L. "The South in Defeat: 1865." Ph.D. dissertation, Duke University, 1956.

Hays, Willard W. "Polemics and Philosophy: A Biography of Albert Taylor Bledsoe." Ph.D. dissertation, University of Tennessee, 1971.

Hickey, Doralyn J. "Benjamin Morgan Palmer: Churchman of the Old South." Ph.D. dissertation, Duke University, 1962.

Huffman, Frank J., Jr. "Old South, New South: Continuity and Change in a Georgia County, 1850–1880." Ph.D. dissertation, Yale University, 1974.

Hunter, Lloyd A. "The Sacred South: Postwar Confederates and the Sacralization of Southern Culture." Ph.D. dissertation, St. Louis University, 1978.

Jabbs, Theodore H. "The Lost Cause: Some Southern Opinion Between 1865 and 1900 About Why the Confederacy Lost the Civil War." M.A. thesis, University of North Carolina, 1967.

Jacobson, Timothy C. "Tradition and Change in the New South, 1865–1910." Ph.D. dissertation, Vanderbilt University, 1974.

Lankevich, George J. "The Grand Army of the Republic in New York State, 1865–1898." Ph.D. dissertation, Columbia University, 1967.

Little, Robert D. "The Ideology of the New South: A Study in the Development of Ideas, 1865–1910." Ph.D. dissertation, University of Chicago, 1950.

McCrary, James Peyton. "John Spencer Bassett: The Scholar as Social Critic." M.A. thesis, University of Virginia, 1966.

Marshall, Howard J. "Gentlemen Without a Country: A Social and Intellectual History of South Carolina, 1860–1900." Ph.D. dissertation, University of North Carolina, 1979.

Moore, Rayburn S. "Southern Writers and Northern Literary Magazines, 1865–1900."
Ph.D. dissertation, Duke University, 1956.

Moss, Melissa. "Edward Valentine, A Southern Artist." M.S. thesis, School of Art of
Virginia Commonwealth University, 1969.

Noyes, Elmer E. "A History of the Grand Army of the Republic in Ohio from 1866 to
1900." Ph.D. dissertation, Ohio State University, 1945.

O'Brien, Michael. "'To Seek a Newer World': Selected Correspondence of Edwin
Mims." M.A. thesis, Vanderbilt University, 1973.

Overy, David H. "Robert Lewis Dabney: Apostle of the Old South." Ph.D. dissertation,
University of Wisconsin, 1967.

Readnour, Harry W. "General Fitzhugh Lee, 1835–1905: A Biographical Study." Ph.D.
dissertation, University of Virginia, 1971.

Ritter, Charles F. "The Press in Florida, Louisiana, and South Carolina and the End of
Reconstruction, 1865–1877: Southern Men With Northern Interests." Ph.D.
dissertation, Catholic University, 1976.

Ruoff, John C. "Southern Womanhood, 1865–1920: An Intellectual and Cultural
Study." Ph.D. dissertation, University of Illinois at Urbana-Champaign, 1976.

Sides, Sudie Duncan. "Women and Slaves: An Interpretation Based on the Writings of
Southern Women." Ph.D. dissertation, University of North Carolina, 1969.

Simpson, Robert R. "The Origin of State Departments of Archives and History in the
South." Ph.D. dissertation, University of Mississippi, 1971.

Simms, L. Moody, Jr. "Philip Alexander Bruce: His Life and Works." Ph.D. dissertation,
University of Virginia, 1966.

Thompson, Marilyn Miller. "Jefferson Davis, the Reluctant Orator: A Study of his
Postwar Speaking (1867–1889)." M.A. thesis, Louisiana State University, 1974.

Towns, Walter S. "Ceremonial Speaking and the Reinforcing of American Nationalism
in the South, 1875–1890." Ph.D. dissertation, University of Florida, 1972.

Walker, Franklin T. "William Peterfield Trent—A Critical Biography." Ph.D. dissertation, George Peabody College for Teachers, 1943.

Webb, James Wallace. "Historical Activity in the South: 1880–1890." M.A. thesis,
Louisiana State University, 1963.

Wolff, Alfred Y., Jr. "The South and the American Imagination: Mythical Views of the
Old South, 1865–1900." Ph.D. dissertation, University of Virginia, 1971.

Index

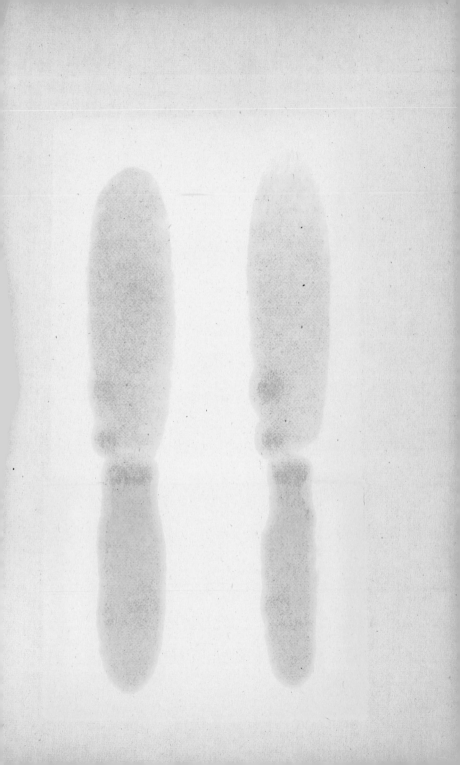